Successful

CELESTIAL NAVIGATION

with H.O. 229

Successful
CELESTIAL
NAVIGATION
with H.O. 229

by G.D. Dunlap

Illustrations by David Q. Scott

International Marine Publishing Company
Camden, Maine 04843

Copyright © 1977 by International Marine Publishing Company
Library of Congress Catalog Card Number: 76-8771
ISBN: 0-87742-075-0

Contents

CHAPTERS

APPENDIXES

Preface

This small treatise on celestial navigation represents the type of project that every technical writer likes to undertake, an informal discussion that is not bound to include specific data to conform to any predetermined formal course of instruction. It has been a conviction of the author for many years that a slightly different, easier-to-understand approach could be used in explaining and illustrating the basic theory of celestial navigation. These ideas are presented in Chapter 1.

Many small volumes on celestial navigation have appeared on the market in recent years, each concentrating on a given set of sight reduction tables and a specific almanac. The choice for this book is the *Nautical Almanac*, simply because it is designed for marine use, and because one volume is good for an entire calendar year. Use of the new H.O. 229 tables is also emphasized: the more practical reason is that they are the new official tables adopted by the U.S. Navy and most other groups. They also serve as a replacement for the out-of-print H.O. 214 tables and are universal in that sight reduction can be performed for any celestial body appearing above the horizon. Any person who learns the new H.O. 229 method can easily use the older H.O. 214 and H.O. 249 tables without undergoing an extensive relearning process.

Chapters 4 and 5 and the data in Appendixes IV and V are taken almost verbatim from *The Book of the Sextant*. This booklet was published primarily as a sextant instruction manual by Weems & Plath, Inc., Annapolis, Maryland 21404. These sections have been used with permission of Weems & Plath, and appreciation is expressed for this.

Special thanks are extended to Captain H. H. Shufeldt for reading and correcting the manuscript. The author has had the privilege of working as a coauthor with Captain Shufeldt on *Dutton's Navigating and Piloting, Piloting and Dead Reckoning* (both published by the United States Naval Institute), and *The Book of the Sextant.*

The data used in this book has formed the basis for a series of lectures in a classroom course in celestial navigation taught by the author for the past three years.

G. Dale Dunlap
Annapolis, Maryland

Chapter 1

Celestial Concepts

In order to practice the *art* of celestial navigation, it is desirable that the navigator be able to visualize some of the basic concepts of the *science* of celestial navigation. In this chapter a brief, illustrated portrayal of these important concepts will be presented. The student will come to understand how a position at sea is computed and plotted with the aid of data obtained from sextant observations of the celestial bodies.

Four basic assumptions, progressive in that each must be understood before the next will appear reasonable, are involved:

1. The celestial bodies can be visualized as being located at an infinite distance from the earth.

2. Light from a celestial body should be pictured as falling on the entire earth in a group of parallel rays.

3. At any given instant of time, the vertical altitude of a celestial body above the horizon, as measured by the sextant, will be the same at any point on a *circle of equal altitude*. A line drawn from the center of a celestial body to the center of the earth would pass through the earth's surface at a point called the *geographic position* (GP) of the body, and this point is the center of the circle of equal altitude. From everywhere on the circumference of this circle, the body will have the same altitude.

1

4. The observation of a single celestial body yields a *line of position* (LOP); the navigator knows only that he is located somewhere on this line. The LOP is plotted as a straight line on the chart. An LOP is actually a small segment or arc of a circle of equal altitude. The complete circle is so large on the surface of the earth that the short portion of the circumference drawn can be considered a straight line without appreciable error resulting.

Before explaining these four points, it should be pointed out that in celestial navigation one always deals with the center of the observed body as it would appear if observed from the center of the earth. When observing the sun or moon, measurement is actually made to the altitude of the upper or lower limb, or part of the rim of the body, but in working the sight, the body's center establishes the true altitude. How the altitude of the center is determined will be discussed in the following paragraphs.

Bodies at Infinity

In this era of space exploration everyone is aware that the sun, moon, planets, and stars are located at greatly varying distances from the earth. However, in working celestial navigation problems, we can assume that they are all located at infinity; in the case of the stars this is literally true for the degree of accuracy required for celestial navigation. For the navigational bodies in the solar system (the sun, moon, and planets), the bodies are at varying finite distances, and corrections to sextant altitudes, taken from an almanac, adjust for the semidiameter (Figure 1-1) and parallax errors (Figure 1-2).

The semidiameter correction is necessary because the distance to the moon, the sun, and to a lesser extent the planets results in their having a visible diameter when viewed from the earth rather than being point sources of light. Parallax results from observations that are made from the surface of the earth rather than from the center of the earth.

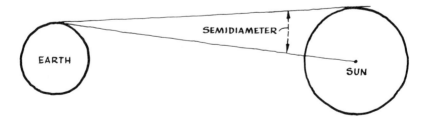

FIGURE 1-1 Semidiameter error.

FIGURE 1-2   *Parallax error.*

This produces an error when one observes celestial bodies that are relatively near to the earth. The maximum parallax error occurs when the body is near the horizon; it becomes zero when the body is directly overhead.

Semidiameter and parallax errors occur because bodies in the solar system are not located at infinity. Adjustments are made to the sextant altitude to correct for these factors. A more complete discussion of this subject is given in Chapter 5. After the corrections are applied, the celestial navigation problem is solved as though all the bodies were located at infinity.

Parallel Light Rays

With the assumption that the navigational bodies are located at an infinite distance from the center of the earth, one fact is evident: the light rays from the body are all parallel when they reach the earth. Within the accuracy required for navigation, the light rays from the closest star would be considered parallel as seen from a series of points extending across the sun–moon–earth system. This is illustrated in Figure 1-3. The closest star is 4.3 light-years away, and most stars are

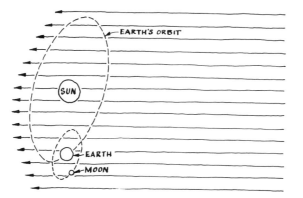

FIGURE 1-3   *Parallel light rays from a single star.*

over 100 light-years distant. By comparison, light travels from the sun to the earth in about 8.3 minutes and from the moon in about 1.25 seconds.

If the earth were a flat plane instead of a sphere, the altitude of a star above this plane at any instant of time would be exactly the same at New York, San Francisco, and all other points (see Figure 1-4). That the earth is spherical in shape is the only reason the altitude of a star, measured in arc above the horizon, at a given instant of time, varies at different locations on the surface of the earth (Figure 1-5).

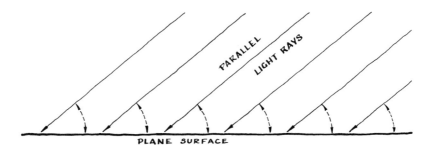

FIGURE 1-4 *Parallel light rays intersect a plane surface at identical angles of observed altitude at all positions on the plane.*

The Circle of Equal Altitude

At any given instant of time a celestial body is directly over (in the zenith of) a GP on earth. The altitude of the body—that is, its angle above the horizon—as observed at the GP will be 90°. The visible horizon from which this measurement is made is a plane, which is tangent to the earth at that geographical location and at that location *only*. If the position of the observer is at some point other than directly under the body, the plane of the horizon will be tilted in relationship to the incoming parallel light rays. This produces a different observed altitude. As shown in Figure 1-6, the altitude becomes progressively less as the observer's distance from the GP of the body increases.

The sextant altitude is the same at any point on a circle on the earth that has the geographic position of the body as the center of the circle (see Figure 1-7). This is the circle of equal altitude. It is so large that it cannot be drawn on the navigation chart, but any short segment of it can be considered a straight line and drawn on the chart. The portion of the segment near the *dead reckoning* (DR) position is called a line of position (LOP). An observation of a single body, most often the

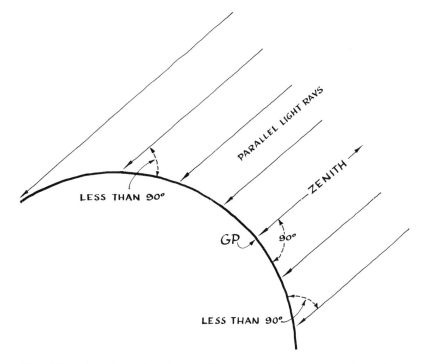

FIGURE 1-5 Parallel light rays from a star intersect a spherical surface (the earth) at different angles, depending on the
location of the observer on the sphere.

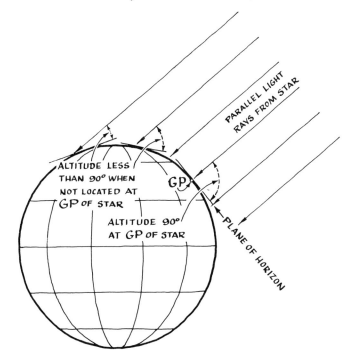

FIGURE 1-6 Altitude decreases as the observer's distance from the
GP of the body increases.

sun, indicates that the position of a ship is somewhere on that LOP. To find which portion of the circle of equal altitude to use, the DR position is determined by advancing a previous position for course steered and distance run.

When sextant observations are made on more than one body, as in the case of morning or evening star sights, the intersection of these lines of position produces the fix, or position (Figure 1-8), of the vessel. The other intersection of the two circles of equal altitude from two stars is located so far from the DR position that there will be no confusion as to which intersection of the circles is being used.

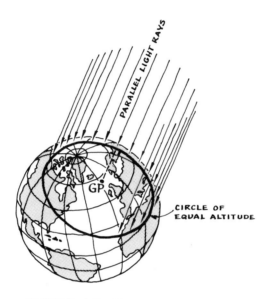

FIGURE 1-7   The circle of equal altitude.

FIGURE 1-8   Intersecting circles of equal altitude produce a fix.

Assuming the Celestial Sphere to be Located at Infinity

For navigational purposes, the celestial bodies are assumed to be located at infinity: it makes no difference that they are actually at greatly varying finite distances from the earth. As previously stated, the corrections applied to the sextant altitude correct the observations of all bodies to make them equal to the value they would have had if the bodies were located at infinity. Using this assumption, the celestial bodies can be visualized as being on a huge celestial sphere, concentric with the earth, and located at an infinite distance. The earth can, for purpose of illustration, be thought of as a small sphere, rotating on its axis once each 24 hours, at the center of this huge celestial sphere (see Figure 1-9). Astronomically speaking, this is not true, but we again emphasize that for purposes of celestial navigation we can assume that it is true. The sight reduction tables are based on the solution of a spherical triangle located on this imaginary celestial sphere, our position on earth being projected out onto the celestial sphere.

The Geographic Position of a Celestial Body

Assuming the celestial sphere exists as described, with the earth at its center, it is obvious that at any instant of time, any given celestial body will be exactly above (in the zenith of) a definite point on earth. This is the geographic position (GP) of the body. With the earth turning on its axis from west to east (never mind that it wobbles a little bit; this is taken into consideration in the almanac tabulations), the GP of the body will move over the earth from east to west. This movement

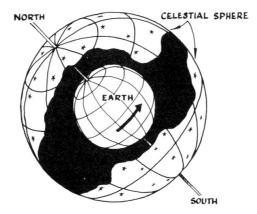

FIGURE 1-9 The celestial sphere.

7

occurs at a predetermined rate along a given parallel of latitude equal in numerical value to the *declination* of the celestial body (see Figures 1-10 and 1-11). Such movement of the GPs of particular bodies was the basis of ancient Polynesian navigation; the seafaring Polynesians knew that a certain star would pass directly over a particular island every night. For modern navigation the almanac tabulates various bodies' GPs for every instant of time.

Terminology Used in Locating the Positions of Celestial Bodies

In determining the positions of celestial bodies on the celestial sphere, as tabulated in the almanac, the terms *declination* and *hour angle* are used instead of *latitude* and *longitude*. Declination, on the celestial sphere, is precisely the same as the latitude of the GP on the earth. It is measured in degrees, minutes, and tenths of a minute of arc north or south of the celestial equator from 0° to 90° and must always be labeled north or south.

The *Greenwich hour angle* (GHA) is analogous to longitude. Longitude on earth is measured east or west from 0°, the Greenwich meridian, to 180°. A *meridian* is a plane passing through a given point on earth and through the north and south poles. The longitude (λ) of a position on earth remains fixed. Since the Greenwich meridian is used as the reference line for measurement of both longitude and time, it is also referred to as the prime meridian. The GHA is the angular distance of the celestial meridian—or hour circle, as it is usually called—of a body measured west from 0° to 360°, 0° being represented by the Greenwich meridian, which is projected out to the celestial sphere and referred to as the Greenwich celestial meridian. An hour circle on the celestial sphere is a great circle passing through a given point, such as the position of a celestial body, and through the celestial poles. An hour circle through the zenith of the observer is called a *celestial meridian*. Remembering that the earth (containing the Greenwich meridian) turns under the celestial sphere, it is easy to see that this projected, imaginary celestial meridian is moving across the sky in an easterly direction at a constant rate. The GHA of any star or other fixed point on the celestial sphere, measured from this moving celestial meridian to a fixed hour circle, is therefore constantly changing, becoming greater as the day progresses. (See Figure 1-11.)

In Chapter 3 the use of the almanac will be explained. At this point let us simply state that the position of celestial bodies is given in terms of declination north or south, 0° to 90°, and Greenwich hour angle, west from 0° to 360°.

Just as GHA is measured from the Greenwich celestial meridian to the hour circle of the body, the *local hour angle* (LHA) is measured

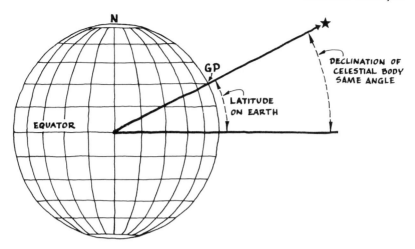

FIGURE 1-10   Declination.

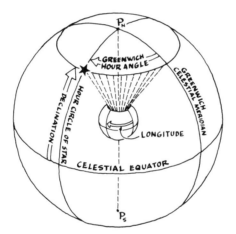

FIGURE 1-11   The Greenwich hour angle (GHA) is synonymous with west longitude at a given instant of time. The GP of a star tracks along a parallel of latitude.

west from the meridian (longitude) of the observer to the hour circle of the body. LHA can therefore be defined as the angular distance west of the local celestial meridian; it is the arc of the celestial equator, or the angle at the celestial pole, between the upper branch of the local celestial meridian and the hour circle of a point on the celestial sphere, measured westward from the local celestial meridian through 360°. The value of west longitude is always subtracted from GHA to obtain

LHA, and the value of east longitude is added to GHA to obtain LHA, as shown in Figure 1-12.

LHA of the body is one of the three entering arguments used in the *Sight Reduction Tables for Marine Navigation, H.O. 229*, which will be explained in a later chapter. In some sight reduction tables, most notably H.O. 214, a meridian angle (*t*) is used instead of the LHA as an entering argument in the tables. Meridian angle is the designation used when measuring the equivalent of the LHA, but in an east or west direction from the local meridian. Whereas LHA is measured westward from the local meridian with values of 0° through 360°, *t* is measured east or west with values from 0° to 180°. If the LHA is less than 180°, it is equivalent to *t* west. If the LHA is greater than 180°, it must be subtracted from 360° to obtain *t* east. (See Figure 1-13.)

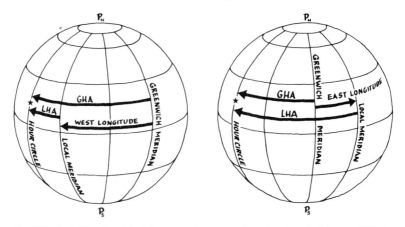

FIGURE 1-12 (Left) Observer in west longitude: LHA = GHA − longitude.
(Right) Observer in east longitude: LHA = GHA + longitude.

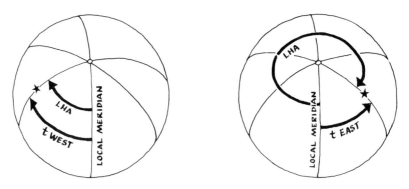

FIGURE 1-13 (Left) t = LHA when LHA < 180°.
(Right) t = 360° − LHA when LHA > 180°.

Sight reduction tables are constructed so that one of the entering arguments is an integral or whole degree of LHA. To obtain the LHA for entering the tables, it is therefore necessary to use an *assumed longitude* (aλ), whose minutes are chosen to produce integral degrees of LHA; this assumed longitude should be within 30′ of the DR longitude. Remember that in west longitude LHA is always obtained by subtracting the value of assumed west longitude from GHA of the body, after adding 360° to the GHA when necessary. In west longitude the minutes of aλ are always the same as the minutes of GHA. In east longitude they are 60 minus the minutes of GHA. For example, if the GHA is 120° 55′ and the DR longitude is 75° 30′W, aλ would be 75° 55′. However, if the DR longitude had been 76° 20′W the aλ would still be 75° 55′, a change in the degree value to assure that aλ is within 30′ of the DR longitude.

Coordinates of Measurement

The celestial equator system of coordinates has been described above without being named. This system uses the *celestial equator* (also called the *equinoctial*) as a plane of reference for determining positions of the navigation bodies on the celestial sphere. The celestial equator is perpendicular to an axis extending from the north celestial pole through the center of the earth to the south celestial pole. Declination and hour angle are the coordinates of measurement (Figure 1-14).

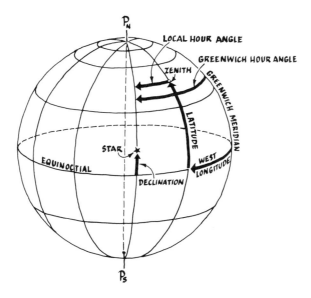

FIGURE 1-14   *Celestial equator system of coordinates.*

The GP of the body as well as the latitude and longitude of the observer are based on the earth system of coordinates, which is similar to the celestial equator system but uses the actual equator and the North and South Poles of the earth. The zenith of the observer's position on earth can be defined on the celestial sphere among the celestial bodies in exactly the same manner as on the surface of the earth. It makes no difference in celestial navigation whether you visualize the zenith of the observer projected on the celestial sphere with the celestial bodies, or visualize the GP of the body on earth with the geographic coordinates of latitude and longitude.

In order to understand how the altitude of an observed body is used in working the spherical triangle to obtain a line of position, it is necessary to become familiar with another set of measurements, one that uses a completely different set of coordinates. This other set is the horizon system of coordinates. The reference plane is the observer's celestial horizon. The axis of the system is perpendicular to this plane and passes through the *zenith* (the point directly overhead) and the *nadir* (the point on the opposite side of the celestial sphere that is intersected by a line passing through the zenith and the center of the earth). See Figure 1-15. The plane of the celestial horizon passes through the center of the earth. The visible horizon at sea, where sea and sky meet, is assumed to be a plane tangent to the earth at the point of observation. The plane of the visible horizon is parallel to the plane of the celestial horizon. Only the sun and moon are near enough to the earth to create a parallax (the difference between altitude measured

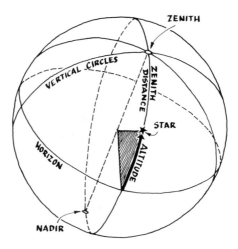

FIGURE 1-15 *Horizon system of coordinates.*

from the visible horizon, which is tangent to the earth at the observer's position, and altitude measured from the celestial horizon, which passes through the center of the earth) that has any practical significance. The parallax correction applied to the sextant altitude (hs) takes care of this difference.

Using the horizon system of measurements, the *altitude* of the celestial body is measured vertically above the celestial horizon on an imaginary arc passing through the celestial body and the zenith of the observer. This arc is part of what is appropriately called a *vertical circle*. There can be an infinite number of these vertical circles passing through the various celestial bodies. The prime vertical is the great circle passing through the east and west points of the horizon and through the zenith. The distance from the celestial body to the zenith is called *zenith distance* (ZD). The zenith distance is therefore 90° minus the altitude.

There is always a reference point common to both of the above systems of coordinates; the zenith of the observer. The spherical triangle, which will be discussed in the next section, combines the measurements obtained from the two different coordinate systems (see Figure 1-16).

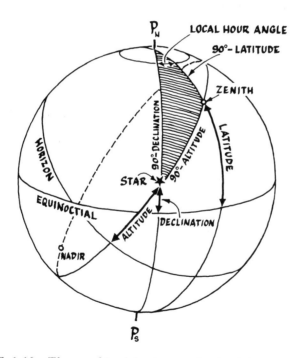

FIGURE 1-16 *The combined horizon and celestial systems of coordinates.*

The Spherical Triangle

The location of an LOP is computed by using the following data: the position of the body being observed, as obtained from the *Nautical Almanac*; the assumed position of the observer, the exact second of time of the observation; and the observed altitude. No mathematics other than addition and subtraction is required, since the formula is built into the sight reduction tables. The navigator should nevertheless be curious enough to want to identify the problem he is solving. The problem is a simple spherical triangle called the celestial triangle, which is shown in Figures 1-16 and 1-17.

The values for two sides (one actual and one assumed) and their included angle are used to solve the spherical triangle. Starting with the included angle, these three values are:

1. Local hour angle (LHA): the difference in arc between the GHA of the body and the assumed longitude (aλ) of the observer, chosen so that it will be an integral degree. The LHA can also be thought of as the angle formed by the two sides at the elevated pole (the pole above the horizon; thus, the North Pole when the observer is in the northern hemisphere).

2. The codeclination of the body: 90° plus or minus the declination (north or south) taken from the almanac.

3. The colatitude: 90° minus the assumed latitude, chosen as the integral degree nearest the DR latitude.

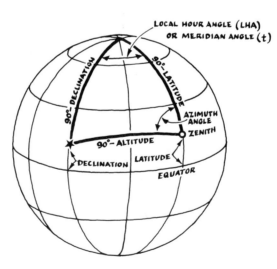

FIGURE 1-17 The celestial triangle.

The sight reduction tables are so arranged that the entering arguments are the *actual* declination and the *assumed* latitude, rather than the cofunctions that make up the sides of the triangle in Figure 1-17. From the tables you extract:

1. The tabulated altitude (called computed altitude in HO 229), which, with its correction for minutes of declination, gives *computed altitude* (Hc). Hc is then compared with the *observed altitude* (Ho) to determine whether the line of position is closer to or farther away from the GP of the body than the assumed position that was chosen for making the sight reduction. The difference between Ho and Hc is called the *altitude intercept* (a). For example: computed altitude from the sight reduction tables, based on the assumed position from which the LOP will be plotted, is 39° 45′.3. Observed altitude, as measured with the sextant and with corrections applied, is 39° 37′.3. The actual position will be somewhere on an LOP plotted 8 miles farther away from the GP of the body than was the assumed position.

2. *Azimuth angle* (Z). This is the direction of the body from the observer's assumed position, measured east or west from the elevated pole—the North Pole when in north latitude, and the South Pole if the latitude is south. The tables include directions for converting the azimuth angle to *true azimuth* (Zn), measured from the north to the eastward through 360°.

As shown in Figure 1-18, the LOP will cross this azimuth line at a 90° angle a given number of miles toward or away from the direction (azimuth) of the GP as measured from the assumed position (AP).

Miles and Minutes

Nautical miles rather than statute miles or kilometers are always used in celestial navigation. The choice is not arbitrary but is made be-

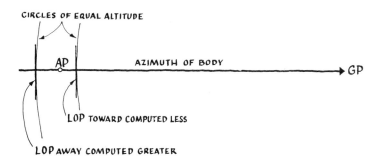

FIGURE 1-18   LOP toward or away; altitude intercept.

cause one nautical mile is equal in length to one minute of arc on a great circle around the earth. A great circle is that line on the surface of a sphere which divides the sphere into two equal parts. It can be formed by the intersection of the surface of the sphere with any plane passing through its center. For instance, if the altitude intercept is 8 minutes of arc, the LOP will cross the azimuth line 8 nautical miles toward or away from the azimuth of the body. Figure 1-19 illustrates the relationship between nautical miles and minutes of arc.

LOP Toward or Away

In order to avoid mistakes in plotting the LOP, one rule should be thoroughly memorized in order to determine whether the LOP will be located toward the GP of the body or away from it as measured from the assumed position along the azimuth line. That rule is "computed greater away" or "Coast Guard Academy." Here is how it is derived. Remember that the LOP is always perpendicular to the azimuth line, and that the latter's direction is determined by the true azimuth of the body as taken from the sight reduction tables. Returning to Figure 1-6,

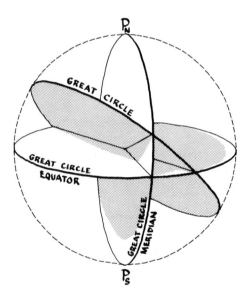

FIGURE 1-19   *The equator, a meridian, or any other plane that divides the sphere into equal hemispheres traces a great circle on the surface of the sphere. Along these great circles, one minute of arc equals one nautical mile.*

note that when the observer is directly under the body the altitude is 90°, and that the altitude becomes progressively less the farther away the ship moves from the GP of the body around the curvature of the earth. The plotting is based on the assumed position (not the DR position), which was used in obtaining the computed altitude. This assumed position (AP) consists of the assumed latitude, which is the integral degree of latitude closest to the DR latitude, and the assumed longitude, which is chosen with the minutes of longitude so determined as to produce an integral degree of LHA. If the computed altitude is the greater, it follows that the observed altitude is the lesser, and the LOP is plotted farther away from the GP than the location of the AP. The problem of LOP toward or away can sometimes cause confusion if the navigator is trying to figure it out under pressure, and, thus, the best approach is to learn the rule and apply it rather than trying to sketch the problem or reason it out each time.

Chapter 2

Time

The correct determination of time is the essence of celestial navigation. Time is a measurement of duration. Since the sun governs the length of our year, each season, and each day, it is used for measuring our time, which is appropriately called solar time. In practice today the U.S. Naval Observatory, which has responsibility for official time keeping in the United States, uses the atomic second as the basis for precise time; this time is called coordinated universal time. For the accuracy needed in celestial navigation, universal time can be considered the same as time measured by the rotation of the earth relative to the sun. One rotation of the earth on its axis, with reference to the sun, is a solar day, and one revolution of the earth around the sun in its orbit is a solar year. Similarly, the measurement of rotation of the earth with reference to a star, or to an arbitrary reference point on the celestial sphere called the Vernal Equinox or the First Point of Aries, is a sidereal day. Sidereal time was used in navigation many years ago, but modern almanac tabulations no longer employ it.

Time and Longitude

There are 360 degrees (°) of longitude in the circumference of the earth, and because the sun makes an apparent rotation around the earth in 24 hours, we have a ratio between arc and time and may convert one to the other. A table for such conversion is contained in Appendix II. Since 360° equals 24 hours, it follows that 15° equals 1 hour, 1° equals 4 minutes of time, 1 minute (of arc) equals 4 seconds of time, and so on.

Apparent and Mean Time

Time that is based on the motion of the true sun is called *apparent time*. It is used by navigators for only a few special computations, as the irregularities in the apparent motion of the true sun do not result in a uniform time basis. A fictitious sun called the mean sun is therefore substituted. This mean sun is assumed to travel around the world at a steady rate—the average or *mean* of the apparent rate of the true sun. The difference between mean and apparent time is called the equation of time and is seldom used today. In timing celestial observations, the time of the observation must be determined to the exact second in terms of Greenwich Mean Time.

Greenwich Mean Time (GMT) is mean solar time measured with reference to the meridian of Greenwich. The day starts at GMT 24 00 00 or 00 00 00, when the mean sun transits the lower branch of the Greenwich meridian. A meridian on earth is defined by a plane passing through a given point on the earth and through the North and South Poles. The *upper branch* of a meridian is that half lying between the poles and passing through the given point, in this case Greenwich (see Figure 2-1). The *lower branch* is the portion of the meridian pass-

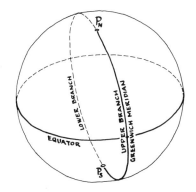

FIGURE 2-1   *The Greenwich meridian.*

ing through the poles and the opposite side of the globe; in this case, the lower branch is the 180th meridian. The transit of the mean sun over the upper branch is at GMT 12 00 00 or Greenwich noon. For navigational purposes it is desirable for the navigator to use a time-piece, preferably a chronometer, that runs on GMT. Since GMT is not used for most other purposes in our daily lives, people generally set their watches and clocks at local zone time.

Local mean time (LMT) is based on some meridian other than that of Greenwich. A day based on LMT begins when the mean sun transits the lower branch of the given local meridian; usually, a meridian that is a multiple of 15° is used as a base. This sort of time is called *zone time* (ZT). *Zone time* is based on keeping the same time (the LMT of the standard meridian) for each 15° band of longitude. This is generally adhered to at sea, but the time zones used at some inland points are based on geographical areas in which it is desirable to use a common time rather than the strict 15°-of-longitude method. For navigation purposes zone 0 extends 7½° each side of the Greenwich meridian. Zone 1 uses the 15° meridian as standard and covers the area from 7½° to 22½° of longitude. (See Figure 2-2, which presents a time zone chart.) In west

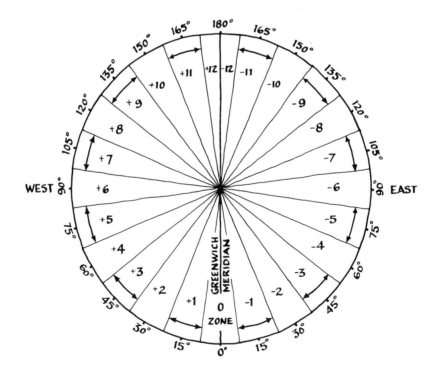

FIGURE 2-2 Zone description diagram for standard time zones.

longitude these time zones carry a plus designation, which indicates the number of hours that must be added to zone time to obtain GMT. For example, the East Coast of the United States is in zone +5, in which the 75th meridian is used as the standard meridian. This time zone is also based on Eastern Standard Time, which is used for nonnavigational purposes. If the time of an observation of a celestial body is 05 34 15 zone time +5, the GMT of the observation would be 10 34 15. In east longitude, the time zones carry a minus designation and the minus zone description is subtracted from zone time to obtain GMT.

Daylight-Saving Time

If a timepiece keeping local time is being used, the navigator must be careful to take into account daylight-saving time. For economic and industrial reasons an area may be on this special time, which, in the United States, is set one hour later than standard time. Thus, on the East Coast of the United States, if daylight-saving time is being used, only 4 hours would be added to obtain GMT. It is sometimes confusing which time is faster or slower; in many rural areas daylight-saving time is referred to simply as "fast time," and this is an easy way to remember the correct designation. From this discussion one can see that it is preferable to keep the chronometer or navigation watch set on GMT in order to avoid confusion.

24-Hour Time

For navigational purposes time is always based on a 24-hour day rather than 12 hours A.M. and 12 hours P.M. To obtain P.M. times, 12 hours are added to the A.M. time. Four digits are always used when recording hours and minutes. For example, 8:45 A.M. is written 0845, and 5:30 P.M. is written 1730. They are spoken, respectively, as "zero-eight-forty-five" and "seventeen-thirty." In writing the time of a celestial observation in hours, minutes, and seconds, a space is left between each—for example, 11 35 43. This enables the navigator to add or subtract times with less chance of error. If the local zone time is 11 35 43 when using +4 time and a timing watch that is 6 seconds fast, 4 hours would be added and 6 seconds subtracted to obtain GMT 15 35 37.

The Time Diagram

As stated previously, time as used in navigation is based on the apparent movement of the mean sun around the earth, as the earth rotates on its axis once each twenty-four hours. To avoid errors in visualizing the relationship of the local meridian, the Greenwich meridian, and the celestial meridian (hour circle) containing the location of the mean sun, it is convenient to draw a sketch called the *time diagram*. To construct such a diagram, imagine an observer in space looking up at the South Pole of the earth, which will then be located at the center of a circle whose circumference represents the celestial equator. Meridians and hour circles will appear as straight lines radiating from the center like spokes of a wheel. The upper branch of the local meridian is *always*, by convention, at the top of the diagram and is illustrated by a solid line labeled *M*; the lower branch, labeled *m*, is illustrated by a dotted line from the center to the bottom of the diagram. All westward directions will increase progressively to the left, or counterclockwise, and eastward directions will increase clockwise, or to the right. (See Figure 2-3.) The upper branch of the Greenwich meridian is represented by a solid line labeled G, and the lower branch by a dotted line *g*. The hour circle of the sun is indicated by the symbol ⊙. Figure 2-3 illustrates the time diagram for an observer in 45° west longitude, and it is obvious that Greenwich will be drawn in 45°, or three hours in time, eastward, or clockwise on the diagram, from the local meridian. If the local hour angle (LHA) of the sun at that time is 165°, it will be evident from the diagram that the sun has already crossed the lower branch of the Greenwich meridian, thus starting a new Greenwich day. It will also be seen that it has not yet crossed the lower branch of the local meridian. Thus, the date at Greenwich is one day greater.

Figure 2-4 depicts the time diagram for an observer at 60° east longitude. If the LHA of the sun is 200°, it will already have crossed the lower branch of the observer's meridian but not the lower branch of the Greenwich meridian. The date at Greenwich is therefore one day less than the local date. Whenever the hour circle of the sun falls between the lower branches of the local and Greenwich meridians, the local date and Greenwich date will be different. In all other cases the local and Greenwich dates will be the same. The relationship of arc to time is always evident. In Figure 2-4 the time at Greenwich will be four hours earlier than the local time, which can be visualized by the fact that the sun will cross the local meridian before it crosses the Greenwich meridian in its westerly progress across the sky. Further uses of the time diagram will be discussed in Chapter 3.

The International Date Line

The majority of yachtsmen in the United States never cross the Pacific and thus do not become involved with the problem of losing

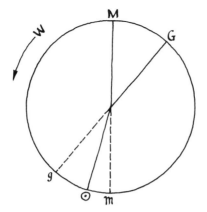

FIGURE 2-3   *The time diagram for an observer in west longitude.*

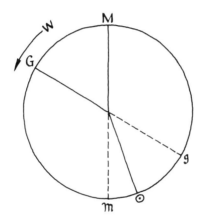

FIGURE 2-4   *The time diagram for an observer in east longitude.*

or gaining a day when crossing the international date line. This line is located for navigational purposes at the 180th meridian. In order to keep a common time in geographical areas near the date line, some shore areas use the date of the opposite side of the line. For those who do not encounter the problem often, it is almost impossible to remember the rule for reducing the local date by one day when sailing east across the line and adding a day when sailing west. The day that is added or subtracted from the local date has no effect on the Greenwich date, which remains the same no matter what time zone the ship is in. Remember that each time zone covers 15° of longitude and that the zone is centered on a standard meridian. With 180° as the standard meridian, the part of the zone that is in west longitude has a zone description of +12, and the part of the zone that is in east longitude has a zone description of −12 (see Figure 2-2). In exactly the same manner as any other problem of converting local time to Greenwich time, 12 hours are added when the ship is in the +12 zone and 12 hours are subtracted when in the −12 zone. If the rule for changing the date cannot be remembered, it can be figured logically by noting that if the vessel has been moving west, the ship's clocks have constantly been set back one hour as each time zone was crossed. This must now be compensated for by increasing the local date by one day as the date line is crossed.

Timing Celestial Observation

The largest source of error in celestial navigation is generally the navigator himself, especially in his attempts to measure and record time exactly. Many methods have been used to obtain the time of the celestial observation. The ideal is for the timepiece used by the observer or his assistant to read GMT and to be free of error. Otherwise, the mental arithmetic or the paper and pencil conversions lead to possible errors, including that of incorrectly applying a plus or a minus.

GMT *must* be available aboard the vessel. This can be accomplished by carrying a chronometer or by having the radio time tick constantly available. Excellent quartz-crystal chronometers are now available; they keep far better time than the older, traditional windup types and are less expensive. They can be used on the smallest yacht or the largest ocean-going vessel. On the best models the accuracy is better than 0.1 second per day over a wide temperature range. The electronic unit is both temperature- and voltage-compensated and is monitored by a vibrating quartz crystal. A number of quartz-crystal chronometers on the market maintain a rate of accuracy of better than 0.5 seconds per day. One of these, the Chelsea Quartz Chronometer, is shown in Figure 2-5. The daily rate of accuracy and whether the rate is constant are important. Statements of accuracy such as "better than a half-minute a year" illustrate dramatically just how good the quartz-crystal chronometers can be, but are insufficient for navigation purposes. Rather than a yearly average, the exact error and rate must be known at a given time.

If a chronometer is not carried, it is necessary to have a good radio receiver capable of picking up time signals. Off the East Coast of the United States, station WWV, which is broadcast from Colorado, is often difficult to pick up without a high-quality receiver. Since the time is broadcast on a number of frequencies, a choice is available for both day and night reception. If reception is poor on one frequency, the user should try a different one. Radio time signals are discussed in greater detail later in this chapter. The most important item concerning time is the actual timing of the observations.

A great variety of timepieces are available; the method of timing used depends on the type of watch or stopwatch being utilized. The timepiece must be capable of being set to the exact second of time. This is generally accomplished by a hack feature that returns the second hand to zero, whence it is restarted by depressing a button. Some models also have a rotating bezel that can be used to read seconds. The following are some of the timing methods that can be used with different timepieces.

FIGURE 2-5 A quartz chronometer (courtesy of Weems & Plath, Inc.)

*Using a stopwatch (timer) and a master navigation watch
or chronometer*

In this method the timer is normally started at the exact second the observation is made, and is then taken to the chronometer. The timer is stopped at any exact reading on the chronometer. When the reading on the timer is subtracted from that of the chronometer, and any chronometer error is applied, the exact time of the observation will be known. We do not normally recommend this system, as much time is required between observations. However, some observers keep several stopwatches and use this system.

Using a second-setting watch

When a watch is available to which the exact second can be set, the mechanism should be stopped and set at the time of the next upcoming signal from WWV, or at the next even minute of time on the chronometer. Listen to the radio time tick and start the watch at the exact instant of the signal. The advantage of this method is that GMT can easily be set on the watch and the time of the observation can be read directly in hours, minutes, and seconds. If the watch is set to local time rather than GMT, the zone description must be applied in order to obtain GMT. When using the second-setting watch, which generally must be read on the fly (that is, without stopping the mechanism), it is best to have an assistant read and record the time, the observer calling "Mark" at the instant of the observation.

Using a stopwatch (timer) and the radio time tick

Start the timer at the start of an exact minute on the time tick or at the start of a whole minute obtained from the chronometer, after applying the correction. Record the GMT when the timer was started. At each sextant observation read the timer and record the time, which is then added to the GMT at which the timer was started. If multiple sights are to be taken, do not stop the timer with each sight or the time will be lost until the navigator can restart the timer to GMT.

Using a split-second timer

By far the best method available for yachtsmen is to use a split-second timer. These timers have a double, or split, second hand. By depressing a button at the time of the observation, one hand stops and can then be read at leisure. When the button is pushed again, this hand rejoins the other part of the second hand, which has continued to run. Any number of observations can be timed using this method, and there is little chance for error. The split-second timer is started from either a corrected chronometer reading or a radio time tick, the time of starting being recorded. The time of each observation is then recorded and added to the time at which the watch was started. (See Figure 2-6.)

Using a split-second chronograph

The split-second feature discussed above is available on some pocket-sized chronographs. The chronograph is set to GMT by comparing it with the radio time tick or the chronometer. The time of each observation can be taken by stopping the split-second hand and recording the GMT. The split-second hand is then started again. Multiple sights can be taken and no corrections are necessary in order to obtain GMT.

Radio Time Signals

Most large commercial vessels carry one or more chronometers, from which the navigator can obtain GMT over long periods of time without using a remote time reference. Even with the best chronometer

FIGURE 2-6   The split-second timer (courtesy of Weems & Plath, Inc.)

available, however, it is good practice to check its accuracy against the radio time signals at periodic intervals. Yachtsmen, most of whom do not have a high-quality chronometer on board, must obtain the time shortly before taking celestial observations. Throughout the world, many different time signals are broadcast; these are listed in H.O. Publication No. 117, *Radio Navigational Aids,* published by the Defense Mapping Agency Hydrographic Center. Some of these signals are broadcast only on a given, published schedule. In our brief description, only the continuous signals will be discussed. These consist primarily of American stations WWV and WWVH; the Canadian station CHU is also convenient for operations off the East Coast of the United States.

WWV and WWVH

The National Bureau of Standards broadcasts continuous time signals from station WWV in Fort Collins, Colorado, and from station WWVH on Kauai in the Hawaiian Islands. The format for these broadcasts is shown in Figure 2-7. In addition to the time tick, a great amount of scientific information is given; this includes standard radio and audio frequencies, standard musical pitch, standard time intervals, time signals, Omega navigation status reports, and special announcements, such as gale warnings for the Atlantic and Pacific oceans.

For the navigator, the time tick for each second is the important service. The voice announcements now designate the time as Coordinated Universal Time, which, for the navigator, is the same as Greenwich Mean Time. This voice announcement of time immediately precedes the start of the minute; WWV uses a male voice and WWVH a female voice. When the tone marker returns, it signifies the start of the minute that has been announced by voice. The ticks for the 59th and 29th seconds are omitted to prepare the navigator for the beginning of the whole minute or half minute when starting a hack watch.

Station WWV broadcasts on 2.5, 5, 10, and 15 MHz (megahertz). Station WWVH broadcasts on all of these same frequencies. For the first 45 seconds of each minute a musical tone is broadcast with the time tick, but it is omitted during the voice announcement. The Canadian station CHU also transmits a beat each second, with certain omissions; the voice announcement is made in English and in French. The navigator who normally uses WWV will have no difficulty ascertaining the time from this signal. CHU transmits on frequencies of 3.33, 7.335, and 14.67 MHz.

Short-wave radio signals used for the time signals produce sky waves rather than ground waves for over-the-horizon transmissions. The signals bounce off the layers of the ionosphere and back to earth, sometimes several times. The signals on a given frequency may there-

WWV BROADCAST FORMAT

VIA TELEPHONE (303) 499-7111
(NOT A TOLL-FREE NUMBER)

U S DEPARTMENT OF COMMERCE
National Bureau of Standards

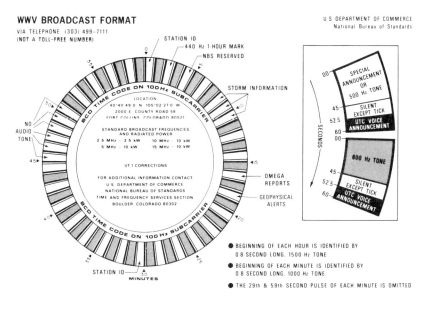

- BEGINNING OF EACH HOUR IS IDENTIFIED BY 0.8 SECOND LONG, 1500 Hz TONE
- BEGINNING OF EACH MINUTE IS IDENTIFIED BY 0.8 SECOND LONG, 1000 Hz TONE
- THE 29th & 59th SECOND PULSE OF EACH MINUTE IS OMITTED

WWVH BROADCAST FORMAT

VIA TELEPHONE (808) 335-4363 (NOT A TOLL-FREE NUMBER)

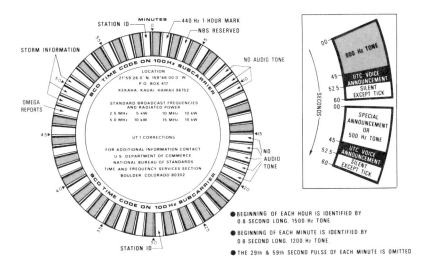

- BEGINNING OF EACH HOUR IS IDENTIFIED BY 0.8-SECOND LONG, 1500 Hz TONE
- BEGINNING OF EACH MINUTE IS IDENTIFIED BY 0.8-SECOND LONG, 1200 Hz TONE
- THE 29th & 59th SECOND PULSE OF EACH MINUTE IS OMITTED

FIGURE 2-7   Radio time broadcast formats.

fore skip an area and still be received at another point farther away from the transmitter. If the signal cannot be received, the navigator should switch to a different frequency. In general, frequencies up to about 10 MHz are received better at night and those above 10 MHz are received better during daylight. This is not an infallible rule, however, and it may be necessary to try several frequencies before receiving a satisfactory signal.

The quality of the receiver is perhaps the most important factor in good reception of signals. The use of an exterior antenna instead of the small telescoping antenna supplied on most portable receiving sets will improve reception. An insulated wire run up a halyard will serve well on a sailboat.

At very great distances from the transmitter, as when making transoceanic passages, the reception may be poor at times, and it is then necessary to choose a best time for reception. In general, reception is best when both the transmitter and receiver are operating in daylight or when both are operating in darkness. When the dark line between daylight and night lies between the two, atmospheric conditions are seldom as good.

Since celestial navigation depends on accurate time, a chronometer or a good radio receiver and a spare should always be aboard and in working order for extended offshore navigation.

Chapter 3

The *Nautical Almanac*

**Using the *Nautical Almanac* to Determine the Position
of Celestial Bodies**

In Chapter 1 positions of the celestial bodies on the celestial sphere (analogous to the GP of the body on earth) were given in terms of Greenwich hour angle (GHA) and declination (dec.). By using the hourly tabulations and the corrections for increments of minutes and seconds that are found in the *Nautical Almanac*, values of GHA can be found for every second of time throughout the year. This is necessary, since hour angle changes in direct relation to time as the earth rotates on its axis.

The declination of a star is almost constant; stars are therefore often referred to as "fixed." There is, of course, a slow change in their declination, for all celestial bodies are moving in space at fantastic speeds. However, the stars are at such a great distance from the earth that the angle, subtended at the earth as they move, is very small, and the declination therefore changes very slowly. The declinations of the stars are tabulated in the *Almanac* only once for every three days, on the opening page of each three-day tabulation. This listing could be much less frequent for most stars without affecting the accuracy of the tabulations. Due to their comparative closeness to the earth and to their interrelationship, navigational bodies within our solar system exhibit a much more rapid change in declination. Declination is listed hourly for the sun, moon, and planets, and requires a further *d* correction for minutes of time, as described below.

Two pages from the *Nautical Almanac*, containing tabulations for three days, are reproduced in Table 3-1 of the present text. These are

31

NOVEMBER 3, 4, 5 (SUN., MON., TUES.)

G.M.T.	ARIES G.H.A.	VENUS −3.5 G.H.A.	Dec.	MARS +1·8 G.H.A.	Dec.	JUPITER −2·2 G.H.A.	Dec.	SATURN +0·2 G.H.A.	Dec.	STARS Name	S.H.A.	Dec.
3 00	41 52·3	184 41·3	S 13 44·8	190 08·0	S 12 26·6	61 42·5	S 9 50·1	291 28·5	N 21 38·4	Acamar	315 39·8	S 40 24·2
01	56 54·8	199 40·7	45·9	205 08·9	27·2	76 45·0	50·1	306 31·0	38·4	Achernar	335 47·6	S 57 21·8
02	71 57·3	214 40·2	46·9	220 09·7	27·8	91 47·5	50·1	321 33·5	38·4	Acrux	173 42·4	S 62 57·5
03	86 59·7	229 39·6	·· 48·0	235 10·5	·· 28·4	106 49·9	·· 50·1	336 36·0	·· 38·4	Adhara	255 35·1	S 28 56·1
04	102 02·2	244 39·0	49·1	250 11·4	29·0	121 52·4	50·1	351 38·4	38·4	Aldebaran	291 22·3	N 16 27·6
05	117 04·6	259 38·4	50·1	265 12·2	29·6	136 54·9	50·0	6 40·9	38·4			
06	132 07·1	274 37·9	S 13 51·2	280 13·1	S 12 30·2	151 57·4	S 9 50·0	21 43·4	N 21 38·4	Alioth	166 46·5	N 56 05·6
07	147 09·6	289 37·3	52·3	295 13·9	30·8	166 59·8	50·0	36 45·9	38·4	Alkaid	153 22·1	N 49 26·2
08	162 12·0	304 36·7	53·3	310 14·7	31·4	182 02·3	50·0	51 48·3	38·5	Al Na'ir	28 19·8	S 47 05·1
S 09	177 14·5	319 36·1	·· 54·4	325 15·6	·· 32·0	197 04·8	·· 50·0	66 50·8	·· 38·5	Alnilam	276 15·5	S 1 12·9
U 10	192 17·0	334 35·6	55·5	340 16·4	32·6	212 07·2	50·0	81 53·3	38·5	Alphard	218 24·6	S 8 32·9
N 11	207 19·4	349 35·0	56·5	355 17·3	33·2	227 09·7	50·0	96 55·8	38·5			
D 12	222 21·9	4 34·4	S 13 57·6	10 18·1	S 12 33·7	242 12·2	S 9 50·0	111 58·3	N 21 38·5	Alphecca	126 35·9	N 26 48·0
A 13	237 24·4	19 33·8	58·6	25 18·9	34·3	257 14·6	50·0	127 00·7	38·5	Alpheratz	358 13·2	N 28 57·4
Y 14	252 26·8	34 33·3	13 59·7	40 19·8	34·9	272 17·1	50·0	142 03·2	38·5	Altair	62 36·6	N 8 48·3
15	267 29·3	49 32·7	14 00·8	55 20·6	·· 35·5	287 19·6	·· 50·0	157 05·7	·· 38·5	Ankaa	353 43·8	S 42 26·5
16	282 31·8	64 32·1	01·8	70 21·4	36·1	302 22·0	50·0	172 08·2	38·5	Antares	113 02·1	S 26 22·6
17	297 34·2	79 31·5	02·9	85 22·3	36·7	317 24·5	50·0	187 10·7	38·5			
18	312 36·7	94 30·9	S 14 03·9	100 23·1	S 12 37·3	332 27·0	S 9 49·9	202 13·1	N 21 38·5	Arcturus	146 22·5	N 19 18·8
19	327 39·1	109 30·4	05·0	115 24·0	37·9	347 29·4	49·9	217 15·6	38·5	Atria	108 30·5	S 68 59·1
20	342 41·6	124 29·8	06·0	130 24·8	38·5	2 31·9	49·9	232 18·1	38·5	Avior	234 29·8	S 59 25·5
21	357 44·1	139 29·2	·· 07·1	145 25·6	·· 39·1	17 34·4	·· 49·9	247 20·6	·· 38·5	Bellatrix	279 02·8	N 6 19·7
22	12 46·5	154 28·6	08·2	160 26·5	39·7	32 36·8	49·9	262 23·0	38·5	Betelgeuse	271 32·4	N 7 24·2
23	27 49·0	169 28·0	09·2	175 27·3	40·2	47 39·3	49·9	277 25·5	38·5			
4 00	42 51·5	184 27·4	S 14 10·3	190 28·1	S 12 40·8	62 41·7	S 9 49·9	292 28·0	N 21 38·5	Canopus	264 08·7	S 52 40·7
01	57 53·9	199 26·9	11·3	205 29·0	41·4	77 44·2	49·9	307 30·5	38·5	Capella	281 16·9	N 45 58·4
02	72 56·4	214 26·3	12·4	220 29·8	42·0	92 46·7	49·9	322 33·0	38·5	Deneb	49 51·3	N 45 11·8
03	87 58·9	229 25·7	·· 13·4	235 30·7	·· 42·6	107 49·1	·· 49·9	337 35·5	·· 38·5	Denebola	183 03·4	N 14 42·7
04	103 01·3	244 25·1	14·5	250 31·5	43·2	122 51·6	49·9	352 37·9	38·5	Diphda	349 24·6	S 18 07·3
05	118 03·8	259 24·5	15·5	265 32·3	43·8	137 54·1	49·8	7 40·4	38·5			
06	133 06·3	274 23·9	S 14 16·6	280 33·2	S 12 44·4	152 56·5	S 9 49·8	22 42·9	N 21 38·5	Dubhe	194 27·4	N 61 52·9
07	148 08·7	289 23·3	17·6	295 34·0	45·0	167 59·0	49·8	37 45·4	38·5	Elnath	278 48·9	N 28 35·2
08	163 11·2	304 22·8	18·7	310 34·8	45·5	183 01·4	49·8	52 47·9	38·6	Eltanin	91 00·0	N 51 29·8
M 09	178 13·6	319 22·2	·· 19·7	325 35·7	·· 46·1	198 03·9	·· 49·8	67 50·3	·· 38·6	Enif	34 15·5	N 9 45·8
O 10	193 16·1	334 21·6	20·8	340 36·5	46·7	213 06·4	49·8	82 52·8	38·6	Fomalhaut	15 55·6	S 29 45·3
N 11	208 18·6	349 21·0	21·8	355 37·3	47·3	228 08·8	49·8	97 55·3	38·6			
D 12	223 21·0	4 20·4	S 14 22·9	10 38·2	S 12 47·9	243 11·3	S 9 49·8	112 57·8	N 21 38·6	Gacrux	172 33·8	S 56 58·2
A 13	238 23·5	19 19·8	23·9	25 39·0	48·5	258 13·7	49·8	128 00·3	38·6	Gienah	176 22·4	S 17 24·1
Y 14	253 26·0	34 19·2	25·0	40 39·8	49·1	273 16·2	49·7	143 02·8	38·6	Hadar	149 29·7	S 60 15·1
15	268 28·4	49 18·6	·· 26·0	55 40·7	·· 49·7	288 18·7	·· 49·7	158 05·2	·· 38·6	Hamal	328 33·1	N 23 20·8
16	283 30·9	64 18·0	27·0	70 41·5	50·3	303 21·1	49·7	173 07·7	38·6	Kaus Aust.	84 22·4	S 34 23·9
17	298 33·4	79 17·5	28·1	85 42·3	50·8	318 23·6	49·7	188 10·2	38·6			
18	313 35·8	94 16·9	S 14 29·1	100 43·2	S 12 51·4	333 26·0	S 9 49·7	203 12·7	N 21 38·6	Kochab	137 19·9	N 74 15·5
19	328 38·3	109 16·3	30·2	115 44·0	52·0	348 28·5	49·7	218 15·2	38·6	Markab	14 07·0	N 15 04·5
20	343 40·7	124 15·7	31·2	130 44·8	52·6	3 31·0	49·7	233 17·7	38·6	Menkar	314 45·0	N 3 59·7
21	358 43·2	139 15·1	·· 32·3	145 45·7	·· 53·2	18 33·4	·· 49·7	248 20·1	·· 38·6	Menkent	148 42·2	S 36 14·8
22	13 45·7	154 14·5	33·3	160 46·5	53·8	33 35·9	49·6	263 22·6	38·6	Miaplacidus	221 45·9	S 69 36·6
23	28 48·1	169 13·9	34·3	175 47·3	54·4	48 38·3	49·6	278 25·1	38·6			
5 00	43 50·6	184 13·3	S 14 35·4	190 48·2	S 12 54·9	63 40·8	S 9 49·6	293 27·6	N 21 38·6	Mirfak	309 21·4	N 49 46·4
01	58 53·1	199 12·7	36·4	205 49·0	55·5	78 43·2	49·6	308 30·1	38·6	Nunki	76 34·3	S 26 19·7
02	73 55·5	214 12·1	37·5	220 49·8	56·1	93 45·7	49·6	323 32·6	38·6	Peacock	54 04·8	S 56 49·1
03	88 58·0	229 11·5	·· 38·5	235 50·7	·· 56·7	108 48·1	·· 49·6	338 35·1	·· 38·6	Pollux	244 02·9	N 28 05·5
04	104 00·5	244 10·9	39·5	250 51·5	57·3	123 50·6	49·6	353 37·5	38·6	Procyon	245 29·9	N 5 17·4
05	119 02·9	259 10·3	40·6	265 52·3	57·9	138 53·1	49·6	8 40·0	38·6			
06	134 05·4	274 09·7	S 14 41·6	280 53·2	S 12 58·5	153 55·5	S 9 49·5	23 42·5	N 21 38·7	Rasalhague	96 33·6	N 12 34·8
07	149 07·9	289 09·1	42·6	295 54·0	59·1	168 58·0	49·5	38 45·0	38·7	Regulus	208 14·4	N 12 05·5
08	164 10·3	304 08·5	43·7	310 54·8	12 59·6	184 00·4	49·5	53 47·5	38·7	Rigel	281 39·6	S 8 13·7
T 09	179 12·8	319 07·9	·· 44·7	325 55·7	13 00·2	199 02·9	·· 49·5	68 50·0	·· 38·7	Rigil Kent.	140 32·0	S 60 43·9
U 10	194 15·2	334 07·3	45·7	340 56·5	00·8	214 05·3	49·5	83 52·5	38·7	Sabik	102 46·0	S 15 41·6
E 11	209 17·7	349 06·7	46·8	355 57·3	01·4	229 07·8	49·5	98 55·0	38·7			
S 12	224 20·2	4 06·1	S 14 47·8	10 58·1	S 13 02·0	244 10·2	S 9 49·5	113 57·4	N 21 38·7	Schedar	350 13·2	N 56 24·3
D 13	239 22·6	19 05·5	48·8	25 59·0	02·6	259 12·7	49·4	128 59·9	38·7	Shaula	97 01·5	S 37 05·2
A 14	254 25·1	34 04·9	49·9	40 59·8	03·1	274 15·1	49·4	144 02·4	38·7	Sirius	258 59·1	S 16 40·8
Y 15	269 27·6	49 04·3	·· 50·9	56 00·6	·· 03·7	289 17·6	·· 49·4	159 04·9	·· 38·7	Spica	159 02·1	S 11 01·4
16	284 30·0	64 03·7	51·9	71 01·5	04·3	304 20·0	49·4	174 07·4	38·7	Suhail	223 13·8	S 43 19·6
17	299 32·5	79 03·1	52·9	86 02·3	04·9	319 22·5	49·4	189 09·9	38·7			
18	314 35·0	94 02·5	S 14 54·0	101 03·1	S 13 05·5	334 24·9	S 9 49·4	204 12·4	N 21 38·7	Vega	80 58·8	N 38 45·5
19	329 37·4	109 01·9	55·0	116 03·9	06·1	349 27·4	49·4	219 14·9	38·7	Zuben'ubi	137 37·8	S 15 56·2
20	344 39·9	124 01·3	56·0	131 04·8	06·6	4 29·8	49·3	234 17·4	38·7			
21	359 42·4	139 00·7	·· 57·0	146 05·6	·· 07·2	19 32·3	·· 49·3	249 19·8	·· 38·7			
22	14 44·8	154 00·1	58·1	161 06·4	07·8	34 34·7	49·3	264 22·3	38·7			
23	29 47·3	168 59·5	59·1	176 07·3	08·4	49 37·2	49·3	279 24·8	38·7			
Mer. Pass. 21 05·1		v −0·6 d 1·0		v 0·8 d 0·6		v 2·5 d 0·0		v 2·5 d 0·0				

	S.H.A.	Mer. Pass.
Venus	141 36·0	11 43
Mars	147 36·7	11 17
Jupiter	19 50·3	19 46
Saturn	249 36·5	4 29

TABLE 3-1 Two daily pages from the Nautical Almanac.

NOVEMBER 3, 4, 5 (SUN., MON., TUES.)

G.M.T.	SUN G.H.A.	SUN Dec.	MOON G.H.A.	v	MOON Dec.	d	H.P.
d h	° ′	° ′	° ′	′	° ′	′	′
3 00	184 06·1	S14 52·4	326 10·1	6·3	N22 12·6	0·2	58·3
01	199 06·1	53·2	340 35·4	6·2	22 12·8	0·1	58·3
02	214 06·1	54·0	355 00·7	6·2	22 12·9	0·1	58·3
03	229 06·1 ··	54·8	9 25·9	6·2	22 12·8	0·2	58·3
04	244 06·1	55·6	23 51·1	6·3	22 12·6	0·4	58·3
05	259 06·1	56·4	38 16·4	6·2	22 12·2	0·5	58·3
06	274 06·1	S14 57·1	52 41·6	6·2	N22 11·7	0·7	58·4
07	289 06·1	57·9	67 06·8	6·2	22 11·0	0·8	58·4
08	304 06·1	58·7	81 32·0	6·1	22 10·2	0·9	58·4
S 09	319 06·1	14 59·5	95 57·1	6·2	22 09·3	1·1	58·4
U 10	334 06·1	15 00·3	110 22·3	6·2	22 08·2	1·2	58·4
N 11	349 06·1	01·1	124 47·5	6·1	22 07·0	1·3	58·4
D 12	4 06·1	S15 01·8	139 12·6	6·2	N22 05·7	1·5	58·5
A 13	19 06·1	02·6	153 37·8	6·2	22 04·2	1·7	58·5
Y 14	34 06·1	03·4	168 03·0	6·1	22 02·5	1·8	58·5
15	49 06·1 ··	04·2	182 28·1	6·2	22 00·7	1·9	58·5
16	64 06·1	05·0	196 53·3	6·1	21 58·8	2·1	58·5
17	79 06·1	05·7	211 18·4	6·2	21 56·7	2·2	58·5
18	94 06·1	S15 06·5	225 43·6	6·2	N21 54·5	2·3	58·5
19	109 06·1	07·3	240 08·8	6·2	21 52·2	2·5	58·6
20	124 06·1	08·1	254 34·0	6·1	21 49·7	2·6	58·6
21	139 06·1 ··	08·9	268 59·1	6·2	21 47·1	2·8	58·6
22	154 06·1	09·6	283 24·3	6·2	21 44·3	2·9	58·6
23	169 06·1	10·4	297 49·5	6·3	21 41·4	3·1	58·6
4 00	184 06·1	S15 11·2	312 14·8	6·2	N21 38·3	3·2	58·6
01	199 06·1	12·0	326 40·0	6·2	21 35·1	3·3	58·6
02	214 06·1	12·7	341 05·2	6·3	21 31·8	3·5	58·7
03	229 06·1 ··	13·5	355 30·5	6·3	21 28·3	3·6	58·7
04	244 06·1	14·3	9 55·8	6·3	21 24·7	3·7	58·7
05	259 06·1	15·1	24 21·1	6·3	21 21·0	3·9	58·7
06	274 06·1	S15 15·8	38 46·4	6·3	N21 17·1	4·0	58·7
07	289 06·1	16·6	53 11·7	6·4	21 13·1	4·2	58·7
08	304 06·1	17·4	67 37·1	6·4	21 08·9	4·3	58·7
M 09	319 06·1 ··	18·2	82 02·5	6·4	21 04·6	4·4	58·7
O 10	334 06·0	18·9	96 27·9	6·4	21 00·2	4·6	58·7
N 11	349 06·0	19·7	110 53·3	6·5	20 55·6	4·7	58·8
D 12	4 06·0	S15 20·5	125 18·8	6·4	N20 50·9	4·8	58·8
A 13	19 06·0	21·3	139 44·2	6·6	20 46·1	5·0	58·8
Y 14	34 06·0	22·0	154 09·8	6·5	20 41·1	5·1	58·8
15	49 06·0 ··	22·8	168 35·3	6·6	20 36·0	5·2	58·8
16	64 06·0	23·6	183 00·9	6·6	20 30·8	5·3	58·8
17	79 06·0	24·3	197 26·5	6·6	20 25·5	5·5	58·8
18	94 06·0	S15 25·1	211 52·1	6·7	N20 20·0	5·7	58·8
19	109 06·0	25·9	226 17·8	6·7	20 14·3	5·7	58·8
20	124 06·0	26·6	240 43·5	6·7	20 08·6	5·9	58·9
21	139 06·0 ··	27·4	255 09·2	6·8	20 02·7	6·0	58·9
22	154 05·9	28·2	269 35·0	6·8	19 56·7	6·1	58·9
23	169 05·9	28·9	284 00·8	6·9	19 50·6	6·3	58·9
5 00	184 05·9	S15 29·7	298 26·7	6·9	N19 44·3	6·4	58·9
01	199 05·9	30·5	312 52·6	6·9	19 37·9	6·5	58·9
02	214 05·9	31·2	327 18·5	7·0	19 31·4	6·6	58·9
03	229 05·9 ··	32·0	341 44·5	7·0	19 24·8	6·8	58·9
04	244 05·9	32·8	356 10·5	7·0	19 18·0	6·9	58·9
05	259 05·9	33·5	10 36·5	7·1	19 11·1	7·0	58·9
06	274 05·9	S15 34·3	25 02·6	7·2	N19 04·1	7·1	59·0
07	289 05·8	35·1	39 28·8	7·2	18 57·0	7·3	59·0
T 08	304 05·8	35·8	53 55·0	7·2	18 49·7	7·3	59·0
U 09	319 05·8 ··	36·6	68 21·2	7·3	18 42·4	7·5	59·0
E 10	334 05·8	37·4	82 47·5	7·3	18 34·9	7·6	59·0
S 11	349 05·8	38·1	97 13·8	7·3	18 27·3	7·7	59·0
D 12	4 05·8	S15 38·9	111 40·1	7·4	N18 19·6	7·8	59·0
A 13	19 05·7	39·6	126 06·5	7·5	18 11·8	8·0	59·0
Y 14	34 05·7	40·4	140 33·0	7·5	18 03·8	8·0	59·0
15	49 05·7 ··	41·2	154 59·5	7·5	17 55·8	8·2	59·0
16	64 05·7	41·9	169 26·0	7·6	17 47·6	8·3	59·0
17	79 05·7	42·7	183 52·6	7·7	17 39·3	8·4	59·0
18	94 05·7	S15 43·4	198 19·3	7·7	N17 30·9	8·5	59·1
19	109 05·6	44·2	212 46·0	7·7	17 22·4	8·6	59·1
20	124 05·6	45·0	227 12·7	7·8	17 13·8	8·7	59·1
21	139 05·6 ··	45·7	241 39·5	7·8	17 05·1	8·8	59·1
22	154 05·6	46·5	256 06·3	7·9	16 56·3	8·9	59·1
23	169 05·6	47·2	270 33·2	7·9	16 47·4	9·0	59·1
	S.D. 16·2	d 0·8	S.D. 15·9		16·0		16·1

Moonrise

Lat.	Twilight Naut.	Twilight Civil	Sun-rise	3	4	5	6
°	h m	h m	h m	h m	h m	h m	h m
N 72	06 16	07 41	09 13	☐	☐	17 48	20 44
N 70	06 11	07 26	08 44	☐	☐	18 55	21 09
68	06 06	07 14	08 21	15 18	17 28	19 31	21 29
66	06 02	07 05	08 04	16 38	18 11	19 56	21 44
64	05 59	06 56	07 50	17 15	18 39	20 16	21 57
62	05 56	06 49	07 39	17 42	19 01	20 32	22 07
60	05 53	06 43	07 29	18 02	19 19	20 45	22 16
N 58	05 50	06 37	07 20	18 19	19 33	20 57	22 24
56	05 48	06 32	07 12	18 34	19 46	21 07	22 31
54	05 46	06 28	07 05	18 46	19 57	21 15	22 37
52	05 43	06 23	06 59	18 57	20 07	21 23	22 43
50	05 41	06 20	06 54	19 06	20 15	21 30	22 48
45	05 36	06 11	06 42	19 27	20 34	21 45	22 58
N 40	05 32	06 04	06 32	19 43	20 48	21 57	23 07
35	05 27	05 57	06 23	19 57	21 01	22 07	23 15
30	05 21	05 51	06 16	20 09	21 12	22 17	23 21
20	05 14	05 40	06 03	20 30	21 31	22 32	23 33
N 10	05 04	05 29	05 51	20 48	21 47	22 46	23 43
0	04 54	05 19	05 40	21 05	22 02	22 58	23 52
S 10	04 42	05 07	05 29	21 22	22 18	23 11	24 02
20	04 27	04 54	05 17	21 40	22 34	23 24	24 12
30	04 08	04 38	05 03	22 00	22 53	23 40	24 23
35	03 56	04 28	04 55	22 12	23 03	23 49	24 29
40	03 41	04 17	04 46	22 26	23 16	23 59	24 37
45	03 23	04 03	04 35	22 43	23 30	24 11	00 11
S 50	02 59	03 46	04 22	23 03	23 48	24 25	00 25
52	02 47	03 37	04 16	23 13	23 57	24 32	00 32
54	02 33	03 28	04 09	23 23	24 06	00 06	00 39
56	02 16	03 17	04 02	23 36	24 16	00 16	00 47
58	01 55	03 05	03 53	23 50	24 28	00 28	00 57
S 60	01 27	02 50	03 43	24 07	00 07	00 42	01 07

Moonset

Lat.	Sun-set	Twilight Civil	Twilight Naut.	3	4	5	6
°	h m	h m	h m	h m	h m	h m	h m
N 72	14 13	15 45	17 09	☐	☐	15 56	14 54
N 70	14 42	16 00	17 15	☐	☐	14 47	14 27
68	15 05	16 11	17 19	14 24	14 15	14 10	14 06
66	15 22	16 21	17 23	13 04	13 32	13 44	13 49
64	15 36	16 30	17 27	12 27	13 03	13 23	13 35
62	15 48	16 37	17 30	12 00	12 41	13 07	13 24
60	15 58	16 43	17 33	11 39	12 23	12 53	13 14
N 58	16 06	16 49	17 36	11 22	12 08	12 41	13 05
56	16 14	16 54	17 39	11 08	11 55	12 30	12 58
54	16 21	16 59	17 41	10 55	11 43	12 21	12 51
52	16 27	17 03	17 43	10 44	11 33	12 13	12 44
50	16 33	17 07	17 45	10 35	11 25	12 05	12 39
45	16 45	17 16	17 50	10 14	11 06	11 49	12 27
N 40	16 55	17 23	17 55	09 57	10 50	11 36	12 17
35	17 04	17 30	18 00	09 43	10 37	11 25	12 08
30	17 11	17 36	18 04	09 31	10 26	11 15	12 00
20	17 24	17 47	18 13	09 10	10 06	10 58	11 47
N 10	17 36	17 58	18 23	08 52	09 49	10 43	11 35
0	17 47	18 09	18 33	08 35	09 32	10 29	11 24
S 10	17 58	18 20	18 46	08 17	09 16	10 15	11 13
20	18 10	18 33	19 01	07 59	08 59	10 00	11 01
30	18 24	18 50	19 20	07 38	08 39	09 43	10 47
35	18 32	19 00	19 32	07 25	08 27	09 32	10 39
40	18 42	19 11	19 47	07 11	08 13	09 21	10 30
45	18 53	19 25	20 06	06 54	07 57	09 07	10 20
S 50	19 06	19 43	20 30	06 33	07 38	08 50	10 06
52	19 12	19 51	20 43	06 23	07 28	08 42	10 00
54	19 19	20 01	20 57	06 12	07 18	08 33	09 54
56	19 27	20 12	21 14	05 59	07 06	08 23	09 46
58	19 36	20 25	21 36	05 44	06 52	08 11	09 37
S 60	19 46	20 40	22 06	05 26	06 35	07 58	09 28

SUN and MOON

Day	SUN Eqn. of Time 00h	SUN Eqn. of Time 12h	SUN Mer. Pass.	MOON Mer. Pass. Upper	MOON Mer. Pass. Lower	Age	Phase
	m s	m s	h m	h m	h m	d	
3	16 24	16 24	11 44	02 21	14 50	19	
4	16 24	16 24	11 44	03 19	15 47	20	●
5	16 24	16 23	11 44	04 16	16 44	21	

generally referred to as the "daily pages." These pages contain separate columns of GHA and declination for the sun, moon, and four planets plus a column for GHA Aries (to be explained in the following paragraph). If similar hourly tabulations were given for each navigational star (there are 57 in the list in Table 3-1, and others can be used), the *Almanac* would be so voluminous as to be unwieldy.

To accommodate the listing of the 57 stars in a reasonable space, they are tabulated in terms of sidereal hour angle (SHA) and declination once on each two facing pages, which cover three days. These values are used without interpolation. GHA Aries is tabulated hourly, and this value, together with the correction for minutes and seconds, is added to the SHA of the star to obtain the GHA of the star at any instant. This discussion has introduced two new terms not explained in Chapter 1. Aries (Υ) is an arbitrary fixed point in the sky; it is also called the *vernal equinox*, as it marks the location in space of the sun when it crosses the celestial equator, or equinoctial, in the spring, when it changes its declination from south to north. Like any other point on the celestial sphere, it constantly changes in GHA due to the rotation of the earth. The symbol Υ, the ram's horns, is often used to designate this first point of Aries, generally referred to simply as Aries. SHA is measured to the west (from 000° to 360°), from the celestial meridian (which is called the *hour circle* on the celestial sphere) of Aries to the hour circle (celestial meridian) of the star. GHAΥ+SHA☆=GHA☆. If this value exceeds 360°, subtract 360° from the total. (See Figures 3-1 and 3-2.)

Two common errors are frequently made in using the *Nautical Almanac*; they can be avoided only by careful attention to detail when using the tables. The first is using the wrong day. Note that three days

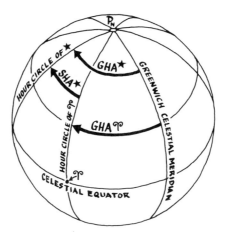

FIGURE 3-1   *GHA* ☆ = *GHA* Υ + *SHA* ☆ *when GHA* Υ + *GHA* ☆ *is less than 360°.*

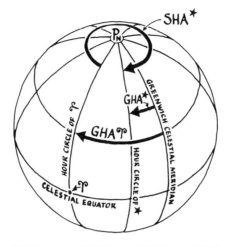

FIGURE 3-2 GHA☆ = GHAƮ + SHA☆ - 360° when GHAƮ + GHA☆ exceeds 360°.

are tabulated on each pair of facing pages. These are separated by a horizontal solid line and are clearly labeled in the GMT column. It is easy to select the correct line for the hour of GMT while using the wrong date. For example, if the observer is in zone +8 on the 16th of the month and makes an observation at 1930 local time, the Greenwich time and date will be 0330 on the 17th. Greenwich time and date must be used when referring to the *Almanac*. The second common source of error results from extracting data from the wrong column, especially in the "Increments and Corrections" section in the yellow pages at the back of the *Almanac*.

Use of the *Almanac* is straightforward. The tabulations on the daily pages list both GHA and declination for each integral hour of GMT. For the minutes and seconds of time, turn to the yellow "Increments and Corrections" pages in the back of the *Almanac*. Two of these pages are reproduced in Table 3-2 of the present text. Minutes are listed at the top of the page, and seconds are listed vertically in the leftmost column of each minute section. It is important to remember that in these pages there are separate columns headed "Sun Planets," "Aries," and "Moon." The correct column must be used to find the addition of minutes and seconds of time to GHA. This is emphasized, as the additions to GHA in the various columns are only slightly different, and the use of the incorrect one would not be readily apparent when performing the sight reduction. However, incorrect use would cause the computation to be erroneous.

In each of these minutes sections there are also columns of *v* or *d* values and adjoining columns listing the correction for each of these

18 (s)	SUN PLANETS (° ′)	ARIES (° ′)	MOON (° ′)	v or d / Corrⁿ	v or d / Corrⁿ	v or d / Corrⁿ
00	4 30·0	4 30·7	4 17·7	0·0 0·0	6·0 1·9	12·0 3·7
01	4 30·3	4 31·0	4 17·9	0·1 0·0	6·1 1·9	12·1 3·7
02	4 30·5	4 31·2	4 18·2	0·2 0·1	6·2 1·9	12·2 3·8
03	4 30·8	4 31·5	4 18·4	0·3 0·1	6·3 1·9	12·3 3·8
04	4 31·0	4 31·7	4 18·7	0·4 0·1	6·4 2·0	12·4 3·8
05	4 31·3	4 32·0	4 18·9	0·5 0·2	6·5 2·0	12·5 3·9
06	4 31·5	4 32·2	4 19·1	0·6 0·2	6·6 2·0	12·6 3·9
07	4 31·8	4 32·5	4 19·4	0·7 0·2	6·7 2·1	12·7 3·9
08	4 32·0	4 32·7	4 19·6	0·8 0·2	6·8 2·1	12·8 3·9
09	4 32·3	4 33·0	4 19·8	0·9 0·3	6·9 2·1	12·9 4·0
10	4 32·5	4 33·2	4 20·1	1·0 0·3	7·0 2·2	13·0 4·0
11	4 32·8	4 33·5	4 20·3	1·1 0·3	7·1 2·2	13·1 4·0
12	4 33·0	4 33·7	4 20·6	1·2 0·4	7·2 2·2	13·2 4·1
13	4 33·3	4 34·0	4 20·8	1·3 0·4	7·3 2·3	13·3 4·1
14	4 33·5	4 34·2	4 21·0	1·4 0·4	7·4 2·3	13·4 4·1
15	4 33·8	4 34·5	4 21·3	1·5 0·5	7·5 2·3	13·5 4·2
16	4 34·0	4 34·8	4 21·5	1·6 0·5	7·6 2·3	13·6 4·2
17	4 34·3	4 35·0	4 21·8	1·7 0·5	7·7 2·4	13·7 4·2
18	4 34·5	4 35·3	4 22·0	1·8 0·6	7·8 2·4	13·8 4·3
19	4 34·8	4 35·5	4 22·2	1·9 0·6	7·9 2·4	13·9 4·3
20	4 35·0	4 35·8	4 22·5	2·0 0·6	8·0 2·5	14·0 4·3
21	4 35·3	4 36·0	4 22·7	2·1 0·6	8·1 2·5	14·1 4·3
22	4 35·5	4 36·3	4 22·9	2·2 0·7	8·2 2·5	14·2 4·4
23	4 35·8	4 36·5	4 23·2	2·3 0·7	8·3 2·6	14·3 4·4
24	4 36·0	4 36·8	4 23·4	2·4 0·7	8·4 2·6	14·4 4·4
25	4 36·3	4 37·0	4 23·7	2·5 0·8	8·5 2·6	14·5 4·5
26	4 36·5	4 37·3	4 23·9	2·6 0·8	8·6 2·7	14·6 4·5
27	4 36·8	4 37·5	4 24·1	2·7 0·8	8·7 2·7	14·7 4·5
28	4 37·0	4 37·8	4 24·4	2·8 0·9	8·8 2·7	14·8 4·6
29	4 37·3	4 38·0	4 24·6	2·9 0·9	8·9 2·7	14·9 4·6
30	4 37·5	4 38·3	4 24·9	3·0 0·9	9·0 2·8	15·0 4·6
31	4 37·8	4 38·5	4 25·1	3·1 1·0	9·1 2·8	15·1 4·7
32	4 38·0	4 38·8	4 25·3	3·2 1·0	9·2 2·8	15·2 4·7
33	4 38·3	4 39·0	4 25·6	3·3 1·0	9·3 2·9	15·3 4·7
34	4 38·5	4 39·3	4 25·8	3·4 1·0	9·4 2·9	15·4 4·7
35	4 38·8	4 39·5	4 26·1	3·5 1·1	9·5 2·9	15·5 4·8
36	4 39·0	4 39·8	4 26·3	3·6 1·1	9·6 3·0	15·6 4·8
37	4 39·3	4 40·0	4 26·5	3·7 1·1	9·7 3·0	15·7 4·8
38	4 39·5	4 40·3	4 26·8	3·8 1·2	9·8 3·0	15·8 4·9
39	4 39·8	4 40·5	4 27·0	3·9 1·2	9·9 3·1	15·9 4·9
40	4 40·0	4 40·8	4 27·2	4·0 1·2	10·0 3·1	16·0 4·9
41	4 40·3	4 41·0	4 27·5	4·1 1·3	10·1 3·1	16·1 5·0
42	4 40·5	4 41·3	4 27·7	4·2 1·3	10·2 3·1	16·2 5·0
43	4 40·8	4 41·5	4 28·0	4·3 1·3	10·3 3·2	16·3 5·0
44	4 41·0	4 41·8	4 28·2	4·4 1·4	10·4 3·2	16·4 5·1
45	4 41·3	4 42·0	4 28·4	4·5 1·4	10·5 3·2	16·5 5·1
46	4 41·5	4 42·3	4 28·7	4·6 1·4	10·6 3·3	16·6 5·1
47	4 41·8	4 42·5	4 28·9	4·7 1·4	10·7 3·3	16·7 5·1
48	4 42·0	4 42·8	4 29·2	4·8 1·5	10·8 3·3	16·8 5·2
49	4 42·3	4 43·0	4 29·4	4·9 1·5	10·9 3·4	16·9 5·2
50	4 42·5	4 43·3	4 29·6	5·0 1·5	11·0 3·4	17·0 5·2
51	4 42·8	4 43·5	4 29·9	5·1 1·6	11·1 3·4	17·1 5·3
52	4 43·0	4 43·8	4 30·1	5·2 1·6	11·2 3·5	17·2 5·3
53	4 43·3	4 44·0	4 30·3	5·3 1·6	11·3 3·5	17·3 5·3
54	4 43·5	4 44·3	4 30·6	5·4 1·7	11·4 3·5	17·4 5·4
55	4 43·8	4 44·5	4 30·8	5·5 1·7	11·5 3·5	17·5 5·4
56	4 44·0	4 44·8	4 31·1	5·6 1·7	11·6 3·6	17·6 5·4
57	4 44·3	4 45·0	4 31·3	5·7 1·8	11·7 3·6	17·7 5·5
58	4 44·5	4 45·3	4 31·5	5·8 1·8	11·8 3·6	17·8 5·5
59	4 44·8	4 45·5	4 31·8	5·9 1·8	11·9 3·7	17·9 5·5
60	4 45·0	4 45·8	4 32·0	6·0 1·9	12·0 3·7	18·0 5·6

19 (s)	SUN PLANETS (° ′)	ARIES (° ′)	MOON (° ′)	v or d / Corrⁿ	v or d / Corrⁿ	v or d / Corrⁿ
00	4 45·0	4 45·8	4 32·0	0·0 0·0	6·0 2·0	12·0 3·9
01	4 45·3	4 46·0	4 32·3	0·1 0·0	6·1 2·0	12·1 3·9
02	4 45·5	4 46·3	4 32·5	0·2 0·1	6·2 2·0	12·2 4·0
03	4 45·8	4 46·5	4 32·7	0·3 0·1	6·3 2·0	12·3 4·0
04	4 46·0	4 46·8	4 33·0	0·4 0·1	6·4 2·1	12·4 4·0
05	4 46·3	4 47·0	4 33·2	0·5 0·2	6·5 2·1	12·5 4·1
06	4 46·5	4 47·3	4 33·4	0·6 0·2	6·6 2·1	12·6 4·1
07	4 46·8	4 47·5	4 33·7	0·7 0·2	6·7 2·2	12·7 4·1
08	4 47·0	4 47·8	4 33·9	0·8 0·3	6·8 2·2	12·8 4·2
09	4 47·3	4 48·0	4 34·2	0·9 0·3	6·9 2·2	12·9 4·2
10	4 47·5	4 48·3	4 34·4	1·0 0·3	7·0 2·3	13·0 4·2
11	4 47·8	4 48·5	4 34·6	1·1 0·4	7·1 2·3	13·1 4·3
12	4 48·0	4 48·8	4 34·9	1·2 0·4	7·2 2·3	13·2 4·3
13	4 48·3	4 49·0	4 35·1	1·3 0·4	7·3 2·4	13·3 4·3
14	4 48·5	4 49·3	4 35·4	1·4 0·5	7·4 2·4	13·4 4·4
15	4 48·8	4 49·5	4 35·6	1·5 0·5	7·5 2·4	13·5 4·4
16	4 49·0	4 49·8	4 35·8	1·6 0·5	7·6 2·5	13·6 4·4
17	4 49·3	4 50·0	4 36·1	1·7 0·6	7·7 2·5	13·7 4·5
18	4 49·5	4 50·3	4 36·3	1·8 0·6	7·8 2·5	13·8 4·5
19	4 49·8	4 50·5	4 36·6	1·9 0·6	7·9 2·6	13·9 4·5
20	4 50·0	4 50·8	4 36·8	2·0 0·7	8·0 2·6	14·0 4·6
21	4 50·3	4 51·0	4 37·0	2·1 0·7	8·1 2·6	14·1 4·6
22	4 50·5	4 51·3	4 37·3	2·2 0·7	8·2 2·7	14·2 4·6
23	4 50·8	4 51·5	4 37·5	2·3 0·7	8·3 2·7	14·3 4·6
24	4 51·0	4 51·8	4 37·7	2·4 0·8	8·4 2·7	14·4 4·7
25	4 51·3	4 52·0	4 38·0	2·5 0·8	8·5 2·8	14·5 4·7
26	4 51·5	4 52·3	4 38·2	2·6 0·8	8·6 2·8	14·6 4·7
27	4 51·8	4 52·5	4 38·5	2·7 0·9	8·7 2·8	14·7 4·8
28	4 52·0	4 52·8	4 38·7	2·8 0·9	8·8 2·9	14·8 4·8
29	4 52·3	4 53·1	4 38·9	2·9 0·9	8·9 2·9	14·9 4·8
30	4 52·5	4 53·3	4 39·2	3·0 1·0	9·0 2·9	15·0 4·9
31	4 52·8	4 53·6	4 39·4	3·1 1·0	9·1 3·0	15·1 4·9
32	4 53·0	4 53·8	4 39·7	3·2 1·0	9·2 3·0	15·2 4·9
33	4 53·3	4 54·1	4 39·9	3·3 1·1	9·3 3·0	15·3 5·0
34	4 53·5	4 54·3	4 40·1	3·4 1·1	9·4 3·1	15·4 5·0
35	4 53·8	4 54·6	4 40·4	3·5 1·1	9·5 3·1	15·5 5·0
36	4 54·0	4 54·8	4 40·6	3·6 1·2	9·6 3·1	15·6 5·1
37	4 54·3	4 55·1	4 40·8	3·7 1·2	9·7 3·2	15·7 5·1
38	4 54·5	4 55·3	4 41·1	3·8 1·2	9·8 3·2	15·8 5·1
39	4 54·8	4 55·6	4 41·3	3·9 1·3	9·9 3·2	15·9 5·2
40	4 55·0	4 55·8	4 41·6	4·0 1·3	10·0 3·3	16·0 5·2
41	4 55·3	4 56·1	4 41·8	4·1 1·3	10·1 3·3	16·1 5·2
42	4 55·5	4 56·3	4 42·0	4·2 1·4	10·2 3·3	16·2 5·3
43	4 55·8	4 56·6	4 42·3	4·3 1·4	10·3 3·3	16·3 5·3
44	4 56·0	4 56·8	4 42·5	4·4 1·4	10·4 3·4	16·4 5·3
45	4 56·3	4 57·1	4 42·8	4·5 1·5	10·5 3·4	16·5 5·4
46	4 56·5	4 57·3	4 43·0	4·6 1·5	10·6 3·4	16·6 5·4
47	4 56·8	4 57·6	4 43·2	4·7 1·5	10·7 3·5	16·7 5·4
48	4 57·0	4 57·8	4 43·5	4·8 1·6	10·8 3·5	16·8 5·5
49	4 57·3	4 58·1	4 43·7	4·9 1·6	10·9 3·5	16·9 5·5
50	4 57·5	4 58·3	4 43·9	5·0 1·6	11·0 3·6	17·0 5·5
51	4 57·8	4 58·6	4 44·2	5·1 1·7	11·1 3·6	17·1 5·6
52	4 58·0	4 58·8	4 44·4	5·2 1·7	11·2 3·6	17·2 5·6
53	4 58·3	4 59·1	4 44·7	5·3 1·7	11·3 3·7	17·3 5·6
54	4 58·5	4 59·3	4 44·9	5·4 1·8	11·4 3·7	17·4 5·7
55	4 58·8	4 59·6	4 45·1	5·5 1·8	11·5 3·7	17·5 5·7
56	4 59·0	4 59·8	4 45·4	5·6 1·8	11·6 3·8	17·6 5·7
57	4 59·3	5 00·1	4 45·6	5·7 1·9	11·7 3·8	17·7 5·8
58	4 59·5	5 00·3	4 45·9	5·8 1·9	11·8 3·8	17·8 5·8
59	4 59·8	5 00·6	4 46·1	5·9 1·9	11·9 3·9	17·9 5·8
60	5 00·0	5 00·8	4 46·3	6·0 2·0	12·0 3·9	18·0 5·9

TABLE 3-2   Two "Increments and Corrections" pages from the Nautical Almanac.

44ᵐ	SUN PLANETS	ARIES	MOON	v or Corrn d		v or Corrn d		v or Corrn d	
s	° ′	° ′	° ′	′	′	′	′	′	′
00	11 00·0	11 01·8	10 29·9	0·0	0·0	6·0	4·5	12·0	8·9
01	11 00·3	11 02·1	10 30·2	0·1	0·1	6·1	4·5	12·1	9·0
02	11 00·5	11 02·3	10 30·4	0·2	0·1	6·2	4·6	12·2	9·0
03	11 00·8	11 02·6	10 30·6	0·3	0·2	6·3	4·7	12·3	9·1
04	11 01·0	11 02·8	10 30·9	0·4	0·3	6·4	4·7	12·4	9·2
05	11 01·3	11 03·1	10 31·1	0·5	0·4	6·5	4·8	12·5	9·3
06	11 01·5	11 03·3	10 31·4	0·6	0·4	6·6	4·9	12·6	9·3
07	11 01·8	11 03·6	10 31·6	0·7	0·5	6·7	5·0	12·7	9·4
08	11 02·0	11 03·8	10 31·8	0·8	0·6	6·8	5·0	12·8	9·5
09	11 02·3	11 04·1	10 32·1	0·9	0·7	6·9	5·1	12·9	9·6
10	11 02·5	11 04·3	10 32·3	1·0	0·7	7·0	5·2	13·0	9·6
11	11 02·8	11 04·6	10 32·6	1·1	0·8	7·1	5·3	13·1	9·7
12	11 03·0	11 04·8	10 32·8	1·2	0·9	7·2	5·3	13·2	9·8
13	11 03·3	11 05·1	10 33·0	1·3	1·0	7·3	5·4	13·3	9·9
14	11 03·5	11 05·3	10 33·3	1·4	1·0	7·4	5·5	13·4	9·9
15	11 03·8	11 05·6	10 33·5	1·5	1·1	7·5	5·6	13·5	10·0
16	11 04·0	11 05·8	10 33·8	1·6	1·2	7·6	5·6	13·6	10·1
17	11 04·3	11 06·1	10 34·0	1·7	1·3	7·7	5·7	13·7	10·2
18	11 04·5	11 06·3	10 34·2	1·8	1·3	7·8	5·8	13·8	10·2
19	11 04·8	11 06·6	10 34·5	1·9	1·4	7·9	5·9	13·9	10·3
20	11 05·0	11 06·8	10 34·7	2·0	1·5	8·0	5·9	14·0	10·4
21	11 05·3	11 07·1	10 34·9	2·1	1·6	8·1	6·0	14·1	10·5
22	11 05·5	11 07·3	10 35·2	2·2	1·6	8·2	6·1	14·2	10·5
23	11 05·8	11 07·6	10 35·4	2·3	1·7	8·3	6·2	14·3	10·6
24	11 06·0	11 07·8	10 35·7	2·4	1·8	8·4	6·2	14·4	10·7
25	11 06·3	11 08·1	10 35·9	2·5	1·9	8·5	6·3	14·5	10·8
26	11 06·5	11 08·3	10 36·1	2·6	1·9	8·6	6·4	14·6	10·8
27	11 06·8	11 08·6	10 36·4	2·7	2·0	8·7	6·5	14·7	10·9
28	11 07·0	11 08·8	10 36·6	2·8	2·1	8·8	6·5	14·8	11·0
29	11 07·3	11 09·1	10 36·9	2·9	2·2	8·9	6·6	14·9	11·1
30	11 07·5	11 09·3	10 37·1	3·0	2·2	9·0	6·7	15·0	11·1
31	11 07·8	11 09·6	10 37·3	3·1	2·3	9·1	6·7	15·1	11·2
32	11 08·0	11 09·8	10 37·6	3·2	2·4	9·2	6·8	15·2	11·3
33	11 08·3	11 10·1	10 37·8	3·3	2·4	9·3	6·9	15·3	11·3
34	11 08·5	11 10·3	10 38·0	3·4	2·5	9·4	7·0	15·4	11·4
35	11 08·8	11 10·6	10 38·3	3·5	2·6	9·5	7·0	15·5	11·5
36	11 09·0	11 10·8	10 38·5	3·6	2·7	9·6	7·1	15·6	11·6
37	11 09·3	11 11·1	10 38·8	3·7	2·7	9·7	7·2	15·7	11·6
38	11 09·5	11 11·3	10 39·0	3·8	2·8	9·8	7·3	15·8	11·7
39	11 09·8	11 11·6	10 39·2	3·9	2·9	9·9	7·3	15·9	11·8
40	11 10·0	11 11·8	10 39·5	4·0	3·0	10·0	7·4	16·0	11·9
41	11 10·3	11 12·1	10 39·7	4·1	3·0	10·1	7·5	16·1	11·9
42	11 10·5	11 12·3	10 40·0	4·2	3·1	10·2	7·6	16·2	12·0
43	11 10·8	11 12·6	10 40·2	4·3	3·2	10·3	7·6	16·3	12·1
44	11 11·0	11 12·8	10 40·4	4·4	3·3	10·4	7·7	16·4	12·2
45	11 11·3	11 13·1	10 40·7	4·5	3·3	10·5	7·8	16·5	12·2
46	11 11·5	11 13·3	10 40·9	4·6	3·4	10·6	7·9	16·6	12·3
47	11 11·8	11 13·6	10 41·1	4·7	3·5	10·7	7·9	16·7	12·4
48	11 12·0	11 13·8	10 41·4	4·8	3·6	10·8	8·0	16·8	12·5
49	11 12·3	11 14·1	10 41·6	4·9	3·6	10·9	8·1	16·9	12·5
50	11 12·5	11 14·3	10 41·9	5·0	3·7	11·0	8·2	17·0	12·6
51	11 12·8	11 14·6	10 42·1	5·1	3·8	11·1	8·2	17·1	12·7
52	11 13·0	11 14·8	10 42·3	5·2	3·9	11·2	8·3	17·2	12·8
53	11 13·3	11 15·1	10 42·6	5·3	3·9	11·3	8·4	17·3	12·8
54	11 13·5	11 15·3	10 42·8	5·4	4·0	11·4	8·5	17·4	12·9
55	11 13·8	11 15·6	10 43·1	5·5	4·1	11·5	8·5	17·5	13·0
56	11 14·0	11 15·8	10 43·3	5·6	4·2	11·6	8·6	17·6	13·1
57	11 14·3	11 16·1	10 43·5	5·7	4·2	11·7	8·7	17·7	13·1
58	11 14·5	11 16·3	10 43·8	5·8	4·3	11·8	8·8	17·8	13·2
59	11 14·8	11 16·6	10 44·0	5·9	4·4	11·9	8·8	17·9	13·3
60	11 15·0	11 16·8	10 44·3	6·0	4·5	12·0	8·9	18·0	13·4

45ᵐ	SUN PLANETS	ARIES	MOON	v or Corrn d		v or Corrn d		v or Corrn d	
s	° ′	° ′	° ′	′	′	′	′	′	′
00	11 15·0	11 16·8	10 44·3	0·0	0·0	6·0	4·6	12·0	9·1
01	11 15·3	11 17·1	10 44·5	0·1	0·1	6·1	4·6	12·1	9·2
02	11 15·5	11 17·3	10 44·7	0·2	0·2	6·2	4·7	12·2	9·3
03	11 15·8	11 17·6	10 45·0	0·3	0·2	6·3	4·8	12·3	9·3
04	11 16·0	11 17·9	10 45·2	0·4	0·3	6·4	4·9	12·4	9·4
05	11 16·3	11 18·1	10 45·4	0·5	0·4	6·5	4·9	12·5	9·5
06	11 16·5	11 18·4	10 45·7	0·6	0·5	6·6	5·0	12·6	9·6
07	11 16·8	11 18·6	10 45·9	0·7	0·5	6·7	5·1	12·7	9·6
08	11 17·0	11 18·9	10 46·2	0·8	0·6	6·8	5·2	12·8	9·7
09	11 17·3	11 19·1	10 46·4	0·9	0·7	6·9	5·2	12·9	9·8
10	11 17·5	11 19·4	10 46·6	1·0	0·8	7·0	5·3	13·0	9·9
11	11 17·8	11 19·6	10 46·9	1·1	0·8	7·1	5·4	13·1	9·9
12	11 18·0	11 19·9	10 47·1	1·2	0·9	7·2	5·5	13·2	10·0
13	11 18·3	11 20·1	10 47·4	1·3	1·0	7·3	5·5	13·3	10·1
14	11 18·5	11 20·4	10 47·6	1·4	1·1	7·4	5·6	13·4	10·2
15	11 18·8	11 20·6	10 47·8	1·5	1·1	7·5	5·7	13·5	10·2
16	11 19·0	11 20·9	10 48·1	1·6	1·2	7·6	5·8	13·6	10·3
17	11 19·3	11 21·1	10 48·3	1·7	1·3	7·7	5·8	13·7	10·4
18	11 19·5	11 21·4	10 48·5	1·8	1·4	7·8	5·9	13·8	10·5
19	11 19·8	11 21·6	10 48·8	1·9	1·4	7·9	6·0	13·9	10·5
20	11 20·0	11 21·9	10 49·0	2·0	1·5	8·0	6·1	14·0	10·6
21	11 20·3	11 22·1	10 49·3	2·1	1·6	8·1	6·1	14·1	10·7
22	11 20·5	11 22·4	10 49·5	2·2	1·7	8·2	6·2	14·2	10·8
23	11 20·8	11 22·6	10 49·7	2·3	1·7	8·3	6·3	14·3	10·8
24	11 21·0	11 22·9	10 50·0	2·4	1·8	8·4	6·4	14·4	10·9
25	11 21·3	11 23·1	10 50·2	2·5	1·9	8·5	6·4	14·5	11·0
26	11 21·5	11 23·4	10 50·5	2·6	2·0	8·6	6·5	14·6	11·1
27	11 21·8	11 23·6	10 50·7	2·7	2·0	8·7	6·6	14·7	11·1
28	11 22·0	11 23·9	10 50·9	2·8	2·1	8·8	6·7	14·8	11·2
29	11 22·3	11 24·1	10 51·2	2·9	2·2	8·9	6·7	14·9	11·3
30	11 22·5	11 24·4	10 51·4	3·0	2·3	9·0	6·8	15·0	11·4
31	11 22·8	11 24·6	10 51·6	3·1	2·4	9·1	6·9	15·1	11·5
32	11 23·0	11 24·9	10 51·9	3·2	2·4	9·2	7·0	15·2	11·5
33	11 23·3	11 25·1	10 52·1	3·3	2·5	9·3	7·1	15·3	11·6
34	11 23·5	11 25·4	10 52·4	3·4	2·6	9·4	7·1	15·4	11·7
35	11 23·8	11 25·6	10 52·6	3·5	2·7	9·5	7·2	15·5	11·8
36	11 24·0	11 25·9	10 52·8	3·6	2·7	9·6	7·3	15·6	11·8
37	11 24·3	11 26·1	10 53·1	3·7	2·8	9·7	7·4	15·7	11·9
38	11 24·5	11 26·4	10 53·3	3·8	2·9	9·8	7·4	15·8	12·0
39	11 24·8	11 26·6	10 53·6	3·9	3·0	9·9	7·5	15·9	12·1
40	11 25·0	11 26·9	10 53·8	4·0	3·0	10·0	7·6	16·0	12·1
41	11 25·3	11 27·1	10 54·0	4·1	3·1	10·1	7·7	16·1	12·2
42	11 25·5	11 27·4	10 54·3	4·2	3·2	10·2	7·7	16·2	12·3
43	11 25·8	11 27·6	10 54·5	4·3	3·3	10·3	7·8	16·3	12·4
44	11 26·0	11 27·9	10 54·7	4·4	3·3	10·4	7·9	16·4	12·4
45	11 26·3	11 28·1	10 55·0	4·5	3·4	10·5	8·0	16·5	12·5
46	11 26·5	11 28·4	10 55·2	4·6	3·5	10·6	8·0	16·6	12·6
47	11 26·8	11 28·6	10 55·5	4·7	3·6	10·7	8·1	16·7	12·7
48	11 27·0	11 28·9	10 55·7	4·8	3·6	10·8	8·2	16·8	12·7
49	11 27·3	11 29·1	10 55·9	4·9	3·7	10·9	8·3	16·9	12·8
50	11 27·5	11 29·4	10 56·2	5·0	3·8	11·0	8·3	17·0	12·9
51	11 27·8	11 29·6	10 56·4	5·1	3·9	11·1	8·4	17·1	13·0
52	11 28·0	11 29·9	10 56·7	5·2	3·9	11·2	8·5	17·2	13·0
53	11 28·3	11 30·1	10 56·9	5·3	4·0	11·3	8·6	17·3	13·1
54	11 28·5	11 30·4	10 57·1	5·4	4·1	11·4	8·6	17·4	13·2
55	11 28·8	11 30·6	10 57·4	5·5	4·2	11·5	8·7	17·5	13·3
56	11 29·0	11 30·9	10 57·6	5·6	4·2	11·6	8·8	17·6	13·3
57	11 29·3	11 31·1	10 57·9	5·7	4·3	11·7	8·9	17·7	13·4
58	11 29·5	11 31·4	10 58·1	5·8	4·4	11·8	8·9	17·8	13·5
59	11 29·8	11 31·6	10 58·3	5·9	4·5	11·9	9·0	17·9	13·6
60	11 30·0	11 31·9	10 58·6	6·0	4·6	12·0	9·1	18·0	13·7

values. These additional corrections are necessary when using the bodies in the solar system.

The values of *v* on the daily pages represent the excesses of the actual hourly changes in GHA over the adopted average values used in computing the "Increments and Corrections" table. The *v* correction is negligible for the sun, and is omitted from the *Almanac*. For the planets, it is listed at the bottom of the GHA columns for each set of three days. The moon's motion appears to be much more erratic, and the *v* correction for the moon is therefore tabulated for each hour of GMT. No *v* correction is required for Aries. The *v* correction is always additive, except at times for Venus, when it is a subtractive correction; it is then preceded by a minus sign.

The values of *d* appearing on the daily pages are the hourly differences in declination. They are listed at the bottom of the three-day columns for the planets and for the sun; for the moon, they are listed for each hour of GMT. The *d* correction can be plus or minus and is determined by inspection of successive entries of the hourly values of declination. If, at the GMT of the observation, the body's declination is increasing numerically, regardless of whether it is north or south, the correction is additive. If the hourly values are decreasing numerically, the correction is subtractive. A space for making this notation is provided on the sight reduction form.

To obtain the correction, the tabulated *v* or *d* value is extracted from the daily pages. This figure is then located in the *v* or *d* column of the "Increments and Corrections" page for the minutes of time in question, and the correction to be applied to the GHA or dec. is extracted from the "Corrections" column. This table simply performs a multiplication. Thus, if the *d* value were 0′.8 and the minutes of time were 45, the correction would be 0′.6.

Adding Units of Arc

Arcs of circles given in degrees, minutes, and tenths of minutes of arc are used in navigation to compute declination, hour angle, latitude, longitude, etc. Those who are in the habit of adding and subtracting only decimal units, as with dollars and cents, may err when using the sexagesimal system, which is based on units of 60. Anytime the addition of minutes of arc produces a sum exceeding 60, units of 60 must be subtracted from the sum, and one degree must be carried to the degree column for each such unit that is subtracted. For example, add

$$
\begin{array}{r}
327° \ 39′.1 \\
4° \ 54′.1 \\
49° \ 51′.3 \\
\hline
382° \ 24′.5
\end{array}
$$

When the minutes column is added, the total is 144'.5; 120 minutes (2°) must therefore be subtracted producing 24'.5. The 2° are then added to the degrees column, producing a sum of 382° 24'.5, and 360° is subtracted from this total, yielding a value of 22° 24'.5.

Using the Almanac

The best way to learn to extract the values of GHA and declination is to work the following problems, whose answers are given in the sight reduction forms in Figure 3-3 (page 40). In order to reduce the volume of sample *Almanac* pages in this chapter, all examples are based on the daily pages for 3, 4, and 5 November and the minutes of time from the 19- and the 45-minute pages of "Increments and Corrections."

Sample Problems for a Star, a Planet, the Sun, and the Moon

Problem: What is the GHA, LHA, and declination for the star Deneb on November 3 at GMT 21 19 33 when the dead reckoning (DR) longitude is 63° 20'W?

Solution: Turn to the daily pages for 3, 4, and 5 November (Table 3-1), follow alphabetically down the list of stars to Deneb, extract SHA 49° 51'.3 and declination N45° 11'.8, and enter these on the sight reduction form, as shown in Figure 3-3. *Note:* When using the stars, there is no further correction to the tabulated value of declination. Turn to the tabulation for 3 November in the daily pages, and in the Aries column opposite 21 hours, extract GHA𝛾 357° 44'.1 and enter it on the form opposite "GHA𝛾" (there is no *v* or *d* correction for Aries). Now turn to the "Increments and Corrections" columns for 19 minutes (Table 3-2), follow down the left-hand column to 33 seconds, and in the Aries column extract the value of 4° 54'.1 and enter this on the form opposite "Corr." so that it can be added to the GHA for the whole hour and to the SHA of the star, using only one addition. These three values total 412° 29'.5, which is over 360°, so one would normally subtract 360°, yielding a GHA Deneb of 52° 29'.5. Short cuts should be taken whenever possible to avoid extra addition or subtraction; remember that the assumed longitude (a𝜆) must be combined with GHA to obtain LHA. In west longitude the a𝜆 is always subtracted from GHA, so it is easier to use the value of 412° 29'.5 for GHA✩ and subtract the a𝜆 from this. With the DR longitude of 63° 20'W, use 63° 29'.5 as the a𝜆, which, when subtracted from GHA, produces an integral degree of LHA of 349°. This is one of the arguments used for entering the sight reduction tables; declination and assumed latitude are the others.

	Date	3 NOV.
Local date and time	Body	DENEB
Name of body observed and limb	Lat.	
DR or EP Latitude	λ DR	W 63° 20'
DR or EP Longitude		

	W. time	17 19 33
Time from watch used by observer	Corr. + 4	4
Watch error and/or zone description	GMT	21 19 33
Greenwich Mean Time and Date of Sight		

Altitude read from sextant

Instrument Correction from sextant certificate + or −

Index Correction as measured   + or −

Dip of horizon from Almanac   always −

Combine hs, I, IC, and Dip to obtain ha

Refraction correction from Almanac − (except ☉ +)

Add'l Corr. TB, or Venus, Mars, or Moon 1st corr.

Sum of corrections or for Moon 2nd corr.

Above corrections applied to ha to obtain Ho (observed alt.)

hs	
I	+ −
IC	
Dip	
ha	
R	
Corr.	
Corr.	
Ho	

GHA from Almanac daily page

GHA for min. and sec. from Almanac yellow pages

SHA for stars, or "v" from Almanac yellow pages

GHA corrected to time of sight

Assumed long. (−W + E) assume minutes for 0 min. LHA

Local Hour Angle, combine GHA & a λ   (subt. 360 if necessary)

Convert LHA (always W) to t angle (East or West) for H. O. 214

GHA ♈	357	44.1
Corr.	4	54.1
SHA ⭐	49	51.3
GHA	412	29.5
a λ	63	29.5
LHA	349	
t (E)(W)		

Tabulated declination from Almanac

d correction from yellow pages of Almanac   + or −

True declination for time of sight

Assumed latitude (nearest integral degree)

Dec. N	45	11.8
d + −		
Dec. N	45	11.8
a L		

Tabulated altitude using Hour Angle, Dec, and a L

Dec. correction from H. O. 214 or H. O. 229

DSD correction H. O. 229

Computed altitude

Observed altitude from above

Altitude intercept (computed greater away) Label A or T

ht	
d corr.	
corr.	
Hc	
Ho	
a A or T	

Azimuth angle from H. O. 214 or H. O. 229

Azimuth angle converted to True Azimuth

Az or Z	
Zn	

FIGURE 3-3   Solutions to sample problems.

Date	4 NOV.
Body	MARS
Lat.	
λ DR	W 64° 55'

W. time	
Corr.	
GMT	21 45 55

hs	
I	
IC	
Dip	
ha	
R	
Corr.	
Corr.	
Ho	

GHA	145	45.7
Corr.	11	28.8
~~SHA~~-v 0.8		0.6
GHA	157	15.1
a λ W	65	15.1
LHA	92	
t (E)(W)		

Dec.	S 12	53.2
d ⊕ 0.6		+ 0.5
Dec.	S 12	53.7
a L		

ht	
d corr.	
corr.	
Hc	
Ho	
a A or T	

Az	
Zn	

Date	5 NOV.
Body	SUN ☉
Lat.	
λ DR	W 77° 45'

W. time	
Corr.	
GMT	11 – 19 – 11

hs	
I	
IC	
Dip	
ha	
R	
Corr.	
Corr.	
Ho	

GHA	349	05.8
Corr.	4	47.8
SHA-v	—	
GHA	353	53.6
a λ	77	53.6
LHA	276	
t (E)(W)	84° E	

Dec.	S 15	38.1
d ⊕ 0.8		0.3
Dec.	S 15	38.4
a L		

ht	
d corr.	
corr.	
Hc	
Ho	
a A or T	

Az	
Zn	

Date	4 NOV.
Body	MOON ☽
Lat.	
λ	

W. time	
Corr.	
GMT	07 45 10

hs	
I	
IC	
Dip	
ha	
R	
Corr.	
Corr.	
Ho	

GHA	53	11.7
Corr.	10	46.6
~~SHA~~-v 6.4		4.9
GHA	64	03.2
a λ		
LHA		
t (E)(W)		

Dec.	N 21	13.1
d + ⊖4.2		– 3.2
Dec.	N 21	09.9
a.L		

ht	
d corr.	
corr.	
Hc	
Ho	
a A or T	

Az	
Zn	

Problem: Find the GHA, LHA, and declination for the planet Mars on November 4 for GMT 21 45 55 when the DR longitude is 64° 55′W.

Solution: Turn to the daily pages for 3, 4, and 5 November. In the section marked "4 Monday" locate the line for 21 hours, follow it across to the column headed "Mars," and extract GHA 145° 45′.7. Enter this on the form, along with the *v* value of 0′.8 taken from the bottom of the Mars column. Now extract the declination of S12° 53′.2 and, from the bottom of the same column, the *d* value of 0′.6. (The *d* value can be plus or minus. In this case it is plus, as the value of declination for 22 hours is greater than that for 21 hours; declination therefore increases numerically with time). Now turn to the "Increments and Corrections" section for 45 minutes and follow the leftmost column down to 55 seconds. In the "Sun Planets" column extract 11° 28′.8, the value of the correction to GHA for 45 minutes, 55 seconds of time, and enter it on the form. With the *Almanac* still open at 45 minutes, look in the "*v* or *d*" column opposite the *v* value of 0′.8, extract the correction of 0′.6, and enter it on the form. Opposite the *d* value of 0′.6, extract the correction of 0′.5 and add it to the declination, yielding a corrected declination of S12° 53′.7. Add the GHA for 21 hours, the correction for minutes and seconds, and the *v* correction to obtain GHA Mars of 157° 15′.1. From the DR longitude of 64° 55′W assume a longitude of 65° 15′.1W and subtract this from the GHA to obtain an integral degree of LHA, 92°, for entering the sight reduction tables. Remember that in west longitude the assumed minutes of longitude are always numerically the same as the minutes of GHA, and are within 30 minutes of the DRλ; in this case it was necessary to change the degrees of aλ from 64° to 65° in order to have the minutes of aλ the same as minutes of GHA and still have the aλ close to the DRλ.

Problem: What is the GHA, LHA, and declination of the sun on November 5, GMT 11 19 11, when the DR longitude is 77° 45′W?

Solution: Turn to the daily pages for 3, 4, and 5 November, and in the section marked "5 Tuesday" locate the line for 11 hours. Follow this line to the column headed "Sun," extract the GHA of 349° 05′.8, and enter this value on the form. There is no *v* value for the sun. Extract the declination of S15° 38′.1 and the *d* value of 0′.8 from the bottom of the column and enter these on the form. Note that the sun increases in declination with time; thus, the correction for the *d* value, when extracted, will be plus. Next, turn to the "Increments and Corrections" section for 19 minutes and follow down the seconds column to 11 seconds. From the "Sun Planets" column, extract the correction for minutes and seconds of 4° 47′.8 and add it to the hourly value to obtain GHA 353° 53′.6. With the *Almanac* still open at 19 minutes, in the "*v* or *d*" column find the value of 0′.8 and from the correction column beside it extract the *d* correction of 0′.3, which is added to the declination of the sun to obtain a corrected declination of S15° 38′.4. Thus, we have the GHA and declination for the exact second of GMT. From the DR longitude of 77° 45′ use an aλ of 77° 53′.6 and subtract it from GHA to obtain the integral degree of LHA, 276°. When using sight reduction tables such as H.O. 214, where meridian angle *t* instead of LHA is the entering argument, subtract 266° from 360° and obtain *t* of 84° E.

Problem: Find the GHA and declination of the moon for November 4 at GMT 07 45 10.

Solution: Turn to the daily pages for 3, 4, and 5 November, and use the section marked "4 Monday." On the line of 07 hours, in the column headed "Moon," extract the GHA of 53° 11′.7 and the *v* value of 6′.4 and enter these on the form. Extract the declination of N21° 13′.1 and the *d* value of 4′.2 and enter these on the form. The next entry, for 08 hours, shows that declination is decreasing with time. Thus, the *d* correction will be minus; note this by circling the minus sign on the form. The *v* and *d* values for the moon are listed hourly instead of at the bottom of the column, as they can be considerably larger than those for the sun and the planets. The other column in the "Moon" section is headed "H.P.," which stands for *horizontal parallax;* this value is used to correct the sextant altitude rather than to locate the position of the moon on the celestial sphere. Now turn to the "Increments and Corrections" columns for 45 minutes, and follow down the leftmost column to 10 seconds. Opposite this, in the "Moon" column, extract 10° 46′.6, the correction to GHA for minutes and seconds of GMT, and enter it on the form. In the "*v* or *d*" correction table in this same 45-minute section, locate the *v* value of 6′.4 and extract the correction of 4′.9, and locate the *d* value of −4′.2 and extract the correction to declination of −3′.2. Enter both of these values on the form. The corrected declination of N21° 09′.9 is obtained by subtracting the correction from the tabulated declination. Adding the GHA entries produces a corrected GHA of 64° 03′.2.

Review

The procedure for extracting the celestial position of a given body from the *Almanac* is always the same for any day and instant of time. By using a standard form and being careful in adding and subtracting degrees and minutes, the location of the celestial body is easily determined. By applying aλ to GHA to obtain LHA, two of the arguments for entering the sight reduction tables are established: the actual declination in degrees, minutes, and tenths, and the LHA in integral degrees. The third argument, assumed latitude (aL) is always the integral degree of latitude nearest the DR latitude.

Using the Time Diagram

In Chapter 2 we introduced the time diagram, a method of illustrating a problem and avoiding gross errors. This diagram can be used to illustrate hour angles, as discussed previously. Hour circles of the bodies are sketched in as radii on the diagram and are labelled ⊙ for the sun, ☆ for a star, ♈ for Aries, and ☾ for the moon.

In Figure 3-4 the longitude, 45°W, is illustrated with a GHA♈ of 100° (measured west from Greenwich) and an SHA☆ of 250°, making the GHA☆ 350°. From the diagram it can be seen that the LHA♈ is 55°, and that the star is east of the observer and rising. It is considered good practice to sketch a time diagram for each observation. It need not be drawn with a protractor and straightedge; an approximate visual representation of the various elements of the problem will suffice.

Figure 3-5 illustrates the above problem concerning the star Deneb; integral degree approximations of the values of arc are used. GHA♈ is 002°, SHA Deneb is 50°, and DR longitude is 63°W. The GHA☆ is 052° (412° − 360°) and LHA☆ is 349°.

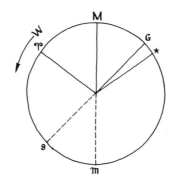

FIGURE 3-4   Using a time diagram; first example.

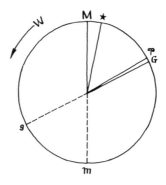

FIGURE 3-5   Using a time diagram; second example.

Chapter 4

The Sextant and its Use

In 1700, Sir Isaac Newton prepared a sketch outlining the principle of the double-reflecting mirrors on which the modern sextant is based, and sent it to Edmond Halley, the then British Astronomer Royal. Unfortunately, the latter did not realize the potential value of an instrument based on Newton's plan, and the sketch was filed and long forgotten.

In 1730, Thomas Godfrey in Philadelphia and John Hadley in England independently and almost simultaneously rediscovered the principle and built instruments incorporating it. Both the Godfrey and Hadley instruments had a physical length of arc of approximately 45°, an eighth of a circle, and were sometimes called *octants*. However, the double-reflecting principle, permitting altitudes of 90° to be measured with the instruments, resulted in their being referred to as *quadrants*. Instruments with a 60° arc that would measure angles as great as 120° were subsequently produced, and the term *sextant* came into general use for all instruments of this type. Modern marine sextants generally have a 65° arc and permit reading altitudes from minus 5°—that is, 5° below the horizontal—to 125°.

The Double-Reflecting Principle

A light ray strikes a mirror at an angle, which is called the angle of incidence. This is the angle that a ray of light falling on a surface makes with a normal to the surface at the point of incidence. The light ray is reflected at an equal angle, called the angle of reflection, which is the angle between a reflected ray and the normal drawn at the point of incidence to a reflecting surface. This is illustrated in Figure 4-1, in which a ray of light from a star is reflected by a mirror placed in a vertical position. The angle of incidence and the angle of reflection are both 40°, as illustrated by the solid lines. The dotted lines show the mirror being tilted 10° from the vertical, with light from another star 20° higher in altitude being reflected from it. As we can see, the angles of incidence and reflection with the mirror in the new position are both 50°. However, the lines illustrating the light reflected by the mirror are in identical positions, and when the sextant is used, both lead to the horizon glass.

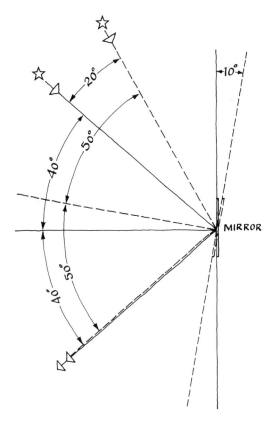

FIGURE 4-1 The double-reflection principle.

The Parts of the Sextant

If the mirror discussed above is considered to be the index mirror of a sextant (see Figures 4-1 and 4-2), it will be seen that the index mirror is rotated around a pivot point by moving the arm of the sextant. The arm, and thus the mirror, is rotated 10° in order to observe a star 20° higher in altitude. This principle can also be stated as follows: the image of an observed celestial body is reflected from the upper or index mirror to the lower or horizon mirror, thence into the field of view of the sextant telescope, where it is brought into coincidence with the sea horizon, which is seen through the clear portion of the horizon glass. The principle of optics involved is stated as follows: the angle between the first and last directions of a ray of light that has undergone two reflections in the same plane is twice the angle that the two reflecting surfaces make with each other. This principle can be proven by geometry and is illustrated in Figure 4-2, in which angle *A*, the difference between the first and last reflections, equals twice angle *B*, which is the angle between the reflecting surfaces. Angle *C* equals angle *D*, and angle *E* equals angle *F*, the angles of incidence and reflection, respectively, of the index and horizon mirrors. The gradations engraved on the sextant arc show the actual altitude of the body rather than the number of degrees the index arm has been moved from the zero set-

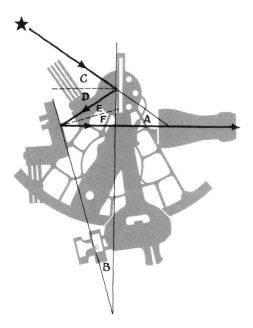

FIGURE 4-2 The light path in a sextant.

ting. This doubling of the angle is the reason why the greatest care and exactness is required in manufacturing a sextant; any error in the construction of the sextant is doubled by its optical system.

The Plath sextant, a modern micrometer drum sextant, is shown in Figure 4-3. *A* is the sextant frame. *B*, the arc or limb (graduated in degrees), is a part of the frame. *C* is the index arm; it is pivoted at the center of the arc, and can be moved along it. An index mark at its lower end permits read-out of whole degrees on the arc. A spring release is fitted at the bottom of the index arm; this permits the arm to be moved quickly along the arc to make large adjustments of altitude. *D*, the index mirror, is mounted over the pivot at the top of the index arm, and turns with it. This mirror is perpendicular to the plane of the arc. *E*, the micrometer drum, is attached to the bottom of the index arm. This drum is an endless tangent screw used to make fine adjustments of altitude readings. The tangent screw engages the teeth cut in the arc; one full turn of the drum moves the index arm along

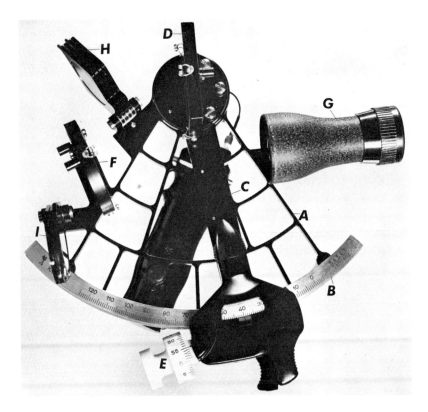

FIGURE 4-3   The parts of a modern micrometer drum sextant.

48

the arc, changing the observed altitude readings by a whole degree. The micrometer drum is usually graduated in minutes of arc; most sextants have a vernier scale that permits the reading of altitude to the nearest $0'.2$, or in some cases to $0'.1$. On other sextants, a single index mark is mounted next to the drum, and tenths of minutes are estimated by the observer. F, the horizon glass, is mounted on the frame, and is perpendicular to the plane of the arc. The horizon glass is divided vertically into two halves; the half nearest the frame is the horizon mirror, and the other half is clear optical glass. The surfaces of the index mirror and of the horizon glass are perpendicular to the plane of the arc. A fine telescope, G, permits stars to be observed when they cannot otherwise be seen, and also permits contact between the body and the horizon to be determined more precisely than is possible with the unaided eye. Some sextants permit the telescope to be moved toward or away from the frame in order to increase the brightness of the body, or of the horizon, as existing conditions warrant. This feature is generally used on sextants with small mirrors, for in this situation the amount of light reflected from a star is critical. On modern sextants with large optical systems, the axis of the telescope is normally aligned with the center of the horizon glass and permits a full view of both the mirror and the clear surface. H locates the index shade glasses. These are made of optically ground glass, are neutrally tinted, and of increasing density. They are mounted so that they are perpendicular to the plane of the arc, and are pivoted so that they can be swung out of the line of vision when not required. A single shade or a combination of two or more shades is used when observing the sun. At times, it is also helpful to use an index shade when observing a brilliant planet or star above a dimly lit horizon. A variable-density polarizing filter, another type of index shade, is mounted on some sextants. The desired density may be obtained by rotating one glass of the two that make up the unit. I indicates the horizon shades, which are similar to and mounted like the index shades. They are used to cut down the glare from a brilliantly illuminated horizon.

A word of caution should be introduced at this point: *never observe the sun's altitude without first obtaining suitable shading by means of the index shades.* The observer must reduce the intensity of the light from the sun. However, this alone is not sufficient; properly designed sunshades also block out damaging rays from the sun that are not in the visible spectrum and that would otherwise damage the human eye without the observer's knowing that this was taking place. This warning is the same in principle as the public warnings that are given whenever there is to be an eclipse of the sun; at such times, people are warned not to try to observe the eclipse simply through smoked glass. If sunshades are broken, they should be replaced only with proper shades supplied by the sextant manufacturer.

Reading the Altitude

The index arm is set on the arc at the approximate altitude of the body to be observed, and the sextant is pointed at the horizon in the direction of the body so that the horizon appears across the center of the clear portion of the horizon glass. Next, the micrometer drum is turned until the body is exactly in contact with the horizon, at which point the altitude in degrees is read from the arc at the index-arm mark; the minutes and tenths of minutes of altitude are then read from the micrometer drum. Whole degrees are read from the arc. In Figure 4-3 the mark on the index arm falls between 39° and 40°, so 39° is noted. The index mark for the micrometer drum reads 55'. Thus, the sextant altitude is 39°55'.

To read the value of tenths of a minute when a vernier is used against the drum, note the graduation on the vernier most nearly in line with a graduation on the drum. Whole minutes are read at the zero (index) mark of the vernier and tenths at the vernier graduation mark most nearly aligned with a drum graduation mark. In Figure 4-3 the index mark on the vernier is most nearly aligned with a graduation on the drum. Thus, the altitude remains 39° 55'.0. In most cases some other vernier graduation will be more nearly aligned. For example, in Figure 4-4 the whole minutes are 38 and the tenths are 4, producing a reading of 38'.4 on the micrometer drum.

Another type of sextant is fitted with an artificial horizon, usually in the form of a chamber filled with liquid, in which a bubble is centered. The image of the body is then brought down to coincide with the center of the bubble, and the altitude is read. Originally, "bubble

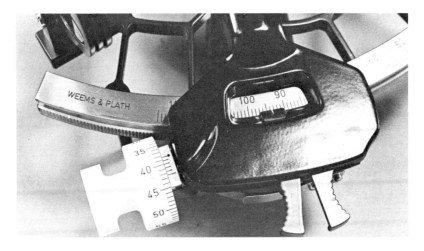

FIGURE 4-4   The sextant vernier.

sextants" were designed for use in aircraft; due to the accelerations always present in a vessel at sea, they were very difficult to use satisfactorily afloat. Detachable bubble-horizon systems are now available for some models of marine sextants; they are designed for surface use, since the bubble is damped to account for a movement which is slower than that encountered by an aircraft bubble sextant. The Plath bubble attachment is illustrated in Figure 4-5. When using a bubble sextant, several observations should be taken and averaged in order to obtain a reasonable approximation of the altitude.

Many sextants have a built-in light system that permits altitude read-out in darkness. The sextant handle serves as a container for one or more penlight batteries, and the switch is usually located conveniently on the handle near the observer's thumb. Such a lighting system is a great convenience for star observations in deep twilight. Some observers prefer a red bulb, which will not interfere with the observer's dark-adapted vision; red lamp dye is available commercially. This lighting system is a necessity on marine sextants fitted with the detachable bubble-horizon system, as the bubble must be illuminated in order to be visible.

Altitude Measurements with the Sextant

When using a marine sextant, the horizon is the reference used in measuring the altitudes of celestial bodies. In order to obtain the true

FIGURE 4-5 *The Plath bubble attachment.*

altitude, it is of the utmost importance that it be measured in the vertical plane.

To obtain an altitude, the observer faces the body and, with the sextant in a vertical position, brings the horizon into the center of his field of view. The spring release is then disengaged, and the index arm is swung until the body appears in the field of view. The tangent screw is then allowed to engage the gear teeth on the arc, and the body is brought in contact with the horizon by turning the micrometer drum.

To determine that the altitude is being measured on the vertical plane, the sextant is "rocked." This consists of rotating the sextant through a few degrees about the line of sight, which causes the image of the body to swing like a pendulum across the horizon. (See Figure 4-6.) The micrometer drum is adjusted so that at the lowest point of its swing, the body just skims the horizon. When this contact is made at the lowest point of the swing, the time is noted and the altitude is read from the sextant.

Most beginners have difficulty holding the sextant steady for more than a few seconds, as they are not in the habit of using their arm muscles in that particular position. Steadiness will improve with practice. Lightweight aluminum alloy sextants are available, and these weigh considerably less than the brass models.

The first step in observing the sun is to turn down the index shades, in order to protect the eye. If there is much glare on the horizon, it may also be helpful to use a horizon shade. Best results are usually obtained by observing the sun's lower limb, or edge; the exception to this rule is when the sun is at a very low altitude, about five degrees or less.

Due to the moon's phases, only one of its limbs is available for

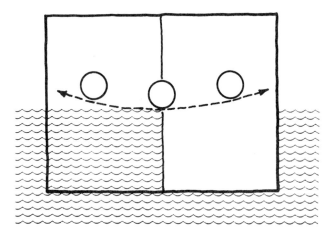

FIGURE 4-6 Rocking the sextant.

observations, except when the moon is full or nearly full. The upper limb is observed about as frequently as the lower. In daylight, no index shade is required, although it may be desirable to use a pale index shade when the moon is brilliant and the horizon is dimly lit.

For practical purposes, stars and planets may be considered point sources of light. The image of a star or planet is brought in direct contact with the horizon. Here again, it may be desirable to use a pale index shade if the body is brilliant and the horizon is dim, as at dusk. Alternately, when the celestial body is dim and the horizon is brightly lit, it is sometimes desirable to use a pale horizon shade, which makes the body appear relatively brighter.

When the horizon is bright and the star is dim, some observers find it helpful, if they are using an old sextant with a small field of view, to invert the sextant (set at zero altitude) and look directly at the star. The usual process of bringing the body down to the horizon—by moving the index arm—is then reversed, and the horizon is brought up to the star. When approximate contact is made between horizon and star, the sextant is returned to the normal position and the altitude is established in the regular way. This procedure is not necessary when using a modern sextant with large, clear optics.

When stars are to be observed at twilight, the best practice is to determine the approximate altitude and azimuth in advance, by using a star finder. The predetermined altitude is then set on the sextant arc, and the horizon is sighted at the approximate azimuth of the star. By scanning back and forth along the horizon, and then slightly above and below it if necessary, the image of the star will come into view in the mirror.

Sextant Practice

As in almost any field of human activity, it takes practice to become proficient in obtaining accurate celestial altitudes. Experiments conducted under contract for the Office of Naval Research involving five observers, each of whom made over 3,000 observations, indicated that the average accuracy of the second thousand sights was better than the average accuracy of the first thousand, and the third thousand was better than the second.

It is usually best for the novice to start with observations of the sun. It will probably be helpful if he can make simultaneous sights with an experienced observer. Excellent practice can be had with the sun at local apparent noon, at which point the sun is on or very close to the observer's meridian. At this time the sun changes altitude very little for a minute or more, and during this period the observed altitudes should be practically identical.

Graphing sights can be helpful to the beginner, or to the expert when maximum accuracy is required, as this permits spotting the random error in single observations; this random error is the single greatest enemy of accurate navigation. To plot sights, it is best to use 20-inch-wide graph paper divided by inches and tenths of inches. Sights should be taken for a period of up to 3 minutes, 20 seconds. With practice and under good conditions, it should be possible to obtain up to 15 good observations during this period. These are then plotted; in doing so, one second of time equals one tenth of an inch on the graph, and one minute of arc equals one inch. After the sights are plotted, a "line of best fit" is drawn in with the aid of a straightedge; this line should approximate the mean rate of change of altitude, and should pass through or as close as possible to the maximum number of plotted observations. This method will clearly indicate sights having a serious random error.

For a skilled observer to take only one sight of a body is poor practice. A better practice is to make quick, multiple observations; by inspection, it is then possible to note if there is an even rate of altitude change over the time periods between sights. At twilight the available time for making observations will elapse quickly, and observations of several stars are desired, limiting the amount of time available for multiple sights of each one. No rigid rules can be laid down as to the number of observations which should be made on each star or of the number of stars to be observed.

Notes on Sextant Observations

The index correction is discussed in Chapter 5. However, it should be pointed out here that the index correction should be determined each time the sextant is used. This may be done by setting the instrument at zero degrees, and then looking at the horizon and bringing the direct and reflected images into coincidence so that the two images form a straight line. This should be done by alternately raising the reflected horizon until it is in coincidence and then depressing it, the index error being noted each time. The several readings are then averaged to obtain the current index correction. If the error is negative—that is, if the sextant reading is under zero degrees, or "off the arc"—the correction is additive, and vice versa. This rule led to the mnemonic phrase, "When it's off, it's on, and when it's on, it's off."

Under conditions of poor lighting, when the horizon is not distinct, the direct and reflected images of a star may be brought into coincidence to establish the index error.

In overcast weather, the sun frequently breaks through for a very short period of time. It is wise, therefore, to have the sextant close at hand, although well secured, so that an observation may be obtained.

Many navigators, even when they are in urgent need of a sight, do not observe the sun when it is screened by thin clouds. This is a mistake; even when the sun's limb appears quite fuzzy, the observation will not be greatly in error. Also, when it is necessary to update the ship's position, many navigators do not observe the sun at low altitudes, even though no other source of information is available. This is also a mistake; if carefully corrected, low-altitude sights, down to one degree or less, are rarely found to be in error by as much as 2 minutes. The "Additional Corrections" from the Altitude Correction Tables in the *Nautical Almanac* should always be used with low-altitude sights. Although the H.O. 214 tables do not give solutions for sights with an altitude of less than about 5°, such observations may be used when the computations are to be made from H.O. 229 or H.O. 249.

As stated above, the accuracy of observations improves with practice. When ashore, an artificial horizon makes practice possible, at altitudes below 45°. A mercury horizon makes it possible to observe the sun, moon, and stars; black, optically ground glass horizons, when leveled, are useful for sun observations, and even a dish of molasses or heavy oil will serve. To avoid damaging the eye when the sun is observed, the reflected image should be screened by means of the horizon shades. Observations should not be made through a glass window, as such glass is not optically flat. With such a reflecting artificial horizon, the true altitude is one-half the altitude read from the sextant, and the correction for refraction should be based on this corrected altitude. In making such observations of the sun, the reflected image may be superimposed on the directly viewed image, resulting in an observation of the center of the body; no correction for semi-diameter of the sun is then required.

The dip correction is not applied to observations made with an artificial horizon; it is applied to all observations made with the sea horizon.

Venus is frequently visible during daylight hours, when its altitude is greater than that of the sun. If obtained at about the same time, observations of the sun and Venus can often furnish an excellent fix. The moon can also be used in conjunction with the sun to obtain daytime fixes.

When observing the moon at night aboard a large ship, it is desirable that the observation be made from a point as low in the vessel as possible, in order to reduce the hazard of using a false horizon. Particularly if there are clouds below the moon, the true horizon may be shaded, and the altitude as measured may be greater than the true altitude.

In observing stars at twilight, it is most desirable to have a clearly defined horizon. At morning twilight, the eastern horizon will brighten and become sharp first; consequently, stars to the east will tend to fade first. The higher and/or the brighter the star is, the longer it will be visible in the eastern sky. It is wise, therefore, during morning sights to commence observing any fairly low stars that are in the general direction of the point where the sun will rise. Next, observe the lower or less bright stars in the other quadrants, then sight the brighter and higher stars to the east and finish with the higher and brighter stars in the other quadrants. At evening twilight, the reverse procedure usually yields the best results. In the tropics, the duration of twilight is very brief, and it is therefore often necessary to work rapidly.

The use of a star finder before making twilight observations is wise. This device allows the observer to prepare in advance a list of stars that are well distributed in azimuth. Their magnitude, or brilliance, and their approximate altitudes and azimuths may be noted on the list when it is prepared. Such a list permits the observer to set the sextant to the desired altitude, and if he then uses a compass to obtain the azimuth, he can usually locate the star readily. Good practice calls for locating at least 5 stars, as evenly distributed through 360 degrees of azimuth as possible, and taking 5 observations of each star.

It is possible to observe stars on a clear, moonless night with a sextant fitted with a good 6-by-30 or 7-by-50 monocular that has coated optics if the observer has dark-adapted vision. The navigators of our fleet submarines in the western Pacific during World War II obtained such sights regularly. To protect his dark-adapted vision, the observer should not expose himself to any artificial lighting whatsoever. However, if this cannot be avoided, red lights should be used, for they have a minimum disturbing effect. A useful trick is to wear an eye patch over the observing eye for an hour before sighting night stars.

Obtaining celestial observations from a yacht presents some problems that are magnified beyond those encountered on a large ship. The platform on a yacht is much less stable, and in general a faster period of roll is present. The yachtsman must often make observations from a rather awkward position in order to avoid falling overboard. A sailboat pitches more than she rolls, the axis of the pitch generally being abaft amidships; observations should therefore be made near this axis. Sights should be obtained when the crest of a wave is directly beneath the observer; he can then assume quite safely that his normal height of eye for that location is correct, as the horizon will be formed by wave crests of the same height as that of the one under the keel.

Star Identification

With practice and study, the navigator will eventually learn to identify the navigational stars simply by viewing them in the heavens.

At the start, however, an artificial aid is very helpful. The H.O. 2102-D Star Finder (Figure 4-7) is the most widely used device for predetermining the approximate altitude and azimuth of a celestial body. The altitudes and azimuth, as taken from the Star Finder enable the observer to detect stars with his sextant telescope when they are not readily visible to the naked eye.

The Star Finder consists of an opaque plastic base, nine templates that are transparent and cover 10° of latitude each, and a red template for plotting additional stars or planets in accordance with their sidereal hour angles and declinations. The base plate is printed on both sides, one for use in north latitude and the other for south latitude. The correct side must be used. The 57 navigational stars are located on this base, and a graduated scale of LHA*Ƴ* is printed around the circumference. Due to the projection used, the position of the stars on the base is *not* a graphic illustration of their relative position in the heavens. The templates also have a north or south side, and the correct side must be used. A series of curves on the templates indicate approximate altitude and azimuth. These templates are referred to as the blue templates, as they are printed in that color.

The Star Finder is set up for use by determining the LHA of Aries.

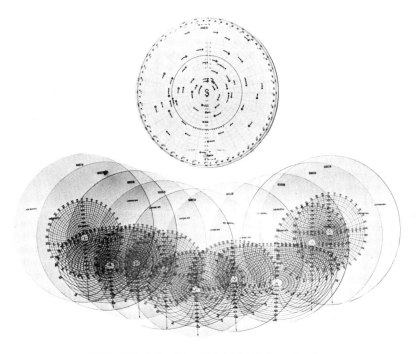

FIGURE 4-7   The HO 2102-D Star Finder.

The normal procedure is to obtain GHAT from the *Almanac*, using GMT twilight and date as an entering argument, and converting this to LHAT by applying longitude (subtract west longitude; add east longitude). Great precision is not required for star identification, and this latter step can be eliminated by entering the *Almanac* with local mean time (LMT) instead of GMT; the entry under GHAT is then LHAT. For this purpose, LMT can be obtained by using zone time that has been corrected by adding 4 minutes for each degree of longitude west of a standard meridian and subtracting when east of a standard meridian. The arrow on the blue template is then set directly at this value of LHAT on the base of the Star Finder, and the altitude and azimuth of each selected navigational star above the horizon will be shown.

Using the Star Finder for Planets

Since the position of the planets in relation to the positions of the fixed stars is constantly changing, they are not printed on the base of the Star Finder, but they can be added by using the red template, which has a convenient slot in it for plotting. The relative daily change in position of the planets is small, and it is not necessary to replot them each day; once a week or so is sufficient. To use the red template, the declination and "360° minus SHA" must be obtained from the *Almanac*. Declination of the planets is listed in the correct column of the *Almanac* under the planet name, as is the GHA of the planet. SHA planet is obtained by subtracting GHAT from GHA planet for the desired time, adding 360° to GHA planet when necessary in order to make the subtraction. The arrow on the red template is set opposite this value of 360° − SHA, on the outer scale on the star base of the Star Finder. Plotting is done through the cutout slot in the template opposite the value of declination, north or south, which is printed along the slot.

Identifying an Unknown Star

Occasionally the navigator will obtain an observation of a star that he has not identified. In such a case, both the altitude and the azimuth should be observed and noted in addition to the usual time of the observation.

If the star is one of those listed on the base plate of the Star Finder, the identification is quite simple. The index arrow of the blue plate is aligned to the appropriate LHA of Aries. The point of intersection of the altitude and azimuth curve of the body is then located on the blue template, and the body listed on the star based at or quite near this position can usually be assumed to be the star observed.

However, if no star appears at or near that point, the red template can be used to determine the approximate declination, and SHA of the star. These two arguments can then be located in the more complete list of stars in the back of the *Almanac*, and the observed star can be identified. To determine the SHA and declination, the red template is placed over the blue template and rotated until the slotted meridian is over the intersection of the altitude and azimuth curve obtained from the observation of the star. The declination is read from the scale along the slotted meridian, and 360° − SHA is read from the base plate underneath the arrow on the red template. This figure subtracted from 360° equals the SHA.

Chapter 5

Sextant Errors, Adjustments, and Corrections

Instrument Errors

Some errors in the sextant are due to slight faults in its manufacture; these are called fixed instrumental errors and cannot be corrected by adjustment. Such errors are caused, for example, by a slight mis-centering of the index arm pivot relative to the arc. On the best instrument the fixed errors never exceed $0'.2$ minutes. This type of error is not consistent at all altitudes. The amount of error, usually stated for every ten degrees of altitude, is found on the manufacturer's certificate on the inside of the lid of the sextant case. Some certificates covering sextants furnished by reputable manufacturers state that the instrument is free of error for practical purposes; it may be assumed, for example, that the fixed error of the Plath sextant is less than ten seconds at all altitudes. Unfortunately, it is impossible to manufacture a sextant that is completely free of error.

Nonadjustable instrument error is the sum of the nonadjustable errors—prismatic, graduation, and centering—of a sextant. The correction for these errors is called the instrument correction (I); it is determined by the manufacturer and recorded on the certificate framed in the sextant box. It varies with the angle measured, may be either positive or negative, and is applied to all angles measured by that particular sextant.

Index Error

The index error (IE) is caused primarily by a slight lack of parallelism between the index mirror and the horizon glass when the instrument is set at zero altitude. at this setting, index error can be recognized by looking at the horizon: if the direct and reflected images do not appear as a continuous line, index error exists. If the sextant is being checked at night, look directly at a star through the telescope, again with the altitude set at zero; index error will cause the reflected image of a star to be either above or below the direct image. Index error may be positive or negative, and is corrected by applying the index correction. Care must be excerised in determining the sign, "+" or "−", of the index correction. If the reading on the micrometer drum when the objects—be they horizon or star—are aligned is 50 or more minutes, the error is negative, the sextant is reading too low, and the correction must therefore be positive (+). For example, if the sextant is set to approximately 0° on the arc and the reading on the drum is 56.5′, the error is −3.5 minutes of arc and the IC would be +3′.5. Conversely, if the reading on the drum is 2′.5, the error is +, the sextant is reading too large an angle, and the IC would be −2.5 minutes of arc. The IC is not fixed, and its value should be determined each time the sextant is used. If the index error is small—say, less than 2′—it is best to use the correction rather than to try to adjust the mirrors. To eliminate or reduce excessive index error, the *horizon* glass must be adjusted so that its lack of parallelism to the index mirror is reduced.

Adjusting the Sextant Mirrors

The horizon glass of the Plath sextant and several other commercial sextants is adjusted within the mirror frame. When the sextant is held exactly vertical, only the upper screw (*A* in Figure 5-1) is used. The one adjusting screw is tightened or loosened slightly with a key supplied with the sextant; this moves the mirror against the mounting springs. When the sextant is adjusted properly, the horizon will appear as in Figure 5-2 with the sextant reading zero. When index error is present, the horizon will appear as in Figure 5-3. The sextant should be checked occasionally to see that the mirrors are perpendicular to the sextant frame, and should be adjusted if a misalignment is found to exist. The observer checks index mirror alignment by holding the

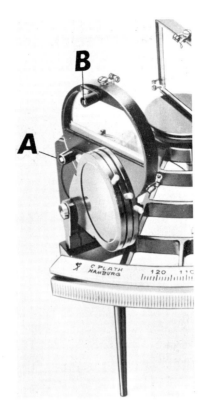

B

A

FIGURE 5-1   Adjusting the sextant mirrors.

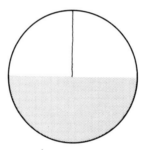

FIGURE 5-2   The horizon on a properly adjusted sextant.

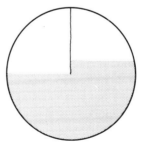

FIGURE 5-3   The horizon on an improperly adjusted sextant.

62

sextant in the left hand with the index mirror toward him; he then looks into the index mirror and shifts the position of the sextant until the image of the limb that is reflected in the index mirror appears to be a continuation of the limb as seen directly, when looking past the index mirror. This is illustrated in Figure 5-4 (left), which shows that the index mirror is misaligned. If the reflected image is inclined to the limb as seen directly, or is not in alignment with it, the index mirror is not perpendicular to the plane of the limb, and the alignment should be corrected by use of the adjusting screw on the back of the index mirror frame.

FIGURE 5-4   (Above) Index mirror aligned. (Below) Index mirror misaligned.

On some sextants, notably the old U.S. Navy Mk II, two screws are used for each adjustment of the mirrors, and the mirror frame is moved in relation to the sextant frame. In this case, one screw must always be backed off slightly before the other is taken up by an equal amount. Failure to do this will result in damage to the adjusting screws.

To check the perpendicularity of the horizon mirror, sight the horizon in the same manner as when determining the index error. The micrometer drum is adjusted until the reflected and direct images of the horizon appear as a straight line with the sextant in a vertical position. The sextant is then turned or rocked around the line of sight; the reflected horizon and the direct horizon should remain in exact alignment, as shown in Figure 5-5. If they do not, as shown in Figure 5-6, the horizon glass must be adjusted until it is perpendicular to the plane of the limb. On sextants whose horizon mirror is adjusted within the frame, the adjusting screw farther away from the sextant frame (B in Figure 5-1) is used. When the mirror is adjusted properly, the horizon will appear as a straight line while the sextant is rotated around the line of sight. To adjust for perpendicularity at night, the sextant, its index set at 0°, is sighted directly at a star. When the micrometer drum is turned, the reflected image of the star should move in a vertical line exactly through the direct image (see Figure 5-7). If the line of movement is to one side or the other of the direct image (Figure 5-8), the horizon mirror is not perpendicular to the frame and should be adjusted.

Since two different adjustments are made on the horizon glass, these adjustments will be interrelated; for example, in adjusting the perpendicularity of the mirror, the index error will be affected. As a general rule, it is best to remove the index error first, adjust for perpendicularity, and then check again for index error. Several adjustments may be necessary if the mirror is badly misaligned.

If extreme difficulty is encountered in bringing a star down to the horizon, it is possible that the line of sight of the telescope is not parallel to the plane of the sextant frame. This is usually difficult to adjust aboard ship, but a quick practical check can be made to determine if the telescope is out of alignment. The sextant is held in a vertical position in the left hand with the horizon mirror toward the observer and the index arm set near 0°. The observer looks into the index mirror, holding the sextant in such a position that the reflected image of the center line of the horizon mirror is directly in line with the actual center line. In this position it should be possible to see straight through the telescope, the line of sight being the same as the path of the light rays of a star when an observation is being made. If the telescope is out of alignment, the observer will be unable to look straight through. On some sextants, the telescope is equipped with screws for adjusting its line of sight. In general, this adjustment should be made in an optical shop.

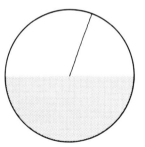

FIGURE 5-5   Perpendicularity of the horizon mirror.

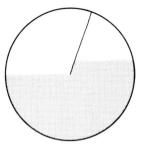

FIGURE 5-6   Nonperpendicularity of the horizon mirror.

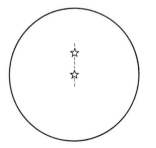

FIGURE 5-7   Perpendicularity checked at night by using a star.

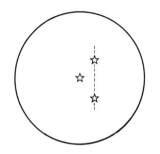

FIGURE 5-8   Nonperpendicularity at night.

Sextant Altitude Corrections

All altitudes observed with the sextant, whether a sea horizon or an artificial horizon is used, require correction. The required corrections fall into two categories: those caused by external conditions, and those due to some optical or mechanical flaw in the instrument. Although the index error is due to a slight misalignment of the sextant optical system, it may vary, and should be measured each time the sextant is used. As we mentioned above, the fixed error (I) cannot be corrected; it is, so to speak, built into the sextant, and if it is larger than about $0'.2$, it must also be allowed for when altitudes are measured.

Dip

A primary external condition that causes error in marine sextant altitudes, unless allowed for, is the height of the observer's eye above the visible horizon. If the observer could measure the altitude of a body with his eye at the level of the water, this correction would not be necessary. As shown in Figure 5-9, the higher the observer's eye above the water, the greater this correction will be. The height of the observer's eye is said to cause the horizon to "dip." The correction for dip is found in the "Dip Correction Table" in the *Nautical Almanac*, which is reproduced in Table 5-1 of the present text. Note that this table is a *critical table*, as are the other altitude correction tables. In such a table, an interval—in this case, height of eye—corresponds to a single value of the correction, and no numerical interpolation is required in the answer column. As a critical entry, the upper of the two possible values of the correction should be used; thus, for a height of eye of 12.6 feet, the value of the correction taken from the table should be $(-) 3'.4$.

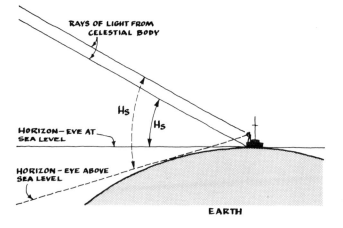

FIGURE 5-9 Dip.

SUN

OCT.–MAR. App. Alt.	Lower Limb	Upper Limb	APR.–SEPT. App. Alt.	Lower Limb	Upper Limb
9 34	+10·8	−21·5	9 39	+10·6	−21·2
9 45	+10·9	−21·4	9 51	+10·7	−21·1
9 56	+11·0	−21·3	10 03	+10·8	−21·0
10 08	+11·1	21·2	10 15	+10·9	20·9
10 21	+11·2	−21·1	10 27	+11·0	−20·8
10 34	+11·3	21·0	10 40	+11·1	−20·7
10 47	+11·4	20·9	10 54	+11·2	20·6
11 01	+11·5	20·8	11 08	+11·3	20·5
11 15	+11·6	20·7	11 23	+11·4	20·4
11 30	+11·7	20·6	11 38	+11·5	20·3
11 46	+11·8	20·5	11 54	+11·6	20·2
12 02	+11·9	20·4	12 10	+11·7	20·1
12 19	+12·0	20·3	12 28	+11·8	20·0
12 37	+12·1	20·2	12 46	+11·9	19·9
12 55	+12·2	20·1	13 05	+12·0	19·8
13 14	+12·3	20·0	13 24	+12·1	19·7
13 35	+12·4	19·9	13 45	+12·2	19·6
13 56	+12·5	19·8	14 07	+12·3	19·5
14 18	+12·6	19·7	14 30	+12·4	19·4
14 42	+12·7	19·6	14 54	+12·5	19·3
15 06	+12·8	19·5	15 19	+12·6	19·2
15 32	+12·9	19·4	15 46	+12·7	19·1
15 59	+13·0	19·3	16 14	+12·8	19·0
16 28	+13·1	19·2	16 44	+12·9	18·9
16 59	+13·2	19·1	17 15	+13·0	18·8
17 32	+13·3	19·0	17 48	+13·1	18·7
18 06	+13·4	18·9	18 24	+13·2	18·6
18 42	+13·5	18·8	19 01	+13·3	18·5
19 21	+13·6	18·7	19 42	+13·4	18·4
20 03	+13·7	18·6	20 25	+13·5	18·3
20 48	+13·8	18·5	21 11	+13·6	18·2
21 35	+13·9	18·4	22 00	+13·7	18·1
22 26	+14·0	18·3	22 54	+13·8	18·0
23 22	+14·1	18·2	23 51	+13·9	17·9
24 21	+14·2	18·1	24 53	+14·0	17·8
25 26	+14·3	18·0	26 00	+14·1	17·7
26 36	+14·4	17·9	27 13	+14·2	17·6
27 52	+14·5	17·8	28 33	+14·3	17·5
29 15	+14·6	17·7	30 00	+14·4	17·4
30 46	+14·7	17·6	31 35	+14·5	17·3
32 26	+14·8	17·5	33 20	+14·6	17·2
34 17	+14·9	17·4	35 17	+14·7	17·1
36 20	+15·0	17·3	37 26	+14·8	17·0
38 36	+15·1	17·2	39 50	+14·9	16·9
41 08	+15·2	17·1	42 31	+15·0	16·8
43 59	+15·3	17·0	45 31	+15·1	16·7
47 10	+15·4	16·9	48 55	+15·2	16·6
50 46	+15·5	16·8	52 44	+15·3	16·5
54 49	+15·6	16·7	57 02	+15·4	16·4
59 23	+15·7	16·6	61 51	+15·5	16·3
64 30	+15·8	16·5	67 17	+15·6	16·2
70 12	+15·9	16·4	73 16	+15·7	16·1
76 26	+16·0	16·3	79 43	+15·8	16·0
83 05	+16·1	16·2	86 32	+15·9	15·9
90 00			90 00		

STARS

App. Alt.	Corrn
9 56	−5·3
10 08	−5·2
10 20	−5·1
10 33	−5·0
10 46	−4·9
11 00	−4·8
11 14	−4·7
11 29	−4·6
11 45	−4·5
12 01	−4·4
12 18	−4·3
12 35	−4·2
12 54	−4·1
13 13	−4·0
13 33	−3·9
13 54	−3·8
14 16	−3·7
14 40	−3·6
15 04	−3·5
15 30	−3·4
15 57	−3·3
16 26	−3·2
16 56	−3·1
17 28	−3·0
18 02	−2·9
18 38	−2·8
19 17	−2·7
19 58	−2·6
20 42	−2·5
21 28	−2·4
22 19	−2·3
23 13	−2·2
24 11	−2·1
25 14	−2·0
26 22	−1·9
27 36	−1·8
28 56	−1·7
30 24	−1·6
32 00	−1·5
33 45	−1·4
35 40	−1·3
37 48	−1·2
40 08	−1·1
42 44	−1·0
45 36	−0·9
48 47	−0·8
52 18	−0·7
56 11	−0·6
60 28	−0·5
65 08	−0·4
70 11	−0·3
75 34	−0·2
81 13	−0·1
87 03	0·0
90 00	

DIP

Ht. of Eye (m)	Corrn	Ht. of Eye (ft)	Ht. of Eye (m)	Corrn
2·4	−2·8	8·0	1·0	− 1·8
2·6	−2·9	8·6	1·5	− 2·2
2·8	−3·0	9·2	2·0	− 2·5
3·0	−3·1	9·8	2·5	− 2·8
3·2	−3·2	10·5	3·0	− 3·0
3·4	−3·3	11·2	See table ←	
3·6	−3·4	11·9		
3·8	−3·5	12·6	m	'
4·0	−3·6	13·3	20	− 7·9
4·3	−3·7	14·1	22	− 8·3
4·5	−3·8	14·9	24	− 8·6
4·7	−3·9	15·7	26	− 9·0
5·0	−4·0	16·5	28	− 9·3
5·2	−4·1	17·4		
5·5	−4·2	18·3	30	− 9·6
5·8	−4·3	19·1	32	−10·0
6·1	−4·4	20·1	34	−10·3
6·3	−4·5	21·0	36	−10·6
6·6	−4·6	22·0	38	−10·8
6·9	−4·7	22·9		
7·2	−4·8	23·9	40	−11·1
7·5	−4·9	24·9	42	−11·4
7·9	−5·0	26·0	44	−11·7
8·2	−5·1	27·1	46	−11·9
8·5	−5·2	28·1	48	−12·2
8·8	−5·3	29·2	ft.	
9·2	−5·4	30·4	2	− 1·4
9·5	−5·5	31·5	4	− 1·9
9·9	−5·6	32·7	6	− 2·4
10·3	−5·7	33·9	8	− 2·7
10·6	−5·8	35·1	10	− 3·1
11·0	−5·9	36·3	See table ←	
11·4	−6·0	37·6		
11·8	−6·1	38·9	ft.	
12·2	−6·2	40·1	70	− 8·1
12·6	−6·3	41·5	75	− 8·4
13·0	−6·4	42·8	80	− 8·7
13·4	−6·5	44·2	85	− 8·9
13·8	−6·6	45·5	90	− 9·2
14·2	−6·7	46·9	95	− 9·5
14·7	−6·8	48·4		
15·1	−6·9	49·8	100	− 9·7
15·5	−7·0	51·3	105	− 9·9
16·0	−7·1	52·8	110	−10·2
16·5	−7·2	54·3	115	−10·4
16·9	−7·3	55·8	120	−10·6
17·4	−7·4	57·4	125	−10·8
17·9	−7·5	58·9		
18·4	−7·6	60·5		
18·8	−7·7	62·1	130	−11·1
19·3	−7·8	63·8	135	−11·3
19·8	−7·9	65·4	140	−11·5
20·4	−8·0	67·1	145	−11·7
20·9	−8·1	68·8	150	−11·9
21·4		70·5	155	−12·1

TABLE 5-1 Altitude correction table from the Nautical Almanac.

The *Nautical Almanac* is a joint British-American publication. Note that the height-of-eye column in the dip correction table can be entered in terms of meters (by using the column headed "m") or feet (the column headed "ft."). Be sure to enter the proper column.

Refraction

Refraction, the bending of light rays passing through media of varying densities, affects the value of the sextant observation. The correction tables allow for such refraction under standard conditions of temperature and barometric pressure.

Refraction (R) affects all altitudes, whether an artificial horizon or the sea horizon is the reference for measurement. When light rays pass from a medium of one density into a medium of another density, they are refracted; a classic example is the stick held with one end under water. Similarly, when a light ray passes from outer space into the earth's atmosphere, it is refracted at an increasing level as it moves into continually denser layers of the atmosphere. The direction of the refraction is downward; the body thereby appears higher than it actually is. This is illustrated in Figure 5-10, which exaggerates refraction in the interest of clarity; it shows the increasing refraction caused by the increasing density of the earth's atmospheric envelope.

Refraction decreases as altitude increases, being zero when the body is at the observer's zenith; conversely, it increases as altitude decreases, reaching its maximum at the observer's sea horizon. Under standard conditions of temperature and atmospheric pressure, the refraction is 34′.5 at 0° altitude. Thus, the sun, with a maximum apparent diameter of 32′.6, is actually completely below the horizon when its lower limb still appears to be slightly above the horizon. The

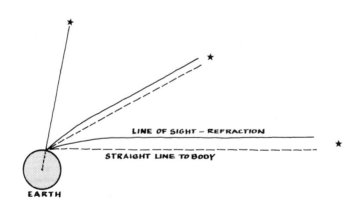

FIGURE 5-10 *Refraction.*

"stars" column of the *Almanac* corrections is a refraction table for standard conditions.

Refraction, as it affects observed altitudes, varies with pressure and temperature in the different atmospheric layers through which it passes. At sea, the navigator is unable to obtain data on upper air conditions. He can, however, modify the correction for refraction that occurs at standard surface weather conditions—a barometric pressure of 29.83 inches (1010 mb) and an air temperature of 50° Fahrenheit (10° centigrade)—by using the appropriate value in the "Additional Corrections" (T and B) in the *Nautical Almanac*. This special almanac table provides an additonal refraction correction for non-standard temperature and barometric pressure situations. It is usually not necessary to use the additional correction table for altitudes over 10°, except under very unusual weather conditions. However, it should always be used when a low-altitude observation is made.

Semidiameter

Semidiameter must be allowed for in measuring altitudes of the sun and moon. Unlike the stars, which may be considered point sources of light, these two bodies appear very sizable to the eye. The marine sextant measures the altitude above the horizon of either the lower or the upper limb. However, in navigation the altitude of the body's center must be used. In order to obtain the altitude of the center of the sun or moon, therefore, the measured altitude of the observed limb must be adjusted for the semidiameter of the body.

The sun's semidiameter varies between 15.8 and 16.3 minutes of arc; its current value is found at the bottom of the "sun" column in the daily pages of the *Nautical Almanac*. If the lower limb of the sun is observed, the value of the semidiameter is added to the sextant altitude; if the upper limb is observed, the semidiameter for the appropriate date is subtracted. Each listing in the "sun" column in Table 5-1 combines the individual corrections for refraction, semidiameter, and parallax. These listings are divided into separate columns for upper-limb and lower-limb observations. (The moon's semidiameter is discussed later in this chapter.)

When greater accuracy is desired in making observations of the sun, the semidiameter (SD) correction obtained from the bottom of the "sun" column in the appropriate daily page in the *Nautical Almanac* should be used, together with the refraction correction for stars and planets, rather than the October–March and April–September combined corrections. This is because the latter corrections are averages over a six-month period of the value of the semidiameter, which actually varies between 15′.8 and 16′.3. The SD correction is additive for the lower limb and subtractive for the upper limb; the sun's center is the point of reference in reducing the observation. When using the actual semidiameter for altitudes below 65°, a correction for parallax should be applied, in addition to the corrections for refraction and dip; this correction is +0′.1.

Parallax

We have noted that in sight reduction the altitude of the center of the body must be used. Similarly, the altitude that is to be reduced must be corrected as though it had been measured at the center of the earth. In the case of the stars this causes no problem, as the stars may be considered to be located at infinity, and their altitudes are equal, whether measured from the plane of the observer's visible horizon or the plane of his celestial horizon, which is parallel to the visible horizon and passes through the center of the earth. However, the sun, the moon, and the planets Venus and Mars are comparatively near the earth, and are affected by parallax. Parallax (P) may be defined as the difference in direction of an object at a finite distance when viewed from two different positions. This is illustrated in Figure 5-11, which shows (on the right side) the rays of a star traveling parallel and therefore intersecting the observer's visible and celestial horizons at equal altitudes. This does not hold true for a body that is comparatively near the earth; as shown on the left-hand side of the figure, there is an appreciable difference in altitude when the body is measured at the earth's surface instead of at its center.

The value of the parallax error is not constant; it varies both with the body's distance from the earth and with its altitude. For a body at a given distance, the value of parallax is maximum when the body is on the horizon, at which point it is called horizontal parallax; its value is zero when the body is directly above the observer's position, at an altitude of 90°. The correction for parallax is always additive. For the sun, it amounts to +0′.1 for altitudes to 65° and less. It is variable for the planets Venus and Mars, and its values for these two planets are found in the inside front cover of the *Nautical Almanac*. It is very large for the moon, and in this respect it is discussed further below.

Venus and Mars pass through phases, as does the moon; that is, their shapes vary between a disc and a crescent. This effect is not always visible to the naked eye, but it affects the appearance of the planet when viewed through the sextant telescope, and it makes a difference in bringing the body in contact with the horizon. The inside front cover of the *Nautical Almanac* contains a combined correction for both the phase effect and parallax for Mars and Venus, a correction that may be positive or negative. Jupiter and Saturn are too distant to require correction for either phase or parallax.

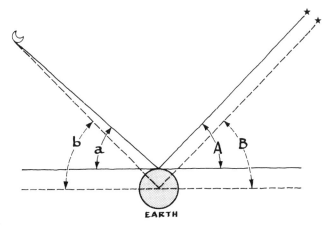

FIGURE 5-11   *The parallax effect. Moon — angles a and b are unequal. Stars — angles A and B are equal.*

The Moon

The moon is our nearest celestial neighbor; its distance from the earth varies somewhat, the mean distance being 207,565 nautical miles. Due to the moon's proximity to us, lunar observations are greatly affected by parallax; they are also affected to a much smaller degree by augmentation. The semidiameter of a body (measured in minutes of arc) varies with its distance from the observer; when the body is at the observer's zenith, it is nearer to him by a distance equal to the earth's radius, than when it is on his horizon. This apparent difference in semidiameter is called augmentation.

Sun, planet, and star observations are not affected by augmentation, as the earth's radius is very small in comparison with the distance involved. With the moon, on the other hand, augmentation must be taken into consideration, since at mean lunar distance the augmentation between the horizon and the zenith amounts to 0'.3.

The altitude correction tables for the moon that are found in the back of the *Nautical Almanac* combine corrections for refraction, parallax, semidiameter, and augmentation. These listings are reproduced in Table 5-2 of the present text. The table consists of two parts: the first is entered with the moon's altitude, interpolating if necessary; the second is entered with the horizontal parallax (H.P.) taken from the hourly value found in the "Moon" column of the daily pages. This second part of the table consists of two columns, one for the moon's lower limb (L) and one for its upper limb (U). All corrections are added to the apparent altitude, but 30' are subtracted from the altitude of the upper limb. These tables make the correction of moon altitudes a simple matter.

App. Alt.	0°–4° Corrn	5°–9° Corrn	10°–14° Corrn	15°–19° Corrn	20°–24° Corrn	25°–29° Corrn	30°–34° Corrn	App. Alt.
00	0 33·8	5 58·2	10 62·1	15 62·8	20 62·2	25 60·8	30 58·9	00
10	35·9	58·5	62·2	62·8	62·1	60·8	58·8	10
20	37·8	58·7	62·2	62·8	62·1	60·7	58·8	20
30	39·6	58·9	62·3	62·8	62·1	60·7	58·7	30
40	41·2	59·1	62·3	62·8	62·0	60·6	58·6	40
50	42·6	59·3	62·4	62·7	62·0	60·6	58·5	50
00	1 44·0	6 59·5	11 62·4	16 62·7	21 62·0	26 60·5	31 58·5	00
10	45·2	59·7	62·4	62·7	61·9	60·4	58·4	10
20	46·3	59·9	62·5	62·7	61·9	60·4	58·3	20
30	47·3	60·0	62·5	62·7	61·9	60·3	58·2	30
40	48·3	60·2	62·5	62·7	61·8	60·3	58·2	40
50	49·2	60·3	62·6	62·7	61·8	60·2	58·1	50
00	2 50·0	7 60·5	12 62·6	17 62·7	22 61·7	27 60·1	32 58·0	00
10	50·8	60·6	62·6	62·6	61·7	60·1	57·9	10
20	51·4	60·7	62·6	62·6	61·6	60·0	57·8	20
30	52·1	60·9	62·7	62·6	61·6	59·9	57·8	30
40	52·7	61·0	62·7	62·6	61·5	59·9	57·7	40
50	53·3	61·1	62·7	62·6	61·5	59·8	57·6	50
00	3 53·8	8 61·2	13 62·7	18 62·5	23 61·5	28 59·7	33 57·5	00
10	54·3	61·3	62·7	62·5	61·4	59·7	57·4	10
20	54·8	61·4	62·7	62·5	61·4	59·6	57·4	20
30	55·2	61·5	62·8	62·5	61·3	59·6	57·3	30
40	55·6	61·6	62·8	62·4	61·3	59·5	57·2	40
50	56·0	61·6	62·8	62·4	61·2	59·4	57·1	50
00	4 56·4	9 61·7	14 62·8	19 62·4	24 61·2	29 59·3	34 57·0	00
10	56·7	61·8	62·8	62·3	61·1	59·3	56·9	10
20	57·1	61·9	62·8	62·3	61·1	59·2	56·9	20
30	57·4	61·9	62·8	62·3	61·0	59·1	56·8	30
40	57·7	62·0	62·8	62·2	60·9	59·1	56·7	40
50	57·9	62·1	62·8	62·2	60·9	59·0	56·6	50

H.P.	L U	L U	L U	L U	L U	L U	L U	H.P.
54·0	0·3 0·9	0·3 0·9	0·4 1·0	0·5 1·1	0·6 1·2	0·7 1·3	0·9 1·5	54·0
54·3	0·7 1·1	0·7 1·2	0·7 1·2	0·8 1·3	0·9 1·4	1·1 1·5	1·2 1·7	54·3
54·6	1·1 1·4	1·1 1·4	1·1 1·4	1·2 1·5	1·3 1·6	1·4 1·7	1·5 1·8	54·6
54·9	1·4 1·6	1·5 1·6	1·5 1·6	1·6 1·7	1·6 1·8	1·8 1·9	1·9 2·0	54·9
55·2	1·8 1·8	1·8 1·8	1·9 1·9	1·9 1·9	2·0 2·0	2·1 2·1	2·2 2·2	55·2
55·5	2·2 2·0	2·2 2·0	2·3 2·1	2·3 2·1	2·4 2·2	2·4 2·3	2·5 2·4	55·5
55·8	2·6 2·2	2·6 2·2	2·6 2·3	2·7 2·3	2·7 2·4	2·8 2·4	2·9 2·5	55·8
56·1	3·0 2·4	3·0 2·5	3·0 2·5	3·0 2·5	3·1 2·6	3·1 2·6	3·2 2·7	56·1
56·4	3·4 2·7	3·4 2·7	3·4 2·7	3·4 2·7	3·4 2·8	3·5 2·8	3·5 2·9	56·4
56·7	3·7 2·9	3·7 2·9	3·8 2·9	3·8 2·9	3·8 3·0	3·8 3·0	3·9 3·0	56·7
57·0	4·1 3·1	4·1 3·1	4·1 3·1	4·1 3·1	4·2 3·1	4·2 3·2	4·2 3·2	57·0
57·3	4·5 3·3	4·5 3·3	4·5 3·3	4·5 3·3	4·5 3·3	4·5 3·4	4·6 3·4	57·3
57·6	4·9 3·5	4·9 3·5	4·9 3·5	4·9 3·5	4·9 3·5	4·9 3·5	4·9 3·6	57·6
57·9	5·3 3·8	5·3 3·8	5·2 3·8	5·2 3·7	5·2 3·7	5·2 3·7	5·2 3·7	57·9
58·2	5·6 4·0	5·6 4·0	5·6 4·0	5·6 4·0	5·6 3·9	5·6 3·9	5·6 3·9	58·2
58·5	6·0 4·2	6·0 4·2	6·0 4·2	6·0 4·2	6·0 4·1	5·9 4·1	5·9 4·1	58·5
58·8	6·4 4·4	6·4 4·4	6·4 4·4	6·3 4·4	6·3 4·3	6·3 4·3	6·2 4·2	58·8
59·1	6·8 4·6	6·8 4·6	6·7 4·6	6·7 4·6	6·7 4·5	6·6 4·5	6·6 4·4	59·1
59·4	7·2 4·8	7·1 4·8	7·1 4·8	7·1 4·8	7·0 4·7	7·0 4·7	6·9 4·6	59·4
59·7	7·5 5·1	7·5 5·0	7·5 5·0	7·5 5·0	7·4 4·9	7·3 4·8	7·2 4·7	59·7
60·0	7·9 5·3	7·9 5·3	7·9 5·2	7·8 5·2	7·8 5·1	7·7 5·0	7·6 4·9	60·0
60·3	8·3 5·5	8·3 5·5	8·2 5·4	8·2 5·4	8·1 5·3	8·0 5·2	7·9 5·1	60·3
60·6	8·7 5·7	8·7 5·7	8·6 5·7	8·6 5·6	8·5 5·5	8·4 5·4	8·2 5·3	60·6
60·9	9·1 5·9	9·0 5·9	9·0 5·9	8·9 5·8	8·8 5·7	8·7 5·6	8·6 5·4	60·9
61·2	9·5 6·2	9·4 6·1	9·4 6·1	9·3 6·0	9·2 5·9	9·1 5·8	8·9 5·6	61·2
61·5	9·8 6·4	9·8 6·3	9·7 6·3	9·7 6·2	9·5 6·1	9·4 5·9	9·2 5·8	61·5

DIP

Ht. of Eye (m)	Corrn	Ht. of Eye (ft.)	Ht. of Eye (m)	Corrn	Ht. of Eye (ft.)
2·4	−2·8	8·0	9·5	−5·5	31·5
2·6	−2·9	8·6	9·9	−5·6	32·7
2·8	−3·0	9·2	10·3	−5·7	33·9
3·0	−3·1	9·8	10·6	−5·8	35·1
3·2	−3·2	10·5	11·0	−5·9	36·3
3·4	−3·3	11·2	11·4	−6·0	37·6
3·6	−3·4	11·9	11·8	−6·1	38·9
3·8	−3·5	12·6	12·2	−6·2	40·1
4·0	−3·6	13·3	12·6	−6·3	41·5
4·3	−3·7	14·1	13·0	−6·4	42·8
4·5	−3·8	14·9	13·4	−6·5	44·2
4·7	−3·9	15·7	13·8	−6·6	45·5
5·0	−4·0	16·5	14·2	−6·7	46·9
5·2	−4·1	17·4	14·7	−6·8	48·4
5·5	−4·2	18·3	15·1	−6·9	49·8
5·8	−4·3	19·1	15·5	−7·0	51·3
6·1	−4·4	20·1	16·0	−7·1	52·8
6·3	−4·5	21·0	16·5	−7·2	54·3
6·6	−4·6	22·0	16·9	−7·3	55·8
6·9	−4·7	22·9	17·4	−7·4	57·4
7·2	−4·8	23·9	17·9	−7·5	58·9
7·5	−4·9	24·9	18·4	−7·6	60·5
7·9	−5·0	26·0	18·8	−7·7	62·1
8·2	−5·1	27·1	19·3	−7·8	63·8
8·5	−5·2	28·1	19·8	−7·9	65·4
8·8	−5·3	29·2	20·4	−8·0	67·1
9·2	−5·4	30·4	20·9	−8·1	68·8
9·5		31·5	21·4		70·5

MOON CORRECTION TABLE

The correction is in two parts; the first correction is taken from the upper part of the table with argument apparent altitude, and the second from the lower part, with argument H.P., in the same column as that from which the first correction was taken. Separate corrections are given in the lower part for lower (L) and upper (U) limbs. All corrections are to be **added** to apparent altitude, *but 30' is to be subtracted from the altitude of the upper limb.*

For corrections for pressure and temperature see page A4.

For bubble sextant observations ignore dip, take the mean of upper and lower limb corrections and subtract 15' from the altitude.

App. Alt. = Apparent altitude = Sextant altitude corrected for index error and dip.

TABLE 5-2 *Altitude correction tables for the moon from the* Nautical Almanac.

Summary

All observations made with the marine sextant should first be corrected for fixed instrumental error (I) (found on the certificate on the inside of the lid of the sextant case), index error, and dip. The correction for index error is written IC, and its value should be established each time the sextant is used. The altitude read from the sextant is labeled *hs;* when this is corrected for the three factors outlined above, it is labeled *ha* (apparent altitude). Using the ha, the value of the refraction correction is found next. If the sun has been observed, semidiameter and parallax are applied next, or the combined table of the three sun corrections can be used. For Venus and Mars, the refraction is applied to ha, together with any additional planet correction given in the *Nautical Almanac.* For Jupiter and Saturn, as well as for the fixed stars, it is only necessary to apply the refraction correction to ha. The correction of moon observations was described in detail above. An additional correction for nonstandard atmospheric conditions is given in the *Almanac* and should be applied when required. Ho (the observed altitude) is the final result. The form used in working a sextant correction is reproduced below.

Altitude read from sextant	hs
Instrument correction from sextant certificate + or −	I
Index correction as measured + or −	IC
Dip of horizon from *Almanac* always −	Dip
Combine hs, I, IC, and Dip to obtain ha	ha
Refraction correction from *Almanac* − (except ☉ +)	R
Add'l Corr. TB, or Venus, Mars, or Moon 1st corr.	Corr.
Sum of corrections or for Moon 2nd corr.	Corr.
Above corrections applied to ha to obtain Ho (observed alt.)	Ho

Examples of Sextant Corrections When Observing a Star, the Sun, and the Moon

Problem: The altitude of a star is read from the sextant as 29° 14′.2. There is no instrument correction, and the IC is +2′. Height of eye is 12 feet. Determine the Ho.

Solution: Enter the hs and the IC on the form. Turn to the appropriate dip table in the *Almanac* (Table 5-1 in the present text), extract the correction of −3′.4, and enter it on the form. Add algebraically the hs, IC, and dip to obtain an ha of 29° 12′.8. Enter the "Stars" correction table of the *Almanac* (also reproduced in Table 5-1) with the ha and extract the refraction correction of −1′.7, which is entered in the form and applied to ha to obtain an Ho of 29° 11′.1.

STAR ☆

hs	29° 14′.2
I	
IC	+2.0
Dip	−3.4
ha	29° 12′.8
R	−1.7
Corr.	
Corr.	
Ho	29° 11′.1

Problem: During November an observation is made of the sun (lower limb) with a sextant altitude of 45° 36′.9. The instrument correction for this altitude, which is taken from the sextant certificate, is +0′.3. IC is +1′.5. Height of eye is 14 feet. Determine the Ho.

Solution: Enter hs, I, and IC on the form. Turn to the dip table (Table 5-1), enter it with 14 feet, extract the correction of −3′.6, and enter this value on the form. Combine the above to obtain an ha of 45° 35′.1. With this ha enter the "Oct.–Mar." column of the sun correction table (Table 5-1) and extract +15′.3 as the combined correction. Add this to the ha to obtain an Ho of 45° 50′.4.

SUN ☉

hs	45° 36′.9
I	+.3
IC	+1.5
Dip	−3.6
ha	45° 35′.1
R	+15.3
Corr.	
Corr.	
Ho	45° 50′.4

Problem: The altitude of the moon is read from the sextant as 21° 22′.3. There is no instrument correction, and the IC is +2′. Height of eye is 12 feet. The observation was made using the upper limb of the moon. The horizontal parallax (H.P.) from the daily pages is 57′.3. Determine the Ho.

Solution: Enter the hs and the IC on the form. From the appropriate dip table in the *Almanac* (Table 5-2 in the present text), extract the correction of −3′.4 and enter this value on the form. Algebraically add the hs, IC, and dip corrections to obtain an ha of 21° 20′.9. Enter the moon tables of the *Almanac* (also reproduced in Table 5-2) in the column headed "20° − 24°," find the section for 21°, and opposite 20′ pick out the first correction of 61′.9 and enter it on the form. Dropping down this same column to the subcolumn headed "U" (designating the upper limb), opposite the H.P. of 57′.3 pick out the second correction of 3′.3 and enter it on the form, together with the special −30′ correction necessary when using the upper limb. By combining the three corrections with the ha, an Ho of 21° 56′.1 is obtained.

MOON ☾	
hs	21° 22′.3
I	
IC	+2.
Dip	−3.4
ha	21° 20′.9
R	+61.9
Corr.	+3.3
Corr.	−30.0
Ho	21° 56′.1

Chapter 6

Sight Reduction Tables

Sight reduction tables are trigonometrical tables designed specifically for solving the celestial triangle. In previous chapters information has been presented on (a) ascertaining the correct time to the nearest second of GMT, (b) figuring the observed altitude (Ho) of a body by correcting the sextant altitude, (c) obtaining the position of a body on the celestial sphere from the *Nautical Almanac,* and (d) choosing the assumed position. When this information is entered on the sight reduction form, it provides the basis for determining the arguments for entering the sight reduction tables. The tables are used to obtain the *computed altitude* (Hc) and the azimuth angle (Z), which would have been observed if the navigator had actually been located at the *assumed position* (AP) and if the timing and sextant observations had been error-free. This computed altitude is then compared with the actual observed altitude (Ho) to produce the altitude difference, which is called the altitude intercept (a) and is used to plot the LOP. To accomplish this purpose, a great variety of tables have been designed and published over the years. The sight reduction can also be performed by using regular trigonometrical tables and a formula. The basic formula for obtaining altitude is:

$$\sin Hc = \sin L \sin d \overset{+}{\underset{\sim}{}} \cos L \cos d \cos t$$

The basic formula for azimuth is:

$$\sin Z = \frac{\cos d \sin t}{\cos Hc}$$

These formulas are presented here so that they can be used with some of the new pocket-size electronic calculators to solve the celestial triangle without the use of tables.

During the 1930s several sets of tables termed the "short methods" were published. These reduced the work involved in previous systems that used standard trigonometric tables. These short methods had the great advantage of being contained in a single small volume that was quite inexpensive. Solution was from the DR position rather than from an assumed position. The short methods most widely used were H.O. 208, "Dreisonstok;" H.O. 211, "Ageton;" and the *Weems Line of Position Book.* The first two were published by the then U.S. Navy Hydrographic Office and have been commercially reprinted. All three required extracting functions of angles from the tables and combining these to obtain the solution. The short methods gradually lost their popularity with the introduction of the so-called inspection tables. H.O. 211 is, however, still recommended in several texts on navigation as an excellent set of tables for computing great circle courses and distances.

Inspection Tables

The inspection tables are so called because both altitude and azimuth, or azimuth angle, are extracted directly from the tables by inspection; no knowledge of trigonometric functions of angles is required. The most widely used of these tables have been H.O. 214 and H.O. 249. H.O. 214 has been in print since World War II but is now being discontinued by the government as the supply of various volumes becomes exhausted. H.O. 249 was designed for aircraft use but has found acceptance in the marine field in cases where the maximum accuracy is not required. This text will concentrate on the H.O. 229 tables, which were designed to replace all former marine tables, including H.O. 214. The navigator who learns to use H.O. 229 will have no difficulty switching to either of the other two, as the entering arguments are similar, and complete instructions are printed in each volume. H.O. 249 is described briefly in the appendix.

H.O. 229 Tables

The H.O. 229 sight reduction tables are printed in six volumes, each volume designated by latitude, as follows:

Volume 1: 0°–15°
Volume 2: 15°–30°
Volume 3: 30°–45°
Volume 4: 45°–60°
Volume 5: 60°–75°
Volume 6: 75°–90°

Since the H.O. 229 tables are basically trigonometrical tables for solving any spherical triangle, the same volume can be used for north or south latitude. Each volume is divided into two sections, each covering 8° of latitude. For example, Volume 3 covers latitude 30°–37° in the first section, or zone, and 38°–45° in the second section. On the east coast of the United States, latitude 45°N is just above Eastport, Maine, and latitude 30°N is just below Jacksonville, Florida. On the west coast, 30°N is well down the Baja California peninsula, and 45°N is just below the entrance to the Columbia River in Oregon. Volume 3 therefore covers the cruising waters of most American yachtsmen. Volume 2 is required for southern Florida, the Gulf of Mexico, and the Bahamas, and Volume 4 is required for the Puget Sound area and the Maritime Provinces of Canada.

The H.O. 229 sight reduction tables are designed to produce altitude to an accuracy of 0′.1 of arc and 0°.1 of azimuth angle.

Arrangement of the Tables

Both a left-hand page and a right-hand page for a given opening of the tables are reproduced in Table 6-1 of the present text (see pages 80-81). The correct volume, and either the first or second section of the volume, is chosen according to the *assumed latitude,* which is the integral degree nearest the DR or estimated latitude of the vessel. The eight column headings on each page are the eight degrees of latitude covered in a given section of the volume, and these headings are the same on all pages in that section; in Table 6-1 these are latitudes 30° through 37°. The page opening is LHA in integral degrees; for each body observed a different page opening is therefore required. Two values of LHA are listed prominently at the top and bottom of each page. It will be noted that two values of LHA are shown together; for example LHA 51°, 309°. The same page of the tables is used for either of the values of LHA shown. The two values are always angles which, if added together, equal 360°. Since LHA and meridian angle (t east) are also angles that equal 360° when combined, meridian angle, t, can be used for entering the tables, for those who prefer this method. It should be noted, however, that the instructions printed on each page for determining true azimuth from azimuth angle will not apply when t is used. Instead, one will know whether the body is rising or setting by knowing whether t is East or West, and therefore whether or not true azimuth and azimuth angle are the same. It should be noted that the LHA at the top and bottom of the left page and at the top of the right page will be identical. The bottom of the right-hand page will contain values of LHA greater than 90°, but less than 270°. This section is necessary as it is possible, except when the observer is at the equator, to observe celestial bodies located more than 90° in hour angle from the observer.

The vertical entering argument listed in the extreme left and right columns of each page is integral degrees of declination (dec.). The integral degree of declination that is *numerically less* than the actual declination is always used. For example, if the declination of a body were 15° 10'.2, 15° would be used; if the declination were 15° 58'.3, 15° would still be used. In this respect H.O. 229 is different from some other tables, such as H.O. 214, and this point is important to remember. The change in altitude according to the number of minutes of actual declination is extracted from the interpolation tables. The use of these tables is discussed later in this chapter.

One final item concerning the arrangement of the tables is particularly important. The left-hand page of any opening of the tables is clearly labeled "Latitude Same name as Declination." This page is used when latitude and declination are both north or both south. The top of the right-hand page is labeled "Latitude Contrary name to Declination." This section is used when latitude is north and declination is south or vice versa. The bottom of the right-hand page is for "Latitude Same name as Declination," but for the values of LHA as discussed above. The two sections of the right-hand page are clearly divided by straight horizontal lines through each column at the point where the altitude values reach zero. In ordinary marine navigation, observations of celestial bodies at negative altitudes are not made, and, thus, no confusion should arise as to which section of the page to use. The instructions printed in the tables explain the use of negative values when the tables are used for purposes other than celestial navigation.

Tabulated Values Found in the Tables

Three different tabulated values are extracted from the appropriate columns of the tables. Referring to Table 6-1, the headings for the values to be extracted are Hc, d, and Z. Hc is the computed altitude for the appropriate integral degree of latitude, LHA, and declination. A correction must be applied to this to compensate for the fact that the actual declination of a body as derived from the *Almanac* is in degrees, minutes, and tenths of minutes. The second tabulated value is d, the difference in successively tabulated values of Hc for a change of 1° in declination at that point in the tables. It could be obtained by sub-

57°, 303° L.H.A. LATITUDE SAME NAME AS DECLINATION

N. Lat. { L.H.A. greater than 180°......Zn=Z ; L.H.A. less than 180°............Zn=360°−Z }

Dec.	30° Hc	30° d	30° Z	31° Hc	31° d	31° Z	32° Hc	32° d	32° Z	33° Hc	33° d	33° Z
°	° ′	′	°	° ′	′	°	° ′	′	°	° ′	′	°
0	28 08.6	+33.8	108.0	27 49.8	+34.7	108.5	27 30.5	+35.7	109.0	27 10.7	+36.6	109.5
1	28 42.4	33.4	107.0	28 24.5	34.4	107.6	28 06.2	35.3	108.1	27 47.3	36.2	108.6
2	29 15.8	33.1	106.1	28 58.9	34.0	106.6	28 41.5	34.9	107.2	28 23.5	35.9	107.7
3	29 48.9	32.6	105.1	29 32.9	33.6	105.7	29 16.4	34.6	106.2	28 59.4	35.5	106.8
4	30 21.5	32.2	104.2	30 06.5	33.2	104.7	29 51.0	34.1	105.3	29 34.9	35.0	105.8
5	30 53.7	+31.7	103.2	30 39.7	+32.7	103.8	30 25.1	+33.7	104.3	30 09.9	+34.7	104.9
6	31 25.4	31.2	102.2	31 12.4	32.3	102.8	30 58.8	33.3	103.4	30 44.6	34.3	104.0
7	31 56.6	30.8	101.2	31 44.7	31.8	101.8	31 32.1	32.8	102.4	31 18.9	33.8	103.0
8	32 27.4	30.3	100.2	32 16.5	31.3	100.8	32 04.9	32.4	101.4	31 52.7	33.4	102.0
9	32 57.7	29.8	99.2	32 47.8	30.9	99.8	32 37.3	31.9	100.4	32 26.1	33.0	101.1
10	33 27.5	+29.3	98.1	33 18.7	+30.3	98.8	33 09.2	+31.4	99.4	32 59.1	+32.4	100.1
11	33 56.8	28.7	97.1	33 49.0	29.8	97.7	33 40.6	30.9	98.4	33 31.5	32.0	99.1
12	34 25.5	28.1	96.0	34 18.8	29.3	96.7	34 11.5	30.4	97.4	34 03.5	31.4	98.0
13	34 53.6	27.6	94.9	34 48.1	28.7	95.6	34 41.9	29.8	96.3	34 34.9	30.9	97.0
14	35 21.2	27.0	93.8	35 16.8	28.2	94.6	35 11.7	29.3	95.3	35 05.8	30.4	96.0
15	35 48.2	+26.4	92.7	35 45.0	+27.5	93.5	35 41.0	+28.6	94.2	35 36.2	+29.8	94.9
16	36 14.6	25.8	91.6	36 12.5	27.0	92.4	36 09.6	28.1	93.1	36 06.0	29.3	93.8
17	36 40.4	25.1	90.5	36 39.5	26.3	91.3	36 37.7	27.5	92.0	36 35.3	28.6	92.7
18	37 05.5	24.5	89.4	37 05.8	25.6	90.1	37 05.2	26.9	90.9	37 03.9	28.0	91.6
19	37 30.0	23.8	88.2	37 31.4	25.0	89.0	37 32.1	26.2	89.8	37 31.9	27.4	90.5
20	37 53.8	+23.1	87.1	37 56.4	+24.4	87.9	37 58.3	+25.5	88.6	37 59.3	+26.8	89.4
21	38 16.9	22.4	85.9	38 20.8	23.6	86.7	38 23.8	24.9	87.5	38 26.1	26.0	88.3
22	38 39.3	21.7	84.7	38 44.4	22.9	85.5	38 48.7	24.1	86.3	38 52.1	25.4	87.1
23	39 01.0	20.9	83.5	39 07.3	22.2	84.3	39 12.8	23.5	85.1	39 17.5	24.7	86.0
24	39 21.9	20.2	82.3	39 29.5	21.5	83.1	39 36.3	22.7	83.9	39 42.2	23.9	84.8
25	39 42.1	+19.4	81.1	39 51.0	+20.6	81.9	39 59.0	+21.9	82.7	40 06.1	+23.2	83.6
26	40 01.5	18.6	79.9	40 11.6	19.9	80.7	40 20.9	21.2	81.5	40 29.3	22.5	82.4
27	40 20.1	17.8	78.6	40 31.5	19.1	79.4	40 42.1	20.4	80.3	40 51.8	21.6	81.1
28	40 37.9	17.0	77.4	40 50.6	18.3	78.2	41 02.5	19.5	79.0	41 13.4	20.9	79.9
29	40 54.9	16.1	76.1	41 08.9	17.4	76.9	41 22.0	18.8	77.8	41 34.3	20.0	78.7
30	41 11.0	+15.3	74.8	41 26.3	+16.6	75.7	41 40.8	+17.8	76.5	41 54.3	+19.2	77.4
31	41 26.3	14.5	73.5	41 42.9	15.7	74.4	41 58.6	17.1	75.2	42 13.5	18.3	76.1
32	41 40.8	13.5	72.2	41 58.6	14.9	73.1	42 15.7	16.1	73.9	42 31.8	17.5	74.8
33	41 54.3	12.6	70.9	42 13.5	13.9	71.8	42 31.8	15.3	72.6	42 49.3	16.5	73.5
34	42 06.9	11.8	69.6	42 27.4	13.1	70.5	42 47.1	14.3	71.3	43 05.8	15.7	72.2
35	42 18.7	+10.8	68.3	42 40.5	+12.1	69.1	43 01.4	+13.4	70.0	43 21.5	+14.7	70.9
36	42 29.5	9.9	66.9	42 52.6	11.2	67.8	43 14.8	12.5	68.7	43 36.2	13.8	69.6
37	42 39.4	8.9	65.6	43 03.8	10.2	66.5	43 27.3	11.5	67.3	43 50.0	12.9	68.2
38	42 48.3	8.0	64.3	43 14.0	9.3	65.1	43 38.8	10.6	66.0	44 02.9	11.8	66.8
39	42 56.3	7.1	62.9	43 23.3	8.3	63.7	43 49.4	9.6	64.6	44 14.7	10.9	65.5
40	43 03.4	+6.0	61.6	43 31.6	+7.3	62.4	43 59.0	+8.6	63.2	44 25.6	+9.9	64.1
41	43 09.4	5.1	60.2	43 38.9	6.3	61.0	44 07.6	7.6	61.9	44 35.5	8.9	62.7
42	43 14.5	4.2	58.8	43 45.2	5.4	59.6	44 15.2	6.6	60.5	44 44.4	7.8	61.3
43	43 18.7	3.1	57.5	43 50.6	4.3	58.3	44 21.8	5.6	59.1	44 52.2	6.9	59.9
44	43 21.8	2.1	56.1	43 54.9	3.4	56.9	44 27.4	4.5	57.7	44 59.1	5.8	58.5
45	43 23.9	+1.2	54.7	43 58.3	+2.3	55.5	44 31.9	+3.6	56.3	45 04.9	+4.7	57.1
46	43 25.1	+0.2	53.3	44 00.6	1.3	54.1	44 35.5	2.5	54.9	45 09.6	3.7	55.7
47	43 25.3	−0.9	52.0	44 01.9	+0.4	52.7	44 38.0	1.4	53.5	45 13.3	2.7	54.3
48	43 24.4	1.8	50.6	44 02.3	−0.7	51.3	44 39.4	+0.5	52.1	45 16.0	1.6	52.9
49	43 22.6	2.8	49.2	44 01.6	1.8	49.9	44 39.9	−0.6	50.7	45 17.6	+0.5	51.5
50	43 19.8	−3.8	47.8	43 59.8	−2.7	48.5	44 39.3	−1.6	49.3	45 18.1	−0.5	50.0
51	43 16.0	4.7	46.5	43 57.1	3.7	47.1	44 37.7	2.7	47.9	45 17.6	1.6	48.6
52	43 11.3	5.8	45.1	43 53.4	4.7	45.8	44 35.0	3.7	46.5	45 16.0	2.6	47.2
53	43 05.5	6.7	43.7	43 48.7	5.8	44.4	44 31.3	4.7	45.1	45 13.4	3.7	45.8
54	42 58.8	7.6	42.4	43 42.9	6.7	43.0	44 26.6	5.8	43.7	45 09.7	4.7	44.4
55	42 51.2	−8.7	41.0	43 36.2	−7.7	41.6	44 20.8	−6.7	42.3	45 05.0	−5.8	42.9
56	42 42.5	9.5	39.7	43 28.5	8.6	40.3	44 14.1	7.8	40.9	44 59.2	6.8	41.5
57	42 33.0	10.5	38.3	43 19.9	9.7	38.9	44 06.3	8.7	39.5	44 52.4	7.8	40.1
58	42 22.5	11.5	37.0	43 10.2	10.6	37.5	43 57.6	9.7	38.1	44 44.6	8.8	38.7
59	42 11.0	12.3	35.7	42 59.6	11.5	36.2	43 47.9	10.7	36.8	44 35.8	9.9	37.3
60	41 58.7	−13.2	34.3	42 48.1	−12.5	34.9	43 37.2	−11.7	35.4	44 25.9	−10.9	36.0
61	41 45.5	14.2	33.0	42 35.6	13.4	33.5	43 25.5	12.6	34.0	44 15.0	11.8	34.6
62	41 31.3	15.0	31.7	42 22.2	14.3	32.2	43 12.9	13.6	32.7	44 03.2	12.8	33.2
63	41 16.3	15.8	30.4	42 07.9	15.1	30.9	42 59.3	14.5	31.4	43 50.4	13.8	31.9
64	41 00.5	16.7	29.2	41 52.8	16.1	29.6	42 44.8	15.4	30.0	43 36.6	14.7	30.5
65	40 43.8	−17.5	27.9	41 36.7	−16.9	28.3	42 29.4	−16.2	28.7	43 21.9	−15.6	29.2
66	40 26.3	18.4	26.6	41 19.8	17.8	27.0	42 13.2	17.2	27.4	43 06.3	16.5	27.9
67	40 07.9	19.1	25.4	41 02.0	18.5	25.7	41 56.0	18.0	26.1	42 49.8	17.5	26.5
68	39 48.8	19.9	24.1	40 43.5	19.4	24.5	41 38.0	18.9	24.9	42 32.3	18.3	25.2
69	39 28.9	20.7	22.9	40 24.1	20.2	23.2	41 19.1	19.7	23.6	42 14.0	19.1	23.9
70	39 08.2	−21.4	21.7	40 03.9	−21.0	22.0	40 59.4	−20.5	22.3	41 54.9	−20.0	22.7
71	38 46.8	22.2	20.5	39 42.9	21.7	20.8	40 38.9	21.3	21.1	41 34.9	20.9	21.4
72	38 24.6	22.9	19.3	39 21.2	22.5	19.6	40 17.6	22.0	19.9	41 14.0	21.6	20.2
73	38 01.7	23.5	18.1	38 58.7	23.2	18.4	39 55.6	22.8	18.6	40 52.4	22.4	18.9
74	37 38.2	24.3	17.0	38 35.5	23.9	17.2	39 32.8	23.6	17.4	40 30.0	23.2	17.7
75	37 13.9	−24.9	15.8	38 11.6	−24.6	16.0	39 09.2	−24.2	16.3	40 06.8	−23.9	16.5
76	36 49.0	25.6	14.7	37 47.0	25.3	14.9	38 45.0	25.0	15.1	39 42.9	24.7	15.3
77	36 23.4	26.1	13.6	37 21.7	25.9	13.7	38 20.0	25.6	13.9	39 18.2	25.3	14.1
78	35 57.3	26.8	12.4	36 55.8	26.5	12.6	37 54.4	26.3	12.8	38 52.9	26.1	12.9
79	35 30.5	27.4	11.3	36 29.3	27.2	11.5	37 28.1	27.0	11.6	38 26.8	26.7	11.8
80	35 03.1	−28.0	10.2	36 02.1	−27.8	10.4	37 01.1	−27.6	10.5	38 00.1	−27.4	10.7
81	34 35.1	28.5	9.2	35 34.3	28.3	9.3	36 33.5	28.2	9.4	37 32.7	28.0	9.5
82	34 06.6	29.1	8.1	35 06.0	29.0	8.2	36 05.3	28.7	8.3	37 04.7	28.6	8.4
83	33 37.5	29.6	7.1	34 37.0	29.4	7.1	35 36.6	29.4	7.2	36 36.1	29.2	7.3
84	33 07.9	30.1	6.0	34 07.6	30.1	6.1	35 07.2	29.9	6.2	36 06.9	29.8	6.2
85	32 37.8	−30.6	5.0	33 37.5	−30.5	5.0	34 37.3	−30.4	5.1	35 37.1	−30.4	5.2
86	32 07.2	31.1	4.0	33 07.0	31.0	4.0	34 06.9	31.0	4.1	35 06.7	30.9	4.1
87	31 36.1	31.6	3.0	32 36.0	31.5	3.0	33 35.9	31.5	3.0	34 35.8	31.4	3.1
88	31 04.5	32.0	2.0	32 04.5	32.0	2.0	33 04.4	32.0	2.0	34 04.4	32.0	2.0
89	30 32.5	32.5	1.0	31 32.5	32.5	1.0	32 32.4	32.4	1.0	33 32.4	32.4	1.0
90	30 00.0	−32.9	0.0	31 00.0	−32.9	0.0	32 00.0	−32.9	0.0	33 00.0	−32.9	0.0
	30°			31°			32°			33°		

34° Hc	34° d	34° Z	35° Hc	35° d	35° Z	36° Hc	36° d	36° Z	37° Hc	37° d	37° Z	Dec.
° ′	′	°	° ′	′	°	° ′	′	°	° ′	′	°	°
26 50.5	+37.4	110.0	26 29.8	+38.3	110.4	26 08.6	+39.2	110.9	25 47.0	+40.0	111.3	0
27 27.9	37.1	109.1	27 08.1	38.0	109.6	26 47.8	38.8	110.0	26 27.0	39.6	110.5	1
28 05.0	36.8	108.2	27 46.1	37.6	108.7	27 26.6	38.5	109.2	27 06.6	39.4	109.7	2
28 41.8	36.4	107.3	28 23.7	37.3	107.8	28 05.1	38.2	108.3	27 46.0	39.0	108.8	3
29 18.2	36.0	106.4	29 01.0	36.9	106.9	28 43.3	37.8	107.4	28 25.0	38.8	108.0	4
29 54.2	+35.7	105.5	29 37.9	+36.6	106.0	29 21.1	+37.5	106.6	29 03.8	+38.3	107.1	5
30 29.9	35.2	104.5	30 14.5	36.2	105.1	29 58.6	37.1	105.7	29 42.1	38.1	106.2	6
31 05.1	34.8	103.6	30 50.7	35.8	104.2	30 35.7	36.7	104.7	30 20.2	37.6	105.3	7
31 39.9	34.4	102.6	31 26.5	35.4	103.2	31 12.4	36.4	103.8	30 57.8	37.3	104.4	8
32 14.3	34.0	101.7	32 01.9	34.9	102.3	31 48.8	35.9	102.9	31 35.1	36.9	103.5	9
32 48.3	+33.4	100.7	32 36.8	+34.5	101.3	32 24.7	+35.5	101.9	32 12.0	+36.4	102.6	10
33 21.7	33.0	99.7	33 11.3	34.0	100.3	33 00.2	35.0	101.0	32 48.4	36.0	101.6	11
33 54.7	32.5	98.7	33 45.3	33.6	99.4	33 35.2	34.6	100.0	33 24.4	35.6	100.7	12
34 27.2	32.0	97.7	34 18.9	33.0	98.4	34 09.8	34.1	99.0	34 00.0	35.1	99.7	13
34 59.2	31.5	96.7	34 51.9	32.6	97.3	34 43.9	33.6	98.0	34 35.1	34.7	98.7	14
35 30.7	+30.9	95.6	35 24.5	+32.0	96.3	35 17.5	+33.1	97.0	35 09.8	+34.1	97.7	15
36 01.6	30.4	94.6	35 56.5	31.5	95.3	35 50.6	32.6	96.0	35 43.9	33.7	96.7	16
36 32.0	29.8	93.5	36 28.0	30.9	94.2	36 23.2	32.0	95.0	36 17.6	33.1	95.7	17
37 01.8	29.2	92.4	36 58.9	30.3	93.2	36 55.2	31.4	93.9	36 50.7	32.5	94.7	18
37 31.0	28.5	91.3	37 29.2	29.7	92.1	37 26.6	30.9	92.8	37 23.2	32.0	93.6	19
37 59.5	+27.9	90.2	37 58.9	+29.1	91.0	37 57.5	+30.2	91.8	37 55.2	+31.4	92.5	20
38 27.4	27.3	89.1	38 28.0	28.5	89.9	38 27.7	29.7	90.7	38 26.6	30.8	91.4	21
38 54.7	26.6	87.9	38 56.5	27.8	88.7	38 57.4	29.0	89.5	38 57.4	30.2	90.3	22
39 21.3	25.9	86.8	39 24.3	27.1	87.6	39 26.4	28.3	88.4	39 27.6	29.5	89.2	23
39 47.2	25.2	85.6	39 51.4	26.4	86.4	39 54.7	27.6	87.3	39 57.1	28.9	88.1	24
40 12.4	+24.5	84.4	40 17.8	+25.7	85.3	40 22.3	+27.0	86.1	40 26.0	+28.1	87.0	25
40 36.9	23.7	83.2	40 43.5	25.0	84.1	40 49.3	26.2	84.9	40 54.1	27.5	85.8	26
41 00.6	22.9	82.0	41 08.5	24.2	82.9	41 15.5	25.4	83.7	41 21.6	26.7	84.6	27
41 23.5	22.1	80.8	41 32.7	23.4	81.6	41 40.9	24.7	82.5	41 48.3	25.9	83.4	28
41 45.6	21.3	79.5	41 56.1	22.6	80.4	42 05.6	23.9	81.3	42 14.2	25.2	82.2	29
42 06.9	+20.5	78.3	42 18.7	+21.8	79.2	42 29.5	+23.1	80.1	42 39.4	+24.4	81.0	30
42 27.4	19.7	77.0	42 40.5	20.9	77.9	42 52.6	22.2	78.8	43 03.8	23.5	79.7	31
42 47.1	18.7	75.7	43 01.4	20.1	76.6	43 14.8	21.4	77.5	43 27.3	22.7	78.5	32
43 05.8	17.9	74.4	43 21.5	19.2	75.3	43 36.2	20.5	76.2	43 50.0	21.9	77.2	33
43 23.7	17.0	73.1	43 40.7	18.3	74.0	43 56.7	19.7	74.9	44 11.9	20.9	75.9	34
43 40.7	+16.0	71.8	43 59.0	+17.4	72.7	44 16.4	+18.7	73.6	44 32.8	+20.0	74.6	35
43 56.7	15.2	70.5	44 16.4	16.4	71.4	44 35.1	17.7	72.3	44 52.8	19.2	73.2	36
44 11.9	14.1	69.1	44 32.8	15.5	70.0	44 52.8	16.9	71.0	45 12.0	18.1	71.9	37
44 26.0	13.2	67.7	44 48.3	14.5	68.7	45 09.7	15.8	69.6	45 30.1	17.2	70.5	38
44 39.2	12.2	66.4	45 02.8	13.5	67.3	45 25.5	14.8	68.2	45 47.3	16.2	69.2	39
44 51.4	+11.2	65.0	45 16.3	+12.5	65.9	45 40.3	+13.9	66.8	46 03.5	+15.2	67.8	40
45 02.6	10.1	63.6	45 28.8	11.5	64.5	45 54.2	12.8	65.4	46 18.7	14.1	66.4	41
45 12.7	9.2	62.2	45 40.3	10.4	63.1	46 07.0	11.8	64.0	46 32.8	13.1	65.0	42
45 21.9	8.1	60.8	45 50.7	9.4	61.7	46 18.8	10.7	62.6	46 45.9	12.0	63.6	43
45 30.0	7.0	59.4	46 00.1	8.4	60.3	46 29.5	9.6	61.2	46 57.9	11.0	62.1	44
45 37.0	+6.1	58.0	46 08.5	+7.2	58.9	46 39.1	+8.6	59.8	47 08.9	+9.9	60.7	45
45 43.1	4.9	56.6	46 15.7	6.2	57.4	46 47.7	7.4	58.3	47 18.8	8.7	59.2	46
45 48.0	3.9	55.1	46 21.9	5.1	56.0	46 55.1	6.4	56.9	47 27.5	7.6	57.8	47
45 51.9	2.7	53.7	46 27.0	4.0	54.5	47 01.5	5.2	55.4	47 35.1	6.5	56.3	48
45 54.6	1.8	52.3	46 31.0	2.9	53.1	47 06.7	4.1	53.9	47 41.6	5.4	54.8	49
45 56.4	+0.6	50.8	46 33.9	+1.8	51.6	47 10.8	+3.0	52.5	47 47.0	+4.2	53.3	50
45 57.0	−0.5	49.4	46 35.7	+0.7	50.2	47 13.8	1.9	51.0	47 51.2	3.1	51.9	51
45 56.5	1.5	47.9	46 36.4	−0.4	48.7	47 15.7	+0.7	49.5	47 54.3	1.9	50.4	52
45 55.0	2.6	46.5	46 36.0	1.5	47.3	47 16.4	−0.4	48.1	47 56.2	+0.7	48.9	53
45 52.4	3.7	45.1	46 34.5	2.7	45.8	47 16.0	1.5	46.6	47 56.9	−0.4	47.4	54
45 48.7	−4.8	43.6	46 31.8	−3.7	44.4	47 14.5	−2.7	45.1	47 56.5	−1.6	45.9	55
45 43.9	5.8	42.2	46 28.1	4.8	42.9	47 11.8	3.8	43.6	47 54.9	2.7	44.4	56
45 38.1	6.9	40.8	46 23.3	5.9	41.5	47 08.0	4.9	42.2	47 52.2	3.9	42.9	57
45 31.2	7.9	39.4	46 17.4	7.0	40.0	47 03.1	6.1	40.7	47 48.3	5.0	41.4	58
45 23.3	9.0	38.0	46 10.4	8.1	38.6	46 57.0	7.1	39.3	47 43.3	6.2	39.9	59
45 14.3	−10.0	36.5	46 02.3	−9.1	37.2	46 49.9	−8.2	37.8	47 37.1	−7.3	38.5	60
45 04.3	11.1	35.2	45 53.2	10.2	35.7	46 41.7	9.4	36.4	47 29.8	8.4	37.0	61
44 53.2	12.0	33.8	45 43.0	11.3	34.3	46 32.3	10.4	34.9	47 21.4	9.6	35.5	62
44 41.2	13.0	32.4	45 31.7	12.2	32.9	46 21.9	11.4	33.5	47 11.8	10.6	34.1	63
44 28.2	14.0	31.0	45 19.5	13.3	31.5	46 10.5	12.5	32.1	47 01.2	11.8	32.6	64
44 14.2	−15.0	29.7	45 06.2	−14.2	30.1	45 58.0	−13.6	30.7	46 49.4	−12.8	31.2	65
43 59.2	15.9	28.3	44 52.0	15.3	28.8	45 44.4	14.5	29.3	46 36.6	13.8	29.8	66
43 43.3	16.8	27.0	44 36.7	16.2	27.4	45 29.9	15.6	27.9	46 22.8	14.9	28.4	67
43 26.5	17.7	25.6	44 20.5	17.1	26.1	45 14.3	16.5	26.5	46 07.9	15.9	27.0	68
43 08.8	18.6	24.3	44 03.4	18.1	24.7	44 57.8	17.5	25.1	45 52.0	16.9	25.6	69
42 50.2	−19.5	23.0	43 45.3	−19.0	23.4	44 40.3	−18.5	23.8	45 35.1	−17.9	24.2	70
42 30.7	20.4	21.7	43 26.3	19.9	22.1	44 21.8	19.3	22.5	45 17.2	18.8	22.8	71
42 10.3	21.2	20.5	43 06.4	20.7	20.8	44 02.5	20.3	21.1	44 58.4	19.8	21.5	72
41 49.1	22.0	19.2	42 45.7	21.6	19.5	43 42.2	21.1	19.8	44 38.6	20.7	20.2	73
41 27.1	22.8	18.0	42 24.1	22.4	18.2	43 21.1	22.0	18.5	44 17.9	21.6	18.8	74
41 04.3	−23.6	16.7	42 01.7	−23.2	17.0	42 59.1	−22.9	17.3	43 56.3	−22.4	17.5	75
40 40.7	24.3	15.5	41 38.5	24.0	15.8	42 36.2	23.7	16.0	43 33.9	23.4	16.3	76
40 16.4	25.1	14.3	41 14.5	24.8	14.5	42 12.5	24.4	14.8	43 10.5	24.1	15.0	77
39 51.3	25.8	13.1	40 49.7	25.5	13.3	41 48.1	25.3	13.5	42 46.4	25.0	13.7	78
39 25.5	26.5	12.0	40 24.2	26.2	12.1	41 22.8	25.9	12.3	42 21.4	25.7	12.5	79
38 59.0	−27.1	10.8	39 58.0	−27.0	11.0	40 56.9	−26.8	11.1	41 55.7	−26.5	11.3	80
38 31.9	27.8	9.7	39 31.0	27.6	9.8	40 30.1	27.4	9.9	41 29.2	27.2	10.1	81
38 04.1	28.5	8.5	39 03.4	28.3	8.6	40 02.7	28.1	8.8	41 02.0	28.0	8.9	82
37 35.6	29.1	7.4	38 35.1	29.0	7.5	39 34.6	28.8	7.6	40 34.0	28.6	7.7	83
37 06.5	29.7	6.3	38 06.1	29.5	6.4	39 05.8	29.5	6.5	40 05.4	29.4	6.6	84
36 36.8	−30.2	5.2	37 36.6	−30.2	5.3	38 36.3	−30.1	5.4	39 36.0	−29.9	5.4	85
36 06.6	30.9	4.2	37 06.4	30.8	4.2	38 06.2	30.7	4.3	39 06.1	30.6	4.3	86
35 35.7	31.4	3.1	36 35.6	31.3	3.1	37 35.5	31.2	3.2	38 35.5	31.3	3.2	87
35 04.3	31.9	2.0	36 04.3	31.9	2.1	37 04.3	31.9	2.1	38 04.2	31.8	2.1	88
34 32.4	32.4	1.0	35 32.4	32.4	1.0	36 32.4	32.4	1.0	37 32.4	32.4	1.1	89
34 00.0	−32.9	0.0	35 00.0	−32.9	0.0	36 00.0	−32.9	0.0	37 00.0	−33.0	0.0	90
34°			35°			36°			37°			

57°, 303° L.H.A. LATITUDE SAME NAME AS DECLINATION

TABLE 6-1 A left-hand page and a right-hand page from the H.O. 229 sight reduction tables.

LATITUDE CONTRARY NAME TO DECLINATION — L.H.A. 57°, 303°

Dec.	30°			31°			32°			33°			34°			35°			36°			37°			Dec.
	Hc	d	Z	Hc	d	Z	Hc	d	Z	Hc	d	Z	Hc	d	Z	Hc	d	Z	Hc	d	Z	Hc	d	Z	
°	° ′	′	°	° ′	′	°	° ′	′	°	° ′	′	°	° ′	′	°	° ′	′	°	° ′	′	°	° ′	′	°	°
0	28 08.6	-34.2	108.0	27 49.8	-35.1	108.5	27 30.5	-36.0	109.0	27 10.7	-36.9	109.5	26 50.5	-37.8	110.0	26 29.8	-38.6	110.4	26 08.6	-39.4	110.9	25 47.0	-40.2	111.3	0
1	27 34.4	34.6	108.9	27 14.7	35.5	109.4	26 54.5	36.4	109.9	26 33.8	37.2	110.4	26 12.7	38.0	110.8	25 51.2	38.9	111.3	25 29.2	39.7	111.7	25 06.8	40.6	112.2	1
2	26 59.8	34.9	109.8	26 39.2	35.8	110.3	26 18.1	36.7	110.8	25 56.6	37.5	111.2	25 34.7	38.4	111.7	25 12.3	39.2	112.1	24 49.5	40.0	112.6	24 26.2	40.7	113.0	2
3	26 24.9	35.3	110.7	26 03.4	36.2	111.2	25 41.4	37.0	111.7	25 19.1	37.9	112.1	24 56.3	38.7	112.5	24 33.1	39.5	113.0	24 09.5	40.3	113.4	23 45.5	41.0	113.8	3
4	25 49.6	35.6	111.6	25 27.2	36.4	112.1	25 04.4	37.3	112.5	24 41.2	38.1	113.0	24 17.6	38.9	113.4	23 53.6	39.7	113.8	23 29.2	40.5	114.2	23 04.5	41.3	114.6	4
5	25 14.0	-35.9	112.5	24 50.8	-36.8	113.0	24 27.1	-37.5	113.4	24 03.1	-38.4	113.8	23 38.7	-39.2	114.2	23 13.9	-40.0	114.6	22 48.7	-40.7	115.0	22 23.2	-41.5	115.4	5
6	24 38.1	36.3	113.4	24 14.0	37.1	113.8	23 49.6	37.9	114.2	23 24.7	38.6	114.6	22 59.5	39.4	115.0	22 33.9	40.2	115.4	22 08.0	40.9	115.8	21 41.7	41.6	116.1	6
7	24 01.8	36.5	114.3	23 36.9	37.3	114.7	23 11.7	38.2	115.1	22 46.1	39.0	115.5	22 20.1	39.7	115.9	21 53.7	40.4	116.2	21 27.1	41.2	116.6	21 00.1	41.9	116.9	7
8	23 25.3	36.8	115.2	22 59.6	37.6	115.6	22 33.5	38.4	115.9	22 07.1	39.1	116.3	21 40.4	40.0	116.7	21 13.3	40.7	117.0	20 45.9	41.4	117.4	20 18.2	42.1	117.7	8
9	22 48.5	37.1	116.0	22 22.0	37.9	116.4	21 55.1	38.6	116.8	21 28.0	39.4	117.1	21 00.4	40.1	117.5	20 32.6	40.9	117.8	20 04.5	41.6	118.1	19 36.1	42.3	118.4	9
10	22 11.4	-37.3	116.9	21 44.1	-38.1	117.2	21 16.5	-38.9	117.6	20 48.6	-39.7	117.9	20 20.3	-40.4	118.3	19 51.7	-41.0	118.6	19 22.9	-41.8	118.9	18 53.8	-42.5	119.2	10
11	21 34.1	37.6	117.7	21 06.0	38.4	118.1	20 37.6	39.1	118.4	20 08.9	39.8	118.7	19 39.9	40.5	119.0	19 10.7	41.3	119.4	18 41.1	41.9	119.6	18 11.3	42.6	119.9	11
12	20 56.5	37.9	118.6	20 27.6	38.6	118.9	19 58.5	39.3	119.2	19 29.1	40.1	119.5	18 59.4	40.8	119.8	18 29.4	41.5	120.1	17 59.2	42.2	120.4	17 28.7	42.8	120.7	12
13	20 18.6	38.0	119.4	19 49.0	38.8	119.7	19 19.2	39.6	120.0	18 49.0	40.2	120.3	18 18.6	40.9	120.6	17 47.9	41.6	120.9	17 17.0	42.3	121.1	16 45.9	43.0	121.4	13
14	19 40.6	38.3	120.2	19 10.2	39.0	120.5	18 39.6	39.7	120.8	18 08.8	40.5	121.1	17 37.7	41.2	121.4	17 06.3	41.8	121.6	16 34.7	42.4	121.9	16 02.9	43.1	122.1	14
15	19 02.3	-38.5	121.0	18 31.2	-39.2	121.3	17 59.9	-39.9	121.6	17 28.3	-40.6	121.9	16 56.5	-41.2	122.1	16 24.5	-41.9	122.4	15 52.3	-42.6	122.6	15 19.8	-43.2	122.9	15
16	18 23.8	38.8	121.8	17 52.0	39.4	122.1	17 20.0	40.1	122.4	16 47.7	40.8	122.6	16 15.3	41.5	122.9	15 42.6	42.1	123.1	15 09.7	42.8	123.4	14 36.6	43.4	123.6	16
17	17 45.0	38.9	122.6	17 12.6	39.6	122.9	16 39.9	40.3	123.2	16 06.9	40.9	123.4	15 33.8	41.6	123.6	15 00.5	42.3	123.9	14 26.9	42.8	124.1	13 53.2	43.5	124.3	17
18	17 06.1	39.1	123.4	16 33.0	39.8	123.7	15 59.6	40.5	123.9	15 26.0	41.1	124.2	14 52.2	41.7	124.4	14 18.2	42.4	124.6	13 44.1	43.0	124.8	13 09.7	43.6	125.0	18
19	16 27.0	39.2	124.2	15 53.2	40.0	124.5	15 19.1	40.6	124.7	14 44.9	41.3	124.9	14 10.5	41.9	125.1	13 35.8	42.5	125.3	13 01.1	43.2	125.5	12 26.1	43.7	125.7	19
20	15 47.8	-39.5	125.0	15 13.2	-40.1	125.2	14 38.5	-40.7	125.5	14 03.6	-41.3	125.7	13 28.6	-42.0	125.9	12 53.3	-42.6	126.1	12 17.9	-43.2	126.2	11 42.4	-43.8	126.4	20
21	15 08.3	39.6	125.8	14 33.1	40.2	126.0	13 57.8	40.9	126.2	13 22.3	41.6	126.4	12 46.6	42.2	126.6	12 10.7	42.7	126.8	11 34.7	43.3	126.9	10 58.6	43.9	127.1	21
22	14 28.7	39.7	126.6	13 52.9	40.4	126.8	13 16.9	41.0	127.0	12 40.7	41.6	127.2	12 04.4	42.2	127.3	11 28.0	42.9	127.5	10 51.4	43.4	127.6	10 14.7	44.0	127.8	22
23	13 49.0	39.9	127.3	13 12.5	40.5	127.5	12 35.9	41.2	127.7	11 59.1	41.8	127.9	11 22.2	42.4	128.1	10 45.1	42.9	128.2	10 08.0	43.6	128.4	9 30.7	44.1	128.5	23
24	13 09.1	40.0	128.1	12 32.0	40.7	128.3	11 54.7	41.2	128.5	11 17.3	41.8	128.6	10 39.8	42.4	128.8	10 02.2	43.0	128.9	9 24.4	43.5	129.0	8 46.6	44.2	129.2	24
25	12 29.1	-40.2	128.9	11 51.3	-40.7	129.0	11 13.5	-41.4	129.2	10 35.5	-42.0	129.4	9 57.4	-42.6	129.5	9 19.2	-43.1	129.6	8 40.9	-43.7	129.7	8 02.4	-44.2	129.9	25
26	11 48.9	40.3	129.6	11 10.6	40.9	129.8	10 32.1	41.5	129.9	9 53.5	42.0	130.1	9 14.8	42.6	130.2	8 36.1	43.2	130.3	7 57.2	43.8	130.4	7 18.2	44.3	130.5	26
27	11 08.6	40.4	130.4	10 29.7	41.0	130.5	9 50.6	41.6	130.7	9 11.5	42.2	130.8	8 32.2	42.7	130.9	7 52.9	43.3	131.0	7 13.4	43.8	131.1	6 33.9	44.3	131.2	27
28	10 28.2	40.5	131.1	9 48.7	41.1	131.3	9 09.0	41.6	131.4	8 29.3	42.2	131.5	7 49.5	42.8	131.6	7 09.6	43.3	131.7	6 29.6	43.8	131.8	5 49.6	44.4	131.9	28
29	9 47.7	40.6	131.9	9 07.6	41.2	132.0	8 27.4	41.7	132.1	7 47.1	42.3	132.2	7 06.7	42.8	132.3	6 26.3	43.4	132.4	5 45.8	43.9	132.5	5 05.2	44.4	132.6	29
30	9 07.1	-40.7	132.6	8 26.4	-41.2	132.8	7 45.7	-41.9	132.9	7 04.8	-42.4	133.0	6 23.9	-42.9	133.0	5 42.9	-43.4	133.1	5 01.9	-44.0	133.2	4 20.8	-44.5	133.2	30
31	8 26.4	40.7	133.4	7 45.2	41.4	133.5	7 03.8	41.8	133.6	6 22.4	42.4	133.7	5 41.0	43.0	133.7	4 59.5	43.5	133.8	4 17.9	44.0	133.9	3 36.3	44.5	133.9	31
32	7 45.7	40.9	134.1	7 03.8	41.4	134.2	6 22.0	42.0	134.3	5 40.0	42.4	134.4	4 58.0	42.9	134.4	4 16.0	43.5	134.5	3 33.9	44.0	134.6	2 51.8	44.5	134.6	32
33	7 04.8	40.9	134.9	6 22.4	41.4	134.9	5 40.0	42.0	135.0	4 57.6	42.5	135.1	4 15.1	43.1	135.1	3 32.5	43.5	135.2	2 49.9	44.0	135.2	2 07.3	44.5	135.3	33
34	6 23.9	41.0	135.6	5 41.0	41.5	135.7	4 58.0	42.0	135.7	4 15.1	42.6	135.8	3 32.0	43.0	135.8	2 49.0	43.6	135.9	2 05.9	44.1	135.9	1 22.8	44.6	135.9	34
35	5 42.9	-41.0	136.3	4 59.5	-41.6	136.4	4 16.0	-42.1	136.5	3 32.5	-42.6	136.5	2 49.0	-43.1	136.5	2 05.4	-43.6	136.6	1 21.8	-44.1	136.6	0 38.2	-44.5	136.6	35
36	5 01.9	41.1	137.1	4 17.9	41.6	137.1	3 33.9	42.1	137.2	2 49.9	42.6	137.2	2 05.9	43.1	137.2	1 21.8	43.6	137.3	0 37.7	-44.0	137.3	0 06.3	+44.6	42.7	36
37	4 20.8	41.1	137.8	3 36.3	41.6	137.8	2 51.8	42.1	137.9	2 07.3	42.6	137.9	1 22.8	43.1	137.9	0 38.2	-43.6	137.9	0 06.3	+44.1	42.1	0 50.9	44.5	42.1	37
38	3 39.7	41.2	138.5	2 54.7	41.7	138.6	2 09.7	42.2	138.6	1 24.7	42.7	138.6	0 39.7	-43.2	138.6	0 05.4	+43.6	41.4	0 50.4	44.1	41.4	1 35.4	44.6	41.4	38
39	2 58.5	41.2	139.3	2 13.0	41.7	139.3	1 27.5	42.1	139.3	0 42.0	-42.6	139.3	0 03.5	+43.1	40.7	0 49.0	43.6	40.7	1 34.5	44.0	40.7	2 20.0	44.5	40.7	39
40	2 17.3	-41.2	140.0	1 31.3	[illegible]	140.0	0 45.4	-42.2	140.0	0 00.6	+42.7	40.0	0 46.6	+43.1	40.0	1 32.6	+43.5	40.0	2 18.5	+44.1	40.0	3 04.5	+44.5	40.0	40
41	1 36.1	41.2	140.7	0 49.6	[illegible]	140.7	0 03.2	-42.2	140.7	0 43.3	42.6	39.3	1 29.7	43.1	39.3	2 16.1	43.6	39.3	3 02.6	44.0	39.3	3 49.0	44.4	39.4	41
42	0 54.9	41.3	141.4	0 07.9	-41.7	141.4	0 39.0	+42.2	38.6	1 25.9	42.6	38.6	2 12.8	43.1	38.6	2 59.7	43.5	38.6	3 46.6	43.9	38.7	4 33.4	44.4	38.7	42
43	0 13.6	-41.2	142.2	0 33.8	+41.7	37.8	1 21.2	42.1	37.8	2 08.5	42.6	37.9	2 55.9	43.1	37.9	3 43.2	43.5	37.9	4 30.5	44.0	38.0	5 17.8	44.4	38.0	43
44	0 27.6	+41.3	37.1	1 15.5	41.7	37.1	2 03.3	42.2	37.1	2 51.1	42.6	37.2	3 39.0	43.0	37.2	4 26.7	43.5	37.2	5 14.5	43.9	37.3	6 02.2	44.3	37.3	44
45	1 08.9	+41.2	36.4	1 57.2	+41.6	36.4	2 45.5	+42.1	36.4	3 33.7	+42.6	36.5	4 22.0	+43.0	36.5	5 10.2	+43.4	36.5	5 58.4	+43.8	36.6	6 46.5	+44.3	36.7	45
46	1 50.1	41.2	35.7	2 38.8	41.7	35.7	3 27.6	42.1	35.7	4 16.3	42.5	35.7	5 05.0	42.9	35.8	5 53.6	43.4	35.9	6 42.2	43.8	35.9	7 30.8	44.2	36.0	46
47	2 31.3	41.2	34.9	3 20.5	41.6	35.0	4 09.7	42.0	35.0	4 58.8	42.5	35.0	5 47.9	42.9	35.1	6 37.0	43.3	35.2	7 26.0	43.7	35.2	8 15.0	44.1	35.3	47
48	3 12.5	41.1	34.2	4 02.1	41.6	34.2	4 51.7	42.0	34.3	5 41.3	42.4	34.3	6 30.8	42.8	34.4	7 20.3	43.2	34.5	8 09.7	43.7	34.5	8 59.1	44.1	34.6	48
49	3 53.6	41.2	33.5	4 43.7	41.5	33.5	5 33.7	41.9	33.6	6 23.7	42.3	33.6	7 13.6	42.8	33.7	8 03.5	43.2	33.8	8 53.4	43.6	33.8	9 43.2	44.0	33.9	49
50	4 34.8	+41.0	32.7	5 25.2	+41.5	32.8	6 15.6	+41.9	32.8	7 06.0	+42.3	32.9	7 56.4	+42.7	33.0	8 46.7	+43.1	33.1	9 37.0	+43.4	33.1	10 27.2	+43.9	33.2	50
51	5 15.8	41.0	32.0	6 06.7	41.4	32.1	6 57.5	41.8	32.1	7 48.3	42.2	32.2	8 39.1	42.6	32.3	9 29.8	43.0	32.4	10 20.4	43.4	32.4	11 11.1	43.7	32.5	51
52	5 56.8	41.0	31.3	6 48.1	41.4	31.3	7 39.3	41.8	31.4	8 30.5	42.2	31.5	9 21.7	42.5	31.6	10 12.8	42.9	31.6	11 03.8	43.3	31.7	11 54.8	43.7	31.9	52
53	6 37.8	40.9	30.5	7 29.5	41.2	30.6	8 21.1	41.7	30.7	9 12.7	42.0	30.8	10 04.2	42.5	30.8	10 55.7	42.8	30.9	11 47.1	43.2	31.0	12 38.5	43.6	31.1	53
54	7 18.7	40.8	29.8	8 10.7	41.3	29.9	9 02.8	41.5	29.9	9 54.7	42.0	30.0	10 46.7	42.3	30.1	11 38.5	42.7	30.2	12 30.3	43.1	30.3	13 22.1	43.5	30.4	54
55	7 59.5	+40.8	29.1	8 52.0	+41.1	29.1	9 44.3	+41.5	29.2	10 36.7	+41.8	29.3	11 29.0	+42.2	29.4	12 21.2	+42.6	29.5	13 13.4	+43.0	29.6	14 05.6	+43.3	29.7	55
56	8 40.3	40.6	28.3	9 33.1	41.0	28.4	10 25.8	41.4	28.5	11 18.5	41.8	28.6	12 11.2	42.1	28.7	13 03.8	42.5	28.8	13 56.4	42.8	28.9	14 48.9	43.2	29.0	56
57	9 20.9	40.6	27.6	10 14.1	40.9	27.7	11 07.2	41.3	27.7	12 00.3	41.6	27.8	12 53.3	42.0	27.9	13 46.3	42.4	28.1	14 39.2	42.7	28.2	15 32.1	43.0	28.3	57
58	10 01.5	40.5	26.9	10 55.0	40.8	26.9	11 48.5	41.2	27.0	12 41.9	41.5	27.1	13 35.3	41.9	27.2	14 28.7	42.2	27.3	15 21.9	42.6	27.4	16 15.1	43.0	27.6	58
59	10 42.0	40.3	26.1	11 35.8	40.7	26.2	12 29.7	41.0	26.3	13 23.4	41.4	26.4	14 17.2	41.7	26.5	15 10.9	42.0	26.6	16 04.5	42.4	26.7	16 58.1	42.7	26.8	59
60	11 22.3	+40.3	25.3	12 16.5	+40.6	25.4	13 10.7	+40.9	25.5	14 04.8	+41.3	25.6	14 58.9	+41.6	25.7	15 52.9	+41.9	25.8	16 46.9	+42.3	26.0	17 40.8	+42.6	26.1	60
61	12 02.6	40.1	24.6	12 57.1	40.5	24.7	13 51.6	40.8	24.8	14 46.1	41.1	24.9	15 40.5	41.4	25.0	16 34.8	41.8	25.1	17 29.2	42.0	25.2	18 23.4	42.4	25.4	61
62	12 42.7	40.0	23.8	13 37.6	40.3	23.9	14 32.4	40.6	24.0	15 27.2	40.9	24.1	16 21.9	41.3	24.2	17 16.6	41.6	24.4	18 11.2	41.9	24.5	19 05.8	42.2	24.6	62
63	13 22.7	39.8	23.0	14 17.9	40.1	23.1	15 13.0	40.5	23.2	16 08.1	40.8	23.4	17 03.2	41.1	23.5	17 58.2	41.4	23.6	18 53.1	41.8	23.7	19 48.0	42.1	23.9	63
64	14 02.5	39.7	22.3	14 58.0	40.0	22.4	15 53.5	40.3	22.5	16 48.9	40.6	22.6	17 44.3	40.9	22.7	18 39.6	41.2	22.8	19 34.9	41.5	23.0	20 30.1	41.8	23.1	64
65	14 42.2	+39.6	21.5	15 38.0	+39.9	21.6	16 33.8	+40.1	21.7	17 29.5	+40.4	21.8	18 25.2	+40.7	21.9	19 20.8	+41.0	22.1	20 16.4	+41.3	22.2	21 11.9	+41.7	22.3	65
66	15 21.8	39.3	20.7	16 17.9	39.6	20.8	17 13.9	40.0	20.9	18 09.9	40.3	21.0	19 05.9	40.6	21.2	20 01.8	40.9	21.3	20 57.7	41.1	21.4	21 53.6	41.4	21.6	66
67	16 01.1	39.2	19.9	16 57.5	39.5	20.0	17 53.9	39.7	20.1	18 50.2	40.0	20.3	19 46.5	40.3	20.4	20 42.7	40.6	20.5	21 38.8	40.9	20.6	22 35.0	41.2	20.8	67
68	16 40.3	39.1	19.1	17 37.0	39.3	19.2	18 33.6	39.6	19.4	19 30.2	39.9	19.5	20 26.8	40.1	19.6	21 23.3	40.4	19.7	22 19.7	40.7	19.9	23 16.2	40.9	20.0	68
69	17 19.4	38.8	18.4	18 16.3	39.1	18.5	19 13.2	39.4	18.6	20 10.1	39.6	18.7	21 06.9	39.9	18.8	22 03.7	40.1	18.9	23 00.4	40.4	19.1	23 57.1	40.7	19.2	69
70	17 58.2	+38.7	17.6	18 55.4	+38.9	17.7	19 52.6	+39.1	17.8	20 49.7	+39.4	17.9	21 46.8	+39.6	18.0	22 43.8	+39.9	18.1	23 40.8	+40.2	18.3	24 37.8	+40.4	18.4	70
71	18 36.9	38.4	16.7	19 34.3	38.7	16.8	20 31.7	38.9	17.0	21 29.1	39.2	17.1	22 26.4	39.4	17.2	23 23.7	39.7	17.3	24 21.0	39.9	17.4	25 18.2	40.2	17.6	71
72	19 15.3	38.2	15.9	20 13.0	38.4	16.0	21 10.6	38.7	16.1	22 08.3	38.9	16.2	23 05.8	39.2	16.4	24 03.4	39.4	16.5	25 00.9	39.6	16.6	25 58.4	39.9	16.8	72
73	19 53.5	38.0	15.1	20 51.4	38.2	15.2	21 49.3	38.5	15.3	22 47.2	38.6	15.4	23 45.0	38.9	15.5	24 42.8	39.1	15.7	25 40.5	39.4	15.8	26 38.3	39.5	15.9	73
74	20 31.5	37.8	14.3	21 29.6	38.0	14.4	22 27.8	38.1	14.5	23 25.8	38.4	14.6	24 23.9	38.6	14.7	25 21.9	38.8	14.8	26 19.9	39.0	14.9	27 17.8	39.3	15.1	74
75	21 09.3	+37.5	13.5	22 07.6	+37.7	13.6	23 05.9	+37.9	13.6	24 04.2	+38.1	13.8	25 02.5	+38.3	13.9	26 00.7	+38.6	14.0	26 58.9	+38.8	14.1	27 57.1	+39.0	14.2	75
76	21 46.8	37.2	12.6	22 45.3	37.5	12.7	23 43.8	37.7	12.8	24 42.3	37.9	12.9	25 40.8	38.0	13.0	26 39.3	38.2	13.1	27 37.7	38.4	13.2	28 36.1	38.6	13.4	76
77	22 24.0	37.0	11.8	23 22.8	37.1	11.9	24 21.5	37.3	12.0	25 20.2	37.5	12.0	26 18.8	37.7	12.1	27 17.5	37.9	12.3	28 16.1	38.1	12.4	29 14.7	38.3	12.5	77
78	23 01.0	36.7	10.9	23 59.9	36.9	11.0	24 58.8	37.1	11.1	25 57.7	37.2	11.2	26 56.5	37.4	11.3	27 55.4	37.5	11.4	28 54.2	37.7	11.5	29 53.0	37.9	11.6	78
79	23 37.7	36.5	10.1	24 36.8	36.6	10.1	25 35.9	36.7	10.2	26 34.9	36.9	10.3	27 33.9	37.1	10.4	28 32.9	37.3	10.5	29 31.9	37.4	10.6	30 30.9	37.5	10.7	79
80	24 14.2	+36.1	9.2	25 13.4	+36.3	9.3	26 12.6	+36.4	9.3	27 11.8	+36.6	9.4	28 11.0	+36.7	9.5	29 10.2	+36.8	9.6	30 09.3	+37.0	9.7	31 08.4	+37.2	9.8	80
81	24 50.3	35.8	8.3	25 49.7	35.9	8.4	26 49.0	36.1	8.5	27 48.4	36.2	8.5	28 47.7	36.3	8.6	29 47.0	36.5	8.7	30 46.3	36.6	8.8	31 45.6	36.8	8.9	81
82	25 26.1	35.5	7.4	26 25.6	35.6	7.5	27 25.1	35.7	7.6	28 24.6	35.8	7.6	29 24.0	36.0	7.7	30 23.5	36.1	7.8	31 22.9	36.2	7.9	32 22.4	36.3	7.9	82
83	26 01.6	35.2	6.5	27 01.2	35.3	6.6	28 00.8	35.4	6.6	29 00.4	35.5	6.7	30 00.0	35.6	6.8	30 59.6	35.6	6.8	31 59.1	35.8	6.9	32 58.7	35.9	7.0	83
84	26 36.8	34.8	5.6	27 36.5	34.9	5.7	28 36.2	35.0	5.7	29 35.9	35.1	5.8	30 35.6	35.1	5.8	31 35.2	35.3	5.9	32 34.9	35.4	6.0	33 34.6	35.5	6.0	84
85	27 11.6	+34.4	4.7	28 11.4	+34.5	4.8	29 11.2	+34.6	4.8	30 11.0	+34.6	4.9	31 10.7	+34.8	4.9	32 10.5	+34.8	5.0	33 10.3	+34.9	5.0	34 10.1	+34.9	5.1	85
86	27 46.0	34.1	3.8	28 45.9	34.1	3.8	29 45.8	34.2	3.9	30 45.6	34.3	3.9	31 45.5	34.3	3.9	32 45.3	34.4	4.0	33 45.2	34.4	4.0	34 45.0	34.6	4.1	86
87	28 20.1	33.7	2.9	29 20.0	33.8	2.9	30 20.0	33.7	2.9	31 19.9	33.8	2.9	32 19.8	33.9	3.0	33 19.7	33.9	3.0	34 19.6	34.0	3.0	35 19.6	34.0	3.1	87
88	28 53.8	33.3	1.9	29 53.8	33.3	1.9	30 53.7	33.4	2.0	31 53.7	33.4	2.0	32 53.7	33.4	2.0	33 53.6	33.5	2.0	34 53.6	33.5	2.0	35 53.6	33.4	2.1	88
89	29 27.1	32.9	1.0	30 27.1	32.9	1.0	31 27.1	32.9	1.0	32 27.1	32.9	1.0	33 27.1	32.9	1.0	34 27.1	32.9	1.0	35 27.1	32.9	1.0	36 27.0	33.0	1.0	89
90	30 00.0	+32.5	0.0	31 00.0	+32.5	0.0	32 00.0	+32.4	0.0	33 00.0	+32.4	0.0	34 00.0	+32.4	0.0	35 00.0	+32.4	0.0	36 00.0	+32.4	0.0	37 00.0	+32.4	0.0	90
	30°			31°			32°			33°			34°			35°			36°			37°			

S. Lat. { L.H.A. greater than 180°......Zn=180°−Z
L.H.A. less than 180°............Zn=180°+Z

LATITUDE SAME NAME AS DECLINATION — L.H.A. 123°, 237°

tracting the values of Hc on successive horizontal lines, but it is tabulated for the convenience of the user. It is important to note and record whether d is preceded by a plus or minus sign. The third tabulation is Z, the abbreviation used for azimuth angle, and its values range from 0° through 180°. Mental interpolation should be used so that the true value of Z for the actual declination is extracted. A half-degree of azimuth is considered sufficiently accurate for plotting purposes. Each page contains a formula for converting this azimuth angle (Z) to *true azimuth* (Zn). To visualize the conversion in the northern hemisphere, if the body is to the east and rising, the true azimuth will be the same as azimuth angle, since both are measured clockwise from the north. If the body is to the west and setting, azimuth angle is measured counterclockwise from the north through 180°. This value must therefore be subtracted from 360° in order to obtain the Zn.

As an example of extracting the tabulated values from the tables, let us assume latitude 35°N, declination S15° 22'.6, and LHA 334° as entering arguments. Since latitude and declination are of opposite name, the right-hand page, as reproduced in Figure 6-1, is used. The values of Hc (34° 14'.6), d (−54'.1), and Z (149°.2; 149°.5 by mental interpolation to the nearest half-degree between 15° and 16° of declination) are extracted from the main tables and entered on the sight reduction form, as shown in Figure 6-2. The formula given in the upper right-hand corner of the left-hand page in Table 6-1 states that in north latitude and with an LHA greater than 180°, Zn = Z; thus, the true azimuth is also 149°.5. The tabulated value of Hc, in most texts referred to as ht (to show that it is the tabulated value uncorrected), must now be corrected for the minutes of latitude—by using the interpolation tables—in order to obtain the final computed altitude, Hc.

LATITUDE **CONTRARY** NAME TO DECLINATION   L.H.A. 26°, 334°

Dec.	30° Hc	d	Z	31° Hc	d	Z	32° Hc	d	Z	33° Hc	d	Z	34° Hc	d	Z	35° Hc	d	Z	36° Hc	d	Z	37° Hc	d	Z	Dec.
0	51 06.7	-48.0	135.7	50 23.5	-48.7	136.6	49 39.6	-49.3	137.4	48 55.2	-49.9	138.2	48 10.2	-50.4	138.9	47 24.8	-51.0	139.6	46 38.8	-51.5	140.3	45 52.4	-52.0	141.0	0
1	50 18.7	-48.4	136.7	49 34.8	-49.1	137.5	48 50.3	-49.7	138.2	48 05.3	-50.3	139.0	47 19.8	-50.8	139.7	46 33.8	-51.4	140.4	45 47.3	-51.8	141.1	45 00.4	-52.2	141.7	1
2	49 30.3	-48.9	137.6	48 45.7	-49.5	138.3	48 00.6	-50.1	139.1	47 15.0	-50.6	139.8	46 29.0	-51.2	140.5	45 42.4	-51.6	141.1	44 55.5	-52.0	141.8	44 08.2	-52.5	142.4	2
3	48 41.4	-49.3	138.5	47 56.2	-49.8	139.2	47 10.5	-50.4	139.9	46 24.4	-50.9	140.6	45 37.8	-51.4	141.2	44 50.8	-51.8	141.9	44 03.5	-52.4	142.5	43 15.7	-52.7	143.0	3
4	47 52.1	-49.7	139.3	47 06.4	-50.2	140.0	46 20.1	-50.7	140.7	45 33.5	-51.2	141.4	44 46.4	-51.6	142.0	43 59.0	-52.1	142.6	43 11.1	-52.5	143.1	42 23.0	-53.0	143.7	4
5	47 02.4	-50.0	140.1	46 16.2	-50.6	140.8	45 29.4	-51.0	141.5	44 42.3	-51.5	142.1	43 54.8	-52.0	142.7	43 06.9	-52.4	143.3	42 18.6	-52.7	143.8	41 30.0	-53.1	144.3	5
6	46 12.4	-50.3	141.0	45 25.6	-50.8	141.6	44 38.4	-51.3	142.2	43 50.8	-51.7	142.8	43 02.8	-52.1	143.4	42 14.5	-52.6	143.9	41 25.9	-53.0	144.4	40 36.9	-53.3	144.9	6
7	45 22.1	-50.6	141.7	44 34.8	-51.1	142.3	43 47.1	-51.5	142.9	42 59.1	-52.0	143.5	42 10.7	-52.4	144.0	41 21.9	-52.8	144.6	40 32.9	-53.2	145.1	39 43.6	-53.6	145.5	7
8	44 31.5	-50.9	142.5	43 43.7	-51.4	143.1	42 55.6	-51.9	143.6	42 07.1	-52.3	144.2	41 18.3	-52.7	144.7	40 29.1	-53.0	145.2	39 39.7	-53.3	145.7	38 50.0	-53.6	146.1	8
9	43 40.6	-51.3	143.2	42 52.3	-51.6	143.8	42 03.7	-52.0	144.3	41 14.8	-52.4	144.8	40 25.6	-52.8	145.3	39 36.1	-53.1	145.8	38 46.4	-53.5	146.3	37 56.4	-53.9	146.7	9
10	42 49.3	-51.4	143.9	42 00.7	-51.9	144.5	41 11.7	-52.3	145.0	40 22.4	-52.7	145.5	39 32.8	-53.0	146.0	38 43.0	-53.4	146.4	37 52.9	-53.7	146.8	37 02.5	-54.0	147.3	10
11	41 57.9	-51.7	144.6	41 08.8	-52.1	145.1	40 19.4	-52.5	145.6	39 29.7	-52.8	146.1	38 39.8	-53.2	146.6	37 49.6	-53.5	147.0	36 59.2	-53.9	147.4	36 08.5	-54.1	147.8	11
12	41 06.2	-52.0	145.3	40 16.7	-52.3	145.8	39 26.9	-52.7	146.3	38 36.9	-53.0	146.7	37 46.6	-53.4	147.1	36 56.1	-53.7	147.6	36 05.3	-53.9	148.0	35 14.4	-54.3	148.3	12
13	40 14.2	-52.1	146.0	39 24.4	-52.6	146.4	38 34.2	-52.8	146.9	37 43.9	-53.2	147.3	36 53.2	-53.5	147.7	36 02.4	-53.8	148.1	35 11.4	-54.2	148.5	34 20.1	-54.4	148.9	13
14	39 22.1	-52.4	146.6	38 31.8	-52.7	147.1	37 41.4	-53.1	147.5	36 50.7	-53.4	147.9	35 59.7	-53.7	148.3	35 08.6	-54.0	148.7	34 17.2	-54.2	149.0	33 25.7	-54.5	149.4	14
15	38 29.7	-52.6	147.2	37 39.1	-52.9	147.7	36 48.3	-53.2	148.1	35 57.3	-53.6	148.5	35 06.0	-53.8	148.8	34 14.6	-54.1	149.2	33 23.0	-54.4	149.5	32 31.2	-54.7	149.9	15
16	37 37.1	-52.7	147.9	36 46.2	-53.1	148.3	35 55.1	-53.4	148.6	35 03.7	-53.6	149.0	34 12.2	-54.0	149.4	33 20.5	-54.2	149.7	32 28.6	-54.5	150.0	31 36.5	-54.7	150.3	16
17	36 44.4	-52.9	148.5	35 53.1	-53.2	148.8	35 01.7	-53.5	149.2	34 10.1	-53.9	149.6	33 18.2	-54.0	149.9	32 26.3	-54.4	150.2	31 34.1	-54.6	150.5	30 41.8	-54.9	150.8	17
18	35 51.5	-53.1	149.0	34 59.9	-53.4	149.4	34 08.2	-53.7	149.8	33 16.2	-53.9	150.1	32 24.2	-54.3	150.4	31 31.9	-54.5	150.7	30 39.5	-54.7	151.0	29 46.9	-54.9	151.3	18

FIGURE 6-1 *A portion of a sight reduction table, reproduced from* H.O. 229.

GHA	
Corr.	
SHA-v	
GHA	
a λ	
LHA	334
t (E)(W)	

Dec.	
d + −	
Dec.	S 15 22.6
a L	35°

ht	34 14.6
d corr. -54.1	− 20.3
corr.	
Hc	33°54'.3
Ho	33°48'.3
a A or Ⓣ	6

Az or Z	149°.5
Zn	149°.5

FIGURE 6-2   Solution to sample problem.

Interpolation Tables

The interpolation tables in H.O. 229 are of a completely new design, and are quite easy to use but difficult to describe. As in most types of problem solving, the solution becomes clear once the basic problem is understood. The interpolation tables simply perform a multiplication. In the above description of the main tables, the value d was explained as the difference in Hc for a change of 1° (60′) of declination in that particular section of the table. If the actual minutes of declination of the body were converted to a percentage of 60′ and the value d multiplied by this percentage, the correction for minutes would be established. The interpolation tables perform this multiplication in two steps. The correction is added to or subtracted from the Hc, depending on whether the sign of the d value in the main tables is plus or minus. If greater precision is required, or if d in the main tables is printed in italic type followed by a dot, an additional small correction, called the double second difference, can be used. This double second difference is always negative and must be subtracted from the tabulated Hc; however, it is seldom needed.

The following description of the interpolation table is taken from the explanation printed in each volume of H.O. 229.

Provision is made for interpolation of the tabular altitude for declination by the tabulation of the altitude difference, d, and by the Interpolation Table included in each volume. The Interpolation Table, abbreviated Int. Tab. in examples, is designed to make possible a reasonably high degree of precision in interpolating the altitude to the nearest $0'.1$ of declination.

The main, vertical, argument of the Interpolation Table is the excess of the actual declination over that used (an integral degree) as the tabular entry. Since it is recommended that the tabular entry used should always be the integral degree of declination numerically less than or equal to the actual declination, this excess should always be the actual minutes of the declination referred to as the declination increment, abbreviated Dec. Inc. The other argument is the tabular altitude difference, d, which for convenience is divided into two parts, the first being a multiple of $10'$ ($10'$, $20'$, $30'$, $40'$, or $50'$) and the second [being] the remainder in the range $0'.0$ to $9'.9$. The minutes of this remainder appear as the horizontal argument, the decimal part as the vertical argument, in the subtable, which is given opposite each range of one minute (10 entries) of the Dec. Inc. used in entering the tables.

The right-hand column of each vertically divided half-page of the Interpolation Table contains a series of critical tables, each corresponding to the range of Dec. Inc. opposite which it is placed, which give the correction for the effect of second differences.

The Interpolation Table was designed so that it could be printed on four pages. The inside front cover and facing page provide for the range $0'.0$ to $31'.9$ of the Dec. Inc., while the inside back cover and facing page provide for the range $28'.0$ to $59'.9$. No special table is provided for interpolation of the azimuth angle, and the differences are not tabulated.

In the sample problem presented on p. 83, the declination was S15° $22'.6$. The integral degree used in entering the tables was 15°. The declination increment, or extra minutes and tenths, is therefore $22'.6$, which becomes the entering argument in the left-hand column of the interpolation tables. (See Figure 6-3, which reproduces a portion of these tables.) The d value extracted from the main tables was $-54'.1$, and the two-part correction would be obtained as follows: enter the horizontal line marked $22'.6$, from the tens column headed $50'$ extract $18'.8$, and then enter the units column headed "$4'$" and the decimal line labeled ".1" and extract the value of $1'.5$ (see Figure 6-3). This pro-

INTERPOLATION TABLE

Dec. Inc.	10′	20′	Tens 30′	40′	(50)	Decimals	Units 0	1	2	3	(4)	5	6	7	8	9	Double Second Diff. and Corr.
16.0	2.6	5.3	8.0	10.6	13.3	.0	0.0 0.3	0.5 0.8	1.1 1.4	1.6 1.9	2.2 2.5						
16.1	2.7	5.3	8.0	10.7	13.4	.1	0.0 0.3	0.6 0.9	1.1 1.4	1.7 2.0	2.2 2.5						
16.2	2.7	5.4	8.1	10.8	13.5	.2	0.1 0.3	0.6 0.9	1.2 1.4	1.7 2.0	2.3 2.5						1.0
16.3	2.7	5.4	8.1	10.9	13.6	.3	0.1 0.4	0.6 0.9	1.2 1.5	1.7 2.0	2.3 2.6						3.0 0.1
16.4	2.7	5.5	8.2	10.9	13.7	.4	0.1 0.4	0.7 0.9	1.2 1.5	1.8 2.0	2.3 2.6						4.9 0.2
16.5	2.8	5.5	8.3	11.0	13.8	.5	0.1 0.4	0.7 1.0	1.2 1.5	1.8 2.1	2.3 2.6						6.9 0.3
16.6	2.8	5.5	8.3	11.1	13.8	.6	0.2 0.4	0.7 1.0	1.3 1.5	1.8 2.1	2.4 2.6						8.9 0.4
16.7	2.8	5.6	8.4	11.2	13.9	.7	0.2 0.5	0.7 1.0	1.3 1.6	1.8 2.1	2.4 2.7						10.8 0.5
16.8	2.8	5.6	8.4	11.2	14.0	.8	0.2 0.5	0.8 1.0	1.3 1.6	1.9 2.1	2.4 2.7						12.8 0.6
16.9	2.9	5.7	8.5	11.3	14.1	.9	0.2 0.5	0.8 1.1	1.3 1.6	1.9 2.2	2.4 2.7						14.8 0.7
																	16.7 0.8
17.0	2.8	5.6	8.5	11.3	14.1	.0	0.0 0.3	0.6 0.9	1.2 1.5	1.7 2.0	2.3						18.7 0.9
17.1		5.7	8.5	11.4	14.x	.x	0.x	0.6 0.9	1.2 1.5	1.8 2.1	3.4						(1.0)
1~	3.6		8.6	11′	3.0	.6	0.2 0.6	0.9	1.2 1.5	3.1 3.4							
21.7	3.6	7.3	10.x	4.5	18.1	.7	0.3 0.6	1.0 1.3		2.4 2.8	3.1 3.5						
21.8	3.7	7.3	10.9	14.6	18.2	.8	0.3 0.6	1.0 1.4	1.7 2.1	2.4 2.8	3.2 3.5						
21.9	3.7	7.3	11.0	14.6	18.3	.9	0.3 0.7	1.0 1.4	1.8 2.1	2.5 2.8	3.2 3.5						
22.0	3.6	7.3	11.0	14.6	18.3	.0	0.0 0.4	0.7 1.1	1.5 1.9	2.2 2.6	3.0 3.4						0.8
22.1	3.7	7.3	11.0	14.7	18.4	(.1)	0.0 0.4	0.8 1.2	(1.5) 1.9	2.3 2.7	3.0 3.4						2.5 0.1
22.2	3.7	7.4	11.1	14.8	18.5	(.2)	0.1 0.4	0.8 1.2	1.6 1.9	2.3 2.7	3.1 3.4						4.2 0.2
22.3	3.7	7.4	11.1	14.9	18.6	.3	0.1 0.5	0.9 1.2	1.6 2.0	2.4 2.7	3.1 3.5						5.9 0.3
22.4	3.7	7.5	11.2	14.9	18.7	.4	0.1 0.5	0.9 1.3	1.6 2.0	2.4 2.8	3.1 3.5						7.6 0.4
22.5	3.8	7.5	11.3	15.0	18.8	.5	0.2 0.6	0.9 1.3	1.7 2.1	2.4 2.8	3.2 3.6						9.3 0.5
(22.6)	3.8	7.5	11.3	15.1	(18.8)	.6	0.2 0.6	1.0 1.3	1.7 2.1	2.5 2.8	3.2 3.6						11.0 0.6
22.7	3.8	7.6	11.4	15.2	18.9	.7	0.3 0.6	1.0 1.4	1.8 2.1	2.5 2.9	3.3 3.6						12.7 0.7
22.8	3.8	7.6	11.4	15.2	19.0	.8	0.3 0.7	1.0 1.4	1.8 2.2	2.5 2.9	3.3 3.7						14.4 0.8
22.9	3.9	7.7	11.5	15.3	19.1	.9	0.3 0.7	1.1 1.5	1.8 2.2	2.6 3.0	3.3 3.7						16.1 0.9
																	17.8 1.0
23.0	3.8	7.6	11.5	15.3	19.1	.0	0.0 0.4	0.8 1.2	1.6 2.0	2.3 2.7	3.1 3.5						19.5 1.1
23.1	3.8	7.7	11.5	15.4	19.2	.1	0.0 0.4	0.8 1.2	1.6 2.0	2.4 2.8	3.2 3.6						21.2 1.2
23.2	3.8	7.7	11.6	15.4	19.3	.2	0.1 0.5	0.9 1.3	1.6 2.0	2.4 2.8	3.2 3.6						22.8 1.3
23.3	3.9	7.8	11.6	15.5	19.4	.3	0.1 0.5	0.9 1.3	1.7 2.1	2.5 2.9	3.3 3.6						24.5 1.4
23.4	3.9	7.8	11.7	15.6	19.5	.4	0.2 0.5	0.9 1.3	1.7 2.1	2.5 2.9	3.3 3.7						26.2 1.5
23.5	3.9	7.8	11.8	15.7	19.6	.5	0.2 0.6	1.0 1.4	1.8 2.2	2.5 2.9	3.3 3.7						27.9 1.6
23.6	3.9	7.9	11.8	15.7	19.7	.6	0.2 0.6	1.0 1.4	1.8 2.2	2.6 3.0	3.4 3.8						29.6 1.7
23.7	4.0	7.9	11.9	15.8	19.8	.7	0.3 0.7	1.1 1.4	1.8 2.2	2.6 3.0	3.4 3.8						31.3 1.8
23.8	4.0	8.0	11.9	15.9	19.9	.8	0.3 0.7	1.1 1.5	1.9 2.3	2.7 3.1	3.4 3.8						33.0 1.9
23.9	4.0	8.0	12.0	16.0	20.0	.9	0.4 0.7	1.1 1.5	1.9 2.3	2.7 3.1	3.5 3.9						34.7 2.0
	10′	20′	30′	40′	50′		0	1 2	3 4	5 6	7 8	9					

FIGURE 6-3 A portion of an interpolation table, reproduced from
H.O. 229.

duces a total correction of 20′.3, which is entered on the sight reduction form (see Figure 6-2) and subtracted from the Hc to obtain the corrected Hc of 33° 54′.3.

If a double second difference had been indicated in the main tables, an additional correction (located in the small critical table at the extreme right in Figure 6-3) would be used. The entering argument for double second differences is the difference, as determined from the main tables, between the d values, immediately above and immediately below the d value being extracted. Examples of this seldom-used correction are given in each volume of H.O. 229.

With the computed altitude (Hc) and true azimuth (Zn) now extracted from the tables, the Hc is compared with the observed altitude (Ho) to obtain the altitude intercept a, in order to determine the point along the azimuth line through which the LOP will be drawn. If the Ho were 33° 48′.3, the intercept would be 6 minutes and therefore 6 miles toward the Zn of 149°.5.

Chapter 7

Plotting the LOP

The celestial line of position (LOP) is plotted from the assumed position (AP) when using sight reduction tables H.O. 214, H.O. 229, or H.O. 249. In selecting the entering arguments for using these tables, the integral degree of latitude nearest the DR latitude is assumed. This is the latitude of the AP. In order to have an integral degree of LHA or meridian angle t, it is necessary to assume a longitude that includes minutes of arc in order to provide the integral degree of LHA or t when the longitude is combined with the GHA. This is the assumed longitude of the AP. Both values are recorded on the sight reduction form. The final results of the computation recorded on the sight reduction form are the true azimuth of the body and the altitude intercept (a). The latter is expressed in minutes of arc and therefore nautical miles toward or away from the body along the azimuth line. Remember that if Ho is greater than Hc, the intercept is drawn from the AP in the direction of the body; if Hc is greater, the intercept is drawn away from the body (computed greater away).

Having drawn the intercept to the correct length, as found by the altitude difference (a), the LOP is drawn at right angles through the end of the intercept. This plotting can best be done by using a plotting protractor. If a protractor is not available, parallel rules can be used to draw the azimuth line. A pair of dividers is then used to establish the length of the intercept. The protractor can then be used to plot the LOP. (See Figure 7-1.)

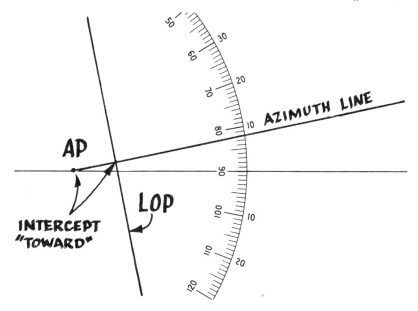

FIGURE 7-1   A line of position (LOP).

Each star in a multiple-star fix will have a different AP; the latitude will be the same for each, but the assumed longitudes will differ. A three-star fix is shown in Figure 7-2; for clarity of illustration, the azimuth lines are dashed and the LOPs are solid lines. This illustration assumes a short elapsed time between sights; therefore, it was not necessary to advance the first two LOPs to the time of the third.

The three LOPs seldom intersect in a point; they generally result in a small triangle, or "cocked hat." The center of this triangle can safely be assumed to be the fix if the three bodies have a spread in azimuth of more than 180°. It is very important, when choosing stars to be observed, that considerable separation in azimuth be maintained. If the azimuths of three or more stars do not span more than 180°, the fix can be located outside the triangle rather than within it, leading to considerable error if the navigator assumes the fix is within the cocked hat.

The LOP on a Universal Plotting Sheet

Using the Oceanographic Office Universal Plotting Sheets, together with the 641 Plotter (see Figure 7-3) with scales to match, is the best method of plotting celestial LOPs and fixes. The parallels of latitude are printed on the plotting sheet together with a compass rose and

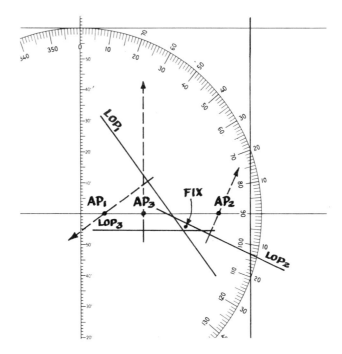

FIGURE 7-2   A three-star fix.

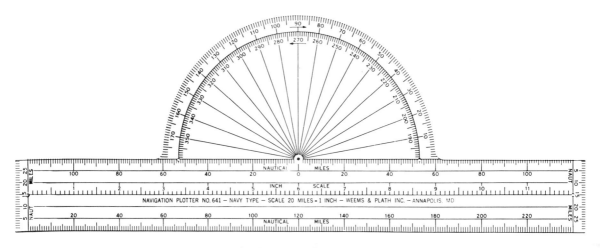

FIGURE 7-3   The 641 Plotter.

latitude scale. The meridians of longitude are drawn in by the user and are spaced according to the mid-latitude. These sheets are therefore universal in the sense that the same sheets can be used for any latitude. Two points are selected on the compass rose, each representing in arc value the mid-latitude, which is 30° in Figure 7-4. These points are located on the compass rose above and below the parallel representing the mid-latitude and a meridian is drawn through them. It will be the correct distance from the central meridian that is printed on the chart. Other meridians are then constructed, using this same horizontal spacing and labeled with the local longitude. West longitude always increases numerically from right to left on the plotting sheets.

Another method is also available for proper spacing of the meridians. A longitude scale is printed in the bottom right-hand corner of each sheet (see Figure 7-5). The linear length of any value of minutes of

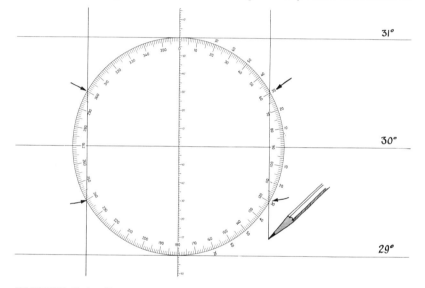

FIGURE 7-4 *Constructing meridians on a Universal Plotting Sheet.*

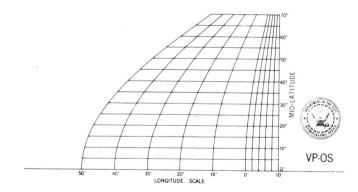

FIGURE 7-5 *The longitude scale of a Universal Plotting Sheet.*

longitude is found by measuring horizontally, after locating the proper latitude in the vertical scale. To construct a plotting sheet for the area of operation, measure 60′ along the appropriate latitude line on the longitude scale, and then transfer this distance with the dividers, east and west from the central meridian printed on the sheet, along each parallel of latitude. Vertical lines can now be drawn through the marked points to represent meridians, properly spaced for the mid-latitude of the sheet.

In addition to publishing the Universal Plotting Sheets, the government publishes several series of plotting sheets covering different specific bands of latitude. On these sheets, the meridians are already drawn in and can be numbered for the appropriate longitude. The degrees of latitude are printed on the parallels of latitude. Many navigators prefer to use these already-completed mercator plotting charts. Lines of position can also be plotted directly on the navigation chart, but the use of a plotting sheet tends to reduce clutter on the navigation chart.

Drawing the LOP

Locate the assumed position in latitude and longitude, and label this point AP. With a pair of dividers, the correct minutes of longitude of the AP can be transferred from the longitude scale to the parallel of latitude representing the assumed latitude. Another method, if dividers are not available, is to use the 641 scale. Tilt the plotter so that 0 is on one meridian and 60 on the scale is on the next meridian. The space between the meridians is thus divided into 60 units. Slide the plotter up or down on the chart, keeping 0 and 60 on the meridians, until the correct minutes of longitude intersect the parallel of latitude, and mark this point; 20 minutes of longitude are shown in Figure 7-6. Lay the plotter on the plotting sheet with the upper straightedge along the parallel of latitude and with the center hole over the AP, as shown by the dotted lines in Figure 7-7. Make a mark at 90° on the scale. This is in effect a meridian drawn through the AP. Place a pencil in the center hole of the plotter and rotate the plotter until the true azimuth is located at the newly constructed meridian (130° in Figure 7-7, shown as solid lines in the illustration). Now place the pencil at any point along the straightedge and slide the plotter along it until the AP is located on the plotter scale at the number of miles toward or away from the AP representing the altitude intercept. In Figure 7-8 this is 15 miles away. The plotter will then be positioned as shown by the dotted lines. Place a dot at the new location of the center hole and one at 90° on the scale. Draw a line through these points; it will be the LOP at 90° to the azimuth line and 15 miles away from the AP. The azimuth line itself is not needed and is therefore not drawn in, since it would only clutter the plotting sheet.

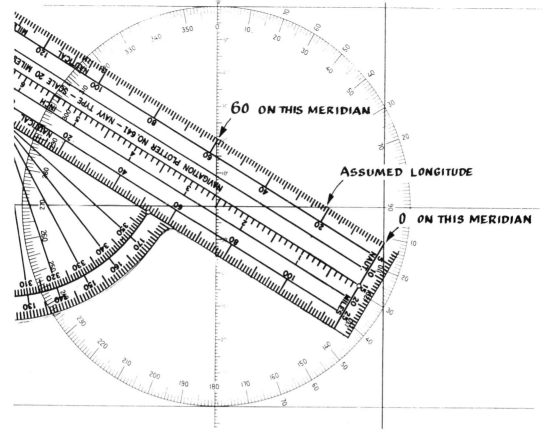

FIGURE 7-6 Drawing the LOP.

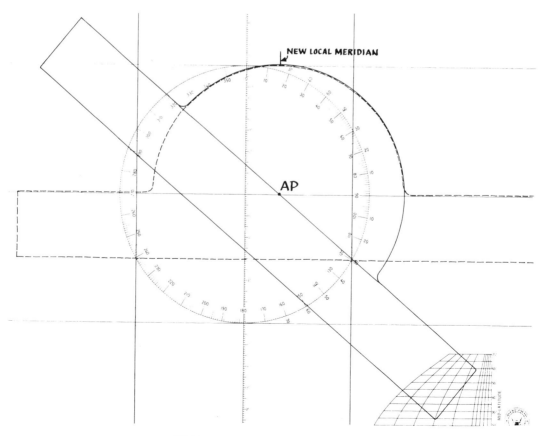

FIGURE 7-7 Drawing the LOP.

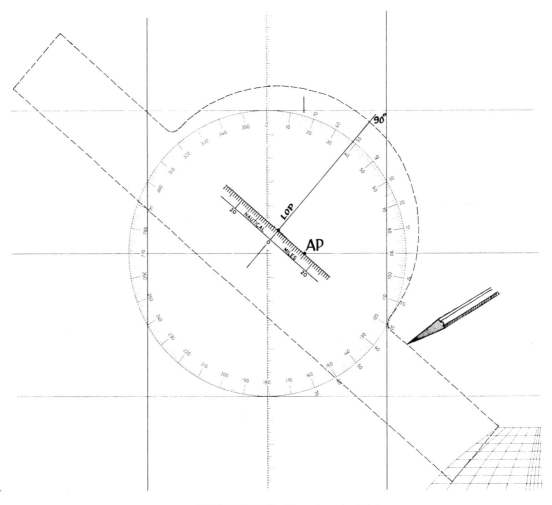

FIGURE 7-8   Drawing the LOP.

Advancing Celestial LOPs (Running Fixes)

An LOP obtained from observing a single celestial body produces only limited data and, at best, an indication of the position of the vessel. It can be assumed that the position lies somewhere along this single LOP. If only the single LOP, which is obtained most often from the sun, is available, the most probable position is generally assumed to be the point on the line that is closest to the DR position. If another LOP is obtained at a later time, the first LOP can be advanced to the time of the second observation. The theory is exactly the same as for advancing terrestrial LOPs in piloting, in which compass bearings are taken of identifiable objects ashore. Since the first line is in effect carried along by a DR plot, the accuracy deteriorates rapidly with time because there is generally no way to determine the precise course and speed made good over the ground. This differs from course and speed through the water by the effect of any unknown currents, steering errors, leeway, and so forth.

To avoid such errors, it is best, when taking multiple-star sights, to make the observations as closely together in time as possible. At the speeds common in small power or sail craft, the advance is often ignored. The fix is obtained by plotting each of the LOPs at their observed time, the time of the middle observation in a three-star fix generally being used as the time of the fix.

At times of poor horizon visibility, or when there is considerable overcast, it is often possible to obtain observations of two stars that might be separated in time by fifteen or twenty minutes during the period of twilight. The first LOP should then be advanced to the time of the second. In this case, the simplest way of plotting is to choose a convenient point on the first LOP, draw a line through this point in the direction of the true course, and, with a pair of dividers, step off the distance run between sights along this course line. Through this point draw in the advanced LOP parallel to the original LOP. In Figure 7-9 assume that an LOP was obtained for star 1 at 0650 and for star 2 at

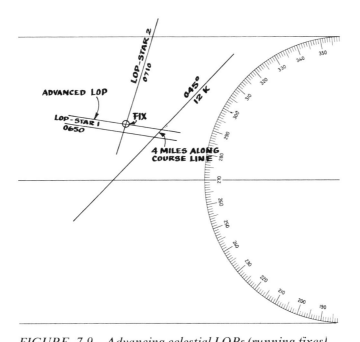

FIGURE 7-9   *Advancing celestial LOPs (running fixes).*

0710. The vessel is on course 045° T, speed 12 K. From the point where LOP 1 crosses the course line, measure a distance of 4 nautical miles (20 minutes at speed 12 K) along the course line and draw in the advanced LOP, labeled as indicated. The point where this advanced LOP intersects the 0710 LOP of star 2 is assumed to be the position obtained by the running fix.

Quite often, a celestial LOP can be used in conjunction with other navigational data, such as a single Loran or RDF LOP. If this is done, the first line must be advanced to the time of the second. Since the determination of position is generally the main objective of the navigator, every opportunity should be taken to combine celestial navigation with any other available data.

The most common use of the running fix is in attempting to determine an approximate longitude at the time of obtaining latitude at local apparent noon (LAN). (See Chapter 8.) In this case a late-morning sun line, observed as much as an hour before noon, is advanced to the time of LAN. If possible, an afternoon sun line is then retarded to the time of LAN. The uncertainty of the course and distance made good during this comparatively long elapsed period of time limits the accuracy of the longitude obtained from the running fix. The data thus obtained should, in most cases, be considered to be better than a purely DR position. Figure 7-10 illustrates a morning sun line taken exactly one hour (for simplicity of illustration) before LAN and another taken one

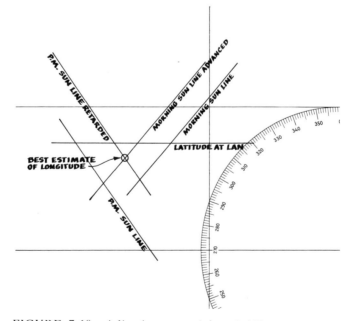

FIGURE 7-10   Adjusting a sun sight to LAN.

hour after LAN, both adjusted to the time of LAN. On a predominantly north or south course, the errors in longitude will be considerably less than on an east or west course, if the errors are due to steering and to uncertainty of the speed made good. The error due to drift in an unknown ocean current will affect the fix by approximately the same amount, regardless of the course being steered. If a good LAN sight were obtained, the latitude could be considered as accurate and the longitude as approximate.

Chapter 8

Special Cases

Local Apparent Noon and the Noon Sight

At sea, the most generally practiced method of celestial navigation is that of observing the sun at local apparent noon (LAN) to obtain the ship's latitude; this applies even aboard vessels that rely principally upon electronic navigation. At LAN the sun transits or crosses the local meridian, which permits a precise determination of latitude.

Since the GHA of the sun is almost exactly repetitive day after day, the solution for the time of LAN is simplified after the first day of a cruise; it is only necessary to apply the vessel's change in longitude, with longitude expressed as units of time, to the time of LAN for the previous day. When one is sailing toward the east, the time of LAN will be earlier, as the ship is moving toward the rising sun; conversely, when one is sailing westward the time will be later.

The noon sight is generally considered the most accurate sight of the day as the sun's change of altitude is minimal as it crosses the meridian (see Figures 8-1 and 8-2). It "hangs" or travels almost horizontally for one or more minutes before starting to descend. Therefore, the determination of the exact second of time of the observation is not vital. A few seconds in watch error is unimportant at LAN, whereas the determination of the exact second is vitally important in most other celestial observations. Since the exact longitude is generally not known,

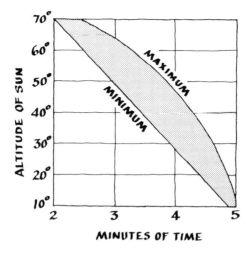

FIGURE 8-1   *Approximate minimum and maximum period of time at LAN when the change in altitude of the sun is 0'.1 of arc or less. This is a function of declination of the sun and latitude of the observer. On this graph the entering argument is the altitude of the sun.*

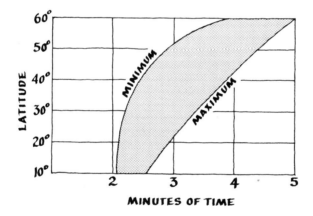

FIGURE 8-2   *Approximate minimum and maximum period of time at LAN when the change in altitude of the sun is 0'.1 of arc or less, based on sun altitudes of 10° through 70°. The entering argument is the latitude of the observer.*

the anticipated time of LAN may be in error. Common practice dictates taking a number of observations, without bothering to record time, starting a few minutes before the estimated time of LAN and continuing for some minutes after. The highest altitudes observed are used in determining latitude. By taking a number of observations, it is easy to determine the highest altitude attained by the sun. If the longitude is not known, observations should be started while the sun is still rising. This may require so many observations that eye strain results, which is another good reason for always carrying forward on the chart as accurate a dead reckoning position (DR) as is possible to attain.

Determining the Time of LAN by Computation

The time of LAN is determined as follows: While the sun is still well to the east, enter the *Nautical Almanac* for the current day and find the tabulated value of the GHA of the sun that is nearest in value to the longitude of the vessel, but east of it. Determine the difference in longitude between the DR longitude and the tabulated GHA of the sun, and convert it to minutes of arc; this will be meridian angle *t* east. Note the GMT for the GHA sun extracted from the *Almanac*. Knowing this time, which is then converted to zone time, it is now necessary to determine by formula the time that will elapse before the sun's GHA and the longitude coincide. Determine the vessel's rate of change of longitude per hour by plotting on the chart, and note whether it is changing to the east or to the west. The sun moves toward the west at a fairly uniform rate of 900′ of arc per hour. Add the vessel's rate of change of longitude to this rate if the vessel is moving toward the east; subtract the vessel's rate if the vessel is sailing toward the west. To find the interval to LAN, divide the meridian angle *t* east, stated in minutes of arc, by the combined rate of change of longitude for the sun and the vessel as determined above, which is also expressed in minutes of arc.

$$\text{Interval to LAN} = \frac{t \text{ east}}{900' + \text{ or } - \text{ vessel change in longitude/hour}}$$

The use of the formula is illustrated in the following example: On November 5 at 1100 (+5) a vessel's DR position is latitude 38° 59′.2N, longitude 71° 20′.5W; course is 080° T, speed 8.5 knots. Convert to GMT as follows: 1100 (+5) = GMT 1600. From the *Nautical Almanac* for that date, note that the GHA sun at GMT 1600 is 64° 05′.′.7. Determine that the difference in longitude between the sun's hour circle, expressed as GHA, and the DR longitude for the same time is 7° 14′.8, which, expressed in minutes of arc, is 434′.8. This is *t* in the formula. Determine from the chart or plotting sheet that the change in longitude on the given course and speed is about 10′.8 per hour. If the vessel is sailing toward the east, the combined change of sun and vessel will be 910′.8 per hour. Divide 438′.8 by 910′.8 to find that the interval to LAN will be about .48 hours. Multiply this value by 60 to obtain

28.8 minutes. The zone time of LAN is therefore about 1129. This formula can be solved very rapidly with a slide rule or electronic calculator.

A shorter but slightly less accurate method is to use the time of meridian passage of the sun given in the lower right-hand corner of the daily pages of the *Almanac*. This is the time of meridian passage on a standard meridian. In the above problem for November 5 this meridian passage is tabulated as 1144 at the standard or zone meridian (75°W). If the 1100 DR of the vessel is advanced to 1144, the DR longitude would have been 71° 12′.4. Using the 4 minutes per degree of movement of the sun, the meridian passage at the 1144 DR longitude (71° 12′.4) would be approximately 15 minutes earlier than at 75°W, or 1129. The only error in this system is that caused by the change in longitude of the vessel between 1144 and 1129. For small vessels this would usually be minimal.

The reason that the meridian passage of the sun over a standard meridian occurs at some time other than 1200 is the difference between *apparent time* and *mean time*, which was discussed in Chapter 2. This difference is the "equation of time," which is given on a daily basis in the small block in the lower right-hand pages of the *Nautical Almanac*.

Finding the Latitude at LAN

The determination of latitude as outlined in this section will be the same for any body crossing the meridian, although the sun at LAN is the body most often observed. When one uses the procedure for stars or the moon, the transit will not occur at noon, but at some other time of the day. Reduction of the noon sight can be accomplished by using any standard sight reduction tables, such as H.O. 229. LHA will be zero, and the other two entering arguments—the integral degree of declination numerically smaller than the actual declination, and the assumed latitude—will be the same as for any other sight reduction. The tabulated altitude is then corrected for the declination difference in the usual way. The altitude intercept is found as usual by determining the difference between Hc and Ho, and the azimuth will be 180° or 360°. The latitude can be determined without plotting on the chart by applying the intercept, in accordance with its sign, to the assumed latitude used in entering the tables.

The noon sight represents a special case of the *navigational triangle*, for the sun, the observer's zenith, and the elevated celestial pole will all lie on the same great circle. A special short solution that does not require the use of tables is therefore possible, in the form of one of the formulas given below. The selection of the appropriate formula depends on the relationship of the latitude and declination.

The solutions are illustrated in Figure 8-3, which is drawn on the plane of the observer's meridian.

I. Latitude and declination same name, but latitude numerically greater than declination:
$$\text{Lat.} = 90° + \text{Dec.} - \text{Ho}$$
II. Latitude and declination opposite name:
$$\text{Lat.} = 90° - (\text{Ho} + \text{Dec.})$$
III. Latitude and declination same name, but declination numerically greater than latitude:
$$\text{Lat.} = \text{Ho} + \text{Dec.} - 90°$$

Since formulas are often difficult to remember under adverse conditions at sea, it is advisable to become thoroughly familiar with how to sketch the diagrams and, therefore, with how to determine which formula is appropriate. Writing the formulas in the almanac is also good practice.

The sextant altitude must be corrected in the normal manner to obtain Ho when determining the latitude at LAN.

Problem: The DR latitude of a ship is N46° 48′, a sextant altitude has been taken and corrected to give Ho 65° 23′.1, and the declination of the sun from the almanac is N 22° 13′.2. Determine the latitude at LAN.

Solution: Since latitude and declination are of the same name, with latitude being numerically greater, the solution is by formula I:

Latitude = 90° + 22° 13′.2 − 65° 23′.1 = 46° 50′.1 north latitude

Off the United States coasts formula I will always apply in the summer, for the sun then has a north declination. In the winter, formula II will apply, as the declination of the sun will be south.

When the sun's declination is within 30° or so of the observer's latitude, excellent running fixes may be obtained in conjunction with the latitude sight at LAN. The sun, when near the observer's latitude, changes azimuth or bearing very rapidly. For example, for an observer in latitude 40°N, when the sun has a declination of N10°, the sun's azimuth will be 143°.9 one hour and twenty minutes before LAN; at LAN its azimuth will be 180°; an hour and twenty minutes after LAN it will be 216°.1. When the sun is nearer the observer's zenith, its change of azimuth is even more rapid, and the period of time required to obtain sun lines of position that differ 35° or more in azimuth will be even shorter.

Advancing the A.M. sun line and retarding the P.M. sun line to the time of LAN will produce a reasonably good noon longitude; any error will be caused principally by any unknown current affecting the estimate of distance run between the sights. Advancing lines of position is covered in Chapter 7.

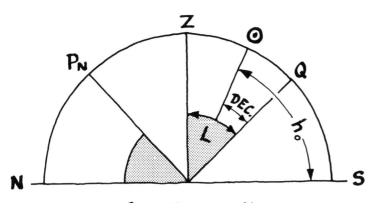

CASE I : L = 90° + DEC. MINUS H_o

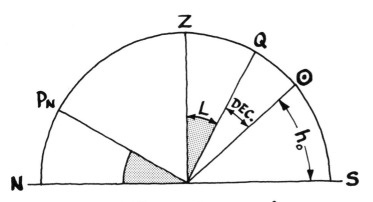

CASE II : L = 90° MINUS (H_o + DEC.)

Z = ZENITH

Q = EQUATOR

☉ = SUN

P_N = NORTH POLE

L = LATITUDE

h_o = OBSERVER'S ALTITUDE

DEC. = DECLINATION

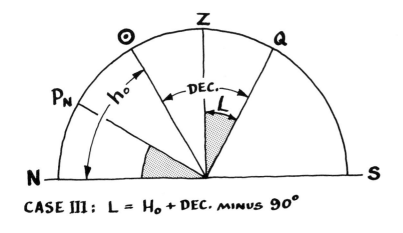

CASE III : L = H_o + DEC. MINUS 90°

FIGURE 8-3   Three solutions to the navigational triangle.

The Longitude LOP

If morning and evening star fixes have not been available for a day or more, it becomes exceedingly important to establish longitude. For example, there are numerous cases of boats completely missing Bermuda during the Newport-to-Bermuda Race. A landfall on a small island is quite easy to miss, especially during periods of low visibility. Although not widely used, a method is available for determining longitude from a single observation of the sun. This observation is made when the sun crosses the prime vertical—that is, the vertical circle passing through the zenith of the observer and the east and west points of the horizon—at which time the true azimuth is either 90° or 270°. However, this method of obtaining the longitude is available only when the sun's declination and the latitude are of the same name, and when the latitude is numerically greater than the declination. In all other cases the sun will not cross the prime vertical. In the discussion of obtaining latitude at LAN, it was noted that obtaining the exact time of the observation was not overly important, as the rate of change of altitude is small at noon. For the longitude sight the exact opposite is true, in that the rate of change of altitude is at a maximum and the exact time of the observation is of prime importance. The observation will seldom be made when the azimuth is exactly 90° or 270°. The observer should, however, strive for this result, especially if the exact latitude is not known, as each degree of azimuth error will tilt the LOP out of the north-south alignment by exactly the same amount.

If compass error (the combination of variation and deviation) is accurately known, and if a compass is so located that azimuths of the sun can be observed, the simplest method of determining the time the sun crosses the prime vertical is merely to begin taking azimuths as the true azimuth of the sun approaches 90° or 270°. If this method is not practical, the data can be obtained with a little effort from the sight reduction tables. It was much easier to obtain this data from the H.O. 214 tables than from the new H.O. 229 tables, in which the primary page opening is by LHA, the desired value. Using the correct latitude section, open the tables to any page and note the azimuth for the nearest degree of DR latitude and declination of the sun. Then check the next page forward and the next page backward in the volume to see if azimuth is increasing or decreasing. It is possible to leaf through the volume rapidly to find the page where the azimuth is 90° or 270° for the given declination and latitude. Note the LHA for the page, and convert this to GHA by applying the DR longitude. For this GHA sun, enter the *Nautical Almanac* and extract the GMT, which is then converted to zone time. In effect, the sight is worked backward to find the time of the desired observation. The procedure is not exact unless interpolations are made, but if several observations are made, close to the determined time, and reduced, the one having an azimuth nearest to east or west can be used. Remember that one of the basic concepts on which celestial navigation is based is the relationship of time and longitude; it is impossible to obtain precise longitude without a precise knowledge of time.

Another method of determining the time when the longitude observation should be made is to precompute what the altitude of the sun will be when on the prime vertical (PV), using this formula:

$$\sin H \text{ on PV} = \frac{\sin \text{ declination}}{\sin \text{ latitude}}$$

Thus, if the latitude is known with reasonable accuracy, the longitude can be determined by commencing to observe the sun just before it reaches the computed altitude, and then by noting the GMT when the exact altitude is reached. If the sextant corrections with sign reversed are applied to the precomputed altitude, the operation is somewhat simplified.

These two methods of computing longitude are obviously rather complex, but they will produce the needed results. The simplest approach is to use a pelorus or a bearing compass to observe the azimuth.

Finding the Time of Sunrise and Sunset and the Duration of Twilight

Star sights must be obtained when both the stars and the horizon are visible during twilight. The duration of this period depends on the declination of the sun, and thus the time of year. It also depends on the latitude of the observer. On the right-hand side of the daily pages in the *Nautical Almanac* there is a column headed "Twilight Civil"; the adjoining column is headed "Sunrise." The period between these two time values is the best period in which to observe morning stars, as both the horizon and most navigational stars are visible then. Civil twilight starts in the morning and ends in the evening when the sun is 6° below the horizon; nautical twilight begins or ends when the sun is 12° below the horizon, and the horizon is consequently very poorly defined. For evening stars, the period between sunset and the time listed under "Civil Twilight" should be used for star observations.

The GMT of the various phenomena on the Greenwich meridian is tabulated in the *Almanac* on the right-hand portion of the daily pages. Refer back to Table 3-1, where an *Almanac* page for 3, 4 and 5 November is reproduced. The time of sunrise and sunset and the time of the beginning of morning twilight and the ending of evening twilight is tabulated. Entries are given for various latitudes, and for other latitudes a mental interpolation between the values tabulated will usually suffice. If an exact interpolation is desired, a table for this purpose, with instructions, is available in the back of the *Almanac*. The times given are GMT on the Greenwich meridian, but they can also be considered as the LMT at any other meridian. The LMT must normally be converted to the zone time being maintained on board the vessel. The simplified method of correcting for longitude is to assume that the time of the phenomenon listed is the time on the central meridian of the local time zone. Four minutes must be added to the time for each degree of longitude west of the standard meridian and subtracted for each degree east of the standard meridian. For example, if the LMT of sunrise at the DR latitude is 0630 and the DR longitude is 73° W, this location is 2° east of the standard meridian of 75° and the zone time of sunrise at 73° W longitude would be 8 minutes earlier, or 0622. Morning star sights can be started at the approximate time of the start of civil twilight, and evening star sights can be started shortly after the time of sunset.

Problem: With a DR position of 31° north latitude and 63° 30′ west longitude, determine the time of the start of civil twilight on 4 November.

Solution: From the sample *Almanac* page in Table 3-1, determine the time at 30°N as 0551 and at 35°N as 0557. Interpolation will give about 0552 as the time at 31°N at any standard meridian. The DR longitude is 3° 30′ west of the standard meridian of 60°, and the start of twilight will thus be 14 minutes later than at the standard meridian (4 minutes for each degree). The start of twilight at the DR position will therefore be about 0606. Note also that at 30°N in the tables the difference in time between civil twilight and sunrise is 25 minutes, which gives a good estimate of the time available for making the observations. This same procedure is used for determining the time of sunset.

Another method of obtaining the correct GMT and zone time of any of the phenomena, such as sunrise and sunset, is given in the *Nautical Almanac*. Since for practical purposes the GMT of the event on the Greenwich meridian can also be considered the LMT on the local meridian, the conversion can be made by the formula, GMT equals LMT plus west longitude or minus east longitude. In using this formula, remember that the longitude must first be converted to time, by means of the conversion table included in the *Almanac* (and duplicated in Appendix II of this book). This produces the GMT on the local meridian, which can be converted to zone time by applying the zone description with the sign reversed.

It is obvious that a DR position must be known in order to determine the time of any of the phenomena; conversely, the approximate

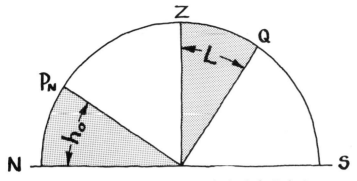

FIGURE 8-4   Determining latitude by Polaris.

time must be known in order to determine the DR position. To obtain greater accuracy, part of the problem might have to be solved twice. First, find in the *Almanac* the time of the phenomenon at the standard meridian, and use this time to determine your DR position. From this DR position, the exact time can be determined as outlined above. Unless the vessel's speed is extremely high, this accuracy will suffice. At 35° latitude, the time will change by one minute for a change in longitude of approximately 12.3 nautical miles.

In practice, the exact time of the start of twilight is not needed. Simply go on deck with the sextant about 10 minutes before the estimated time of civil twilight, and start to work as soon as the horizon can be defined, using the sextant with its telescope in place. In Chapter 4 suggestions are given as to the best method of determining which stars to observe first in order to take full advantage of the limited time of twilight for obtaining a fix.

Determining Latitude by Polaris

If a visible star were located exactly at the north celestial pole, the observed altitude would always be equal to the north latitude of the observer. Figure 8-4, which is drawn on the plane of a meridian, illustrates this concept. The star Polaris is located less than 1° from the north celestial pole, and its altitude, with suitable corrections, can therefore be used to determine latitude. As all other stars, Polaris goes around the pole in a diurnal circle, and its altitude is the same as the pole's twice a day. Correction tables based on LHA*T* are printed in the *Nautical Almanac*. A good approximation of the longitude, which is used in determining LHA, is necessary in order to obtain accuracy in determining latitude. An explanation of the three-section correction table in the *Nautical Almanac* is given at the bottom of the table. In addition, a

POLARIS (POLE STAR) TABLES
FOR DETERMINING LATITUDE FROM SEXTANT ALTITUDE AND FOR AZIMUTH

L.H.A. ARIES	0 – 9	10 – 19	20 – 29	30 – 39	40 – 49	50 – 59	60 – 69	70 – 79	80 – 89	90 – 99	100 – 109	110 – 119
	a_0	a_0	a_0	a_0	a_0	a_0	a_0	a_0	a_0	a_0	a_0	a_0
0	0 15·6	0 11·5	0 08·9	0 07·8	0 08·3	0 10·4	0 13·9	0 18·9	0 25·0	0 32·2	0 40·2	0 48·7
1	15·1	11·2	08·7	07·8	08·5	10·7	14·4	19·4	25·7	33·0	41·0	49·6
2	14·7	10·9	08·6	07·8	08·6	11·0	14·8	20·0	26·4	33·7	41·9	50·5
3	14·2	10·6	08·4	07·8	08·8	11·3	15·3	20·6	27·1	34·5	42·7	51·4
4	13·8	10·3	08·3	07·8	09·0	11·6	15·7	21·2	27·8	35·3	43·6	52·3
5	0 13·4	0 10·0	0 08·2	0 07·9	0 09·2	0 12·0	0 16·2	0 21·8	0 28·5	0 36·1	0 44·4	0 53·1
6	13·0	09·8	08·1	07·9	09·4	12·3	16·7	22·4	29·2	36·9	45·3	54·0
7	12·6	09·5	08·0	08·0	09·6	12·7	17·2	23·0	29·9	37·7	46·1	54·9
8	12·2	09·3	07·9	08·1	09·8	13·1	17·8	23·7	30·7	38·5	47·0	55·8
9	11·9	09·1	07·9	08·2	10·1	13·5	18·3	24·3	31·4	39·4	47·9	56·7
10	0 11·5	0 08·9	0 07·8	0 08·3	0 10·4	0 13·9	0 18·9	0 25·0	0 32·2	0 40·2	0 48·7	0 57·6

Lat.	a_1	a_1	a_1	a_1	a_1	a_1	a_1	a_1	a_1	a_1	a_1	a_1
0	0·5	0·6	0·6	0·6	0·6	0·5	0·5	0·4	0·3	0·2	0·2	0·2
10	·5	·6	·6	·6	·6	·5	·5	·4	·4	·3	·2	·2
20	·5	·6	·6	·6	·6	·6	·5	·5	·4	·4	·3	·3
30	·6	·6	·6	·6	·6	·6	·5	·5	·5	·4	·4	·4
40	0·6	0·6	0·6	0·6	0·6	0·6	0·6	0·5	0·5	0·5	0·5	0·5
45	·6	·6	·6	·6	·6	·6	·6	·6	·6	·5	·5	·5
50	·6	·6	·6	·6	·6	·6	·6	·6	·6	·6	·6	·6
55	·6	·6	·6	·6	·6	·6	·6	·6	·7	·7	·7	·7
60	·6	·6	·6	·6	·6	·6	·7	·7	·7	·8	·8	·8
62	0·7	0·6	0·6	0·6	0·6	0·6	0·7	0·7	0·8	0·8	0·8	0·9
64	·7	·6	·6	·6	·6	·7	·7	·8	·8	·9	0·9	0·9
66	·7	·6	·6	·6	·6	·7	·7	·8	·9	0·9	1·0	1·0
68	0·7	0·6	0·6	0·6	0·6	0·7	0·7	0·8	0·9	1·0	1·0	1·1

Month	a_2	a_2	a_2	a_2	a_2	a_2	a_2	a_2	a_2	a_2	a_2	a_2
Jan.	0·7	0·7	0·7	0·7	0·8	0·8	0·8	0·8	0·7	0·7	0·7	0·7
Feb.	·6	·7	·7	·7	·8	·8	·8	·8	·9	·9	·8	·8
Mar.	·5	·5	·6	·7	·7	·8	·8	·9	·9	·9	·9	0·9
Apr.	0·3	0·4	0·5	0·5	0·6	0·7	0·7	0·8	0·8	0·9	0·9	1·0
May	·2	·3	·3	·4	·4	·5	·6	·6	·7	·8	·8	0·9
June	·2	·2	·2	·3	·3	·4	·4	·5	·6	·6	·7	·8
July	0·2	0·2	0·2	0·2	0·2	0·3	0·3	0·4	0·4	0·5	0·5	0·6
Aug.	·4	·3	·3	·3	·3	·3	·3	·3	·3	·3	·4	·4
Sept.	·5	·5	·4	·4	·3	·3	·3	·3	·3	·3	·3	·3
Oct.	0·7	0·7	0·6	0·6	0·5	0·4	0·4	0·3	0·3	0·3	0·3	0·2
Nov.	0·9	0·9	·8	·7	·7	·6	·5	·5	·4	·3	·3	·3
Dec.	1·0	1·0	0·9	0·9	0·8	0·8	0·7	0·6	0·5	0·5	0·4	0·3

Lat.	AZIMUTH											
0	0·4	0·2	0·1	0·0	359·8	359·7	359·5	359·4	359·3	359·2	359·2	359·2
20	0·4	0·3	0·1	0·0	359·8	359·6	359·5	359·4	359·3	359·2	359·1	359·1
40	0·5	0·3	0·1	359·9	359·7	359·6	359·4	359·2	359·1	359·0	358·9	358·9
50	0·6	0·4	0·2	359·9	359·7	359·5	359·3	359·1	358·9	358·8	358·7	358·7
55	0·7	0·4	0·2	359·9	359·7	359·4	359·2	359·0	358·8	358·7	358·6	358·5
60	0·8	0·5	0·2	359·9	359·6	359·3	359·1	358·8	358·6	358·5	358·4	358·3
65	0·9	0·6	0·2	359·9	359·5	359·2	358·9	358·6	358·4	358·2	358·1	358·0

Latitude = Apparent altitude (corrected for refraction) − 1° + a_0 + a_1 + a_2

The table is entered with L.H.A. Aries to determine the column to be used; each column refers to a range of 10°. a_0 is taken, with mental interpolation, from the upper table with the units of L.H.A. Aries in degrees as argument; a_1, a_2 are taken, without interpolation, from the second and third tables with arguments latitude and month respectively. a_0, a_1, a_2 are always positive. The final table gives the azimuth of *Polaris*.

ILLUSTRATION

On 1974 January 22 at G.M.T. 23ʰ 13ᵐ 48ˢ in longitude W. 37° 14′ the corrected sextant altitude of *Polaris* was 49° 31′·6.

From the daily pages:		
G.H.A. Aries (23ʰ)	106	54·5
Increment (13ᵐ 48ˢ)	3	27·6
Longitude (west)	37	14
L.H.A. Aries	73	08

Corr. Sext. Alt.	49 31·6
a_0 (argument 73 08′)	0 20·7
a_1 (lat. 50 approx.)	0·6
a_2 (January)	0·8
Sum − 1° Lat.	48 53·7

TABLE 8-1 Altitude correction tables for Polaris from the Nautical Almanac.

sample problem from the *Almanac* is reprinted at the bottom of Table 8-1.

To obtain a latitude by Polaris make the usual corrections to sextant altitude to obtain Ho. Determine GHAΥ from the almanac for the time of the observation and apply your best estimate of longitude to obtain LHAΥ in degrees and minutes of arc. This value of LHAΥ is then used as the entering argument in the Polaris tables, which are located on the last white pages of the almanac. The corrections thus obtained when applied to Ho produce latitude.

Chapter 9

The Complete Celestial Solution

The following examples include a three-star fix, a sun line, and a single LOP calculated from the observation of a planet. It is suggested that the student work through these problems to determine how each of the entries in the sight reduction form was obtained. In each case, the sextant used had an IC of +0.2, and the height of eye of the observer was 11 feet. Observations were made on November 4. In working these three problems, refer to Table 3-1 (the daily pages from the *Nautical Almanac*), Tables 3-2 and 9-1 (the necessary "Increments and Corrections" pages from the *Almanac*), Table 5-1 (the "Altitude Correction Table" from the *Almanac*), and Tables 6-1, 9-2, and 9-3 (the appropriate main tables and interpolation tables from H.O. 229).

Various types of sight reduction forms are printed and sold by different companies. Once "what is being solved" is learned, the exact arrangement of the form is unimportant. The forms used in this text were designed by the author and contain all data in a single vertical column. The data can therefore be copied in the margin of a notebook, and several columns used opposite each entry. This permits a permanent record of your navigation if desired.

56^m	SUN PLANETS	ARIES	MOON	v or Corr^n d		v or Corr^n d		v or Corr^n d	
s	° ′	° ′	° ′	′	′	′	′	′	′
00	14 00·0	14 02·3	13 21·7	0·0	0·0	6·0	5·7	12·0	11·3
01	14 00·3	14 02·6	13 22·0	0·1	0·1	6·1	5·7	12·1	11·4
02	14 00·5	14 02·8	13 22·2	0·2	0·2	6·2	5·8	12·2	11·5
03	14 00·8	14 03·1	13 22·4	0·3	0·3	6·3	5·9	12·3	11·6
04	14 01·0	14 03·3	13 22·7	0·4	0·4	6·4	6·0	12·4	11·7
05	14 01·3	14 03·6	13 22·9	0·5	0·5	6·5	6·1	12·5	11·8
06	14 01·5	14 03·8	13 23·2	0·6	0·6	6·6	6·2	12·6	11·9
07	14 01·8	14 04·1	13 23·4	0·7	0·7	6·7	6·3	12·7	12·0
08	14 02·0	14 04·3	13 23·6	0·8	0·8	6·8	6·4	12·8	12·1
09	14 02·3	14 04·6	13 23·9	0·9	0·8	6·9	6·5	12·9	12·1
10	14 02·5	14 04·8	13 24·1	1·0	0·9	7·0	6·6	13·0	12·2
11	14 02·8	14 05·1	13 24·4	1·1	1·0	7·1	6·7	13·1	12·3
12	14 03·0	14 05·3	13 24·6	1·2	1·1	7·2	6·8	13·2	12·4
13	14 03·3	14 05·6	13 24·8	1·3	1·2	7·3	6·9	13·3	12·5
14	14 03·5	14 05·8	13 25·1	1·4	1·3	7·4	7·0	13·4	12·6
15	14 03·8	14 06·1	13 25·3	1·5	1·4	7·5	7·1	13·5	12·7
16	14 04·0	14 06·3	13 25·6	1·6	1·5	7·6	7·2	13·6	12·8
17	14 04·3	14 06·6	13 25·8	1·7	1·6	7·7	7·3	13·7	12·9
18	14 04·5	14 06·8	13 26·0	1·8	1·7	7·8	7·3	13·8	13·0
19	14 04·8	14 07·1	13 26·3	1·9	1·8	7·9	7·4	13·9	13·1
20	14 05·0	14 07·3	13 26·5	2·0	1·9	8·0	7·5	14·0	13·2
21	14 05·3	14 07·6	13 26·7	2·1	2·0	8·1	7·6	14·1	13·3
22	14 05·5	14 07·8	13 27·0	2·2	2·1	8·2	7·7	14·2	13·4
23	14 05·8	14 08·1	13 27·2	2·3	2·2	8·3	7·8	14·3	13·5
24	14 06·0	14 08·3	13 27·5	2·4	2·3	8·4	7·9	14·4	13·6
25	14 06·3	14 08·6	13 27·7	2·5	2·4	8·5	8·0	14·5	13·7
26	14 06·5	14 08·8	13 27·9	2·6	2·4	8·6	8·1	14·6	13·7
27	14 06·8	14 09·1	13 28·2	2·7	2·5	8·7	8·2	14·7	13·8
28	14 07·0	14 09·3	13 28·4	2·8	2·6	8·8	8·3	14·8	13·9
29	14 07·3	14 09·6	13 28·7	2·9	2·7	8·9	8·4	14·9	14·0
30	14 07·5	14 09·8	13 28·9	3·0	2·8	9·0	8·5	15·0	14·1
31	14 07·8	14 10·1	13 29·1	3·1	2·9	9·1	8·6	15·1	14·2
32	14 08·0	14 10·3	13 29·4	3·2	3·0	9·2	8·7	15·2	14·3
33	14 08·3	14 10·6	13 29·6	3·3	3·1	9·3	8·8	15·3	14·4
34	14 08·5	14 10·8	13 29·8	3·4	3·2	9·4	8·9	15·4	14·5
35	14 08·8	14 11·1	13 30·1	3·5	3·3	9·5	8·9	15·5	14·6
36	14 09·0	14 11·3	13 30·3	3·6	3·4	9·6	9·0	15·6	14·7
37	14 09·3	14 11·6	13 30·6	3·7	3·5	9·7	9·1	15·7	14·8
38	14 09·5	14 11·8	13 30·8	3·8	3·6	9·8	9·2	15·8	14·9
39	14 09·8	14 12·1	13 31·0	3·9	3·7	9·9	9·3	15·9	15·0
40	14 10·0	14 12·3	13 31·3	4·0	3·8	10·0	9·4	16·0	15·1
41	14 10·3	14 12·6	13 31·5	4·1	3·9	10·1	9·5	16·1	15·2
42	14 10·5	14 12·8	13 31·8	4·2	4·0	10·2	9·6	16·2	15·3
43	14 10·8	14 13·1	13 32·0	4·3	4·0	10·3	9·7	16·3	15·3
44	14 11·0	14 13·3	13 32·2	4·4	4·1	10·4	9·8	16·4	15·4
45	14 11·3	14 13·6	13 32·5	4·5	4·2	10·5	9·9	16·5	15·5
46	14 11·5	14 13·8	13 32·7	4·6	4·3	10·6	10·0	16·6	15·6
47	14 11·8	14 14·1	13 32·9	4·7	4·4	10·7	10·1	16·7	15·7
48	14 12·0	14 14·3	13 33·2	4·8	4·5	10·8	10·2	16·8	15·8
49	14 12·3	14 14·6	13 33·4	4·9	4·6	10·9	10·3	16·9	15·9
50	14 12·5	14 14·8	13 33·7	5·0	4·7	11·0	10·4	17·0	16·0
51	14 12·8	14 15·1	13 33·9	5·1	4·8	11·1	10·5	17·1	16·1
52	14 13·0	14 15·3	13 34·1	5·2	4·9	11·2	10·5	17·2	16·2
53	14 13·3	14 15·6	13 34·4	5·3	5·0	11·3	10·6	17·3	16·3
54	14 13·5	14 15·8	13 34·6	5·4	5·1	11·4	10·7	17·4	16·4
55	14 13·8	14 16·1	13 34·9	5·5	5·2	11·5	10·8	17·5	16·5
56	14 14·0	14 16·3	13 35·1	5·6	5·3	11·6	10·9	17·6	16·6
57	14 14·3	14 16·6	13 35·3	5·7	5·4	11·7	11·0	17·7	16·7
58	14 14·5	14 16·8	13 35·6	5·8	5·5	11·8	11·1	17·8	16·8
59	14 14·8	14 17·1	13 35·8	5·9	5·6	11·9	11·2	17·9	16·9
60	14 15·0	14 17·3	13 36·1	6·0	5·7	12·0	11·3	18·0	17·0

57^m	SUN PLANETS	ARIES	MOON	v or Corr^n d		v or Corr^n d		v or Corr^n d	
s	° ′	° ′	° ′	′	′	′	′	′	′
00	14 15·0	14 17·3	13 36·1	0·0	0·0	6·0	5·8	12·0	11·5
01	14 15·3	14 17·6	13 36·3	0·1	0·1	6·1	5·8	12·1	11·6
02	14 15·5	14 17·8	13 36·5	0·2	0·2	6·2	5·9	12·2	11·7
03	14 15·8	14 18·1	13 36·8	0·3	0·3	6·3	6·0	12·3	11·8
04	14 16·0	14 18·3	13 37·0	0·4	0·4	6·4	6·1	12·4	11·9
05	14 16·3	14 18·6	13 37·2	0·5	0·5	6·5	6·2	12·5	12·0
06	14 16·5	14 18·8	13 37·5	0·6	0·6	6·6	6·3	12·6	12·1
07	14 16·8	14 19·1	13 37·7	0·7	0·7	6·7	6·4	12·7	12·2
08	14 17·0	14 19·3	13 38·0	0·8	0·8	6·8	6·5	12·8	12·3
09	14 17·3	14 19·6	13 38·2	0·9	0·9	6·9	6·6	12·9	12·4
10	14 17·5	14 19·8	13 38·4	1·0	1·0	7·0	6·7	13·0	12·5
11	14 17·8	14 20·1	13 38·7	1·1	1·1	7·1	6·8	13·1	12·6
12	14 18·0	14 20·3	13 38·9	1·2	1·2	7·2	6·9	13·2	12·7
13	14 18·3	14 20·6	13 39·2	1·3	1·2	7·3	7·0	13·3	12·7
14	14 18·5	14 20·9	13 39·4	1·4	1·3	7·4	7·1	13·4	12·8
15	14 18·8	14 21·1	13 39·6	1·5	1·4	7·5	7·2	13·5	12·9
16	14 19·0	14 21·4	13 39·9	1·6	1·5	7·6	7·3	13·6	13·0
17	14 19·3	14 21·6	13 40·1	1·7	1·6	7·7	7·4	13·7	13·1
18	14 19·5	14 21·9	13 40·3	1·8	1·7	7·8	7·5	13·8	13·2
19	14 19·8	14 22·1	13 40·6	1·9	1·8	7·9	7·6	13·9	13·3
20	14 20·0	14 22·4	13 40·8	2·0	1·9	8·0	7·7	14·0	13·4
21	14 20·3	14 22·6	13 41·1	2·1	2·0	8·1	7·8	14·1	13·5
22	14 20·5	14 22·9	13 41·3	2·2	2·1	8·2	7·9	14·2	13·6
23	14 20·8	14 23·1	13 41·5	2·3	2·2	8·3	8·0	14·3	13·7
24	14 21·0	14 23·4	13 41·8	2·4	2·3	8·4	8·1	14·4	13·8
25	14 21·3	14 23·6	13 42·0	2·5	2·4	8·5	8·1	14·5	13·9
26	14 21·5	14 23·9	13 42·3	2·6	2·5	8·6	8·2	14·6	14·0
27	14 21·8	14 24·1	13 42·5	2·7	2·6	8·7	8·3	14·7	14·1
28	14 22·0	14 24·4	13 42·7	2·8	2·7	8·8	8·4	14·8	14·2
29	14 22·3	14 24·6	13 43·0	2·9	2·8	8·9	8·5	14·9	14·3
30	14 22·5	14 24·9	13 43·2	3·0	2·9	9·0	8·6	15·0	14·4
31	14 22·8	14 25·1	13 43·4	3·1	3·0	9·1	8·7	15·1	14·5
32	14 23·0	14 25·4	13 43·7	3·2	3·1	9·2	8·8	15·2	14·6
33	14 23·3	14 25·6	13 43·9	3·3	3·2	9·3	8·9	15·3	14·7
34	14 23·5	14 25·9	13 44·2	3·4	3·3	9·4	9·0	15·4	14·8
35	14 23·8	14 26·1	13 44·4	3·5	3·4	9·5	9·1	15·5	14·9
36	14 24·0	14 26·4	13 44·6	3·6	3·5	9·6	9·2	15·6	15·0
37	14 24·3	14 26·6	13 44·9	3·7	3·5	9·7	9·3	15·7	15·0
38	14 24·5	14 26·9	13 45·1	3·8	3·6	9·8	9·4	15·8	15·1
39	14 24·8	14 27·1	13 45·4	3·9	3·7	9·9	9·5	15·9	15·2
40	14 25·0	14 27·4	13 45·6	4·0	3·8	10·0	9·6	16·0	15·3
41	14 25·3	14 27·6	13 45·8	4·1	3·9	10·1	9·7	16·1	15·4
42	14 25·5	14 27·9	13 46·1	4·2	4·0	10·2	9·8	16·2	15·5
43	14 25·8	14 28·1	13 46·3	4·3	4·1	10·3	9·9	16·3	15·6
44	14 26·0	14 28·4	13 46·5	4·4	4·2	10·4	10·0	16·4	15·7
45	14 26·3	14 28·6	13 46·8	4·5	4·3	10·5	10·1	16·5	15·8
46	14 26·5	14 28·9	13 47·0	4·6	4·4	10·6	10·2	16·6	15·9
47	14 26·8	14 29·1	13 47·3	4·7	4·5	10·7	10·3	16·7	16·0
48	14 27·0	14 29·4	13 47·5	4·8	4·6	10·8	10·4	16·8	16·1
49	14 27·3	14 29·6	13 47·7	4·9	4·7	10·9	10·4	16·9	16·2
50	14 27·5	14 29·9	13 48·0	5·0	4·8	11·0	10·5	17·0	16·3
51	14 27·8	14 30·1	13 48·2	5·1	4·9	11·1	10·6	17·1	16·4
52	14 28·0	14 30·4	13 48·5	5·2	5·0	11·2	10·7	17·2	16·5
53	14 28·3	14 30·6	13 48·7	5·3	5·1	11·3	10·8	17·3	16·6
54	14 28·5	14 30·9	13 48·9	5·4	5·2	11·4	10·9	17·4	16·7
55	14 28·8	14 31·1	13 49·2	5·5	5·3	11·5	11·0	17·5	16·8
56	14 29·0	14 31·4	13 49·4	5·6	5·4	11·6	11·1	17·6	16·9
57	14 29·3	14 31·6	13 49·7	5·7	5·5	11·7	11·2	17·7	17·0
58	14 29·5	14 31·9	13 49·9	5·8	5·6	11·8	11·3	17·8	17·1
59	14 29·8	14 32·1	13 50·1	5·9	5·7	11·9	11·4	17·9	17·2
60	14 30·0	14 32·4	13 50·4	6·0	5·8	12·0	11·5	18·0	17·3

TABLE 9-1   "Increments and Corrections" page from the Nautical Almanac.

N. Lat. {L.H.A. greater than 180°......Zn=Z; L.H.A. less than 180°............Zn=360°−Z}

Dec.	30° Hc	d	Z	31° Hc	d	Z	32° Hc	d	Z	33° Hc	d	Z
°	° ′	′	°	° ′	′	°	° ′	′	°	° ′	′	°
0	9 30.7	+30.3	95.6	9 24.8	+31.3	95.7	9 18.7	+32.2	95.9	9 12.5	+33.0	96.0
1	10 01.0	30.3	94.7	9 56.1	31.1	94.9	9 50.9	32.0	95.0	9 45.5	33.0	95.2
2	10 31.3	30.0	93.8	10 27.2	31.0	94.0	10 22.9	31.9	94.2	10 18.5	32.8	94.3
3	11 01.3	29.9	92.9	10 58.2	30.8	93.1	10 54.8	31.8	93.3	10 51.3	32.6	93.5
4	11 31.2	29.8	92.0	11 29.0	30.7	92.2	11 26.6	31.5	92.4	11 23.9	32.5	92.6
5	12 01.0	+29.6	91.1	11 59.7	+30.5	91.4	11 58.1	+31.5	91.6	11 56.4	+32.3	91.8
6	12 30.6	29.4	90.3	12 30.2	30.3	90.5	12 29.6	31.2	90.7	12 28.7	32.2	90.9
7	13 00.0	29.2	89.4	13 00.5	30.2	89.6	13 00.8	31.1	89.8	13 00.9	32.0	90.1
8	13 29.2	29.1	88.5	13 30.7	30.0	88.7	13 31.9	30.9	88.9	13 32.9	31.8	89.2
9	13 58.3	28.8	87.6	14 00.7	29.7	87.8	14 02.8	30.7	88.1	14 04.7	31.7	88.3
10	14 27.1	+28.6	86.7	14 30.4	+29.6	86.9	14 33.5	+30.5	87.2	14 36.4	+31.4	87.4
11	14 55.7	28.4	85.8	15 00.0	29.4	86.0	15 04.0	30.3	86.3	15 07.8	31.2	86.6
12	15 24.1	28.2	84.8	15 29.4	29.1	85.1	15 34.3	30.1	85.4	15 39.0	31.0	85.7
13	15 52.3	28.0	83.9	15 58.5	28.9	84.2	16 04.4	29.9	84.5	16 10.0	30.8	84.8
14	16 20.3	27.7	83.0	16 27.4	28.7	83.3	16 34.3	29.6	83.6	16 40.8	30.6	83.9
15	16 48.0	+27.4	82.1	16 56.1	+28.4	82.4	17 03.9	+29.4	82.7	17 11.4	+30.3	83.0
16	17 15.4	27.2	81.1	17 24.5	28.2	81.5	17 33.3	29.1	81.8	17 41.7	30.1	82.1
17	17 42.6	27.0	80.2	17 52.7	27.9	80.5	18 02.4	28.8	80.8	18 11.8	29.8	81.2
18	18 09.6	26.6	79.3	18 20.6	27.6	79.6	18 31.2	28.6	79.9	18 41.6	29.5	80.3
19	18 36.2	26.4	78.3	18 48.2	27.4	78.7	18 59.8	28.4	79.0	19 11.1	29.3	79.3
20	19 02.6	+26.1	77.4	19 15.6	+27.0	77.7	19 28.2	+28.0	78.1	19 40.4	+29.0	78.4
21	19 28.7	25.8	76.4	19 42.6	26.8	76.8	19 56.2	27.7	77.1	20 09.4	28.6	77.5
22	19 54.5	25.5	75.5	20 09.4	26.4	75.8	20 23.9	27.4	76.2	20 38.0	28.4	76.5
23	20 20.0	25.1	74.5	20 35.8	26.2	74.9	20 51.3	27.1	75.2	21 06.4	28.1	75.6
24	20 45.1	24.9	73.5	21 02.0	25.8	73.9	21 18.4	26.8	74.3	21 34.5	27.7	74.6
25	21 10.0	+24.5	72.6	21 27.8	+25.4	72.9	21 45.2	+26.4	73.3	22 02.2	+27.4	73.7
26	21 34.5	24.1	71.6	21 53.2	25.2	72.0	22 11.6	26.1	72.3	22 29.6	27.1	72.7
27	21 58.6	23.8	70.6	22 18.4	24.7	71.0	22 37.7	25.8	71.4	22 56.7	26.7	71.8
28	22 22.4	23.4	69.6	22 43.1	24.4	70.0	23 03.5	25.3	70.4	23 23.4	26.3	70.8
29	22 45.8	23.1	68.6	23 07.5	24.0	69.0	23 28.8	25.0	69.4	23 49.7	26.0	69.8
30	23 08.9	+22.6	67.6	23 31.5	+23.7	68.0	23 53.8	+24.6	68.4	24 15.7	+25.6	68.8
31	23 31.5	22.3	66.6	23 55.2	23.2	67.0	24 18.4	24.3	67.4	24 41.3	25.2	67.8
32	23 53.8	21.9	65.6	24 18.4	22.9	66.0	24 42.7	23.8	66.4	25 06.5	24.8	66.8
33	24 15.7	21.5	64.6	24 41.3	22.4	65.0	25 06.5	23.4	65.4	25 31.3	24.3	65.8
34	24 37.2	21.0	63.5	25 03.7	22.0	63.9	25 29.9	22.9	64.4	25 55.6	24.0	64.8
35	24 58.2	+20.6	62.5	25 25.7	+21.6	62.9	25 52.8	+22.6	63.3	26 19.6	+23.5	63.8
36	25 18.8	20.2	61.5	25 47.3	21.1	61.9	26 15.4	22.1	62.3	26 43.1	23.0	62.8
37	25 39.0	19.8	60.4	26 08.4	20.7	60.8	26 37.5	21.6	61.3	27 06.1	22.6	61.7
38	25 58.8	19.2	59.4	26 29.1	20.3	59.8	26 59.1	21.2	60.2	27 28.7	22.1	60.7
39	26 18.0	18.8	58.3	26 49.4	19.7	58.7	27 20.3	20.7	59.2	27 50.8	21.7	59.6
40	26 36.8	+18.4	57.3	27 09.1	+19.3	57.7	27 41.0	+20.2	58.1	28 12.5	+21.1	58.6
41	26 55.2	17.8	56.2	27 28.4	18.8	56.6	28 01.2	19.7	57.1	28 33.6	20.7	57.5
42	27 13.0	17.4	55.1	27 47.2	18.3	55.5	28 20.9	19.2	56.0	28 54.3	20.1	56.4
43	27 30.4	16.9	54.0	28 05.5	17.7	54.5	28 40.1	18.7	54.9	29 14.4	19.7	55.4
44	27 47.3	16.3	53.0	28 23.2	17.3	53.4	28 58.8	18.2	53.8	29 34.1	19.0	54.3
45	28 03.6	+15.8	51.9	28 40.5	+16.7	52.3	29 17.0	+17.6	52.7	29 53.1	+18.6	53.2
46	28 19.4	15.4	50.8	28 57.2	16.2	51.2	29 34.6	17.1	51.6	30 11.7	18.0	52.1
47	28 34.8	14.7	49.7	29 13.4	15.7	50.1	29 51.7	16.6	50.5	30 29.7	17.4	51.0
48	28 49.5	14.3	48.6	29 29.1	15.1	49.0	30 08.3	15.9	49.4	30 47.1	16.9	49.9
49	29 03.8	13.6	47.5	29 44.2	14.5	47.9	30 24.2	15.4	48.3	31 04.0	16.3	48.8
50	29 17.4	+13.2	46.3	29 58.7	+14.0	46.8	30 39.6	+14.9	47.2	31 20.3	+15.6	47.6
51	29 30.6	12.5	45.2	30 12.7	13.4	45.6	30 54.5	14.2	46.1	31 35.9	15.1	46.5
52	29 43.1	12.0	44.1	30 26.1	12.8	44.5	31 08.7	13.6	44.9	31 51.0	14.5	45.4
53	29 55.1	11.4	43.0	30 38.9	12.2	43.4	31 22.3	13.1	43.8	32 05.5	13.8	44.2
54	30 06.5	10.8	41.8	30 51.1	11.6	42.2	31 35.4	12.4	42.6	32 19.3	13.3	43.1
55	30 17.3	+10.2	40.7	31 02.7	+11.0	41.1	31 47.8	+11.8	41.5	32 32.6	+12.6	41.9
56	30 27.5	9.7	39.6	31 13.7	10.4	39.9	31 59.6	11.1	40.3	32 45.2	11.9	40.7
57	30 37.2	9.0	38.4	31 24.1	9.7	38.8	32 10.7	10.5	39.2	32 57.1	11.3	39.6
58	30 46.2	8.4	37.3	31 33.8	9.2	37.6	32 21.2	9.9	38.0	33 08.4	10.6	38.4
59	30 54.6	7.8	36.1	31 43.0	8.5	36.5	32 31.1	9.2	36.8	33 19.0	10.0	37.2
60	31 02.4	+7.2	34.9	31 51.5	+7.8	35.3	32 40.3	+8.6	35.7	33 29.0	+9.2	36.0
61	31 09.6	6.5	33.8	31 59.3	7.3	34.1	32 48.9	7.9	34.5	33 38.2	8.6	34.8
62	31 16.1	5.9	32.6	32 06.6	6.5	33.0	32 56.8	7.2	33.3	33 46.8	8.0	33.7
63	31 22.0	5.3	31.5	32 13.1	6.0	31.8	33 04.0	6.6	32.1	33 54.8	7.2	32.5
64	31 27.3	4.7	30.3	32 19.1	5.2	30.6	33 10.6	5.9	30.9	34 02.0	6.5	31.3
65	31 32.0	+4.0	29.1	32 24.3	+4.6	29.4	33 16.5	+5.2	29.7	34 08.5	+5.8	30.1
66	31 36.0	3.4	28.0	32 28.9	4.0	28.2	33 21.7	4.5	28.6	34 14.3	5.1	28.9
67	31 39.4	2.7	26.8	32 32.9	3.2	27.1	33 26.2	3.9	27.4	34 19.4	4.4	27.7
68	31 42.1	2.1	25.6	32 36.1	2.6	25.9	33 30.1	3.1	26.2	34 23.8	3.7	26.5
69	31 44.2	1.4	24.4	32 38.7	2.0	24.7	33 33.2	2.4	25.0	34 27.5	3.0	25.3
70	31 45.6	+0.8	23.3	32 40.7	+1.2	23.5	33 35.6	+1.8	23.8	34 30.5	+2.3	24.0
71	31 46.4	+0.1	22.1	32 41.9	+0.6	22.3	33 37.4	1.1	22.6	34 32.8	1.5	22.8
72	31 46.5	−0.5	20.9	32 42.5	0.0	21.1	33 38.5	+0.3	21.4	34 34.3	0.8	21.6
73	31 46.0	1.1	19.7	32 42.5	−0.8	19.9	33 38.8	−0.3	20.2	34 35.1	+0.1	20.4
74	31 44.9	1.8	18.6	32 41.7	1.4	18.8	33 38.5	1.0	19.0	34 35.2	−0.6	19.2
75	31 43.1	−2.5	17.4	32 40.3	−2.1	17.6	33 37.5	−1.8	17.8	34 34.6	−1.4	18.0
76	31 40.6	3.1	16.2	32 38.2	2.8	16.4	33 35.7	2.4	16.6	34 33.2	2.1	16.8
77	31 37.5	3.7	15.0	32 35.4	3.4	15.2	33 33.3	3.1	15.4	34 31.1	2.8	15.5
78	31 33.8	4.4	13.9	32 32.0	4.1	14.0	33 30.2	3.8	14.2	34 28.3	3.5	14.3
79	31 29.4	5.0	12.7	32 27.9	4.8	12.8	33 26.4	4.5	13.0	34 24.8	4.2	13.1
80	31 24.4	−5.7	11.5	32 23.1	−5.4	11.6	33 21.9	−5.2	11.8	34 20.6	−4.9	11.9
81	31 18.7	6.3	10.4	32 17.7	6.1	10.5	33 16.7	5.9	10.6	34 15.7	5.7	10.7
82	31 12.4	6.9	9.2	32 11.6	6.7	9.3	33 10.8	6.5	9.4	34 10.0	6.3	9.5
83	31 05.5	7.5	8.0	32 04.9	7.4	8.1	33 04.3	7.2	8.2	34 03.7	7.1	8.3
84	30 58.0	8.2	6.9	31 57.5	8.0	6.9	32 57.1	7.9	7.0	33 56.6	7.7	7.1
85	30 49.8	−8.7	5.7	31 49.5	−8.6	5.8	32 49.2	−8.5	5.8	33 48.9	−8.4	5.9
86	30 41.1	9.4	4.6	31 40.9	9.3	4.6	32 40.7	9.2	4.7	33 40.5	9.1	4.7
87	30 31.7	10.0	3.4	31 31.6	9.9	3.5	32 31.5	9.9	3.5	33 31.4	9.8	3.5
88	30 21.7	10.5	2.3	31 21.7	10.6	2.3	32 21.6	10.5	2.3	33 21.6	10.5	2.4
89	30 11.2	11.2	1.1	31 11.1	11.1	1.1	32 11.1	11.1	1.2	33 11.1	11.1	1.2
90	30 00.0	−11.7	0.0	31 00.0	−11.8	0.0	32 00.0	−11.8	0.0	33 00.0	−11.8	0.0

Dec.	34° Hc	d	Z	35° Hc	d	Z	36° Hc	d	Z	37° Hc	d	Z
°	° ′	′	°	° ′	′	°	° ′	′	°	° ′	′	°
0	9 06.1	+33.9	96.2	8 59.5	+34.8	96.4	8 52.8	+35.6	96.5	8 45.9	+36.5	96.7
1	9 40.0	33.8	95.4	9 34.3	34.7	95.5	9 28.4	35.6	95.7	9 22.4	36.4	95.9
2	10 13.8	33.7	94.5	10 09.0	34.5	94.7	10 04.0	35.4	94.9	9 58.8	36.2	95.1
3	10 47.5	33.5	93.7	10 43.5	34.4	93.9	10 39.4	35.3	94.1	10 35.0	36.2	94.3
4	11 21.0	33.4	92.8	11 17.9	34.3	93.0	11 14.7	35.1	93.2	11 11.2	36.0	93.4
5	11 54.4	+33.3	92.0	11 52.2	+34.1	92.2	11 49.8	+35.0	92.4	11 47.2	+35.8	92.6
6	12 27.7	33.0	91.1	12 26.3	34.0	91.4	12 24.8	34.8	91.6	12 23.0	35.7	91.8
7	13 00.7	32.9	90.3	13 00.3	33.8	90.5	12 59.6	34.7	90.7	12 58.7	35.6	91.0
8	13 33.6	32.8	89.4	13 34.1	33.6	89.7	13 34.3	34.5	89.9	13 34.3	35.4	90.2
9	14 06.4	32.5	88.6	14 07.7	33.5	88.8	14 08.8	34.4	89.1	14 09.7	35.2	89.3
10	14 38.9	+32.4	87.7	14 41.2	+33.2	88.0	14 43.2	+34.1	88.2	14 44.9	+35.0	88.5
11	15 11.3	32.1	86.8	15 14.4	33.1	87.1	15 17.3	34.0	87.4	15 19.9	34.9	87.6
12	15 43.4	31.9	85.9	15 47.5	32.8	86.2	15 51.3	33.7	86.5	15 54.8	34.6	86.8
13	16 15.3	31.8	85.1	16 20.3	32.7	85.4	16 25.0	33.6	85.7	16 29.4	34.5	85.9
14	16 47.1	31.4	84.2	16 53.0	32.4	84.5	16 58.6	33.3	84.8	17 03.9	34.2	85.1
15	17 18.5	+31.3	83.3	17 25.4	+32.2	83.6	17 31.9	+33.1	83.9	17 38.1	+34.0	84.2
16	17 49.8	31.0	82.4	17 57.6	31.9	82.7	18 05.0	32.9	83.0	18 12.1	33.8	83.4
17	18 20.8	30.8	81.5	18 29.5	31.7	81.8	18 37.9	32.6	82.2	18 45.9	33.5	82.5
18	18 51.6	30.4	80.6	19 01.2	31.4	80.9	19 10.5	32.3	81.3	19 19.4	33.3	81.6
19	19 22.0	30.3	79.7	19 32.6	31.2	80.0	19 42.8	32.1	80.4	19 52.7	33.0	80.7
20	19 52.3	+29.9	78.8	20 03.8	+30.8	79.1	20 14.9	+31.8	79.5	20 25.7	+32.7	79.8
21	20 22.2	29.6	77.8	20 34.6	30.6	78.2	20 46.7	31.5	78.6	20 58.4	32.5	78.9
22	20 51.8	29.4	76.9	21 05.2	30.3	77.3	21 18.2	31.3	77.7	21 30.9	32.1	78.0
23	21 21.2	29.0	76.0	21 35.5	30.0	76.4	21 49.5	30.9	76.7	22 03.0	31.9	77.1
24	21 50.2	28.7	75.0	22 05.5	29.6	75.4	22 20.4	30.6	75.8	22 34.9	31.5	76.2
25	22 18.9	+28.3	74.1	22 35.1	+29.3	74.5	22 51.0	+30.2	74.9	23 06.4	+31.2	75.3
26	22 47.2	28.1	73.1	23 04.4	29.0	73.5	23 21.2	30.0	73.9	23 37.6	30.9	74.4
27	23 15.3	27.6	72.2	23 33.4	28.7	72.6	23 51.2	29.6	73.0	24 08.5	30.5	73.4
28	23 42.9	27.3	71.2	24 02.1	28.2	71.6	24 20.8	29.2	72.0	24 39.0	30.2	72.5
29	24 10.2	27.0	70.2	24 30.3	27.9	70.7	24 50.0	28.8	71.1	25 09.2	29.8	71.5
30	24 37.2	+26.5	69.2	24 58.2	+27.5	69.7	25 18.8	+28.5	70.1	25 39.0	+29.4	70.6
31	25 03.7	26.2	68.3	25 25.7	27.1	68.7	25 47.3	28.1	69.1	26 08.4	29.1	69.6
32	25 29.9	25.7	67.3	25 52.8	26.8	67.7	26 15.4	27.7	68.2	26 37.5	28.6	68.6
33	25 55.6	25.4	66.3	26 19.6	26.3	66.7	26 43.1	27.2	67.2	27 06.1	28.2	67.6
34	26 21.0	24.9	65.3	26 45.9	25.8	65.7	27 10.3	26.8	66.2	27 34.3	27.8	66.6
35	26 45.9	+24.4	64.2	27 11.7	+25.4	64.7	27 37.1	+26.4	65.2	28 02.1	+27.4	65.6
36	27 10.3	24.0	63.2	27 37.1	25.0	63.7	28 03.5	26.0	64.1	28 29.5	26.9	64.6
37	27 34.3	23.6	62.2	28 02.1	24.5	62.6	28 29.5	25.4	63.1	28 56.4	26.4	63.6
38	27 57.9	23.1	61.1	28 26.6	24.1	61.6	28 54.9	25.0	62.1	29 22.8	25.9	62.6
39	28 21.0	22.6	60.1	28 50.7	23.5	60.6	29 19.9	24.5	61.1	29 48.7	25.5	61.5
40	28 43.6	+22.1	59.0	29 14.2	+23.1	59.5	29 44.4	+24.0	60.0	30 14.2	+25.0	60.5
41	29 05.7	21.6	58.0	29 37.3	22.5	58.5	30 08.4	23.5	58.9	30 39.2	24.4	59.4
42	29 27.3	21.0	56.9	29 59.8	22.0	57.4	30 31.9	23.0	57.9	31 03.6	23.9	58.4
43	29 48.3	20.6	55.8	30 21.8	21.5	56.3	30 54.9	22.4	56.8	31 27.5	23.4	57.3
44	30 08.9	20.0	54.7	30 43.3	21.0	55.2	31 17.3	21.9	55.7	31 50.9	22.8	56.2
45	30 28.9	+19.5	53.7	31 04.3	+20.4	54.1	31 39.2	+21.3	54.6	32 13.7	+22.3	55.1
46	30 48.4	18.9	52.6	31 24.7	19.8	53.0	32 00.5	20.8	53.5	32 36.0	21.7	54.0
47	31 07.3	18.3	51.4	31 44.5	19.2	51.9	32 21.3	20.1	52.4	32 57.7	21.0	52.9
48	31 25.6	17.8	50.3	32 03.7	18.7	50.8	32 41.4	19.6	51.3	33 18.7	20.5	51.8
49	31 43.4	17.1	49.2	32 22.4	18.0	49.7	33 01.0	18.9	50.2	33 39.2	19.9	50.7
50	32 00.5	+16.6	48.1	32 40.4	+17.5	48.6	33 19.9	+18.4	49.0	33 59.1	+19.2	49.5
51	32 17.1	15.9	46.9	32 57.9	16.8	47.4	33 38.3	17.7	47.9	34 18.3	18.6	48.4
52	32 33.0	15.3	45.8	33 14.7	16.2	46.3	33 56.0	17.0	46.8	34 36.9	17.9	47.3
53	32 48.3	14.7	44.7	33 30.9	15.5	45.1	34 13.0	16.4	45.6	34 54.8	17.3	46.1
54	33 03.0	14.1	43.5	33 46.4	14.9	44.0	34 29.4	15.7	44.4	35 12.1	16.6	44.9
55	33 17.1	+13.4	42.3	34 01.3	+14.2	42.8	34 45.1	+15.1	43.3	35 28.7	+15.8	43.7
56	33 30.5	12.7	41.2	34 15.5	13.5	41.6	35 00.2	14.3	42.1	35 44.5	15.2	42.6
57	33 43.2	12.1	40.0	34 29.0	12.9	40.4	35 14.5	13.7	40.9	35 59.7	14.5	41.4
58	33 55.3	11.3	38.8	34 41.9	12.1	39.2	35 28.2	12.9	39.7	36 14.2	13.7	40.2
59	34 06.6	10.7	37.6	34 54.0	11.5	38.1	35 41.1	12.3	38.5	36 27.9	13.1	39.0
60	34 17.3	+10.1	36.4	35 05.5	+10.7	36.9	35 53.4	+11.5	37.3	36 41.0	+12.2	37.7
61	34 27.4	9.3	35.3	35 16.2	10.1	35.7	36 04.9	10.7	36.1	36 53.2	11.5	36.5
62	34 36.7	8.6	34.1	35 26.3	9.3	34.4	36 15.6	10.0	34.9	37 04.7	10.8	35.3
63	34 45.3	7.9	32.8	35 35.6	8.5	33.2	36 25.6	9.3	33.6	37 15.5	9.9	34.1
64	34 53.2	7.1	31.6	35 44.1	7.9	32.0	36 34.9	8.5	32.4	37 25.4	9.2	32.8
65	35 00.3	+6.5	30.4	35 52.0	+7.1	30.8	36 43.4	+7.7	31.2	37 34.6	+8.4	31.6
66	35 06.8	5.7	29.2	35 59.1	6.3	29.6	36 51.1	7.0	29.9	37 43.0	7.6	30.3
67	35 12.5	5.0	28.0	36 05.4	5.6	28.3	36 58.1	6.2	28.7	37 50.6	6.9	29.1
68	35 17.5	4.2	26.8	36 11.0	4.8	27.1	37 04.3	5.4	27.4	37 57.5	6.0	27.8
69	35 21.7	3.5	25.6	36 15.8	4.0	25.9	37 09.7	4.6	26.2	38 03.5	5.1	26.5
70	35 25.2	+2.8	24.3	36 19.8	+3.3	24.6	37 14.3	+3.8	24.9	38 08.6	+4.4	25.3
71	35 28.0	2.0	23.1	36 23.1	2.5	23.4	37 18.1	3.1	23.7	38 13.0	3.6	24.0
72	35 30.0	1.3	21.9	36 25.6	1.8	22.1	37 21.2	2.2	22.4	38 16.6	2.7	22.7
73	35 31.3	+0.5	20.6	36 27.4	1.0	20.9	37 23.4	1.4	21.2	38 19.3	1.9	21.5
74	35 31.8	−0.2	19.4	36 28.4	+0.2	19.7	37 24.8	+0.6	19.9	38 21.2	1.1	20.2
75	35 31.6	−1.0	18.2	36 28.6	0.6	18.4	37 25.4	−0.1	18.7	38 22.3	+0.2	18.9
76	35 30.6	1.7	17.0	36 28.0	1.4	17.2	37 25.3	1.0	17.4	38 22.5	−0.6	17.6
77	35 28.9	2.4	15.7	36 26.6	2.1	15.9	37 24.3	1.8	16.1	38 21.9	1.4	16.4
78	35 26.5	3.3	14.5	36 24.5	2.9	14.7	37 22.5	2.5	14.9	38 20.5	2.3	15.1
79	35 23.2	3.9	13.3	36 21.6	3.6	13.4	37 20.0	3.4	13.6	38 18.2	3.0	13.8
80	35 19.3	−4.7	12.1	36 18.0	4.5	12.2	37 16.6	4.2	12.4	38 15.2	−3.9	12.5
81	35 14.6	5.4	10.8	36 13.5	5.2	11.0	37 12.4	4.9	11.1	38 11.3	4.7	11.3
82	35 09.2	6.1	9.6	36 08.3	5.9	9.7	37 07.5	5.8	9.9	38 06.6	5.6	10.0
83	35 03.1	6.9	8.4	36 02.4	6.7	8.5	37 01.7	6.5	8.6	38 01.0	6.3	8.7
84	34 56.2	7.6	7.2	35 55.7	7.5	7.3	36 55.2	7.3	7.4	37 54.7	7.1	7.5
85	34 48.6	−8.3	6.0	35 48.2	−8.1	6.1	36 47.9	−8.1	6.1	37 47.6	−8.0	6.2
86	34 40.3	9.1	4.8	35 40.1	9.0	4.8	36 39.8	8.8	4.9	37 39.6	8.7	5.0
87	34 31.2	9.7	3.6	35 31.1	9.6	3.6	36 31.0	9.6	3.7	37 30.9	9.5	3.7
88	34 21.5	10.4	2.4	35 21.5	10.4	2.4	36 21.4	10.3	2.4	37 21.4	10.3	2.5
89	34 11.1	11.1	1.2	35 11.1	11.1	1.2	36 11.1	11.1	1.2	37 11.1	11.1	1.2
90	34 00.0	−11.8	0.0	35 00.0	11.8	0.0	36 00.0	11.8	0.0	37 00.0	11.8	0.0

79°, 281° L.H.A. LATITUDE SAME NAME AS DECLINATION

TABLE 9-2 Sight reduction tables from H.O. 229. (This page and following three pages.)

LATITUDE CONTRARY NAME TO DECLINATION — L.H.A. 35°, 325°

Dec.	30°			31°			32°			33°			34°			35°			36°			37°			Dec.
	Hc	d	Z	Hc	d	Z	Hc	d	Z	Hc	d	Z	Hc	d	Z	Hc	d	Z	Hc	d	Z	Hc	d	Z	
°	° ′	′	°	° ′	′	°	° ′	′	°	° ′	′	°	° ′	′	°	° ′	′	°	° ′	′	°	° ′	′	°	°
0	45 11.2	-42.8	125.5	44 36.0	-43.7	126.3	44 00.1	-44.4	127.1	43 23.6	-45.2	127.9	42 46.4	-45.9	128.6	42 08.7	-46.6	129.3	41 30.4	-47.3	130.0	40 51.6	-47.9	130.7	0
1	44 28.4	43.3	126.5	43 52.3	44.1	127.3	43 15.7	44.9	128.0	42 38.4	45.6	128.8	42 00.5	46.3	129.5	41 22.1	47.0	130.2	40 43.1	47.6	130.8	40 03.7	48.3	131.5	1
2	43 45.1	43.8	127.5	43 08.2	44.5	128.2	42 30.8	45.3	129.0	41 52.8	46.0	129.7	41 14.2	46.6	130.3	40 35.1	47.3	131.0	39 55.5	47.9	131.6	39 15.4	48.5	132.2	2
3	43 01.3	44.3	128.4	42 23.7	45.0	129.1	41 45.5	45.7	129.8	41 06.8	46.4	130.5	40 27.6	47.0	131.2	39 47.8	47.6	131.8	39 07.6	48.2	132.4	38 26.9	48.8	133.0	3
4	42 17.0	44.7	129.3	41 38.7	45.4	130.0	40 59.8	46.0	130.7	40 20.4	46.7	131.4	39 40.6	47.4	132.0	39 00.2	47.9	132.6	38 19.4	48.6	133.2	37 38.1	49.1	133.7	4
5	41 32.3	-45.0	130.2	40 53.3	-45.8	130.9	40 13.8	-46.5	131.5	39 33.7	-47.0	132.2	38 53.2	-47.6	132.8	38 12.3	-48.3	133.4	37 30.8	-48.7	133.9	36 49.0	-49.3	134.5	5
6	40 47.3	45.5	131.1	40 07.5	46.1	131.8	39 27.3	46.7	132.4	38 46.7	47.4	133.0	38 05.6	48.0	133.5	37 24.0	48.5	134.1	36 42.1	49.1	134.6	35 59.7	49.6	135.2	6
7	40 01.8	45.9	132.0	39 21.4	46.5	132.6	38 40.6	47.1	133.2	37 59.3	47.7	133.8	37 17.6	48.2	134.3	36 35.5	48.8	134.8	35 53.0	49.3	135.4	35 10.1	49.8	135.9	7
8	39 15.9	46.2	132.8	38 34.9	46.8	133.4	37 53.5	47.4	134.0	37 11.6	47.9	134.5	36 29.4	48.5	135.0	35 46.7	49.0	135.6	35 03.7	49.6	136.1	34 20.3	50.0	136.5	8
9	38 29.7	46.5	133.6	37 48.1	47.1	134.2	37 06.1	47.7	134.7	36 23.7	48.3	135.3	35 40.9	48.8	135.8	34 57.7	49.3	136.3	34 14.1	49.7	136.7	33 30.3	50.3	137.2	9
10	37 43.2	-46.8	134.4	37 01.0	-47.4	135.0	36 18.4	-40.0	135.5	35 35.4	-48.5	136.0	34 52.1	-49.0	136.5	34 08.4	-49.5	137.0	33 24.4	-50.0	137.4	32 40.0	-50.4	137.9	10
11	36 56.4	47.2	135.2	36 13.6	47.7	135.7	35 30.4	48.2	136.2	34 46.9	48.7	136.7	34 03.1	49.3	137.2	33 18.9	49.7	137.6	32 34.4	50.2	138.1	31 49.6	50.6	138.5	11
12	36 09.2	47.4	136.0	35 25.9	48.0	136.5	34 42.2	48.5	137.0	33 58.2	49.0	137.4	33 13.8	49.5	137.9	32 29.2	50.0	138.3	31 44.2	50.4	138.7	30 59.0	50.8	139.1	12
13	35 21.8	47.8	136.7	34 37.9	48.2	137.2	33 53.7	48.7	137.7	33 09.2	49.2	138.1	32 24.3	49.6	138.6	31 39.2	50.1	139.0	30 53.8	50.5	139.4	30 08.2	51.0	139.7	13
14	34 34.0	47.9	137.5	33 49.7	48.5	137.9	33 05.0	49.0	138.4	32 20.0	49.5	138.8	31 34.7	49.9	139.2	30 49.1	50.3	139.6	30 03.3	50.8	140.0	29 17.2	51.1	140.3	14
15	33 46.1	-48.3	138.2	33 01.2	-48.8	138.6	32 16.0	-49.2	139.1	31 30.5	-49.6	139.5	30 44.8	-50.1	139.9	29 58.8	-50.5	140.2	29 12.5	-50.9	140.6	28 26.1	-51.3	140.9	15
16	32 57.8	48.5	138.9	32 12.4	48.9	139.3	31 26.8	49.4	139.7	30 40.9	49.9	140.1	29 54.7	50.2	140.5	29 08.3	50.7	140.9	28 21.6	51.0	141.2	27 34.8	51.5	141.5	16
17	32 09.3	48.7	139.6	31 23.5	49.1	140.0	30 37.4	49.6	140.4	29 51.0	50.0	140.8	29 04.5	50.5	141.1	28 17.6	50.8	141.5	27 30.6	51.2	141.8	26 43.3	51.5	142.1	17
18	31 20.6	48.9	140.3	30 34.4	49.4	140.7	29 47.8	49.8	141.1	29 01.0	50.2	141.4	28 14.0	50.6	141.7	27 26.8	51.0	142.1	26 39.4	51.4	142.4	25 51.8	51.8	142.7	18
19	30 31.7	49.1	141.0	29 45.0	49.5	141.3	28 58.0	49.9	141.7	28 10.8	50.3	142.0	27 23.4	50.7	142.4	26 35.8	51.1	142.7	25 48.0	51.5	143.0	25 00.0	51.8	143.2	19
20	29 42.6	-49.3	141.6	28 55.5	-49.8	142.0	28 08.1	-50.2	142.3	27 20.5	-50.5	142.6	26 32.7	-50.9	143.0	25 44.7	-51.3	143.2	24 56.5	-51.6	143.5	24 08.2	-51.9	143.8	20
21	28 53.3	49.5	142.3	28 05.7	49.9	142.6	27 17.9	50.3	142.9	26 30.0	50.7	143.2	25 41.8	51.0	143.5	24 53.4	51.3	143.8	24 04.9	51.7	144.1	23 16.3	52.1	144.3	21
22	28 03.8	49.7	142.9	27 15.8	50.0	143.3	26 27.6	50.4	143.6	25 39.3	50.8	143.8	24 50.8	51.2	144.1	24 02.1	51.6	144.4	23 13.2	51.8	144.6	22 24.2	52.2	144.9	22
23	27 14.1	49.8	143.6	26 25.8	50.3	143.9	25 37.2	50.6	144.2	24 48.5	51.0	144.4	23 59.6	51.3	144.7	23 10.5	51.6	144.9	22 21.4	52.0	145.2	21 32.0	52.2	145.4	23
24	26 24.3	50.0	144.2	25 35.5	50.3	144.5	24 46.6	50.7	144.8	23 57.5	51.0	145.0	23 08.3	51.4	145.3	22 18.9	51.7	145.5	21 29.4	52.1	145.7	20 39.8	52.4	145.9	24
25	25 34.3	-50.2	144.8	24 45.2	-50.6	145.1	23 55.9	-50.9	145.3	23 06.5	-51.2	145.6	22 16.9	-51.5	145.8	21 27.2	-51.9	146.0	20 37.3	-52.1	146.3	19 47.4	-52.5	146.5	25
26	24 44.1	50.3	145.4	23 54.6	50.6	145.7	23 05.0	51.0	145.9	22 15.3	51.4	146.2	21 25.4	51.7	146.4	20 35.3	51.9	146.6	19 45.2	52.3	146.8	18 54.9	52.5	147.0	26
27	23 53.8	50.4	146.0	23 04.0	50.8	146.3	22 14.0	51.1	146.5	21 23.9	51.4	146.7	20 33.7	51.7	146.9	19 43.4	52.0	147.1	18 52.9	52.3	147.3	18 02.4	52.6	147.5	27
28	23 03.4	50.6	146.6	22 13.2	50.9	146.8	21 22.9	51.2	147.1	20 32.5	51.5	147.3	19 42.0	51.8	147.5	18 51.4	52.2	147.6	18 00.6	52.4	147.8	17 09.8	52.7	148.0	28
29	22 12.8	50.7	147.2	21 22.3	51.0	147.4	20 31.7	51.3	147.6	19 41.0	51.6	147.8	18 50.2	52.0	148.0	17 59.2	52.2	148.2	17 08.2	52.5	148.3	16 17.1	52.8	148.5	29
30	21 22.1	-50.8	147.8	20 31.3	-51.1	148.0	19 40.4	-51.4	148.2	18 49.4	-51.8	148.3	17 58.2	-52.0	148.5	17 07.0	-52.3	148.7	16 15.7	-52.5	148.8	15 24.3	-52.8	149.0	30
31	20 31.3	50.9	148.3	19 40.2	51.2	148.5	18 49.0	51.6	148.7	17 57.6	51.8	148.9	17 06.2	52.1	149.0	16 14.7	52.3	149.2	15 23.2	52.7	149.3	14 31.5	52.9	149.5	31
32	19 40.4	51.0	148.9	18 49.0	51.4	149.1	17 57.4	51.6	149.2	17 05.8	51.9	149.4	16 14.1	52.1	149.6	15 22.4	52.5	149.7	14 30.5	52.7	149.8	13 38.6	52.9	150.0	32
33	18 49.4	51.2	149.5	17 57.6	51.4	149.6	17 05.8	51.7	149.8	16 13.9	51.9	149.9	15 22.0	52.3	150.1	14 29.9	52.4	150.2	13 37.8	52.7	150.3	12 45.7	53.0	150.4	33
34	17 58.2	51.2	150.0	17 06.2	51.5	150.2	16 14.1	51.7	150.3	15 22.0	52.1	150.5	14 29.7	52.2	150.6	13 37.5	52.6	150.7	12 45.1	52.8	150.8	11 52.7	53.1	150.9	34
35	17 07.0	-51.3	150.6	16 14.7	-51.5	150.7	15 22.4	-51.9	150.8	14 29.9	-52.1	151.0	13 37.5	-52.4	151.1	12 44.9	-52.6	151.2	11 52.3	-52.9	151.3	10 59.6	-53.1	151.4	35
36	16 15.7	51.4	151.1	15 23.2	51.7	151.2	14 30.5	51.9	151.4	13 37.8	52.1	151.5	12 45.1	52.4	151.6	11 52.3	52.7	151.7	10 59.4	52.9	151.8	10 06.5	53.1	151.9	36
37	15 24.3	51.4	151.6	14 31.5	51.7	151.8	13 38.6	52.0	151.9	12 45.7	52.2	152.0	11 52.7	52.5	152.1	10 59.6	52.7	152.2	10 06.5	52.9	152.3	9 13.4	53.1	152.3	37
38	14 32.9	51.6	152.2	13 39.8	51.8	152.3	12 46.6	52.0	152.4	11 53.5	52.3	152.5	11 00.2	52.5	152.6	10 06.9	52.7	152.7	9 13.6	53.0	152.7	8 20.3	53.2	152.8	38
39	13 41.3	51.6	152.7	12 48.0	51.8	152.8	11 54.6	52.1	152.9	11 01.2	52.3	153.0	10 07.7	52.6	153.1	9 14.2	52.8	153.2	8 20.6	53.0	153.2	7 27.1	53.3	153.3	39
40	12 49.7	-51.6	153.2	11 56.2	-51.9	153.3	11 02.5	-52.1	153.4	10 08.9	-52.4	153.5	9 15.1	-52.6	153.6	8 21.4	-52.8	153.6	7 27.6	-53.0	153.7	6 33.8	-53.2	153.8	40
41	11 58.1	51.7	153.7	11 04.3	52.0	153.8	10 10.4	52.2	153.9	9 16.5	52.4	154.0	8 22.5	52.6	154.1	7 28.6	52.9	154.1	6 34.6	53.1	154.2	5 40.6	53.3	154.2	41
42	11 06.4	51.8	154.3	10 12.3	52.0	154.3	9 18.2	52.2	154.4	8 24.1	52.5	154.5	7 29.9	52.6	154.5	6 35.7	52.8	154.6	5 41.5	53.1	154.6	4 47.3	53.3	154.7	42
43	10 14.6	51.8	154.8	9 20.3	52.0	154.8	8 26.0	52.3	154.9	7 31.6	52.4	155.0	6 37.3	52.7	155.0	5 42.9	52.9	155.1	4 48.4	53.1	155.1	3 54.0	53.3	155.1	43
44	9 22.8	51.9	155.3	8 28.3	52.1	155.3	7 33.7	52.3	155.4	6 39.2	52.6	155.5	5 44.6	52.8	155.5	4 50.0	53.0	155.5	3 55.3	53.1	155.6	3 00.7	53.3	155.6	44
45	8 30.9	-51.9	155.8	7 36.2	-52.1	155.8	6 41.4	-52.3	155.9	5 46.6	-52.5	155.9	4 51.8	-52.7	156.0	3 57.0	-52.9	156.0	3 02.2	-53.1	156.0	2 07.4	-53.3	156.1	45
46	7 39.0	51.9	156.3	6 44.1	52.2	156.3	5 49.1	52.4	156.4	4 54.1	52.5	156.4	3 59.1	52.7	156.5	3 04.1	53.0	156.5	2 09.1	53.2	156.5	1 14.1	53.4	156.5	46
47	6 47.1	52.0	156.8	5 51.9	52.2	156.8	4 56.7	52.3	156.9	4 01.6	52.6	156.9	3 06.4	52.8	156.9	2 11.1	52.9	157.0	1 15.9	53.1	157.0	0 20.7	53.3	157.0	47
48	5 55.1	52.0	157.3	4 59.7	52.1	157.3	4 04.4	52.4	157.4	3 09.0	52.6	157.4	2 13.6	52.8	157.4	1 18.2	53.0	157.4	0 22.8	53.2	157.4	0 32.6	+53.3	22.6	48
49	5 03.1	52.0	157.8	4 07.6	52.3	157.8	3 12.0	52.4	157.9	2 16.4	52.6	157.9	1 20.8	52.8	157.9	0 25.2	52.9	157.9	0 30.4	+53.1	22.1	1 25.9	53.4	22.1	49
50	4 11.1	-52.0	158.3	3 15.3	-52.2	158.3	2 19.6	-52.4	158.3	1 23.8	-52.6	158.4	0 28.0	-52.7	158.4	0 27.7	+53.0	21.6	1 23.5	+53.1	21.6	2 19.3	+53.3	21.7	50
51	3 19.1	52.1	158.8	2 23.1	52.2	158.8	1 27.2	52.5	158.8	0 31.2	-52.6	158.8	0 24.7	+52.8	21.2	1 20.7	53.0	21.2	2 16.6	53.2	21.2	3 12.6	53.3	21.2	51
52	2 27.0	52.1	159.3	1 30.9	52.3	159.3	0 34.7	-52.4	159.3	0 21.4	+52.6	20.7	1 17.5	52.8	20.7	2 13.7	52.9	20.7	3 09.8	53.1	20.7	4 05.9	53.3	20.7	52
53	1 34.9	52.0	159.8	0 38.6	-52.2	159.8	0 17.7	+52.4	20.2	1 14.0	52.6	20.2	2 10.3	52.8	20.2	3 06.6	52.9	20.2	4 02.9	53.1	20.2	4 59.2	53.3	20.3	53
54	0 42.9	-52.1	160.3	0 13.6	+52.3	19.7	1 10.1	52.4	19.7	2 06.6	52.6	19.7	3 03.1	52.7	19.7	3 59.5	53.0	19.8	4 56.0	53.1	19.8	5 52.5	53.2	19.8	54
55	0 09.2	+52.1	19.2	1 05.9	+52.2	19.2	2 02.5	+52.4	19.2	2 59.2	+52.5	19.2	3 55.8	+52.8	19.3	4 52.5	+52.9	19.3	5 49.1	+53.1	19.3	6 45.7	+53.2	19.3	55
56	1 01.3	52.0	18.7	1 58.1	52.2	18.7	2 54.9	52.4	18.7	3 51.7	52.6	18.8	4 48.6	52.7	18.8	5 45.4	52.8	18.8	6 42.2	53.0	18.8	7 38.9	53.2	18.9	56
57	1 53.3	52.1	18.2	2 50.3	52.3	18.2	3 47.3	52.4	18.2	4 44.3	52.5	18.3	5 41.3	52.7	18.3	6 38.2	52.9	18.3	7 35.2	53.0	18.4	8 32.1	53.2	18.4	57
58	2 45.4	52.1	17.7	3 42.6	52.2	17.7	4 39.7	52.4	17.8	5 36.8	52.6	17.8	6 34.0	52.6	17.8	7 31.1	52.8	17.9	8 28.2	53.0	17.9	9 25.3	53.1	17.9	58
59	3 37.5	52.0	17.2	4 34.8	52.1	17.2	5 32.1	52.3	17.3	6 29.4	52.4	17.3	7 26.6	52.7	17.3	8 23.9	52.8	17.4	9 21.2	52.9	17.4	10 18.4	53.1	17.5	59
60	4 29.5	+52.0	16.7	5 26.9	+52.2	16.7	6 24.4	+52.3	16.8	7 21.8	+52.5	16.8	8 19.3	+52.6	16.8	9 16.7	+52.7	16.9	10 14.1	+52.9	16.9	11 11.5	+53.0	17.0	60
61	5 21.5	52.0	16.2	6 19.1	52.1	16.2	7 16.7	52.3	16.3	8 14.3	52.4	16.3	9 11.9	52.5	16.4	10 09.4	52.7	16.4	11 07.0	52.8	16.5	12 04.5	53.0	16.5	61
62	6 13.5	51.9	15.7	7 11.2	52.1	15.7	8 09.0	52.2	15.8	9 06.7	52.4	15.8	10 04.4	52.5	15.9	11 02.1	52.7	15.9	11 59.8	52.8	16.0	12 57.5	52.9	16.0	62
63	7 05.4	52.0	15.2	8 03.3	52.1	15.2	9 01.2	52.2	15.3	9 59.1	52.3	15.3	10 56.9	52.5	15.4	11 54.8	52.6	15.4	12 52.6	52.8	15.5	13 50.4	52.9	15.6	63
64	7 57.4	51.9	14.7	8 55.4	52.0	14.7	9 53.4	52.2	14.8	10 51.4	52.3	14.8	11 49.4	52.4	14.9	12 47.4	52.5	14.9	13 45.4	52.6	15.0	14 43.3	52.8	15.1	64
65	8 49.3	+51.8	14.2	9 47.4	+52.0	14.2	10 45.6	+52.1	14.3	11 43.7	+52.2	14.3	12 41.8	+52.4	14.4	13 39.9	+52.5	14.4	14 38.0	+52.7	14.5	15 36.1	+52.8	14.6	65
66	9 41.1	51.8	13.7	10 39.4	51.9	13.7	11 37.7	52.0	13.8	12 35.9	52.2	13.8	13 34.2	52.3	13.9	14 32.4	52.5	13.9	15 30.7	52.5	14.0	16 28.9	52.6	14.1	66
67	10 32.9	51.8	13.2	11 31.3	51.9	13.2	12 29.7	52.0	13.3	13 28.1	52.1	13.3	14 26.5	52.2	13.4	15 24.9	52.3	13.4	16 23.2	52.5	13.5	17 21.5	52.6	13.6	67
68	11 24.7	51.7	12.7	12 23.2	51.8	12.7	13 21.7	51.9	12.8	14 20.2	52.1	12.8	15 18.7	52.2	12.9	16 17.2	52.3	12.9	17 15.7	52.4	13.0	18 14.1	52.6	13.1	68
69	12 16.4	51.6	12.1	13 15.0	51.8	12.2	14 13.6	51.9	12.2	15 12.3	52.0	12.3	16 10.9	52.1	12.4	17 09.5	52.2	12.4	18 08.1	52.3	12.5	19 06.7	52.4	12.6	69
70	13 08.0	+51.6	11.6	14 06.8	+51.6	11.7	15 05.5	+51.8	11.7	16 04.3	+51.9	11.8	17 03.0	+52.0	11.8	18 01.7	+52.1	11.9	19 00.4	+52.2	12.0	19 59.1	+52.3	12.0	70
71	13 59.6	51.5	11.1	14 58.4	51.6	11.1	15 57.3	51.7	11.2	16 56.2	51.8	11.3	17 55.0	51.9	11.3	18 53.8	52.1	11.4	19 52.6	52.2	11.5	20 51.4	52.3	11.5	71
72	14 51.1	51.4	10.6	15 50.0	51.6	10.6	16 49.0	51.7	10.7	17 48.0	51.7	10.7	18 46.9	51.9	10.8	19 45.9	51.9	10.9	20 44.8	52.0	10.9	21 43.7	52.1	11.0	72
73	15 42.5	51.4	10.0	16 41.6	51.4	10.1	17 40.7	51.5	10.1	18 39.7	51.7	10.2	19 38.8	51.7	10.3	20 37.8	51.8	10.3	21 36.8	52.0	10.4	22 35.8	52.1	10.5	73
74	16 33.9	51.2	9.5	17 33.0	51.4	9.5	18 32.2	51.5	9.6	19 31.4	51.5	9.7	20 30.5	51.6	9.7	21 29.6	51.8	9.8	22 28.8	51.8	9.9	23 27.9	51.9	9.9	74
75	17 25.1	+51.2	9.0	18 24.4	+51.3	9.0	19 23.7	+51.3	9.1	20 22.9	+51.4	9.1	21 22.1	+51.6	9.2	22 21.4	+51.6	9.2	23 20.6	+51.7	9.3	24 19.8	+51.8	9.4	75
76	18 16.3	51.1	8.4	19 15.7	51.1	8.5	20 15.0	51.3	8.5	21 14.3	51.4	8.6	22 13.7	51.4	8.6	23 13.0	51.5	8.7	24 12.3	51.6	8.8	25 11.6	51.7	8.8	76
77	19 07.4	51.0	7.8	20 06.8	51.1	7.9	21 06.3	51.1	7.9	22 05.7	51.2	8.0	23 05.1	51.3	8.1	24 04.5	51.4	8.1	25 03.9	51.5	8.2	26 03.3	51.5	8.3	77
78	19 58.4	50.9	7.3	20 57.9	51.0	7.3	21 57.4	51.0	7.4	22 56.9	51.1	7.4	23 56.4	51.2	7.5	24 55.9	51.2	7.6	25 55.4	51.3	7.6	26 54.8	51.4	7.7	78
79	20 49.3	50.7	6.7	21 48.9	50.8	6.8	22 48.4	50.9	6.8	23 48.0	51.0	6.9	24 47.6	51.0	6.9	25 47.1	51.1	7.0	26 46.7	51.2	7.0	27 46.2	51.3	7.1	79
80	21 40.0	+50.7	6.2	22 39.7	+50.7	6.2	23 39.3	+50.8	6.2	24 39.0	+50.8	6.3	25 38.6	+50.9	6.3	26 38.2	+51.0	6.4	27 37.9	+51.0	6.5	28 37.5	+51.1	6.5	80
81	22 30.7	50.5	5.6	23 30.4	50.6	5.6	24 30.1	50.7	5.7	25 29.8	50.7	5.7	26 29.5	50.8	5.8	27 29.2	50.8	5.8	28 28.9	50.9	5.9	29 28.6	50.9	5.9	81
82	23 21.2	50.4	5.0	24 21.0	50.4	5.0	25 20.8	50.4	5.1	26 20.5	50.6	5.1	27 20.3	50.6	5.2	28 20.0	50.7	5.2	29 19.8	50.7	5.3	30 19.5	50.8	5.3	82
83	24 11.6	50.3	4.4	25 11.4	50.3	4.4	26 11.2	50.4	4.5	27 11.1	50.4	4.5	28 10.9	50.4	4.5	29 10.7	50.5	4.6	30 10.5	50.5	4.6	31 10.3	50.6	4.7	83
84	25 01.9	50.1	3.8	26 01.7	50.2	3.8	27 01.6	50.2	3.9	28 01.5	50.2	3.9	29 01.3	50.3	3.9	30 01.2	50.3	4.0	31 01.0	50.4	4.0	32 00.9	50.4	4.1	84
85	25 52.0	+49.9	3.2	26 51.9	+50.0	3.2	27 51.8	+50.0	3.2	28 51.7	+50.0	3.3	29 51.6	+50.1	3.3	30 51.5	+50.1	3.3	31 51.4	+50.1	3.4	32 51.3	+50.2	3.4	85
86	26 41.9	49.8	2.6	27 41.9	49.8	2.6	28 41.8	49.8	2.6	29 41.7	49.9	2.6	30 41.7	49.9	2.7	31 41.6	49.9	2.7	32 41.5	50.0	2.7	33 41.5	49.9	2.8	86
87	27 31.7	49.6	1.9	28 31.7	49.6	2.0	29 31.6	49.7	2.0	30 31.6	49.7	2.0	31 31.6	49.7	2.0	32 31.5	49.7	2.0	33 31.5	49.7	2.1	34 31.4	49.8	2.1	87
88	28 21.3	49.5	1.3	29 21.3	49.4	1.3	30 21.3	49.4	1.3	31 21.3	49.4	1.3	32 21.3	49.4	1.4	33 21.2	49.5	1.4	34 21.2	49.5	1.4	35 21.2	49.5	1.4	88
89	29 10.8	49.2	0.7	30 10.7	49.3	0.7	31 10.7	49.3	0.7	32 10.7	49.3	0.7	33 10.7	49.3	0.7	34 10.7	49.3	0.7	35 10.7	49.3	0.7	36 10.7	49.3	0.7	89
90	30 00.0	+49.0	0.0	31 00.0	+49.0	0.0	32 00.0	+49.0	0.0	33 00.0	+49.0	0.0	34 00.0	+49.0	0.0	35 00.0	+49.0	0.0	36 00.0	+49.0	0.0	37 00.0	+49.0	0.0	90
	30°			31°			32°			33°			34°			35°			36°			37°			

S. Lat. { L.H.A. greater than 180°......Zn=180°−Z
L.H.A. less than 180°............Zn=180°+Z

LATITUDE SAME NAME AS DECLINATION — L.H.A. 145°, 215°

Dec.	38°			39°			40°			41°			42°			43°			44°			45°			Dec.
	Hc	d	Z	Hc	d	Z	Hc	d	Z	Hc	d	Z	Hc	d	Z	Hc	d	Z	Hc	d	Z	Hc	d	Z	
°	° ′	′	°	° ′	′	°	° ′	′	°	° ′	′	°	° ′	′	°	° ′	′	°	° ′	′	°	° ′	′	°	°
0	31 07.8	-43.3	118.2	30 39.2	-44.0	118.7	30 10.2	-44.7	119.2	29 40.7	-45.4	119.7	29 10.8	-46.1	120.2	28 40.4	-46.8	120.7	28 09.6	-47.4	121.1	27 38.4	-48.0	121.6	0
1	30 24.5	43.6	119.0	29 55.2	44.3	119.5	29 25.5	45.0	120.0	28 55.3	45.7	120.4	28 24.7	46.4	120.9	27 53.6	46.9	121.4	27 22.2	47.6	121.8	26 50.4	48.2	122.3	1
2	29 40.9	43.9	119.8	29 10.9	44.6	120.2	28 40.5	45.3	120.7	28 09.6	45.9	121.2	27 38.3	46.5	121.6	27 06.7	47.2	122.1	26 34.6	47.8	122.5	26 02.2	48.4	122.9	2
3	28 57.0	44.1	120.5	28 26.3	44.8	121.0	27 55.2	45.5	121.5	27 23.7	46.1	121.9	26 51.8	46.8	122.3	26 19.5	47.4	122.8	25 46.8	47.9	123.2	25 13.8	48.5	123.6	3
4	28 12.9	44.4	121.3	27 41.5	45.1	121.8	27 09.7	45.7	122.2	26 37.6	46.4	122.6	26 05.0	46.9	123.0	25 32.1	47.5	123.4	24 58.9	48.2	123.8	24 25.3	48.7	124.2	4
5	27 28.5	-44.7	122.1	26 56.4	-45.3	122.5	26 24.0	-45.9	122.9	25 51.2	-46.5	123.3	25 18.1	-47.2	123.7	24 44.6	-47.8	124.1	24 10.7	-48.3	124.5	23 36.6	-48.8	124.9	5
6	26 43.8	44.8	122.8	26 11.1	45.5	123.2	25 38.1	46.2	123.6	25 04.7	46.8	124.0	24 30.9	47.3	124.4	23 56.8	47.9	124.8	23 22.4	48.4	125.1	22 47.8	49.0	125.5	6
7	25 59.0	45.1	123.6	25 25.6	45.7	124.0	24 51.9	46.3	124.3	24 17.9	46.9	124.7	23 43.6	47.5	125.1	23 08.9	48.0	125.4	22 34.0	48.6	125.8	21 58.8	49.2	126.1	7
8	25 13.9	45.4	124.3	24 39.9	45.9	124.7	24 05.6	46.5	125.0	23 31.0	47.1	125.4	22 56.1	47.7	125.8	22 20.9	48.3	126.1	21 45.4	48.8	126.4	21 09.6	49.3	126.7	8
9	24 28.5	45.5	125.0	23 54.0	46.2	125.4	23 19.1	46.7	125.7	22 43.9	47.3	126.1	22 08.4	47.8	126.4	21 32.6	48.3	126.7	20 56.6	48.9	127.0	20 20.3	49.3	127.3	9
10	23 43.0	-45.7	125.7	23 07.8	-46.3	126.1	22 32.4	-46.9	126.4	21 56.6	-47.4	126.7	21 20.6	-48.0	127.1	20 44.3	-48.5	127.4	20 07.7	-49.0	127.7	19 31.0	-49.6	128.0	10
11	22 57.3	45.9	126.4	22 21.5	46.4	126.8	21 45.5	47.1	127.1	21 09.2	47.6	127.4	20 32.6	48.1	127.7	19 55.8	48.7	128.0	19 18.7	49.1	128.3	18 41.4	49.6	128.5	11
12	22 11.4	46.1	127.1	21 35.1	46.7	127.4	20 58.4	47.1	127.8	20 21.6	47.7	128.1	19 44.5	48.3	128.3	19 07.1	48.7	128.6	18 29.6	49.3	128.9	17 51.8	49.7	129.1	12
13	21 25.3	46.2	127.8	20 48.4	46.8	128.1	20 11.3	47.4	128.4	19 33.9	47.9	128.7	18 56.2	48.4	129.0	18 18.4	48.9	129.2	17 40.3	49.3	129.5	17 02.1	49.9	129.7	13
14	20 39.1	46.4	128.5	20 01.6	46.9	128.8	19 23.9	47.5	129.1	18 46.0	48.0	129.3	18 07.8	48.4	129.6	17 29.5	49.0	129.8	16 51.0	49.5	130.1	16 12.2	49.9	130.3	14
15	19 52.7	-46.6	129.2	19 14.7	-47.1	129.5	18 36.4	-47.6	129.7	17 58.0	-48.1	130.0	17 19.4	-48.7	130.2	16 40.5	-49.1	130.4	16 01.5	-49.6	130.7	15 22.3	-50.0	130.9	15
16	19 06.1	46.7	129.8	18 27.6	47.2	130.1	17 48.8	47.7	130.4	17 09.9	48.2	130.6	16 30.7	48.7	130.8	15 51.4	49.2	131.0	15 11.9	49.6	131.3	14 32.3	50.1	131.5	16
17	18 19.4	46.8	130.5	17 40.4	47.4	130.8	17 01.1	47.8	131.0	16 21.7	48.4	131.2	15 42.0	48.8	131.4	15 02.2	49.2	131.6	14 22.3	49.7	131.8	13 42.2	50.2	132.0	17
18	17 32.6	47.0	131.2	16 53.0	47.4	131.4	16 13.3	48.0	131.6	15 33.3	48.4	131.8	14 53.2	48.9	132.0	14 13.0	49.4	132.2	13 32.6	49.8	132.4	12 52.0	50.2	132.6	18
19	16 45.6	47.0	131.8	16 05.6	47.6	132.0	15 25.3	48.1	132.2	14 44.9	48.6	132.4	14 04.3	49.0	132.6	13 23.6	49.5	132.8	12 42.8	49.9	133.0	12 01.8	50.3	133.1	19
20	15 58.6	-47.2	132.5	15 18.0	-47.7	132.7	14 37.2	-48.1	132.9	13 56.3	-48.6	133.1	13 15.3	-49.1	133.2	12 34.1	-49.5	133.4	11 52.9	-50.0	133.6	11 11.5	-50.4	133.7	20
21	15 11.4	47.3	133.1	14 30.3	47.8	133.3	13 49.1	48.3	133.5	13 07.7	48.7	133.7	12 26.2	49.1	133.8	11 44.6	49.6	134.0	11 02.9	50.0	134.1	10 21.1	50.4	134.3	21
22	14 24.1	47.4	133.7	13 42.5	47.9	133.9	13 00.8	48.3	134.1	12 19.0	48.8	134.3	11 37.1	49.2	134.4	10 55.0	49.6	134.5	10 12.9	50.1	134.7	9 30.7	50.5	134.8	22
23	13 36.7	47.6	134.4	12 54.6	47.9	134.5	12 12.5	48.4	134.7	11 30.2	48.8	134.9	10 47.9	49.3	135.0	10 05.4	49.7	135.1	9 22.8	50.1	135.2	8 40.2	50.6	135.4	23
24	12 49.1	47.5	135.0	12 06.7	48.1	135.2	11 24.1	48.5	135.3	10 41.4	49.0	135.4	9 58.6	49.4	135.6	9 15.7	49.8	135.7	8 32.7	50.2	135.8	7 49.6	50.5	135.9	24
25	12 01.6	-47.7	135.6	11 18.6	-48.1	135.8	10 35.6	-48.6	135.9	9 52.4	-48.9	136.0	9 09.2	-49.4	136.1	8 25.9	-49.8	136.3	7 42.5	-50.2	136.4	6 59.1	-50.6	136.4	25
26	11 13.9	47.8	136.2	10 30.5	48.2	136.4	9 47.0	48.6	136.5	9 03.5	49.1	136.6	8 19.8	49.4	136.7	7 36.1	49.9	136.8	6 52.3	50.2	136.9	6 08.5	50.7	137.0	26
27	10 26.1	47.8	136.9	9 42.3	48.2	137.0	8 58.4	48.7	137.1	8 14.4	49.1	137.2	7 30.4	49.5	137.3	6 46.2	49.9	137.4	6 02.1	50.3	137.5	5 17.8	50.6	137.5	27
28	9 38.3	47.9	137.5	8 54.1	48.4	137.6	8 09.7	48.7	137.7	7 25.3	49.1	137.8	6 40.9	49.6	137.9	5 56.3	49.9	137.9	5 11.8	50.3	138.0	4 27.2	50.7	138.1	28
29	8 50.4	47.9	138.1	8 05.7	48.3	138.2	7 21.0	48.8	138.3	6 36.2	49.2	138.4	5 51.3	49.6	138.4	5 06.4	49.9	138.5	4 21.5	50.4	138.5	3 36.5	50.7	138.6	29
30	8 02.5	-48.0	138.7	7 17.4	-48.4	138.8	6 32.2	-48.8	138.9	5 47.0	-49.2	138.9	5 01.7	-49.6	139.0	4 16.5	-50.0	139.0	3 31.1	-50.3	139.1	2 45.8	-50.8	139.1	30
31	7 14.5	48.1	139.3	6 29.0	48.5	139.4	5 43.4	48.8	139.4	4 57.8	49.2	139.5	4 12.1	49.6	139.6	3 26.5	50.0	139.6	2 40.8	50.4	139.6	1 55.0	50.7	139.7	31
32	6 26.4	48.0	139.9	5 40.5	48.5	140.0	4 54.6	48.9	140.0	4 08.6	49.3	140.1	3 22.5	49.6	140.1	2 36.5	50.0	140.2	1 50.4	50.4	140.2	1 04.3	50.7	140.2	32
33	5 38.4	48.2	140.5	4 52.0	48.5	140.6	4 05.7	48.9	140.6	3 19.3	49.3	140.7	2 32.9	49.7	140.7	1 46.5	50.1	140.7	1 00.0	50.4	140.7	0 13.6	-50.8	140.7	33
34	4 50.2	48.1	141.1	4 03.5	48.5	141.2	3 16.8	49.0	141.2	2 30.0	49.3	141.2	1 43.2	49.6	141.2	0 56.4	50.0	141.3	0 09.6	-50.4	141.3	0 37.2	+50.7	38.7	34
35	4 02.1	-48.2	141.7	3 15.0	-48.6	141.7	2 27.8	-48.9	141.8	1 40.7	-49.3	141.8	0 53.6	-49.7	141.8	0 06.4	-50.0	141.8	0 40.8	+50.3	38.2	1 27.9	+50.8	38.2	35
36	3 13.9	48.2	142.3	2 26.4	48.6	142.3	1 38.9	48.9	142.4	0 51.4	49.3	142.4	0 03.9	-49.7	142.4	0 43.6	+50.1	37.6	1 31.1	50.4	37.6	2 18.7	50.7	37.7	36
37	2 25.7	48.2	142.9	1 37.8	48.6	142.9	0 50.0	49.0	142.9	0 02.1	-49.3	142.9	0 45.8	+49.7	37.1	1 33.7	50.0	37.1	2 21.5	50.4	37.1	3 09.4	50.7	37.1	37
38	1 37.5	48.3	143.5	0 49.2	48.6	143.5	0 01.0	-49.0	143.5	0 47.2	+49.3	36.5	1 35.5	49.6	36.5	2 23.7	50.0	36.5	3 11.9	50.3	36.6	4 00.1	50.7	36.6	38
39	0 49.2	48.2	144.1	0 00.6	-48.6	144.1	0 48.0	+48.9	35.9	1 36.5	49.3	35.9	2 25.1	49.7	35.9	3 13.7	50.0	36.0	4 02.2	50.4	36.0	4 50.8	50.6	36.1	39
40	0 01.0	-48.2	144.7	0 48.0	+48.5	35.3	1 36.9	+48.9	35.3	2 25.8	+49.3	35.4	3 14.8	+49.6	35.4	4 03.7	+49.9	35.4	4 52.6	+50.3	35.5	5 41.4	+50.6	35.5	40
41	0 47.2	+48.3	34.7	1 36.5	48.6	34.7	2 25.8	49.0	34.8	3 15.1	49.3	34.8	4 04.4	49.6	34.8	4 53.6	50.0	34.9	5 42.9	50.2	34.9	6 32.0	50.6	35.0	41
42	1 35.5	48.2	34.1	2 25.1	48.6	34.1	3 14.8	48.9	34.2	4 04.4	49.2	34.2	4 54.0	49.6	34.3	5 43.6	49.9	34.3	6 33.1	50.3	34.4	7 22.6	50.6	34.4	42
43	2 23.7	48.2	33.5	3 13.7	48.5	33.6	4 03.7	48.9	33.6	4 53.6	49.3	33.6	5 43.6	49.5	33.7	6 33.5	49.9	33.8	7 23.4	50.1	33.8	8 13.2	50.5	33.9	43
44	3 11.9	48.2	32.9	4 02.2	48.6	33.0	4 52.6	48.8	33.0	5 42.9	49.1	33.1	6 33.1	49.5	33.1	7 23.4	49.8	33.2	8 13.5	50.2	33.3	9 03.7	50.4	33.4	44
45	4 00.1	+48.1	32.3	4 50.8	+48.4	32.4	5 41.4	+48.8	32.4	6 32.0	+49.2	32.5	7 22.6	+49.5	32.6	8 13.2	+49.8	32.6	9 03.7	+50.1	32.7	9 54.1	+50.4	32.8	45
46	4 48.2	48.2	31.7	5 39.2	48.5	31.8	6 30.2	48.8	31.8	7 21.2	49.1	31.9	8 12.1	49.4	32.0	9 03.0	49.7	32.1	9 53.8	50.0	32.2	10 44.5	50.4	32.3	46
47	5 36.4	48.0	31.1	6 27.7	48.4	31.2	7 19.0	48.7	31.3	8 10.3	49.0	31.3	9 01.5	49.4	31.4	9 52.7	49.7	31.5	10 43.8	50.0	31.6	11 34.9	50.3	31.7	47
48	6 24.4	48.1	30.5	7 16.1	48.4	30.6	8 07.7	48.7	30.7	8 59.3	49.0	30.7	9 50.9	49.3	30.8	10 42.4	49.6	30.9	11 33.8	49.9	31.0	12 25.2	50.2	31.1	48
49	7 12.5	48.0	29.9	8 04.5	48.3	30.0	8 56.4	48.6	30.1	9 48.3	48.9	30.2	10 40.2	49.2	30.3	11 32.0	49.5	30.4	12 23.7	49.8	30.5	13 15.4	50.1	30.6	49
50	8 00.5	+47.9	29.3	8 52.8	+48.2	29.4	9 45.0	+48.6	29.5	10 37.2	+48.9	29.6	11 29.4	+49.2	29.7	12 21.5	+49.5	29.8	13 13.5	+49.8	29.9	14 05.5	+50.1	30.0	50
51	8 48.4	47.9	28.7	9 41.0	48.2	28.8	10 33.6	48.5	28.9	11 26.1	48.8	29.0	12 18.6	49.0	29.1	13 11.0	49.4	29.2	14 03.3	49.7	29.3	14 55.6	50.0	29.4	51
52	9 36.3	47.8	28.1	10 29.2	48.1	28.2	11 22.1	48.4	28.3	12 14.9	48.7	28.4	13 07.6	49.1	28.5	14 00.4	49.3	28.6	14 53.0	49.6	28.7	15 45.6	49.9	28.9	52
53	10 24.1	47.8	27.5	11 17.3	48.1	27.6	12 10.5	48.3	27.7	13 03.6	48.6	27.8	13 56.7	48.9	27.9	14 49.7	49.2	28.0	15 42.6	49.5	28.2	16 35.5	49.7	28.3	53
54	11 11.9	47.7	26.9	12 05.4	48.0	27.0	12 58.8	48.3	27.1	13 52.2	48.6	27.2	14 45.6	48.8	27.3	15 38.9	49.1	27.4	16 32.1	49.4	27.6	17 25.2	49.7	27.7	54
55	11 59.6	+47.6	26.3	12 53.4	+47.8	26.4	13 47.1	+48.2	26.5	14 40.8	+48.4	26.6	15 34.4	+48.7	26.7	16 28.0	+49.0	26.8	17 21.5	+49.3	27.0	18 14.9	+49.6	27.1	55
56	12 47.2	47.5	25.6	13 41.2	47.8	25.7	14 35.3	48.0	25.9	15 29.2	48.4	26.0	16 23.1	48.7	26.1	17 17.0	48.9	26.2	18 10.8	49.2	26.[illegible]	19 04.5	49.5	26.5	56
57	13 34.7	47.4	25.0	14 29.0	47.7	25.1	15 23.3	48.0	25.2	16 17.6	48.2	25.4	17 11.8	48.5	25.5	18 05.9	48.8	25.6	19 00.0	49.0	25.8	19 54.0	49.3	25.9	57
58	14 22.1	47.3	24.4	15 16.7	47.6	24.5	16 11.3	47.8	24.6	17 05.8	48.1	24.7	18 00.3	48.4	24.9	18 54.7	48.7	25.0	19 49.0	49.0	25.2	20 43.3	49.2	25.3	58
59	15 09.4	47.2	23.7	16 04.3	47.5	23.9	16 59.1	47.8	24.0	17 53.9	48.0	24.1	18 48.7	48.2	24.2	19 43.4	48.5	24.4	20 38.0	48.8	24.5	21 32.5	49.1	24.7	59
60	15 56.6	+47.1	23.1	16 51.8	+47.3	23.2	17 46.9	+47.6	23.3	18 41.9	+47.9	23.5	19 36.9	+48.2	23.6	20 31.9	+48.4	23.8	21 26.8	+48.6	23.9	22 21.6	+48.9	24.1	60
61	16 43.7	47.0	22.5	17 39.1	47.2	22.6	18 34.5	47.5	22.7	19 29.8	47.8	22.8	20 25.1	48.0	23.0	21 20.3	48.2	23.1	22 15.4	48.6	23.3	23 10.5	48.8	23.5	61
62	17 30.7	46.8	21.8	18 26.3	47.1	21.9	19 22.0	47.3	22.1	20 17.6	47.6	22.2	21 13.1	47.8	22.3	22 08.5	48.2	22.5	23 04.0	48.3	22.7	23 59.3	48.6	22.8	62
63	18 17.5	46.7	21.2	19 13.4	47.0	21.3	20 09.3	47.2	21.4	21 05.2	47.4	21.5	22 00.9	47.7	21.7	22 56.7	47.9	21.8	23 52.3	48.2	22.0	24 47.9	48.5	22.2	63
64	19 04.2	46.6	20.5	20 00.4	46.8	20.6	20 56.5	47.1	20.7	21 52.6	47.3	20.9	22 48.6	47.6	21.0	23 44.6	47.8	21.2	24 40.5	48.0	21.4	25 36.4	48.2	21.5	64
65	19 50.8	+46.4	19.8	20 47.2	+46.6	19.9	21 43.6	+46.8	20.1	22 39.9	+47.1	20.2	23 36.2	+47.3	20.4	24 32.4	+47.6	20.5	25 28.5	+47.9	20.7	26 24.6	+48.1	20.9	65
66	20 37.2	46.2	19.1	21 33.8	46.5	19.3	22 30.4	46.8	19.4	23 27.0	47.0	19.5	24 23.5	47.2	19.7	25 20.0	47.4	19.9	26 16.4	47.6	20.0	27 12.7	47.9	20.2	66
67	21 23.4	46.1	18.5	22 20.3	46.3	18.6	23 17.2	46.5	18.7	24 14.0	46.7	18.9	25 10.7	47.0	19.0	26 07.4	47.2	19.2	27 04.0	47.5	19.3	28 00.6	47.7	19.5	67
68	22 09.5	45.9	17.8	23 06.6	46.1	17.9	24 03.7	46.3	18.0	25 00.7	46.6	18.2	25 57.7	46.8	18.3	26 54.6	47.0	18.5	27 51.5	47.3	18.6	28 48.3	47.5	18.8	68
69	22 55.4	45.7	17.1	23 52.7	46.0	17.2	24 50.0	46.2	17.3	25 47.3	46.4	17.5	26 44.5	46.6	17.6	27 41.6	46.9	17.8	28 38.8	47.0	17.9	29 35.8	47.3	18.1	69
70	23 41.1	+45.6	16.4	24 38.7	+45.7	16.5	25 36.2	+45.9	16.6	26 33.7	+46.1	16.8	27 31.1	+46.3	16.9	28 28.5	+46.5	17.1	29 25.8	+46.8	17.2	30 23.1	+47.0	17.4	70
71	24 26.7	45.3	15.7	25 24.4	45.5	15.8	26 22.1	45.8	15.9	27 19.8	45.9	16.1	28 17.4	46.2	16.2	29 15.0	46.4	16.4	30 12.6	46.5	16.5	31 10.1	46.8	16.7	71
72	25 12.0	45.1	14.9	26 09.9	45.3	15.1	27 07.9	45.5	15.2	28 05.7	45.7	15.3	29 03.6	45.9	15.5	30 01.4	46.1	15.6	30 59.1	46.4	15.8	31 56.9	46.5	16.0	72
73	25 57.1	44.9	14.2	26 55.2	45.1	14.3	27 53.4	45.2	14.5	28 51.4	45.5	14.6	29 49.5	45.6	14.7	30 47.5	45.8	14.9	31 45.5	46.0	15.0	32 43.4	46.2	15.2	73
74	26 42.0	44.6	13.5	27 40.3	44.8	13.6	28 38.6	45.0	13.7	29 36.9	45.2	13.8	30 35.1	45.4	14.0	31 33.3	45.6	14.1	32 31.5	45.8	14.3	33 29.6	46.0	14.4	74
75	27 26.6	+44.4	12.7	28 25.1	+44.6	12.8	29 23.6	+44.8	13.0	30 22.1	+44.9	13.1	31 20.5	+45.1	13.2	32 18.9	+45.3	13.4	33 17.3	+45.4	13.5	34 15.6	+45.6	13.7	75
76	28 11.0	44.2	12.0	29 09.7	44.3	12.1	30 08.4	44.5	12.2	31 07.0	44.7	12.3	32 05.6	44.8	12.4	33 04.2	45.0	12.6	34 02.7	45.2	12.7	35 01.2	45.4	12.9	76
77	28 55.2	43.9	11.2	29 54.0	44.1	11.3	30 52.9	44.2	11.4	31 51.7	44.3	11.5	32 50.4	44.6	11.7	33 49.2	44.7	11.8	34 47.9	44.9	11.9	35 46.6	45.0	12.1	77
78	29 39.1	43.6	10.4	30 38.1	43.7	10.5	31 37.1	43.9	10.6	32 36.0	44.1	10.7	33 35.0	44.2	10.9	34 33.9	44.3	11.0	35 32.8	44.5	11.1	36 31.6	44.7	11.3	78
79	30 22.7	43.3	9.6	31 21.8	43.5	9.7	32 21.0	43.6	9.8	33 20.1	43.7	9.9	34 19.2	43.9	10.0	35 18.2	44.1	10.2	36 17.3	44.2	10.3	37 16.3	44.3	10.4	79
80	31 06.0	+43.0	8.8	32 05.3	+43.1	8.9	33 04.6	+43.2	9.0	34 03.8	+43.4	9.1	35 03.1	+43.5	9.2	36 02.3	+43.6	9.3	37 01.5	+43.8	9.4	38 00.6	+44.0	9.6	80
81	31 49.0	42.7	8.0	32 48.4	42.8	8.1	33 47.8	43.0	8.2	34 47.2	43.1	8.3	35 46.6	43.2	8.4	36 45.9	43.3	8.5	37 45.3	43.4	8.6	38 44.6	43.5	8.7	81
82	32 31.7	42.4	7.2	33 31.2	42.5	7.2	34 30.8	42.5	7.3	35 30.3	42.6	7.4	36 29.8	42.7	7.5	37 29.2	42.9	7.6	38 28.7	43.0	7.7	39 28.1	43.2	7.8	82
83	33 14.1	42.0	6.3	34 13.7	42.1	6.4	35 13.3	42.2	6.5	36 12.9	42.3	6.5	37 12.5	42.4	6.6	38 12.1	42.5	6.7	39 11.7	42.6	6.8	40 11.3	42.7	6.9	83
84	33 56.1	41.6	5.5	34 55.8	41.7	5.5	35 55.5	41.8	5.6	36 55.2	41.9	5.7	37 54.9	42.0	5.7	38 54.6	42.1	5.8	39 54.3	42.2	5.9	40 54.0	42.3	6.0	84
85	34 37.7	+41.3	4.6	35 37.5	+41.4	4.6	36 37.3	+41.5	4.7	37 37.1	+41.5	4.8	38 36.9	+41.6	4.8	39 36.7	+41.6	4.9	40 36.5	+41.7	5.0	41 36.3	+41.8	5.0	85
86	35 19.0	40.9	3.7	36 18.9	40.9	3.7	37 18.8	41.0	3.8	38 18.6	41.1	3.8	39 18.5	41.1	3.9	40 18.3	41.2	4.0	41 18.2	41.2	4.0	42 18.1	41.2	4.1	86
87	35 59.9	40.5	2.8	36 59.8	40.5	2.8	37 59.8	40.5	2.9	38 59.7	40.6	2.9	39 59.6	40.6	3.0	40 59.5	40.7	3.0	41 59.4	40.8	3.0	42 59.3	40.8	3.1	87
88	36 40.4	40.0	1.9	37 40.3	40.1	1.9	38 40.3	40.1	1.9	39 40.3	40.1	2.0	40 40.2	40.2	2.0	41 40.2	40.2	2.0	42 40.2	40.2	2.1	43 40.1	40.2	2.1	88
89	37 20.4	39.6	0.9	38 20.4	39.6	1.0	39 20.4	39.6	1.0	40 20.4	39.6	1.0	41 20.4	39.6	1.0	42 20.4	39.6	1.0	43 20.4	39.6	1.0	44 20.3	39.7	1.1	89
90	38 00.0	+39.1	0.0	39 00.0	+39.1	0.0	40 00.0	+39.1	0.0	41 00.0	+39.1	0.0	42 00.0	+39.1	0.0	43 00.0	+39.1	0.0	44 00.0	+39.1	0.0	45 00.0	+39.1	0.0	90
	38°			39°			40°			41°			42°			43°			44°			45°			

S. Lat. { L.H.A. greater than 180°......Zn=180°−Z; L.H.A. less than 180°............Zn=180°+Z

LATITUDE CONTRARY NAME TO DECLINATION — L.H.A. 33°, 327°

Dec.	38° Hc	38° d	38° Z	39° Hc	39° d	39° Z	40° Hc	40° d	40° Z	41° Hc	41° d	41° Z	42° Hc	42° d	42° Z	43° Hc	43° d	43° Z	44° Hc	44° d	44° Z	45° Hc	45° d	45° Z	Dec.
°	° ′	′	°	° ′	′	°	° ′	′	°	° ′	′	°	° ′	′	°	° ′	′	°	° ′	′	°	° ′	′	°	°
0	41 22.0	−49.3	133.5	40 40.5	−49.9	134.1	39 58.5	−50.4	134.7	39 16.1	−51.0	135.3	38 33.2	−51.4	135.9	37 50.0	−51.9	136.4	37 06.3	−52.3	136.9	36 22.3	−52.7	137.4	0
1	40 32.7	49.7	134.2	39 50.6	50.2	134.8	39 08.1	50.7	135.4	38 25.1	51.2	136.0	37 41.8	51.7	136.5	36 58.1	52.1	137.0	36 14.0	52.5	137.5	35 29.6	53.0	138.0	1
2	39 43.0	49.9	135.0	39 00.4	50.4	135.5	38 17.4	51.0	136.1	37 33.9	51.4	136.6	36 50.1	51.8	137.2	36 06.0	52.3	137.7	35 21.5	52.7	138.1	34 36.6	53.1	138.6	2
3	38 53.1	50.2	135.7	38 10.0	50.7	136.2	37 26.4	51.1	136.8	36 42.5	51.6	137.3	35 58.3	52.1	137.8	35 13.7	52.5	138.3	34 28.8	52.9	138.7	33 43.5	53.2	139.2	3
4	38 02.9	50.4	136.4	37 19.3	50.9	136.9	36 35.3	51.4	137.4	35 50.9	51.8	137.9	35 06.2	52.2	138.4	34 21.2	52.6	138.8	33 35.9	53.0	139.3	32 50.3	53.4	139.7	4
5	37 12.5	−50.7	137.1	36 28.4	−51.2	137.6	35 43.9	−51.6	138.1	34 59.1	−52.0	138.5	34 14.0	−52.4	139.0	33 28.6	−52.8	139.4	32 42.9	−53.2	139.8	31 56.9	−53.6	140.3	5
6	36 21.8	50.9	137.7	35 37.2	51.3	138.2	34 52.3	51.7	138.7	34 07.1	52.1	139.1	33 21.6	52.6	139.6	32 35.8	53.0	140.0	31 49.7	53.3	140.4	31 03.3	53.6	140.8	6
7	35 30.9	51.0	138.4	34 45.9	51.5	138.8	34 00.6	51.9	139.3	33 15.0	52.4	139.7	32 29.0	52.7	140.1	31 42.8	53.1	140.5	30 56.4	53.5	140.9	30 09.7	53.8	141.3	7
8	34 39.9	51.3	139.0	33 54.4	51.7	139.5	33 08.7	52.2	139.9	32 22.6	52.5	140.3	31 36.3	52.9	140.7	30 49.7	53.2	141.1	30 02.9	53.5	141.5	29 15.9	53.9	141.8	8
9	33 48.6	51.5	139.7	33 02.7	51.9	140.1	32 16.5	52.2	140.5	31 30.1	52.6	140.9	30 43.4	53.0	141.3	29 56.5	53.3	141.6	29 09.4	53.7	142.0	28 22.0	54.0	142.3	9
10	32 57.1	−51.6	140.3	32 10.8	−52.0	140.7	31 24.3	−52.4	141.1	30 37.5	−52.8	141.4	29 50.4	−53.1	141.8	29 03.2	−53.5	142.2	28 15.7	−53.8	142.5	27 28.0	−54.1	142.8	10
11	32 05.5	51.9	140.9	31 18.8	52.2	141.3	30 31.9	52.6	141.6	29 44.7	52.9	142.0	28 57.3	53.2	142.3	28 09.7	53.6	142.7	27 21.9	53.9	143.0	26 33.9	54.2	143.3	11
12	31 13.6	51.9	141.5	30 26.6	52.4	141.8	29 39.3	52.7	142.2	28 51.8	53.1	142.5	28 04.1	53.4	142.9	27 16.1	53.7	143.2	26 28.0	54.0	143.5	25 39.7	54.3	143.8	12
13	30 21.7	52.2	142.0	29 34.2	52.4	142.4	28 46.6	52.8	142.7	27 58.7	53.1	143.1	27 10.7	53.5	143.4	26 22.4	53.8	143.7	25 34.0	54.1	144.0	24 45.4	54.4	144.2	13
14	29 29.5	52.2	142.6	28 41.8	52.7	143.0	27 53.8	53.0	143.3	27 05.6	53.3	143.6	26 17.2	53.6	143.9	25 28.6	53.8	144.2	24 39.9	54.2	144.4	23 51.0	54.4	144.7	14
15	28 37.3	−52.4	143.2	27 49.1	−52.7	143.5	27 00.8	−53.1	143.8	26 12.3	−53.4	144.1	25 23.6	−53.7	144.4	24 34.8	−54.0	144.7	23 45.7	−54.2	144.9	22 56.6	−54.6	145.2	15
16	27 44.9	52.6	143.7	26 56.4	52.9	144.0	26 07.7	53.1	144.3	25 18.9	53.5	144.6	24 29.9	53.8	144.9	23 40.8	54.1	145.1	22 51.5	54.4	145.4	22 02.0	54.6	145.6	16
17	26 52.3	52.6	144.3	26 03.5	52.9	144.6	25 14.6	53.3	144.8	24 25.4	53.6	145.1	23 36.1	53.8	145.4	22 46.7	54.2	145.6	21 57.1	54.4	145.8	21 07.4	54.7	146.1	17
18	25 59.7	52.8	144.8	25 10.6	53.1	145.1	24 21.3	53.4	145.3	23 31.8	53.6	145.6	22 42.3	54.0	145.8	21 52.5	54.2	146.1	21 02.7	54.5	146.3	20 12.7	54.7	146.5	18
19	25 06.9	52.9	145.3	24 17.5	53.2	145.6	23 27.9	53.5	145.8	22 38.2	53.8	146.1	21 48.3	54.0	146.3	20 58.3	54.3	146.5	20 08.2	54.6	146.7	19 18.0	54.8	146.9	19
20	24 14.0	−53.0	145.9	23 24.3	−53.3	146.1	22 34.4	−53.6	146.3	21 44.4	−53.8	146.6	20 54.3	−54.1	146.8	20 04.0	−54.4	147.0	19 13.6	−54.6	147.2	18 23.2	−54.9	147.4	20
21	23 21.0	53.1	146.4	22 31.0	53.4	146.6	21 40.8	53.6	146.8	20 50.6	54.0	147.0	20 00.2	54.2	147.2	19 09.6	54.4	147.4	18 19.0	54.7	147.6	17 28.3	54.9	147.8	21
22	22 27.9	53.1	146.9	21 37.6	53.4	147.1	20 47.2	53.7	147.3	19 56.6	54.0	147.5	19 06.0	54.3	147.7	18 15.2	54.5	147.9	17 24.3	54.7	148.0	16 33.4	55.0	148.2	22
23	21 34.8	53.3	147.4	20 44.2	53.6	147.6	19 53.5	53.9	147.8	19 02.6	54.0	148.0	18 11.7	54.3	148.1	17 20.7	54.5	148.3	16 29.6	54.8	148.5	15 38.4	55.0	148.6	23
24	20 41.5	53.4	147.9	19 50.6	53.6	148.1	18 59.6	53.8	148.3	18 08.6	54.2	148.4	17 17.4	54.4	148.6	16 26.2	54.7	148.8	15 34.8	54.8	148.9	14 43.4	55.1	149.0	24
25	19 48.1	−53.4	148.4	18 57.0	−53.7	148.5	18 05.8	−54.0	148.7	17 14.4	−54.1	148.9	16 23.0	−54.4	149.0	15 31.5	−54.6	149.2	14 40.0	−54.9	149.3	13 48.3	−55.1	149.4	25
26	18 54.7	53.5	148.8	18 03.3	53.8	149.0	17 11.8	54.0	149.2	16 20.3	54.3	149.3	15 28.6	54.5	149.5	14 36.9	54.7	149.6	13 45.1	54.9	149.7	12 53.2	55.1	149.9	26
27	18 01.2	53.6	149.3	17 09.5	53.8	149.5	16 17.8	54.0	149.6	15 26.0	54.3	149.8	14 34.1	54.5	149.9	13 42.2	54.8	150.0	12 50.2	55.0	150.2	11 58.1	55.2	150.3	27
28	17 07.6	53.6	149.8	16 15.7	53.9	149.9	15 23.8	54.2	150.1	14 31.7	54.3	150.2	13 39.6	54.6	150.3	12 47.4	54.7	150.5	11 55.2	55.0	150.6	11 02.9	55.2	150.7	28
29	16 14.0	53.7	150.3	15 21.8	53.9	150.4	14 29.6	54.1	150.5	13 37.4	54.4	150.7	12 45.0	54.6	150.8	11 52.7	54.9	150.9	11 00.2	55.0	151.0	10 07.7	55.2	151.1	29
30	15 20.3	−53.8	150.7	14 27.9	−54.0	150.8	13 35.5	−54.2	151.0	12 43.0	−54.5	151.1	11 50.4	−54.6	151.2	10 57.8	−54.8	151.3	10 05.2	−55.1	151.4	9 12.5	−55.3	151.5	30
31	14 26.5	53.8	151.2	13 33.9	54.0	151.3	12 41.3	54.3	151.4	11 48.5	54.4	151.5	10 55.8	54.7	151.6	10 03.0	54.9	151.7	9 10.1	55.1	151.8	8 17.2	55.2	151.9	31
32	13 32.7	53.9	151.6	12 39.9	54.1	151.7	11 47.0	54.3	151.8	10 54.1	54.5	151.9	10 01.1	54.7	152.0	9 08.1	54.9	152.1	8 15.0	55.1	152.2	7 22.0	55.3	152.2	32
33	12 38.8	53.9	152.1	11 45.8	54.1	152.2	10 52.7	54.3	152.3	9 59.6	54.6	152.4	9 06.4	54.8	152.4	8 13.2	55.0	152.5	7 19.9	55.1	152.6	6 26.7	55.4	152.6	33
34	11 44.9	53.9	152.5	10 51.7	54.2	152.6	9 58.4	54.4	152.7	9 05.0	54.5	152.8	8 11.6	54.7	152.9	7 18.2	54.9	152.9	6 24.8	55.1	153.0	5 31.3	55.3	153.0	34
35	10 51.0	−54.0	153.0	9 57.5	−54.2	153.1	9 04.0	−54.4	153.1	8 10.5	−54.6	153.2	7 16.9	−54.8	153.3	6 23.3	−55.0	153.3	5 29.7	−55.2	153.4	4 36.0	−55.3	153.4	35
36	9 57.0	54.0	153.4	9 03.3	54.2	153.5	8 09.6	54.4	153.6	7 15.9	54.7	153.6	6 22.1	54.8	153.7	5 28.3	55.0	153.7	4 34.5	55.2	153.8	3 40.7	55.4	153.8	36
37	9 03.0	54.1	153.9	8 09.1	54.3	153.9	7 15.2	54.5	154.0	6 21.2	54.6	154.0	5 27.3	54.8	154.1	4 33.3	55.0	154.1	3 39.3	55.2	154.2	2 45.3	55.4	154.2	37
38	8 08.9	54.1	154.3	7 14.8	54.2	154.4	6 20.7	54.4	154.4	5 26.6	54.6	154.5	4 32.5	54.9	154.5	3 38.3	55.0	154.5	2 44.1	55.2	154.6	1 49.9	55.3	154.6	38
39	7 14.8	54.1	154.7	6 20.6	54.3	154.8	5 26.3	54.5	154.8	4 32.0	54.7	154.9	3 37.6	54.8	154.9	2 43.3	55.0	154.9	1 48.9	55.2	154.9	0 54.6	−55.4	155.0	39
40	6 20.7	−54.1	155.2	5 26.3	−54.3	155.2	4 31.8	−54.5	155.3	3 37.3	−54.7	155.3	2 42.8	−54.9	155.3	1 48.3	−55.1	155.3	0 53.7	−55.2	155.3	0 00.8	+55.4	24.7	40
41	5 26.6	54.1	155.6	4 32.0	54.4	155.6	3 37.3	54.5	155.7	2 42.6	54.7	155.7	1 47.9	54.8	155.7	0 53.2	−55.0	155.7	0 01.5	+55.2	24.3	0 56.2	55.3	24.3	41
42	4 32.5	54.2	156.0	3 37.6	54.3	156.1	2 42.8	54.5	156.1	1 47.9	54.7	156.1	0 53.1	−54.9	156.1	0 01.8	+55.0	23.9	0 56.7	55.2	23.9	1 51.5	55.4	23.9	42
43	3 38.3	54.2	156.5	2 43.3	54.4	156.5	1 48.3	54.6	156.5	0 53.2	−54.7	156.5	0 01.8	+54.9	23.5	0 56.8	55.1	23.5	1 51.9	55.2	23.5	2 46.9	55.4	23.5	43
44	2 44.1	54.2	156.9	1 48.9	54.3	156.9	0 53.7	−54.5	156.9	0 01.5	+54.7	23.1	0 56.7	54.8	23.1	1 51.9	55.0	23.1	2 47.1	55.2	23.1	3 42.3	55.3	23.1	44
45	1 49.9	−54.1	157.3	0 54.6	−54.4	157.3	0 00.8	+54.5	22.7	0 56.2	+54.7	22.7	1 51.5	+54.9	22.7	2 46.9	+55.0	22.7	3 42.3	+55.1	22.7	4 37.6	+55.3	22.7	45
46	0 55.8	54.2	157.8	0 00.2	−54.3	157.8	0 55.3	54.6	22.2	1 50.9	54.7	22.2	2 46.4	54.8	22.3	3 41.9	55.0	22.3	4 37.4	55.2	22.3	5 32.9	55.4	22.3	46
47	0 01.6	−54.2	158.2	0 54.1	+54.4	21.8	1 49.9	54.5	21.8	2 45.6	54.6	21.8	3 41.2	54.9	21.9	4 36.9	55.0	21.9	5 32.6	55.1	21.9	6 28.3	55.3	22.0	47
48	0 52.6	+54.2	21.4	1 48.5	54.4	21.4	2 44.4	54.5	21.4	3 40.2	54.7	21.4	4 36.1	54.8	21.4	5 31.9	55.0	21.5	6 27.7	55.2	21.5	7 23.6	55.2	21.6	48
49	1 46.8	54.2	20.9	2 42.9	54.3	21.0	3 38.9	54.5	21.0	4 34.9	54.7	21.0	5 30.9	54.8	21.0	6 26.9	55.0	21.1	7 22.9	55.1	21.1	8 18.8	55.3	21.2	49
50	2 41.0	+54.2	20.5	3 37.2	+54.3	20.5	4 33.4	+54.5	20.6	5 29.6	+54.6	20.6	6 25.7	+54.8	20.6	7 21.9	+54.9	20.7	8 18.0	+55.1	20.7	9 14.1	+55.2	20.8	50
51	3 35.2	54.1	20.1	4 31.5	54.3	20.1	5 27.9	54.4	20.1	6 24.2	54.6	20.2	7 20.5	54.8	20.2	8 16.8	54.9	20.3	9 13.1	55.0	20.3	10 09.3	55.2	20.4	51
52	4 29.3	54.2	19.7	5 25.8	54.3	19.7	6 22.3	54.5	19.7	7 18.8	54.6	19.8	8 15.3	54.7	19.8	9 11.7	54.9	19.9	10 08.1	55.1	19.9	11 04.5	55.2	20.0	52
53	5 23.5	54.1	19.2	6 20.1	54.3	19.3	7 16.8	54.4	19.3	8 13.4	54.6	19.3	9 10.0	54.7	19.4	10 06.6	54.8	19.4	11 03.2	55.0	19.5	11 59.7	55.1	19.6	53
54	6 17.6	54.1	18.8	7 14.4	54.3	18.8	8 11.2	54.4	18.9	9 08.0	54.5	18.9	10 04.7	54.7	19.0	11 01.4	54.9	19.0	11 58.2	54.9	19.1	12 54.8	55.1	19.2	54
55	7 11.7	+54.1	18.4	8 08.7	+54.2	18.4	9 05.6	+54.4	18.4	10 02.5	+54.5	18.5	10 59.4	+54.6	18.6	11 56.3	+54.7	18.6	12 53.1	+54.9	18.7	13 49.9	+55.1	18.8	55
56	8 05.8	54.1	17.9	9 02.9	54.2	18.0	10 00.0	54.3	18.0	10 57.0	54.5	18.1	11 54.0	54.6	18.1	12 51.0	54.8	18.2	13 48.0	54.9	18.3	14 45.0	55.0	18.4	56
57	8 59.9	54.0	17.5	9 57.1	54.1	17.5	10 54.3	54.3	17.6	11 51.5	54.4	17.6	12 48.6	54.6	17.7	13 45.8	54.7	17.8	14 42.9	54.8	17.9	15 40.0	55.0	17.9	57
58	9 53.9	54.0	17.0	10 51.2	54.2	17.1	11 48.6	54.2	17.1	12 45.9	54.4	17.2	13 43.2	54.5	17.3	14 40.5	54.6	17.4	15 37.7	54.8	17.4	16 35.0	54.9	17.5	58
59	10 47.9	53.9	16.6	11 45.4	54.1	16.6	12 42.8	54.3	16.7	13 40.3	54.3	16.8	14 37.7	54.5	16.9	15 35.1	54.6	16.9	16 32.5	54.8	17.0	17 29.9	54.9	17.1	59
60	11 41.8	+53.9	16.1	12 39.5	+54.0	16.2	13 37.1	+54.1	16.3	14 34.6	+54.3	16.3	15 32.2	+54.4	16.4	16 29.7	+54.6	16.5	17 27.3	+54.6	16.6	18 24.8	+54.8	16.7	60
61	12 35.7	53.9	15.7	13 33.5	54.0	15.8	14 31.2	54.1	15.8	15 28.9	54.3	15.9	16 26.6	54.4	16.0	17 24.3	54.5	16.1	18 21.9	54.7	16.2	19 19.6	54.7	16.2	61
62	13 29.6	53.8	15.2	14 27.5	53.9	15.3	15 25.3	54.1	15.4	16 23.2	54.2	15.5	17 21.0	54.3	15.5	18 18.8	54.4	15.6	19 16.6	54.5	15.7	20 14.3	54.7	15.8	62
63	14 23.4	53.8	14.8	15 21.4	53.9	14.9	16 19.4	54.0	14.9	17 17.4	54.1	15.0	18 15.3	54.3	15.1	19 13.2	54.4	15.2	20 11.1	54.5	15.3	21 09.0	54.6	15.4	63
64	15 17.2	53.7	14.3	16 15.3	53.8	14.4	17 13.4	53.9	14.5	18 11.5	54.0	14.6	19 09.6	54.1	14.6	20 07.6	54.3	14.7	21 05.6	54.4	14.8	22 03.6	54.5	14.9	64
65	16 10.9	+53.6	13.9	17 09.1	+53.8	13.9	18 07.3	+53.9	14.0	19 05.5	+54.0	14.1	20 03.7	+54.1	14.2	21 01.9	+54.2	14.3	22 00.0	+54.4	14.4	22 58.1	+54.5	14.5	65
66	17 04.5	53.6	13.4	18 02.9	53.7	13.5	19 01.2	53.8	13.6	19 59.5	54.0	13.6	20 57.8	54.1	13.7	21 56.1	54.2	13.8	22 54.4	54.2	13.9	23 52.6	54.4	14.0	66
67	17 58.1	53.5	12.9	18 56.6	53.6	13.0	19 55.0	53.8	13.1	20 53.5	53.8	13.2	21 51.9	53.9	13.3	22 50.3	54.0	13.4	23 48.6	54.2	13.5	24 47.0	54.3	13.6	67
68	18 51.6	53.5	12.5	19 50.2	53.5	12.5	20 48.8	53.6	12.6	21 47.3	53.8	12.7	22 45.8	53.9	12.8	23 44.3	54.0	12.9	24 42.8	54.1	13.0	25 41.3	54.2	13.1	68
69	19 45.1	53.3	12.0	20 43.7	53.5	12.0	21 42.4	53.6	12.1	22 41.1	53.6	12.2	23 39.7	53.8	12.3	24 38.3	53.9	12.4	25 36.9	54.0	12.5	26 35.5	54.1	12.6	69
70	20 38.4	+53.3	11.5	21 37.2	+53.4	11.6	22 36.0	+53.5	11.6	23 34.7	+53.6	11.7	24 33.5	+53.7	11.8	25 32.2	+53.8	11.9	26 30.9	+53.9	12.0	27 29.6	+54.0	12.1	70
71	21 31.7	53.2	11.0	22 30.6	53.3	11.1	23 29.5	53.3	11.1	24 28.3	53.5	11.2	25 27.2	53.5	11.3	26 26.0	53.7	11.4	27 24.8	53.8	11.5	28 23.6	53.8	11.6	71
72	22 24.9	53.1	10.5	23 23.9	53.2	10.6	24 22.8	53.3	10.6	25 21.8	53.4	10.7	26 20.7	53.5	10.8	27 19.7	53.5	10.9	28 18.6	53.6	11.0	29 17.4	53.8	11.1	72
73	23 18.0	53.0	10.0	24 17.1	53.0	10.1	25 16.1	53.2	10.1	26 15.2	53.2	10.2	27 14.2	53.4	10.3	28 13.2	53.5	10.4	29 12.2	53.6	10.5	30 11.2	53.7	10.6	73
74	24 11.0	52.9	9.5	25 10.1	53.0	9.5	26 09.3	53.1	9.6	27 08.4	53.2	9.7	28 07.6	53.2	9.8	29 06.7	53.3	9.9	30 05.8	53.4	10.0	31 04.9	53.5	10.1	74
75	25 03.9	+52.7	9.0	26 03.1	+52.9	9.0	27 02.4	+52.9	9.1	28 01.6	+53.0	9.2	29 00.8	+53.2	9.3	30 00.0	+53.2	9.4	30 59.2	+53.3	9.5	31 58.4	+53.4	9.6	75
76	25 56.6	52.7	8.4	26 56.0	52.7	8.5	27 55.3	52.8	8.6	28 54.6	53.0	8.7	29 54.0	52.9	8.7	30 53.2	53.1	8.8	31 52.5	53.2	8.9	32 51.8	53.2	9.0	76
77	26 49.3	52.5	7.9	27 48.7	52.7	8.0	28 48.1	52.7	8.0	29 47.6	52.7	8.1	30 46.9	52.9	8.2	31 46.3	53.0	8.3	32 45.7	53.0	8.4	33 45.0	53.1	8.5	77
78	27 41.8	52.5	7.3	28 41.4	52.4	7.4	29 40.8	52.6	7.5	30 40.3	52.7	7.6	31 39.8	52.7	7.6	32 39.3	52.7	7.7	33 38.7	52.9	7.8	34 38.1	53.0	7.9	78
79	28 34.3	52.2	6.8	29 33.8	52.4	6.9	30 33.4	52.4	6.9	31 33.0	52.4	7.0	32 32.5	52.6	7.1	33 32.0	52.7	7.2	34 31.6	52.7	7.2	35 31.1	52.8	7.3	79
80	29 26.5	+52.2	6.2	30 26.2	+52.2	6.3	31 25.8	+52.3	6.4	32 25.4	+52.4	6.4	33 25.1	+52.4	6.5	34 24.7	+52.4	6.6	35 24.3	+52.5	6.7	36 23.9	+52.6	6.7	80
81	30 18.7	52.0	5.7	31 18.4	52.0	5.7	32 18.1	52.1	5.8	33 17.8	52.1	5.9	34 17.5	52.2	5.9	35 17.1	52.3	6.0	36 16.8	52.3	6.1	37 16.5	52.4	6.1	81
82	31 10.7	51.8	5.1	32 10.4	51.9	5.1	33 10.2	51.9	5.2	34 09.9	52.0	5.3	35 09.7	52.0	5.3	36 09.4	52.1	5.4	37 09.1	52.2	5.5	38 08.9	52.2	5.5	82
83	32 02.5	51.6	4.5	33 02.3	51.7	4.5	34 02.1	51.8	4.6	35 01.9	51.8	4.6	36 01.7	51.9	4.7	37 01.5	51.9	4.8	38 01.3	51.9	4.8	39 01.1	52.0	4.9	83
84	32 54.1	51.5	3.9	33 54.0	51.5	3.9	34 53.9	51.5	4.0	35 53.7	51.6	4.0	36 53.6	51.6	4.1	37 53.4	51.7	4.1	38 53.2	51.8	4.2	39 53.1	51.8	4.3	84
85	33 45.6	+51.3	3.3	34 45.5	+51.3	3.3	35 45.4	+51.4	3.4	36 45.3	+51.4	3.4	37 45.2	+51.4	3.4	38 45.1	+51.5	3.5	39 45.0	+51.5	3.5	40 44.9	+51.5	3.6	85
86	34 36.9	51.1	2.6	35 36.8	51.2	2.7	36 36.8	51.1	2.7	37 36.7	51.2	2.7	38 36.6	51.2	2.8	39 36.6	51.2	2.8	40 36.5	51.3	2.9	41 36.4	51.3	2.9	86
87	35 28.0	50.9	2.0	36 28.0	50.9	2.0	37 27.9	51.0	2.1	38 27.9	50.9	2.1	39 27.8	51.0	2.1	40 27.8	51.0	2.1	41 27.8	51.0	2.2	42 27.7	51.1	2.2	87
88	36 18.9	50.7	1.4	37 18.9	50.7	1.4	38 18.9	50.7	1.4	39 18.8	50.7	1.4	40 18.8	50.7	1.4	41 18.8	50.7	1.5	42 18.8	50.7	1.5	43 18.8	50.7	1.5	88
89	37 09.6	50.4	0.7	38 09.6	50.4	0.7	39 09.6	50.4	0.7	40 09.5	50.5	0.7	41 09.5	50.5	0.7	42 09.5	50.5	0.7	43 09.5	50.5	0.7	44 09.5	50.5	0.8	89
90	38 00.0	+50.2	0.0	39 00.0	+50.2	0.0	40 00.0	+50.2	0.0	41 00.0	+50.2	0.0	42 00.0	+50.2	0.0	43 00.0	+50.2	0.0	44 00.0	+50.2	0.0	45 00.0	+50.2	0.0	90
	38°			39°			40°			41°			42°			43°			44°			45°			

S. Lat. { L.H.A. greater than 180°......Zn=180°−Z
L.H.A. less than 180°............Zn=180°+Z }

LATITUDE SAME NAME AS DECLINATION — L.H.A. 147°, 213°

INTERPOLATION TABLE

Dec. Inc.	Tens 10′	20′	30′	40′	50′	Decimals	Units 0′	1′	2′	3′	4′	5′	6′	7′	8′	9′	Double Second Diff. and Corr.
0.0	0.0	0.0	0.0	0.0	0.0	.0	0.0	0.0	0.0	0.0	0.0	0.0	0.0	0.1	0.1	0.1	
0.1	0.0	0.0	0.0	0.0	0.1	.1	0.0	0.0	0.0	0.0	0.0	0.0	0.1	0.1	0.1	0.1	0.0 0.0
0.2	0.0	0.0	0.1	0.1	0.1	.2	0.0	0.0	0.0	0.0	0.0	0.0	0.1	0.1	0.1	0.1	48.2
0.3	0.0	0.1	0.1	0.2	0.2	.3	0.0	0.0	0.0	0.0	0.0	0.0	0.1	0.1	0.1	0.1	
0.4	0.1	0.1	0.2	0.3	0.3	.4	0.0	0.0	0.0	0.0	0.0	0.0	0.1	0.1	0.1	0.1	
0.5	0.1	0.2	0.3	0.3	0.4	.5	0.0	0.0	0.0	0.0	0.0	0.0	0.1	0.1	0.1	0.1	
0.6	0.1	0.2	0.3	0.4	0.5	.6	0.0	0.0	0.0	0.0	0.0	0.0	0.1	0.1	0.1	0.1	16.2 0.1
0.7	0.1	0.3	0.4	0.5	0.6	.7	0.0	0.0	0.0	0.0	0.0	0.0	0.1	0.1	0.1	0.1	48.6
0.8	0.2	0.3	0.4	0.6	0.7	.8	0.0	0.0	0.0	0.0	0.0	0.0	0.1	0.1	0.1	0.1	
0.9	0.2	0.3	0.5	0.6	0.8	.9	0.0	0.0	0.0	0.0	0.0	0.0	0.1	0.1	0.1	0.1	
1.0	0.1	0.3	0.5	0.6	0.8	.0	0.0	0.0	0.0	0.1	0.1	0.1	0.1	0.2	0.2	0.2	
1.1	0.2	0.3	0.5	0.7	0.9	.1	0.0	0.0	0.1	0.1	0.1	0.1	0.2	0.2	0.2	0.2	
1.2	0.2	0.4	0.6	0.8	1.0	.2	0.0	0.0	0.1	0.1	0.1	0.1	0.2	0.2	0.2	0.2	
1.3	0.2	0.4	0.6	0.9	1.1	.3	0.0	0.0	0.1	0.1	0.1	0.1	0.2	0.2	0.2	0.2	8.2 0.1
1.4	0.2	0.5	0.7	0.9	1.2	.4	0.0	0.0	0.1	0.1	0.1	0.1	0.2	0.2	0.2	0.2	24.6 0.2
1.5	0.3	0.5	0.8	1.0	1.3	.5	0.0	0.0	0.1	0.1	0.1	0.1	0.2	0.2	0.2	0.2	41.0
1.6	0.3	0.5	0.8	1.1	1.3	.6	0.0	0.0	0.1	0.1	0.1	0.1	0.2	0.2	0.2	0.2	
1.7	0.3	0.6	0.9	1.2	1.4	.7	0.0	0.0	0.1	0.1	0.1	0.1	0.2	0.2	0.2	0.2	
1.8	0.3	0.6	0.9	1.2	1.5	.8	0.0	0.0	0.1	0.1	0.1	0.1	0.2	0.2	0.2	0.2	
1.9	0.4	0.7	1.0	1.3	1.6	.9	0.0	0.0	0.1	0.1	0.1	0.1	0.2	0.2	0.2	0.2	
2.0	0.3	0.6	1.0	1.3	1.6	.0	0.0	0.0	0.1	0.1	0.2	0.2	0.2	0.3	0.3	0.4	
2.1	0.3	0.7	1.0	1.4	1.7	.1	0.0	0.0	0.1	0.1	0.2	0.2	0.3	0.3	0.3	0.4	
2.2	0.3	0.7	1.1	1.4	1.8	.2	0.0	0.0	0.1	0.1	0.2	0.2	0.3	0.3	0.3	0.4	
2.3	0.4	0.8	1.1	1.5	1.9	.3	0.0	0.1	0.1	0.1	0.2	0.2	0.3	0.3	0.3	0.4	5.0 0.1
2.4	0.4	0.8	1.2	1.6	2.0	.4	0.0	0.1	0.1	0.1	0.2	0.2	0.3	0.3	0.3	0.4	15.0 0.2
2.5	0.4	0.8	1.3	1.7	2.1	.5	0.0	0.1	0.1	0.1	0.2	0.2	0.3	0.3	0.4	0.4	25.0 0.3
2.6	0.4	0.9	1.3	1.7	2.2	.6	0.0	0.1	0.1	0.1	0.2	0.2	0.3	0.3	0.4	0.4	35.1
2.7	0.5	0.9	1.4	1.8	2.3	.7	0.0	0.1	0.1	0.2	0.2	0.2	0.3	0.3	0.4	0.4	
2.8	0.5	1.0	1.4	1.9	2.4	.8	0.0	0.1	0.1	0.2	0.2	0.2	0.3	0.3	0.4	0.4	
2.9	0.5	1.0	1.5	2.0	2.5	.9	0.0	0.1	0.1	0.2	0.2	0.2	0.3	0.3	0.4	0.4	
3.0	0.5	1.0	1.5	2.0	2.5	.0	0.0	0.1	0.1	0.2	0.2	0.3	0.3	0.4	0.5	0.5	
3.1	0.5	1.0	1.5	2.0	2.6	.1	0.0	0.1	0.1	0.2	0.2	0.3	0.4	0.4	0.5	0.5	
3.2	0.5	1.0	1.6	2.1	2.6	.2	0.0	0.1	0.1	0.2	0.2	0.3	0.4	0.4	0.5	0.5	3.6 0.1
3.3	0.5	1.1	1.6	2.2	2.7	.3	0.0	0.1	0.1	0.2	0.3	0.3	0.4	0.4	0.5	0.5	10.9 0.2
3.4	0.6	1.1	1.7	2.3	2.8	.4	0.0	0.1	0.1	0.2	0.3	0.3	0.4	0.4	0.5	0.5	18.2 0.3
3.5	0.6	1.2	1.8	2.3	2.9	.5	0.0	0.1	0.1	0.2	0.3	0.3	0.4	0.4	0.5	0.6	25.5 0.4
3.6	0.6	1.2	1.8	2.4	3.0	.6	0.0	0.1	0.2	0.2	0.3	0.3	0.4	0.4	0.5	0.6	32.8 0.5
3.7	0.6	1.3	1.9	2.5	3.1	.7	0.0	0.1	0.2	0.2	0.3	0.3	0.4	0.4	0.5	0.6	40.1
3.8	0.7	1.3	1.9	2.6	3.2	.8	0.0	0.1	0.2	0.2	0.3	0.3	0.4	0.5	0.5	0.6	
3.9	0.7	1.3	2.0	2.6	3.3	.9	0.1	0.1	0.2	0.2	0.3	0.3	0.4	0.5	0.5	0.6	
4.0	0.6	1.3	2.0	2.6	3.3	.0	0.0	0.1	0.1	0.2	0.3	0.4	0.4	0.5	0.6	0.7	
4.1	0.7	1.3	2.0	2.7	3.4	.1	0.0	0.1	0.2	0.2	0.3	0.4	0.5	0.5	0.6	0.7	2.9 0.1
4.2	0.7	1.4	2.1	2.8	3.5	.2	0.0	0.1	0.2	0.2	0.3	0.4	0.5	0.5	0.6	0.7	8.6 0.2
4.3	0.7	1.4	2.1	2.9	3.6	.3	0.0	0.1	0.2	0.2	0.3	0.4	0.5	0.5	0.6	0.7	14.4 0.3
4.4	0.7	1.5	2.2	2.9	3.7	.4	0.0	0.1	0.2	0.3	0.3	0.4	0.5	0.6	0.6	0.7	20.2 0.4
4.5	0.8	1.5	2.3	3.0	3.8	.5	0.0	0.1	0.2	0.3	0.3	0.4	0.5	0.6	0.6	0.7	25.9 0.5
4.6	0.8	1.5	2.3	3.1	3.8	.6	0.0	0.1	0.2	0.3	0.3	0.4	0.5	0.6	0.6	0.7	31.7 0.6
4.7	0.8	1.6	2.4	3.2	3.9	.7	0.1	0.1	0.2	0.3	0.4	0.4	0.5	0.6	0.7	0.7	37.5
4.8	0.8	1.6	2.4	3.2	4.0	.8	0.1	0.1	0.2	0.3	0.4	0.4	0.5	0.6	0.7	0.7	
4.9	0.9	1.7	2.5	3.3	4.1	.9	0.1	0.1	0.2	0.3	0.4	0.4	0.5	0.6	0.7	0.7	
5.0	0.8	1.6	2.5	3.3	4.1	.0	0.0	0.1	0.2	0.3	0.4	0.5	0.5	0.6	0.7	0.8	
5.1	0.8	1.7	2.5	3.4	4.2	.1	0.0	0.1	0.2	0.3	0.4	0.5	0.6	0.7	0.7	0.8	2.4 0.1
5.2	0.8	1.7	2.6	3.4	4.3	.2	0.0	0.1	0.2	0.3	0.4	0.5	0.6	0.7	0.8	0.8	7.2 0.2
5.3	0.9	1.8	2.6	3.5	4.4	.3	0.0	0.1	0.2	0.3	0.4	0.5	0.6	0.7	0.8	0.9	12.0 0.3
5.4	0.9	1.8	2.7	3.6	4.5	.4	0.0	0.1	0.2	0.3	0.4	0.5	0.6	0.7	0.8	0.9	16.8 0.4
5.5	0.9	1.8	2.8	3.7	4.6	.5	0.0	0.1	0.2	0.3	0.4	0.5	0.6	0.7	0.8	0.9	21.6 0.5
5.6	0.9	1.9	2.8	3.7	4.7	.6	0.1	0.1	0.2	0.3	0.4	0.5	0.6	0.7	0.8	0.9	26.4 0.6
5.7	1.0	1.9	2.9	3.8	4.8	.7	0.1	0.2	0.2	0.3	0.4	0.5	0.6	0.7	0.8	0.9	31.2 0.7
5.8	1.0	2.0	2.9	3.9	4.9	.8	0.1	0.2	0.3	0.3	0.4	0.5	0.6	0.7	0.8	0.9	36.0
5.9	1.0	2.0	3.0	4.0	5.0	.9	0.1	0.2	0.3	0.4	0.4	0.5	0.6	0.7	0.8	0.9	
6.0	1.0	2.0	3.0	4.0	5.0	.0	0.0	0.1	0.2	0.3	0.4	0.5	0.6	0.8	0.9	1.0	
6.1	1.0	2.0	3.0	4.0	5.1	.1	0.0	0.1	0.2	0.3	0.4	0.6	0.7	0.8	0.9	1.0	2.1 0.1
6.2	1.0	2.0	3.1	4.1	5.1	.2	0.0	0.1	0.2	0.3	0.5	0.6	0.7	0.8	0.9	1.0	6.2 0.2
6.3	1.0	2.1	3.1	4.2	5.2	.3	0.0	0.1	0.2	0.4	0.5	0.6	0.7	0.8	0.9	1.0	10.4 0.3
6.4	1.1	2.1	3.2	4.3	5.3	.4	0.0	0.2	0.3	0.4	0.5	0.6	0.7	0.8	0.9	1.0	14.5 0.4
6.5	1.1	2.2	3.3	4.3	5.4	.5	0.1	0.2	0.3	0.4	0.5	0.6	0.7	0.8	0.9	1.0	18.6 0.5
6.6	1.1	2.2	3.3	4.4	5.5	.6	0.1	0.2	0.3	0.4	0.5	0.6	0.7	0.8	0.9	1.0	22.8 0.6
6.7	1.1	2.3	3.4	4.5	5.6	.7	0.1	0.2	0.3	0.4	0.5	0.6	0.7	0.8	0.9	1.1	26.9 0.7
6.8	1.2	2.3	3.4	4.6	5.7	.8	0.1	0.2	0.3	0.4	0.5	0.6	0.7	0.8	1.0	1.1	31.1 0.8
6.9	1.2	2.3	3.5	4.6	5.8	.9	0.1	0.2	0.3	0.4	0.5	0.6	0.7	0.9	1.0	1.1	35.2
7.0	1.2	2.3	3.5	4.6	5.8	.0	0.0	0.1	0.2	0.4	0.5	0.6	0.7	0.9	1.0	1.1	1.8 0.1
7.1	1.2	2.3	3.5	4.7	5.9	.1	0.0	0.1	0.3	0.4	0.5	0.6	0.8	0.9	1.0	1.1	5.5 0.2
7.2	1.2	2.4	3.6	4.8	6.0	.2	0.0	0.1	0.3	0.4	0.5	0.6	0.8	0.9	1.0	1.1	9.1 0.3
7.3	1.2	2.4	3.6	4.9	6.1	.3	0.0	0.2	0.3	0.4	0.5	0.7	0.8	0.9	1.0	1.2	12.8 0.4
7.4	1.2	2.5	3.7	4.9	6.2	.4	0.0	0.2	0.3	0.4	0.5	0.7	0.8	0.9	1.0	1.2	16.5 0.5
7.5	1.3	2.5	3.8	5.0	6.3	.5	0.1	0.2	0.3	0.4	0.6	0.7	0.8	0.9	1.1	1.2	20.1 0.6
7.6	1.3	2.5	3.8	5.1	6.3	.6	0.1	0.2	0.3	0.4	0.6	0.7	0.8	0.9	1.1	1.2	23.8 0.7
7.7	1.3	2.6	3.9	5.2	6.4	.7	0.1	0.2	0.3	0.5	0.6	0.7	0.8	1.0	1.1	1.2	27.4 0.8
7.8	1.3	2.6	3.9	5.2	6.5	.8	0.1	0.2	0.3	0.5	0.6	0.7	0.8	1.0	1.1	1.2	31.1 0.9
7.9	1.4	2.7	4.0	5.3	6.6	.9	0.1	0.2	0.4	0.5	0.6	0.7	0.9	1.0	1.1	1.2	34.7
	10	20	30	40	50		0′	1′	2′	3′	4′	5′	6′	7′	8′	9′	

Dec. Inc.	Tens 10′	20′	30′	40′	50′	Decimals	Units 0′	1′	2′	3′	4′	5′	6′	7′	8′	9′	Double Second Diff. and Corr.
8.0	1.3	2.6	4.0	5.3	6.6	.0	0.0	0.1	0.3	0.4	0.6	0.7	0.8	1.0	1.1	1.3	
8.1	1.3	2.7	4.0	5.4	6.7	.1	0.0	0.2	0.3	0.4	0.6	0.7	0.9	1.0	1.1	1.3	
8.2	1.3	2.7	4.1	5.4	6.8	.2	0.0	0.2	0.3	0.5	0.6	0.7	0.9	1.0	1.2	1.3	1.6 0
8.3	1.4	2.8	4.1	5.5	6.9	.3	0.0	0.2	0.3	0.5	0.6	0.8	0.9	1.0	1.2	1.3	4.8 0
8.4	1.4	2.8	4.2	5.6	7.0	.4	0.1	0.2	0.3	0.5	0.6	0.8	0.9	1.0	1.2	1.3	8.0 0
8.5	1.4	2.8	4.3	5.7	7.1	.5	0.1	0.2	0.4	0.5	0.6	0.8	0.9	1.1	1.2	1.3	11.2 0
8.6	1.4	2.9	4.3	5.7	7.2	.6	0.1	0.2	0.4	0.5	0.7	0.8	0.9	1.1	1.2	1.4	14.5 0
8.7	1.5	2.9	4.4	5.8	7.3	.7	0.1	0.2	0.4	0.5	0.7	0.8	0.9	1.1	1.2	1.4	17.7 0
8.8	1.5	3.0	4.4	5.9	7.4	.8	0.1	0.3	0.4	0.5	0.7	0.8	1.0	1.1	1.2	1.4	20.9 0
8.9	1.5	3.0	4.5	6.0	7.5	.9	0.1	0.3	0.4	0.6	0.7	0.8	1.0	1.1	1.3	1.4	24.1 0 27.3 0
9.0	1.5	3.0	4.5	6.0	7.5	.0	0.0	0.2	0.3	0.5	0.6	0.8	0.9	1.1	1.3	1.4	30.5 1
9.1	1.5	3.0	4.5	6.0	7.6	.1	0.0	0.2	0.3	0.5	0.6	0.8	1.0	1.1	1.3	1.4	33.7 1
9.2	1.5	3.0	4.6	6.1	7.6	.2	0.0	0.2	0.3	0.5	0.7	0.8	1.0	1.1	1.3	1.5	36.9
9.3	1.5	3.1	4.6	6.2	7.7	.3	0.0	0.2	0.4	0.5	0.7	0.8	1.0	1.2	1.3	1.5	
9.4	1.6	3.1	4.7	6.3	7.8	.4	0.1	0.2	0.4	0.5	0.7	0.9	1.0	1.2	1.3	1.5	
9.5	1.6	3.2	4.8	6.3	7.9	.5	0.1	0.2	0.4	0.6	0.7	0.9	1.0	1.2	1.3	1.5	
9.6	1.6	3.2	4.8	6.4	8.0	.6	0.1	0.3	0.4	0.6	0.7	0.9	1.0	1.2	1.4	1.5	
9.7	1.6	3.3	4.9	6.5	8.1	.7	0.1	0.3	0.4	0.6	0.7	0.9	1.1	1.2	1.4	1.5	1.4 0
9.8	1.7	3.3	4.9	6.6	8.2	.8	0.1	0.3	0.4	0.6	0.8	0.9	1.1	1.2	1.4	1.6	4.2 0
9.9	1.7	3.3	5.0	6.6	8.3	.9	0.1	0.3	0.5	0.6	0.8	0.9	1.1	1.3	1.4	1.6	7.1 0 9.9 0
10.0	1.6	3.3	5.0	6.6	8.3	.0	0.0	0.2	0.3	0.5	0.7	0.9	1.0	1.2	1.4	1.6	12.7 0
10.1	1.7	3.3	5.0	6.7	8.4	.1	0.0	0.2	0.4	0.5	0.7	0.9	1.1	1.2	1.4	1.6	15.5 0
10.2	1.7	3.4	5.1	6.8	8.5	.2	0.0	0.2	0.4	0.6	0.7	0.9	1.1	1.3	1.4	1.6	18.4 0
10.3	1.7	3.4	5.1	6.9	8.6	.3	0.1	0.2	0.4	0.6	0.8	0.9	1.1	1.3	1.5	1.6	21.2 0
10.4	1.7	3.5	5.2	6.9	8.7	.4	0.1	0.2	0.4	0.6	0.8	0.9	1.1	1.3	1.5	1.6	24.0 0 26.8 1
10.5	1.8	3.5	5.3	7.0	8.8	.5	0.1	0.3	0.4	0.6	0.8	1.0	1.1	1.3	1.5	1.7	29.7 1
10.6	1.8	3.5	5.3	7.1	8.8	.6	0.1	0.3	0.5	0.6	0.8	1.0	1.2	1.3	1.5	1.7	32.5 1
10.7	1.8	3.6	5.4	7.2	8.9	.7	0.1	0.3	0.5	0.6	0.8	1.0	1.2	1.3	1.5	1.7	35.3
10.8	1.8	3.6	5.4	7.2	9.0	.8	0.1	0.3	0.5	0.7	0.8	1.0	1.2	1.4	1.5	1.7	
10.9	1.9	3.7	5.5	7.3	9.1	.9	0.2	0.3	0.5	0.7	0.9	1.0	1.2	1.4	1.6	1.7	
11.0	1.8	3.6	5.5	7.3	9.1	.0	0.0	0.2	0.4	0.6	0.8	1.0	1.1	1.3	1.5	1.7	
11.1	1.8	3.7	5.5	7.4	9.2	.1	0.0	0.2	0.4	0.6	0.8	1.0	1.2	1.4	1.6	1.7	1.3 0
11.2	1.8	3.7	5.6	7.4	9.3	.2	0.0	0.2	0.4	0.6	0.8	1.0	1.2	1.4	1.6	1.8	3.8 0
11.3	1.9	3.8	5.6	7.5	9.4	.3	0.1	0.2	0.4	0.6	0.8	1.0	1.2	1.4	1.6	1.8	6.3 0
11.4	1.9	3.8	5.7	7.6	9.5	.4	0.1	0.3	0.5	0.7	0.8	1.0	1.2	1.4	1.6	1.8	8.9 0
11.5	1.9	3.8	5.8	7.7	9.6	.5	0.1	0.3	0.5	0.7	0.9	1.1	1.2	1.4	1.6	1.8	11.4 0
11.6	1.9	3.9	5.8	7.7	9.7	.6	0.1	0.3	0.5	0.7	0.9	1.1	1.3	1.5	1.6	1.8	14.0 0
11.7	2.0	3.9	5.9	7.8	9.8	.7	0.1	0.3	0.5	0.7	0.9	1.1	1.3	1.5	1.7	1.9	16.5 0
11.8	2.0	4.0	5.9	7.9	9.9	.8	0.2	0.3	0.5	0.7	0.9	1.1	1.3	1.5	1.7	1.9	19.0 0
11.9	2.0	4.0	6.0	8.0	10.0	.9	0.2	0.4	0.6	0.7	0.9	1.1	1.3	1.5	1.7	1.9	21.6 0 24.1 1
12.0	2.0	4.0	6.0	8.0	10.0	.0	0.0	0.2	0.4	0.6	0.8	1.0	1.2	1.5	1.7	1.9	26.7 1
12.1	2.0	4.0	6.0	8.0	10.1	.1	0.0	0.2	0.4	0.6	0.9	1.1	1.3	1.5	1.7	1.9	29.2 1
12.2	2.0	4.0	6.1	8.1	10.1	.2	0.0	0.2	0.5	0.7	0.9	1.1	1.3	1.5	1.7	1.9	31.7 1
12.3	2.0	4.1	6.1	8.2	10.2	.3	0.1	0.3	0.5	0.7	0.9	1.1	1.3	1.5	1.7	1.9	34.3
12.4	2.1	4.1	6.2	8.3	10.3	.4	0.1	0.3	0.5	0.7	0.9	1.1	1.3	1.5	1.7	2.0	
12.5	2.1	4.2	6.3	8.3	10.4	.5	0.1	0.3	0.5	0.7	0.9	1.1	1.4	1.6	1.8	2.0	1.2 0
12.6	2.1	4.2	6.3	8.4	10.5	.6	0.1	0.3	0.5	0.7	1.0	1.2	1.4	1.6	1.8	2.0	3.5 0
12.7	2.1	4.3	6.4	8.5	10.6	.7	0.1	0.4	0.6	0.8	1.0	1.2	1.4	1.6	1.8	2.0	5.8 0
12.8	2.2	4.3	6.4	8.6	10.7	.8	0.2	0.4	0.6	0.8	1.0	1.2	1.4	1.6	1.8	2.0	8.1 0
12.9	2.2	4.3	6.5	8.6	10.8	.9	0.2	0.4	0.6	0.8	1.0	1.2	1.4	1.6	1.9	2.1	10.5 0 12.8 0
13.0	2.1	4.3	6.5	8.6	10.8	.0	0.0	0.2	0.4	0.7	0.9	1.1	1.3	1.6	1.8	2.0	15.1 0
13.1	2.2	4.3	6.5	8.7	10.9	.1	0.0	0.2	0.5	0.7	0.9	1.1	1.4	1.6	1.8	2.0	17.4 0
13.2	2.2	4.4	6.6	8.8	11.0	.2	0.0	0.3	0.5	0.7	0.9	1.2	1.4	1.6	1.8	2.1	19.8 0
13.3	2.2	4.4	6.6	8.9	11.1	.3	0.1	0.3	0.5	0.7	1.0	1.2	1.4	1.6	1.9	2.1	22.1 1
13.4	2.2	4.5	6.7	8.9	11.2	.4	0.1	0.3	0.5	0.8	1.0	1.2	1.4	1.7	1.9	2.1	24.4 1
13.5	2.3	4.5	6.8	9.0	11.3	.5	0.1	0.3	0.6	0.8	1.0	1.2	1.5	1.7	1.9	2.1	26.7 1
13.6	2.3	4.5	6.8	9.1	11.3	.6	0.1	0.4	0.6	0.8	1.0	1.3	1.5	1.7	1.9	2.2	29.1 1
13.7	2.3	4.6	6.9	9.2	11.4	.7	0.2	0.4	0.6	0.8	1.1	1.3	1.5	1.7	2.0	2.2	31.4 1
13.8	2.3	4.6	6.9	9.2	11.5	.8	0.2	0.4	0.6	0.9	1.1	1.3	1.5	1.8	2.0	2.2	33.7 1
13.9	2.4	4.7	7.0	9.3	11.6	.9	0.2	0.4	0.7	0.9	1.1	1.3	1.6	1.8	2.0	2.2	36.0
14.0	2.3	4.6	7.0	9.3	11.6	.0	0.0	0.2	0.5	0.7	1.0	1.2	1.4	1.7	1.9	2.2	
14.1	2.3	4.7	7.0	9.4	11.7	.1	0.0	0.3	0.5	0.7	1.0	1.2	1.5	1.7	2.0	2.2	
14.2	2.3	4.7	7.1	9.4	11.8	.2	0.0	0.3	0.5	0.8	1.0	1.3	1.5	1.7	2.0	2.2	1.1 0
14.3	2.4	4.8	7.1	9.5	11.9	.3	0.1	0.3	0.6	0.8	1.0	1.3	1.5	1.8	2.0	2.2	3.2 0
14.4	2.4	4.8	7.2	9.6	12.0	.4	0.1	0.3	0.6	0.8	1.1	1.3	1.5	1.8	2.0	2.3	5.3 0
14.5	2.4	4.8	7.3	9.7	12.1	.5	0.1	0.4	0.6	0.8	1.1	1.3	1.6	1.8	2.1	2.3	7.5 0
14.6	2.4	4.9	7.3	9.7	12.2	.6	0.1	0.4	0.6	0.9	1.1	1.4	1.6	1.8	2.1	2.3	9.6 0
14.7	2.5	4.9	7.4	9.8	12.3	.7	0.2	0.4	0.7	0.9	1.1	1.4	1.6	1.9	2.1	2.3	11.7 0
14.8	2.5	5.0	7.4	9.9	12.4	.8	0.2	0.4	0.7	0.9	1.2	1.4	1.6	1.9	2.1	2.4	13.9 0
14.9	2.5	5.0	7.5	10.0	12.5	.9	0.2	0.5	0.7	0.9	1.2	1.4	1.7	1.9	2.2	2.4	16.0 0 18.1 0
15.0	2.5	5.0	7.5	10.0	12.5	.0	0.0	0.3	0.5	0.8	1.0	1.3	1.5	1.8	2.1	2.3	20.3 1
15.1	2.5	5.0	7.5	10.0	12.6	.1	0.0	0.3	0.5	0.8	1.1	1.3	1.6	1.8	2.1	2.4	22.4 1
15.2	2.5	5.0	7.6	10.1	12.6	.2	0.1	0.3	0.6	0.8	1.1	1.3	1.6	1.9	2.1	2.4	24.5 1
15.3	2.5	5.1	7.6	10.2	12.7	.3	0.1	0.3	0.6	0.9	1.1	1.4	1.6	1.9	2.1	2.4	26.7 1
15.4	2.6	5.1	7.7	10.3	12.8	.4	0.1	0.4	0.6	0.9	1.1	1.4	1.7	1.9	2.2	2.4	28.8 1 30.9 1
15.5	2.6	5.2	7.8	10.3	12.9	.5	0.1	0.4	0.6	0.9	1.2	1.4	1.7	1.9	2.2	2.5	33.1 1
15.6	2.6	5.2	7.8	10.4	13.0	.6	0.2	0.4	0.7	0.9	1.2	1.4	1.7	2.0	2.2	2.5	35.2
15.7	2.6	5.3	7.9	10.5	13.1	.7	0.2	0.4	0.7	1.0	1.2	1.5	1.7	2.0	2.2	2.5	
15.8	2.7	5.3	7.9	10.6	13.2	.8	0.2	0.5	0.7	1.0	1.2	1.5	1.8	2.0	2.3	2.5	
15.9	2.7	5.3	8.0	10.6	13.3	.9	0.2	0.5	0.7	1.0	1.3	1.5	1.8	2.0	2.3	2.6	
	10′	20′	30′	40′	50′		0′	1′	2′	3′	4′	5′	6′	7′	8′	9′	

The Double-Second-Difference correction (Corr.) is always to be added to the tabulated altitude.

TABLE 9-3 Interpolation tables from H.O. 229. (This page and following three pages.)

INTERPOLATION TABLE

Altitude Difference (d)

10′	20′	30′	40′	50′	Decimals	0′	1′	2′	3′	4′	5′	6′	7′	8′	9′
2.6	5.3	8.0	10.6	13.3	.0	0.0	0.3	0.5	0.8	1.1	1.4	1.6	1.9	2.2	2.5
2.7	5.3	8.0	10.7	13.4	.1	0.0	0.3	0.6	0.9	1.1	1.4	1.7	2.0	2.2	2.5
2.7	5.4	8.1	10.8	13.5	.2	0.1	0.3	0.6	0.9	1.2	1.4	1.7	2.0	2.3	2.5
2.7	5.4	8.1	10.9	13.6	.3	0.1	0.4	0.6	0.9	1.2	1.5	1.7	2.0	2.3	2.6
2.7	5.5	8.2	10.9	13.7	.4	0.1	0.4	0.7	0.9	1.2	1.5	1.8	2.0	2.3	2.6
2.8	5.5	8.3	11.0	13.8	.5	0.1	0.4	0.7	1.0	1.2	1.5	1.8	2.1	2.3	2.6
2.8	5.5	8.3	11.1	13.8	.6	0.2	0.4	0.7	1.0	1.3	1.5	1.8	2.1	2.4	2.6
2.8	5.6	8.4	11.2	13.9	.7	0.2	0.5	0.7	1.0	1.3	1.6	1.8	2.1	2.4	2.7
2.8	5.6	8.4	11.2	14.0	.8	0.2	0.5	0.8	1.0	1.3	1.6	1.9	2.1	2.4	2.7
2.9	5.7	8.5	11.3	14.1	.9	0.2	0.5	0.8	1.1	1.3	1.6	1.9	2.2	2.4	2.7
2.8	5.6	8.5	11.3	14.1	.0	0.0	0.3	0.6	0.9	1.2	1.5	1.7	2.0	2.3	2.6
2.8	5.7	8.5	11.4	14.2	.1	0.0	0.3	0.6	0.9	1.2	1.5	1.8	2.1	2.4	2.7
2.8	5.7	8.6	11.4	14.3	.2	0.1	0.3	0.6	0.9	1.2	1.5	1.8	2.1	2.4	2.7
2.9	5.8	8.6	11.5	14.4	.3	0.1	0.4	0.7	1.0	1.3	1.5	1.8	2.1	2.4	2.7
2.9	5.8	8.7	11.6	14.5	.4	0.1	0.4	0.7	1.0	1.3	1.6	1.9	2.2	2.4	2.7
2.9	5.8	8.8	11.7	14.6	.5	0.1	0.4	0.7	1.0	1.3	1.6	1.9	2.2	2.5	2.8
2.9	5.9	8.8	11.7	14.7	.6	0.2	0.5	0.8	1.0	1.3	1.6	1.9	2.2	2.5	2.8
3.0	5.9	8.9	11.8	14.8	.7	0.2	0.5	0.8	1.1	1.4	1.7	2.0	2.2	2.5	2.8
3.0	6.0	8.9	11.9	14.9	.8	0.2	0.5	0.8	1.1	1.4	1.7	2.0	2.3	2.6	2.9
3.0	6.0	9.0	12.0	15.0	.9	0.3	0.6	0.8	1.1	1.4	1.7	2.0	2.3	2.6	2.9
3.0	6.0	9.0	12.0	15.0	.0	0.0	0.3	0.6	0.9	1.2	1.5	1.8	2.2	2.5	2.8
3.0	6.0	9.0	12.0	15.1	.1	0.0	0.3	0.6	1.0	1.3	1.6	1.9	2.2	2.5	2.8
3.0	6.0	9.1	12.1	15.1	.2	0.1	0.4	0.7	1.0	1.3	1.6	1.9	2.2	2.5	2.8
3.0	6.1	9.1	12.2	15.2	.3	0.1	0.4	0.7	1.0	1.3	1.6	1.9	2.3	2.6	2.9
3.1	6.1	9.2	12.3	15.3	.4	0.1	0.4	0.7	1.0	1.4	1.7	2.0	2.3	2.6	2.9
3.1	6.2	9.3	12.3	15.4	.5	0.2	0.5	0.8	1.1	1.4	1.7	2.0	2.3	2.6	2.9
3.1	6.2	9.3	12.4	15.5	.6	0.2	0.5	0.8	1.1	1.4	1.7	2.0	2.3	2.7	3.0
3.1	6.3	9.4	12.5	15.6	.7	0.2	0.5	0.8	1.1	1.4	1.8	2.1	2.4	2.7	3.0
3.2	6.3	9.4	12.6	15.7	.8	0.2	0.6	0.9	1.2	1.5	1.8	2.1	2.4	2.7	3.0
3.2	6.3	9.5	12.6	15.8	.9	0.3	0.6	0.9	1.2	1.5	1.8	2.1	2.4	2.7	3.1
3.1	6.3	9.5	12.6	15.8	.0	0.0	0.3	0.6	1.0	1.3	1.6	1.9	2.3	2.6	2.9
3.2	6.3	9.5	12.7	15.9	.1	0.0	0.4	0.7	1.0	1.3	1.7	2.0	2.3	2.6	3.0
3.2	6.4	9.6	12.8	16.0	.2	0.1	0.4	0.7	1.0	1.4	1.7	2.0	2.3	2.7	3.0
3.2	6.4	9.6	12.9	16.1	.3	0.1	0.4	0.7	1.1	1.4	1.7	2.0	2.4	2.7	3.0
3.2	6.5	9.7	12.9	16.2	.4	0.1	0.5	0.8	1.1	1.4	1.8	2.1	2.4	2.7	3.1
3.3	6.5	9.8	13.0	16.3	.5	0.2	0.5	0.8	1.1	1.5	1.8	2.1	2.4	2.8	3.1
3.3	6.5	9.8	13.1	16.3	.6	0.2	0.5	0.8	1.2	1.5	1.8	2.1	2.5	2.8	3.1
3.3	6.6	9.9	13.2	16.4	.7	0.2	0.6	0.9	1.2	1.5	1.9	2.2	2.5	2.8	3.2
3.3	6.6	9.9	13.2	16.5	.8	0.3	0.6	0.9	1.2	1.6	1.9	2.2	2.5	2.9	3.2
3.4	6.7	10.0	13.3	16.6	.9	0.3	0.6	0.9	1.3	1.6	1.9	2.2	2.6	2.9	3.2
3.3	6.6	10.0	13.3	16.6	.0	0.0	0.3	0.7	1.0	1.4	1.7	2.0	2.4	2.7	3.1
3.3	6.7	10.0	13.4	16.7	.1	0.0	0.4	0.7	1.1	1.4	1.7	2.1	2.4	2.8	3.1
3.3	6.7	10.1	13.4	16.8	.2	0.1	0.4	0.8	1.1	1.4	1.8	2.1	2.5	2.8	3.1
3.4	6.8	10.1	13.5	16.9	.3	0.1	0.4	0.8	1.1	1.5	1.8	2.2	2.5	2.8	3.2
3.4	6.8	10.2	13.6	17.0	.4	0.1	0.5	0.8	1.2	1.5	1.8	2.2	2.5	2.9	3.2
3.4	6.8	10.3	13.7	17.1	.5	0.2	0.5	0.9	1.2	1.5	1.9	2.2	2.6	2.9	3.2
3.4	6.9	10.3	13.7	17.2	.6	0.2	0.5	0.9	1.2	1.6	1.9	2.3	2.6	2.9	3.3
3.5	6.9	10.4	13.8	17.3	.7	0.2	0.6	0.9	1.3	1.6	1.9	2.3	2.6	3.0	3.3
3.5	7.0	10.4	13.9	17.4	.8	0.3	0.6	1.0	1.3	1.6	2.0	2.3	2.7	3.0	3.3
3.5	7.0	10.5	14.0	17.5	.9	0.3	0.6	1.0	1.3	1.7	2.0	2.4	2.7	3.0	3.4
3.5	7.0	10.5	14.0	17.5	.0	0.0	0.4	0.7	1.1	1.4	1.8	2.1	2.5	2.9	3.2
3.5	7.0	10.5	14.0	17.6	.1	0.0	0.4	0.8	1.1	1.5	1.8	2.2	2.5	2.9	3.3
3.5	7.0	10.6	14.1	17.6	.2	0.1	0.4	0.8	1.1	1.5	1.9	2.2	2.6	2.9	3.3
3.5	7.1	10.6	14.2	17.7	.3	0.1	0.5	0.8	1.2	1.5	1.9	2.3	2.6	3.0	3.3
3.6	7.1	10.7	14.3	17.8	.4	0.1	0.5	0.9	1.2	1.6	1.9	2.3	2.7	3.0	3.4
3.6	7.2	10.8	14.3	17.9	.5	0.2	0.5	0.9	1.3	1.6	2.0	2.3	2.7	3.0	3.4
3.6	7.2	10.8	14.4	18.0	.6	0.2	0.6	0.9	1.3	1.6	2.0	2.4	2.7	3.1	3.4
3.6	7.3	10.9	14.5	18.1	.7	0.3	0.6	1.0	1.3	1.7	2.0	2.4	2.8	3.1	3.5
3.7	7.3	10.9	14.6	18.2	.8	0.3	0.6	1.0	1.4	1.7	2.1	2.4	2.8	3.2	3.5
3.7	7.3	11.0	14.6	18.3	.9	0.3	0.7	1.0	1.4	1.8	2.1	2.5	2.8	3.2	3.5
3.6	7.3	11.0	14.6	18.3	.0	0.0	0.4	0.7	1.1	1.5	1.9	2.2	2.6	3.0	3.4
3.7	7.3	11.0	14.7	18.4	.1	0.0	0.4	0.8	1.2	1.5	1.9	2.3	2.7	3.0	3.4
3.7	7.4	11.1	14.8	18.5	.2	0.1	0.4	0.8	1.2	1.6	1.9	2.3	2.7	3.1	3.4
3.7	7.4	11.1	14.9	18.6	.3	0.1	0.5	0.9	1.2	1.6	2.0	2.4	2.7	3.1	3.5
3.7	7.5	11.2	14.9	18.7	.4	0.1	0.5	0.9	1.3	1.6	2.0	2.4	2.8	3.1	3.5
3.8	7.5	11.3	15.0	18.8	.5	0.2	0.6	0.9	1.3	1.7	2.1	2.4	2.8	3.2	3.6
3.8	7.5	11.3	15.1	18.8	.6	0.2	0.6	1.0	1.3	1.7	2.1	2.5	2.8	3.2	3.6
3.8	7.6	11.4	15.2	18.9	.7	0.3	0.6	1.0	1.4	1.8	2.1	2.5	2.9	3.3	3.6
3.8	7.6	11.4	15.2	19.0	.8	0.3	0.7	1.0	1.4	1.8	2.2	2.5	2.9	3.3	3.7
3.9	7.7	11.5	15.3	19.1	.9	0.3	0.7	1.1	1.5	1.8	2.2	2.6	3.0	3.3	3.7
3.8	7.6	11.5	15.3	19.1	.0	0.0	0.4	0.8	1.2	1.6	2.0	2.3	2.7	3.1	3.5
3.8	7.7	11.5	15.4	19.2	.1	0.0	0.4	0.8	1.2	1.6	2.0	2.4	2.8	3.2	3.6
3.8	7.7	11.6	15.4	19.3	.2	0.1	0.5	0.9	1.3	1.6	2.0	2.4	2.8	3.2	3.6
3.9	7.8	11.6	15.5	19.4	.3	0.1	0.5	0.9	1.3	1.7	2.1	2.5	2.9	3.3	3.6
3.9	7.8	11.7	15.6	19.5	.4	0.2	0.5	0.9	1.3	1.7	2.1	2.5	2.9	3.3	3.7
3.9	7.8	11.8	15.7	19.6	.5	0.2	0.6	1.0	1.4	1.8	2.2	2.5	2.9	3.3	3.7
3.9	7.9	11.8	15.7	19.7	.6	0.2	0.6	1.0	1.4	1.8	2.2	2.6	3.0	3.4	3.8
4.0	7.9	11.9	15.8	19.8	.7	0.3	0.7	1.1	1.4	1.8	2.2	2.6	3.0	3.4	3.8
4.0	8.0	11.9	15.9	19.9	.8	0.3	0.7	1.1	1.5	1.9	2.3	2.7	3.1	3.4	3.8
4.0	8.0	12.0	16.0	20.0	.9	0.4	0.7	1.1	1.5	1.9	2.3	2.7	3.1	3.5	3.9
10′	20′	30′	40′	50′		0′	1′	2′	3′	4′	5′	6′	7′	8′	9′

Double Second Diff. and Corr.

Double Second Diff.	Corr.
1.0	
	0.1
3.0	
	0.2
4.9	
	0.3
6.9	
	0.4
8.9	
	0.5
10.8	
	0.6
12.8	
	0.7
14.8	
	0.8
16.7	
	0.9
18.7	
	1.0
20.7	
	1.1
22.7	
	1.2
24.6	
	1.3
26.6	
	1.4
28.6	
	1.5
30.5	
	1.6
32.5	
	1.7
34.5	

Double Second Diff.	Corr.
0.9	
	0.1
2.8	
	0.2
4.6	
	0.3
6.5	
	0.4
8.3	
	0.5
10.2	
	0.6
12.0	
	0.7
13.9	
	0.8
15.7	
	0.9
17.6	
	1.0
19.4	
	1.1
21.3	
	1.2
23.1	
	1.3
25.0	
	1.4
26.8	
	1.5
28.7	
	1.6
30.5	
	1.7
32.3	
	1.8
34.2	

Double Second Diff.	Corr.
0.9	
	0.1
2.6	
	0.2
4.4	
	0.3
6.2	
	0.4
7.9	
	0.5
9.7	
	0.6
11.4	
	0.7
13.2	
	0.8
14.9	
	0.9
16.7	
	1.0
18.5	
	1.1
20.2	
	1.2
22.0	
	1.3
23.7	
	1.4
25.5	
	1.5
27.3	
	1.6
29.0	
	1.7
30.8	
	1.8
32.5	
	1.9
34.3	

Double Second Diff.	Corr.
0.8	
	0.1
2.5	
	0.2
4.2	
	0.3
5.9	
	0.4
7.6	
	0.5
9.3	
	0.6
11.0	
	0.7
12.7	
	0.8
14.4	
	0.9
16.1	
	1.0
17.8	
	1.1
19.5	
	1.2
21.2	
	1.3
22.8	
	1.4
24.5	
	1.5
26.2	
	1.6
27.9	
	1.7
29.6	
	1.8
31.3	
	1.9
33.0	
	2.0
34.7	

Dec. Inc.	10′	20′	30′	40′	50′	Decimals	0′	1′	2′	3′	4′	5′	6′	7′	8′	9′
24.0	4.0	8.0	12.0	16.0	20.0	.0	0.0	0.4	0.8	1.2	1.6	2.0	2.4	2.9	3.3	3.7
24.1	4.0	8.0	12.0	16.0	20.1	.1	0.0	0.4	0.9	1.3	1.7	2.1	2.5	2.9	3.3	3.7
24.2	4.0	8.0	12.1	16.1	20.1	.2	0.1	0.5	0.9	1.3	1.7	2.1	2.5	2.9	3.3	3.8
24.3	4.0	8.1	12.1	16.2	20.2	.3	0.1	0.5	0.9	1.3	1.8	2.2	2.6	3.0	3.4	3.8
24.4	4.1	8.1	12.2	16.3	20.3	.4	0.2	0.6	1.0	1.4	1.8	2.2	2.6	3.0	3.4	3.8
24.5	4.1	8.2	12.3	16.3	20.4	.5	0.2	0.6	1.0	1.4	1.8	2.2	2.7	3.1	3.5	3.9
24.6	4.1	8.2	12.3	16.4	20.5	.6	0.2	0.7	1.1	1.5	1.9	2.3	2.7	3.1	3.5	3.9
24.7	4.1	8.3	12.4	16.5	20.6	.7	0.3	0.7	1.1	1.5	1.9	2.3	2.7	3.1	3.6	4.0
24.8	4.2	8.3	12.4	16.6	20.7	.8	0.3	0.7	1.1	1.6	2.0	2.4	2.8	3.2	3.6	4.0
24.9	4.2	8.3	12.5	16.6	20.8	.9	0.4	0.8	1.2	1.6	2.0	2.4	2.8	3.2	3.6	4.0
25.0	4.1	8.3	12.5	16.6	20.8	.0	0.0	0.4	0.8	1.3	1.7	2.1	2.5	3.0	3.4	3.8
25.1	4.2	8.3	12.5	16.7	20.9	.1	0.0	0.5	0.9	1.3	1.7	2.2	2.6	3.0	3.4	3.9
25.2	4.2	8.4	12.6	16.8	21.0	.2	0.1	0.5	0.9	1.4	1.8	2.2	2.6	3.1	3.5	3.9
25.3	4.2	8.4	12.6	16.9	21.1	.3	0.1	0.6	1.0	1.4	1.8	2.3	2.7	3.1	3.5	4.0
25.4	4.2	8.5	12.7	16.9	21.2	.4	0.2	0.6	1.0	1.4	1.9	2.3	2.7	3.1	3.6	4.0
25.5	4.3	8.5	12.8	17.0	21.3	.5	0.2	0.6	1.1	1.5	1.9	2.3	2.8	3.2	3.6	4.0
25.6	4.3	8.5	12.8	17.1	21.3	.6	0.3	0.7	1.1	1.5	2.0	2.4	2.8	3.2	3.7	4.1
25.7	4.3	8.6	12.9	17.2	21.4	.7	0.3	0.7	1.1	1.6	2.0	2.4	2.8	3.3	3.7	4.1
25.8	4.3	8.6	12.9	17.2	21.5	.8	0.3	0.8	1.2	1.6	2.0	2.5	2.9	3.3	3.7	4.2
25.9	4.4	8.7	13.0	17.3	21.6	.9	0.4	0.8	1.2	1.7	2.1	2.5	2.9	3.4	3.8	4.2
26.0	4.3	8.6	13.0	17.3	21.6	.0	0.0	0.4	0.9	1.3	1.8	2.2	2.6	3.1	3.5	4.0
26.1	4.3	8.7	13.0	17.4	21.7	.1	0.0	0.5	0.9	1.4	1.8	2.3	2.7	3.1	3.6	4.0
26.2	4.3	8.7	13.1	17.4	21.8	.2	0.1	0.5	1.0	1.4	1.9	2.3	2.7	3.2	3.6	4.1
26.3	4.4	8.8	13.1	17.5	21.9	.3	0.1	0.6	1.0	1.5	1.9	2.3	2.8	3.2	3.7	4.1
26.4	4.4	8.8	13.2	17.6	22.0	.4	0.2	0.6	1.1	1.5	1.9	2.4	2.8	3.3	3.7	4.2
26.5	4.4	8.8	13.3	17.7	22.1	.5	0.2	0.7	1.1	1.5	2.0	2.4	2.9	3.3	3.8	4.2
26.6	4.4	8.9	13.3	17.7	22.2	.6	0.3	0.7	1.1	1.6	2.0	2.5	2.9	3.4	3.8	4.2
26.7	4.5	8.9	13.4	17.8	22.3	.7	0.3	0.8	1.2	1.6	2.1	2.5	3.0	3.4	3.8	4.3
26.8	4.5	9.0	13.4	17.9	22.4	.8	0.4	0.8	1.2	1.7	2.1	2.6	3.0	3.4	3.9	4.3
26.9	4.5	9.0	13.5	18.0	22.5	.9	0.4	0.8	1.3	1.7	2.2	2.6	3.0	3.5	3.9	4.4
27.0	4.5	9.0	13.5	18.0	22.5	.0	0.0	0.5	0.9	1.4	1.8	2.3	2.7	3.2	3.7	4.1
27.1	4.5	9.0	13.5	18.0	22.6	.1	0.0	0.5	1.0	1.4	1.9	2.3	2.8	3.3	3.7	4.2
27.2	4.5	9.0	13.6	18.1	22.6	.2	0.1	0.5	1.0	1.5	1.9	2.4	2.8	3.3	3.8	4.2
27.3	4.5	9.1	13.6	18.2	22.7	.3	0.1	0.6	1.1	1.5	2.0	2.4	2.9	3.3	3.8	4.3
27.4	4.6	9.1	13.7	18.3	22.8	.4	0.2	0.6	1.1	1.6	2.0	2.5	2.9	3.4	3.8	4.3
27.5	4.6	9.2	13.8	18.3	22.9	.5	0.2	0.7	1.1	1.6	2.1	2.5	3.0	3.4	3.9	4.4
27.6	4.6	9.2	13.8	18.4	23.0	.6	0.3	0.7	1.2	1.6	2.1	2.6	3.0	3.5	3.9	4.4
27.7	4.6	9.3	13.9	18.5	23.1	.7	0.3	0.8	1.2	1.7	2.2	2.6	3.1	3.5	4.0	4.4
27.8	4.7	9.3	13.9	18.6	23.2	.8	0.4	0.8	1.3	1.7	2.2	2.7	3.1	3.6	4.0	4.5
27.9	4.7	9.3	14.0	18.6	23.3	.9	0.4	0.9	1.3	1.8	2.2	2.7	3.2	3.6	4.1	4.5
28.0	4.6	9.3	14.0	18.6	23.3	.0	0.0	0.5	0.9	1.4	1.9	2.4	2.8	3.3	3.8	4.3
28.1	4.7	9.3	14.0	18.7	23.4	.1	0.0	0.5	1.0	1.5	1.9	2.4	2.9	3.4	3.8	4.3
28.2	4.7	9.4	14.1	18.8	23.5	.2	0.1	0.6	1.0	1.5	2.0	2.5	2.9	3.4	3.9	4.4
28.3	4.7	9.4	14.1	18.9	23.6	.3	0.1	0.6	1.1	1.6	2.0	2.5	3.0	3.5	3.9	4.4
28.4	4.7	9.5	14.2	18.9	23.7	.4	0.2	0.7	1.1	1.6	2.1	2.6	3.0	3.5	4.0	4.5
28.5	4.8	9.5	14.3	19.0	23.8	.5	0.2	0.7	1.2	1.7	2.1	2.6	3.1	3.6	4.0	4.5
28.6	4.8	9.5	14.3	19.1	23.8	.6	0.3	0.8	1.2	1.7	2.2	2.7	3.1	3.6	4.1	4.6
28.7	4.8	9.6	14.4	19.2	23.9	.7	0.3	0.8	1.3	1.8	2.2	2.7	3.2	3.7	4.1	4.6
28.8	4.8	9.6	14.4	19.2	24.0	.8	0.4	0.9	1.3	1.8	2.3	2.8	3.2	3.7	4.2	4.7
28.9	4.9	9.7	14.5	19.3	24.1	.9	0.4	0.9	1.4	1.9	2.3	2.8	3.3	3.8	4.2	4.7
29.0	4.8	9.6	14.5	19.3	24.1	.0	0.0	0.5	1.0	1.5	2.0	2.5	2.9	3.4	3.9	4.4
29.1	4.8	9.7	14.5	19.4	24.2	.1	0.0	0.5	1.0	1.5	2.0	2.5	3.0	3.5	4.0	4.5
29.2	4.8	9.7	14.6	19.4	24.3	.2	0.1	0.6	1.1	1.6	2.1	2.6	3.0	3.5	4.0	4.5
29.3	4.9	9.8	14.6	19.5	24.4	.3	0.1	0.6	1.1	1.6	2.1	2.6	3.1	3.6	4.1	4.6
29.4	4.9	9.8	14.7	19.6	24.5	.4	0.2	0.7	1.2	1.7	2.2	2.7	3.1	3.6	4.1	4.6
29.5	4.9	9.8	14.8	19.7	24.6	.5	0.2	0.7	1.2	1.7	2.2	2.7	3.2	3.7	4.2	4.7
29.6	4.9	9.9	14.8	19.7	24.7	.6	0.3	0.8	1.3	1.8	2.3	2.8	3.2	3.7	4.2	4.7
29.7	5.0	9.9	14.9	19.8	24.8	.7	0.3	0.8	1.3	1.8	2.3	2.8	3.3	3.8	4.3	4.8
29.8	5.0	10.0	14.9	19.9	24.9	.8	0.4	0.9	1.4	1.9	2.4	2.9	3.3	3.8	4.3	4.8
29.9	5.0	10.0	15.0	20.0	25.0	.9	0.4	0.9	1.4	1.9	2.4	2.9	3.4	3.9	4.4	4.9
30.0	5.0	10.0	15.0	20.0	25.0	.0	0.0	0.5	1.0	1.5	2.0	2.5	3.0	3.6	4.1	4.6
30.1	5.0	10.0	15.0	20.0	25.1	.1	0.1	0.6	1.1	1.6	2.1	2.6	3.1	3.6	4.1	4.6
30.2	5.0	10.0	15.1	20.1	25.1	.2	0.1	0.6	1.1	1.6	2.1	2.6	3.2	3.7	4.2	4.7
30.3	5.0	10.1	15.1	20.2	25.2	.3	0.2	0.7	1.2	1.7	2.2	2.7	3.2	3.7	4.2	4.7
30.4	5.1	10.1	15.2	20.3	25.3	.4	0.2	0.7	1.2	1.7	2.2	2.7	3.3	3.8	4.3	4.8
30.5	5.1	10.2	15.3	20.3	25.4	.5	0.3	0.8	1.3	1.8	2.3	2.8	3.3	3.8	4.3	4.8
30.6	5.1	10.2	15.3	20.4	25.5	.6	0.3	0.8	1.3	1.8	2.3	2.8	3.4	3.9	4.4	4.9
30.7	5.1	10.3	15.4	20.5	25.6	.7	0.4	0.9	1.4	1.9	2.4	2.9	3.4	3.9	4.4	4.9
30.8	5.2	10.3	15.4	20.6	25.7	.8	0.4	0.9	1.4	1.9	2.4	2.9	3.5	4.0	4.5	5.0
30.9	5.2	10.3	15.5	20.6	25.8	.9	0.5	1.0	1.5	2.0	2.5	3.0	3.5	4.0	4.5	5.0
31.0	5.1	10.3	15.5	20.6	25.8	.0	0.0	0.5	1.0	1.6	2.1	2.6	3.1	3.7	4.2	4.7
31.1	5.2	10.3	15.5	20.7	25.9	.1	0.1	0.6	1.1	1.6	2.2	2.7	3.2	3.7	4.3	4.8
31.2	5.2	10.4	15.6	20.8	26.0	.2	0.1	0.6	1.2	1.7	2.2	2.7	3.3	3.8	4.3	4.8
31.3	5.2	10.4	15.6	20.9	26.1	.3	0.2	0.7	1.2	1.7	2.3	2.8	3.3	3.8	4.4	4.9
31.4	5.2	10.5	15.7	20.9	26.2	.4	0.2	0.7	1.3	1.8	2.3	2.8	3.4	3.9	4.4	4.9
31.5	5.3	10.5	15.8	21.0	26.3	.5	0.3	0.8	1.3	1.8	2.4	2.9	3.4	3.9	4.5	5.0
31.6	5.3	10.5	15.8	21.1	26.3	.6	0.3	0.8	1.4	1.9	2.4	2.9	3.5	4.0	4.5	5.0
31.7	5.3	10.6	15.9	21.2	26.4	.7	0.4	0.9	1.4	1.9	2.5	3.0	3.5	4.0	4.6	5.1
31.8	5.3	10.6	15.9	21.2	26.5	.8	0.4	0.9	1.5	2.0	2.5	3.0	3.6	4.1	4.6	5.1
31.9	5.4	10.7	16.0	21.3	26.6	.9	0.5	1.0	1.5	2.0	2.6	3.1	3.6	4.1	4.7	5.2
	10′	20′	30′	40′	50′		0′	1′	2′	3′	4′	5′	6′	7′	8′	9′

Double Second Diff. and Corr.

Double Second Diff.	Corr.
0.8	
	0.1
2.5	
	0.2
4.1	
	0.3
5.8	
	0.4
7.4	
	0.5
9.1	
	0.6
10.7	
	0.7
12.3	
	0.8
14.0	
	0.9
15.6	
	1.0
17.3	
	1.1
18.9	
	1.2
20.6	
	1.3
22.2	
	1.4
23.9	
	1.5
25.5	
	1.6
27.2	
	1.7
28.8	
	1.8
30.4	
	1.9
32.1	
	2.0
33.7	
	2.1
35.4	

Double Second Diff.	Corr.
0.8	
	0.1
2.4	
	0.2
4.0	
	0.3
5.7	
	0.4
7.3	
	0.5
8.9	
	0.6
10.5	
	0.7
12.1	
	0.8
13.7	
	0.9
15.4	
	1.0
17.0	
	1.1
18.6	
	1.2
20.2	
	1.3
21.8	
	1.4
23.4	
	1.5
25.1	
	1.6
26.7	
	1.7
28.3	
	1.8
29.9	
	1.9
31.5	
	2.0
33.1	
	2.1
34.7	

Double Second Diff.	Corr.
0.8	
	0.1
2.4	
	0.2
4.0	
	0.3
5.6	
	0.4
7.2	
	0.5
8.8	
	0.6
10.4	
	0.7
12.0	
	0.8
13.6	
	0.9
15.2	
	1.0
16.8	
	1.1
18.4	
	1.2
20.0	
	1.3
21.6	
	1.4
23.2	
	1.5
24.8	
	1.6
26.4	
	1.7
28.0	
	1.8
29.6	
	1.9
31.2	
	2.0
32.8	
	2.1
34.4	

Double Second Diff.	Corr.
0.8	
	0.1
2.4	
	0.2
4.0	
	0.3
5.6	
	0.4
7.2	
	0.5
8.8	
	0.6
10.4	
	0.7
12.0	
	0.8
13.6	
	0.9
15.2	
	1.0
16.8	
	1.1
18.4	
	1.2
20.0	
	1.3
21.6	
	1.4
23.2	
	1.5
24.8	
	1.6
26.4	
	1.7
28.0	
	1.8
29.6	
	1.9
31.2	
	2.0
32.8	
	2.1
34.4	

The Double-Second-Difference correction (Corr.) is always to be added to the tabulated altitude.

INTERPOLATION TABLE

Dec. Inc.	10′	20′	30′	40′	50′	Decimals	0′	1′	2′	3′	4′	5′	6′	7′	8′	9′
	Tens						Units									
28.0	4.6	9.3	14.0	18.6	23.3	**.0**	0.0	0.5	0.9	1.4	1.9	2.4	2.8	3.3	3.8	4.3
28.1	4.7	9.3	14.0	18.7	23.4	**.1**	0.0	0.5	1.0	1.5	1.9	2.4	2.9	3.4	3.8	4.3
28.2	4.7	9.4	14.1	18.8	23.5	**.2**	0.1	0.6	1.0	1.5	2.0	2.5	2.9	3.4	3.9	4.4
28.3	4.7	9.4	14.1	18.9	23.6	**.3**	0.1	0.6	1.1	1.6	2.0	2.5	3.0	3.5	3.9	4.4
28.4	4.7	9.5	14.2	18.9	23.7	**.4**	0.2	0.7	1.1	1.6	2.1	2.6	3.0	3.5	4.0	4.5
28.5	4.8	9.5	14.3	19.0	23.8	**.5**	0.2	0.7	1.2	1.7	2.1	2.6	3.1	3.6	4.0	4.5
28.6	4.8	9.5	14.3	19.1	23.8	**.6**	0.3	0.8	1.2	1.7	2.2	2.7	3.1	3.6	4.1	4.6
28.7	4.8	9.6	14.4	19.2	23.9	**.7**	0.3	0.8	1.3	1.8	2.2	2.7	3.2	3.7	4.1	4.6
28.8	4.8	9.6	14.4	19.2	24.0	**.8**	0.4	0.9	1.3	1.8	2.3	2.8	3.2	3.7	4.2	4.7
28.9	4.9	9.7	14.5	19.3	24.1	**.9**	0.4	0.9	1.4	1.9	2.3	2.8	3.3	3.8	4.2	4.7
29.0	4.8	9.6	14.5	19.3	24.1	**.0**	0.0	0.5	1.0	1.5	2.0	2.5	2.9	3.4	3.9	4.4
29.1	4.8	9.7	14.5	19.4	24.2	**.1**	0.0	0.5	1.0	1.5	2.0	2.5	3.0	3.5	4.0	4.5
29.2	4.8	9.7	14.6	19.4	24.3	**.2**	0.1	0.6	1.1	1.6	2.1	2.6	3.0	3.5	4.0	4.5
29.3	4.9	9.8	14.6	19.5	24.4	**.3**	0.1	0.6	1.1	1.6	2.1	2.6	3.1	3.6	4.1	4.6
29.4	4.9	9.8	14.7	19.6	24.5	**.4**	0.2	0.7	1.2	1.7	2.2	2.7	3.1	3.6	4.1	4.6
29.5	4.9	9.8	14.8	19.7	24.6	**.5**	0.2	0.7	1.2	1.7	2.2	2.7	3.2	3.7	4.2	4.7
29.6	4.9	9.9	14.8	19.7	24.7	**.6**	0.3	0.8	1.3	1.8	2.3	2.8	3.2	3.7	4.2	4.7
29.7	5.0	9.9	14.9	19.8	24.8	**.7**	0.3	0.8	1.3	1.8	2.3	2.8	3.3	3.8	4.3	4.8
29.8	5.0	10.0	14.9	19.9	24.9	**.8**	0.4	0.9	1.4	1.9	2.4	2.9	3.3	3.8	4.3	4.8
29.9	5.0	10.0	15.0	20.0	25.0	**.9**	0.4	0.9	1.4	1.9	2.4	2.9	3.4	3.9	4.4	4.9
30.0	5.0	10.0	15.0	20.0	25.0	**.0**	0.0	0.5	1.0	1.5	2.0	2.5	3.0	3.6	4.1	4.6
30.1	5.0	10.0	15.0	20.0	25.1	**.1**	0.1	0.6	1.1	1.6	2.1	2.6	3.1	3.6	4.1	4.6
30.2	5.0	10.0	15.1	20.1	25.1	**.2**	0.1	0.6	1.1	1.6	2.1	2.6	3.2	3.7	4.2	4.7
30.3	5.0	10.1	15.1	20.2	25.2	**.3**	0.2	0.7	1.2	1.7	2.2	2.7	3.2	3.7	4.2	4.7
30.4	5.1	10.1	15.2	20.3	25.3	**.4**	0.2	0.7	1.2	1.7	2.2	2.7	3.3	3.8	4.3	4.8
30.5	5.1	10.2	15.3	20.3	25.4	**.5**	0.3	0.8	1.3	1.8	2.3	2.8	3.3	3.8	4.3	4.8
30.6	5.1	10.2	15.3	20.4	25.5	**.6**	0.3	0.8	1.3	1.8	2.3	2.8	3.4	3.9	4.4	4.9
30.7	5.1	10.3	15.4	20.5	25.6	**.7**	0.4	0.9	1.4	1.9	2.4	2.9	3.4	3.9	4.4	4.9
30.8	5.2	10.3	15.4	20.6	25.7	**.8**	0.4	0.9	1.4	1.9	2.4	2.9	3.5	4.0	4.5	5.0
30.9	5.2	10.3	15.5	20.6	25.8	**.9**	0.5	1.0	1.5	2.0	2.5	3.0	3.5	4.0	4.5	5.0
31.0	5.1	10.3	15.5	20.6	25.8	**.0**	0.0	0.5	1.0	1.6	2.1	2.6	3.1	3.7	4.2	4.7
31.1	5.2	10.3	15.5	20.7	25.9	**.1**	0.1	0.6	1.1	1.6	2.2	2.7	3.2	3.7	4.3	4.8
31.2	5.2	10.4	15.6	20.8	26.0	**.2**	0.1	0.6	1.2	1.7	2.2	2.7	3.3	3.8	4.3	4.8
31.3	5.2	10.4	15.6	20.9	26.1	**.3**	0.2	0.7	1.2	1.7	2.3	2.8	3.3	3.8	4.4	4.9
31.4	5.2	10.5	15.7	20.9	26.2	**.4**	0.2	0.7	1.3	1.8	2.3	2.8	3.4	3.9	4.4	4.9
31.5	5.3	10.5	15.8	21.0	26.3	**.5**	0.3	0.8	1.3	1.8	2.4	2.9	3.4	3.9	4.5	5.0
31.6	5.3	10.5	15.8	21.1	26.3	**.6**	0.3	0.8	1.4	1.9	2.4	2.9	3.5	4.0	4.5	5.0
31.7	5.3	10.6	15.9	21.2	26.4	**.7**	0.4	0.9	1.4	1.9	2.5	3.0	3.5	4.0	4.6	5.1
31.8	5.3	10.6	15.9	21.2	26.5	**.8**	0.4	0.9	1.5	2.0	2.5	3.0	3.6	4.1	4.6	5.1
31.9	5.4	10.7	16.0	21.3	26.6	**.9**	0.5	1.0	1.5	2.0	2.6	3.1	3.6	4.1	4.7	5.2
32.0	5.3	10.6	16.0	21.3	26.6	**.0**	0.0	0.5	1.1	1.6	2.2	2.7	3.2	3.8	4.3	4.9
32.1	5.3	10.7	16.0	21.4	26.7	**.1**	0.1	0.6	1.1	1.7	2.2	2.8	3.3	3.8	4.4	4.9
32.2	5.3	10.7	16.1	21.4	26.8	**.2**	0.1	0.6	1.2	1.7	2.3	2.8	3.4	3.9	4.4	5.0
32.3	5.4	10.8	16.1	21.5	26.9	**.3**	0.2	0.7	1.2	1.8	2.3	2.9	3.4	4.0	4.5	5.0
32.4	5.4	10.8	16.2	21.6	27.0	**.4**	0.2	0.8	1.3	1.8	2.4	2.9	3.5	4.0	4.5	5.1
32.5	5.4	10.8	16.3	21.7	27.1	**.5**	0.3	0.8	1.4	1.9	2.4	3.0	3.5	4.1	4.6	5.1
32.6	5.4	10.9	16.3	21.7	27.2	**.6**	0.3	0.9	1.4	1.9	2.5	3.0	3.6	4.1	4.7	5.2
32.7	5.5	10.9	16.4	21.8	27.3	**.7**	0.4	0.9	1.5	2.0	2.5	3.1	3.6	4.2	4.7	5.3
32.8	5.5	11.0	16.4	21.9	27.4	**.8**	0.4	1.0	1.5	2.1	2.6	3.1	3.7	4.2	4.8	5.3
32.9	5.5	11.0	16.5	22.0	27.5	**.9**	0.5	1.0	1.6	2.1	2.7	3.2	3.7	4.3	4.8	5.4
33.0	5.5	11.0	16.5	22.0	27.5	**.0**	0.0	0.6	1.1	1.7	2.2	2.8	3.3	3.9	4.5	5.0
33.1	5.5	11.0	16.5	22.0	27.6	**.1**	0.1	0.6	1.2	1.7	2.3	2.8	3.4	4.0	4.5	5.1
33.2	5.5	11.0	16.6	22.1	27.6	**.2**	0.1	0.7	1.2	1.8	2.3	2.9	3.5	4.0	4.6	5.1
33.3	5.5	11.1	16.6	22.2	27.7	**.3**	0.2	0.7	1.3	1.8	2.4	3.0	3.5	4.1	4.6	5.2
33.4	5.6	11.1	16.7	22.3	27.8	**.4**	0.2	0.8	1.3	1.9	2.5	3.0	3.6	4.1	4.7	5.2
33.5	5.6	11.2	16.8	22.3	27.9	**.5**	0.3	0.8	1.4	2.0	2.5	3.1	3.6	4.2	4.7	5.3
33.6	5.6	11.2	16.8	22.4	28.0	**.6**	0.3	0.9	1.5	2.0	2.6	3.1	3.7	4.2	4.8	5.4
33.7	5.6	11.3	16.9	22.5	28.1	**.7**	0.4	0.9	1.5	2.1	2.6	3.2	3.7	4.3	4.9	5.4
33.8	5.7	11.3	16.9	22.6	28.2	**.8**	0.4	1.0	1.6	2.1	2.7	3.2	3.8	4.4	4.9	5.5
33.9	5.7	11.3	17.0	22.6	28.3	**.9**	0.5	1.1	1.6	2.2	2.7	3.3	3.9	4.4	5.0	5.5
34.0	5.6	11.3	17.0	22.6	28.3	**.0**	0.0	0.6	1.1	1.7	2.3	2.9	3.4	4.0	4.6	5.2
34.1	5.7	11.3	17.0	22.7	28.4	**.1**	0.1	0.6	1.2	1.8	2.4	2.9	3.5	4.1	4.7	5.2
34.2	5.7	11.4	17.1	22.8	28.5	**.2**	0.1	0.7	1.3	1.8	2.4	3.0	3.6	4.1	4.7	5.3
34.3	5.7	11.4	17.1	22.9	28.6	**.3**	0.2	0.7	1.3	1.9	2.5	3.0	3.6	4.2	4.8	5.3
34.4	5.7	11.5	17.2	22.9	28.7	**.4**	0.2	0.8	1.4	2.0	2.5	3.1	3.7	4.3	4.8	5.4
34.5	5.8	11.5	17.3	23.0	28.8	**.5**	0.3	0.9	1.4	2.0	2.6	3.2	3.7	4.3	4.9	5.5
34.6	5.8	11.5	17.3	23.1	28.8	**.6**	0.3	0.9	1.5	2.1	2.6	3.2	3.8	4.4	4.9	5.5
34.7	5.8	11.6	17.4	23.2	28.9	**.7**	0.4	1.0	1.6	2.1	2.7	3.3	3.9	4.4	5.0	5.6
34.8	5.8	11.6	17.4	23.2	29.0	**.8**	0.5	1.0	1.6	2.2	2.8	3.3	3.9	4.5	5.1	5.6
34.9	5.9	11.7	17.5	23.3	29.1	**.9**	0.5	1.1	1.7	2.2	2.8	3.4	4.0	4.5	5.1	5.7
35.0	5.8	11.6	17.5	23.3	29.1	**.0**	0.0	0.6	1.2	1.8	2.4	3.0	3.5	4.1	4.7	5.3
35.1	5.8	11.7	17.5	23.4	29.2	**.1**	0.1	0.7	1.2	1.8	2.4	3.0	3.6	4.2	4.8	5.4
35.2	5.8	11.7	17.6	23.4	29.3	**.2**	0.1	0.7	1.3	1.9	2.5	3.1	3.7	4.3	4.9	5.4
35.3	5.9	11.8	17.6	23.5	29.4	**.3**	0.2	0.8	1.4	2.0	2.5	3.1	3.7	4.3	4.9	5.5
35.4	5.9	11.8	17.7	23.6	29.5	**.4**	0.2	0.8	1.4	2.0	2.6	3.2	3.8	4.4	5.0	5.6
35.5	5.9	11.8	17.8	23.7	29.6	**.5**	0.3	0.9	1.5	2.1	2.7	3.3	3.8	4.4	5.0	5.6
35.6	5.9	11.9	17.8	23.7	29.7	**.6**	0.4	0.9	1.5	2.1	2.7	3.3	3.9	4.5	5.1	5.7
35.7	6.0	11.9	17.9	23.8	29.8	**.7**	0.4	1.0	1.6	2.2	2.8	3.4	4.0	4.6	5.1	5.7
35.8	6.0	12.0	17.9	23.9	29.9	**.8**	0.5	1.1	1.7	2.2	2.8	3.4	4.0	4.6	5.2	5.8
35.9	6.0	12.0	18.0	24.0	30.0	**.9**	0.5	1.1	1.7	2.3	2.9	3.5	4.1	4.7	5.3	5.9
	10′	20′	30′	40′	50′		0′	1′	2′	3′	4′	5′	6′	7′	8′	9′

Double Second Diff. and Corr. (Dec. Inc. 28.0–35.9)

28.0–29.9 Diff.	Corr.	30.0–31.9 Diff.	Corr.	32.0–33.9 Diff.	Corr.	34.0–35.9 Diff.	Corr.
0.8		0.8		0.8		0.8	
	0.1		0.1		0.1		0.1
2.4		2.4		2.4		2.5	
	0.2		0.2		0.2		0.2
4.0		4.0		4.0		4.1	
	0.3		0.3		0.3		0.3
5.6		5.6		5.7		5.8	
	0.4		0.4		0.4		0.4
7.2		7.2		7.3		7.4	
	0.5		0.5		0.5		0.5
8.8		8.8		8.9		9.1	
	0.6		0.6		0.6		0.6
10.4		10.4		10.5		10.7	
	0.7		0.7		0.7		0.7
12.0		12.0		12.1		12.3	
	0.8		0.8		0.8		0.8
13.6		13.6		13.7		14.0	
	0.9		0.9		0.9		0.9
15.2		15.2		15.4		15.6	
	1.0		1.0		1.0		1.0
16.8		16.8		17.0		17.3	
	1.1		1.1		1.1		1.1
18.4		18.4		18.6		18.9	
	1.2		1.2		1.2		1.2
20.0		20.0		20.2		20.6	
	1.3		1.3		1.3		1.3
21.6		21.6		21.8		22.2	
	1.4		1.4		1.4		1.4
23.2		23.2		23.4		23.9	
	1.5		1.5		1.5		1.5
24.8		24.8		25.1		25.5	
	1.6		1.6		1.6		1.6
26.4		26.4		26.7		27.2	
	1.7		1.7		1.7		1.7
28.0		28.0		28.3		28.8	
	1.8		1.8		1.8		1.8
29.6		29.6		29.9		30.4	
	1.9		1.9		1.9		1.9
31.2		31.2		31.5		32.1	
	2.0		2.0		2.0		2.0
32.8		32.8		33.1		33.7	
	2.1		2.1		2.1		2.1
34.4		34.4		34.7		35.4	

Dec. Inc.	10′	20′	30′	40′	50′	Decimals	0′	1′	2′	3′	4′	5′	6′	7′	8′	9′
	Tens						Units									
36.0	6.0	12.0	18.0	24.0	30.0	**.0**	0.0	0.6	1.2	1.8	2.4	3.0	3.6	4.3	4.9	5.5
36.1	6.0	12.0	18.0	24.0	30.1	**.1**	0.1	0.7	1.3	1.9	2.5	3.1	3.7	4.3	4.9	5.5
36.2	6.0	12.0	18.1	24.1	30.1	**.2**	0.1	0.7	1.3	1.9	2.6	3.2	3.8	4.4	5.0	5.6
36.3	6.0	12.1	18.1	24.2	30.2	**.3**	0.2	0.8	1.4	2.0	2.6	3.2	3.8	4.4	5.0	5.7
36.4	6.1	12.1	18.2	24.3	30.3	**.4**	0.2	0.9	1.5	2.1	2.7	3.3	3.9	4.5	5.1	5.7
36.5	6.1	12.2	18.3	24.3	30.4	**.5**	0.3	0.9	1.5	2.1	2.7	3.3	4.0	4.6	5.2	5.8
36.6	6.1	12.2	18.3	24.4	30.5	**.6**	0.4	1.0	1.6	2.2	2.8	3.4	4.0	4.6	5.2	5.8
36.7	6.1	12.3	18.4	24.5	30.6	**.7**	0.4	1.0	1.6	2.3	2.9	3.5	4.1	4.7	5.3	5.9
36.8	6.2	12.3	18.4	24.6	30.7	**.8**	0.5	1.1	1.7	2.3	2.9	3.5	4.1	4.7	5.4	6.0
36.9	6.2	12.3	18.5	24.6	30.8	**.9**	0.5	1.2	1.8	2.4	3.0	3.6	4.2	4.8	5.4	6.0
37.0	6.1	12.3	18.5	24.6	30.8	**.0**	0.0	0.6	1.2	1.9	2.5	3.1	3.7	4.4	5.0	5.6
37.1	6.2	12.3	18.5	24.7	30.9	**.1**	0.1	0.7	1.3	1.9	2.6	3.2	3.8	4.4	5.1	5.7
37.2	6.2	12.4	18.6	24.8	31.0	**.2**	0.1	0.7	1.4	2.0	2.6	3.2	3.9	4.5	5.1	5.7
37.3	6.2	12.4	18.6	24.9	31.1	**.3**	0.2	0.8	1.4	2.1	2.7	3.3	3.9	4.6	5.2	5.8
37.4	6.2	12.5	18.7	24.9	31.2	**.4**	0.2	0.9	1.5	2.1	2.7	3.4	4.0	4.6	5.2	5.9
37.5	6.3	12.5	18.8	25.0	31.3	**.5**	0.3	0.9	1.6	2.2	2.8	3.4	4.1	4.7	5.3	5.9
37.6	6.3	12.5	18.8	25.1	31.3	**.6**	0.4	1.0	1.6	2.2	2.9	3.5	4.1	4.7	5.4	6.0
37.7	6.3	12.6	18.9	25.2	31.4	**.7**	0.4	1.1	1.7	2.3	2.9	3.6	4.2	4.8	5.4	6.1
37.8	6.3	12.6	18.9	25.2	31.5	**.8**	0.5	1.1	1.7	2.4	3.0	3.6	4.2	4.9	5.5	6.1
37.9	6.4	12.7	19.0	25.3	31.6	**.9**	0.6	1.2	1.8	2.4	3.1	3.7	4.3	4.9	5.6	6.2
38.0	6.3	12.6	19.0	25.3	31.6	**.0**	0.0	0.6	1.3	1.9	2.6	3.2	3.8	4.5	5.1	5.8
38.1	6.3	12.7	19.0	25.4	31.7	**.1**	0.1	0.7	1.3	2.0	2.6	3.3	3.9	4.6	5.2	5.8
38.2	6.3	12.7	19.1	25.4	31.8	**.2**	0.1	0.8	1.4	2.1	2.7	3.3	4.0	4.6	5.3	5.9
38.3	6.4	12.8	19.1	25.5	31.9	**.3**	0.2	0.8	1.5	2.1	2.8	3.4	4.0	4.7	5.3	6.0
38.4	6.4	12.8	19.2	25.6	32.0	**.4**	0.3	0.9	1.5	2.2	2.8	3.5	4.1	4.7	5.4	6.0
38.5	6.4	12.8	19.3	25.7	32.1	**.5**	0.3	1.0	1.6	2.2	2.9	3.5	4.2	4.8	5.5	6.1
38.6	6.4	12.9	19.3	25.7	32.2	**.6**	0.4	1.0	1.7	2.3	3.0	3.6	4.2	4.9	5.5	6.2
38.7	6.5	12.9	19.4	25.8	32.3	**.7**	0.4	1.1	1.7	2.4	3.0	3.7	4.3	4.9	5.6	6.2
38.8	6.5	13.0	19.4	25.9	32.4	**.8**	0.5	1.2	1.8	2.4	3.1	3.7	4.4	5.0	5.6	6.3
38.9	6.5	13.0	19.5	26.0	32.5	**.9**	0.6	1.2	1.9	2.5	3.1	3.8	4.4	5.1	5.7	6.4
39.0	6.5	13.0	19.5	26.0	32.5	**.0**	0.0	0.7	1.3	2.0	2.6	3.3	3.9	4.6	5.3	5.9
39.1	6.5	13.0	19.5	26.0	32.6	**.1**	0.1	0.7	1.4	2.0	2.7	3.4	4.0	4.7	5.3	6.0
39.2	6.5	13.0	19.6	26.1	32.6	**.2**	0.1	0.8	1.4	2.1	2.8	3.4	4.1	4.7	5.4	6.1
39.3	6.5	13.1	19.6	26.2	32.7	**.3**	0.2	0.9	1.5	2.2	2.8	3.5	4.1	4.8	5.5	6.1
39.4	6.6	13.1	19.7	26.3	32.8	**.4**	0.3	0.9	1.6	2.2	2.9	3.6	4.2	4.9	5.5	6.2
39.5	6.6	13.2	19.8	26.3	32.9	**.5**	0.3	1.0	1.6	2.3	3.0	3.6	4.3	4.9	5.6	6.3
39.6	6.6	13.2	19.8	26.4	33.0	**.6**	0.4	1.1	1.7	2.4	3.0	3.7	4.3	5.0	5.7	6.3
39.7	6.6	13.3	19.9	26.5	33.1	**.7**	0.5	1.1	1.8	2.4	3.1	3.8	4.4	5.1	5.7	6.4
39.8	6.7	13.3	19.9	26.6	33.2	**.8**	0.5	1.2	1.8	2.5	3.2	3.8	4.5	5.1	5.8	6.5
39.9	6.7	13.3	20.0	26.6	33.3	**.9**	0.6	1.3	1.9	2.6	3.2	3.9	4.5	5.2	5.9	6.5
40.0	6.6	13.3	20.0	26.6	33.3	**.0**	0.0	0.7	1.3	2.0	2.7	3.4	4.0	4.7	5.4	6.1
40.1	6.7	13.3	20.0	26.7	33.4	**.1**	0.1	0.7	1.4	2.1	2.8	3.4	4.1	4.8	5.5	6.1
40.2	6.7	13.4	20.1	26.8	33.5	**.2**	0.1	0.8	1.5	2.2	2.8	3.5	4.2	4.9	5.5	6.2
40.3	6.7	13.4	20.1	26.9	33.6	**.3**	0.2	0.9	1.6	2.2	2.9	3.6	4.3	4.9	5.6	6.3
40.4	6.7	13.5	20.2	26.9	33.7	**.4**	0.3	0.9	1.6	2.3	3.0	3.6	4.3	5.0	5.7	6.3
40.5	6.8	13.5	20.3	27.0	33.8	**.5**	0.3	1.0	1.7	2.4	3.0	3.7	4.4	5.1	5.7	6.4
40.6	6.8	13.5	20.3	27.1	33.8	**.6**	0.4	1.1	1.8	2.4	3.1	3.8	4.5	5.1	5.8	6.5
40.7	6.8	13.6	20.4	27.2	33.9	**.7**	0.5	1.1	1.8	2.5	3.2	3.8	4.5	5.2	5.9	6.5
40.8	6.8	13.6	20.4	27.2	34.0	**.8**	0.5	1.2	1.9	2.6	3.2	3.9	4.6	5.3	5.9	6.6
40.9	6.9	13.7	20.5	27.3	34.1	**.9**	0.6	1.3	2.0	2.6	3.3	4.0	4.7	5.3	6.0	6.7
41.0	6.8	13.6	20.5	27.3	34.1	**.0**	0.0	0.7	1.4	2.1	2.8	3.5	4.1	4.8	5.5	6.2
41.1	6.8	13.7	20.5	27.4	34.2	**.1**	0.1	0.8	1.5	2.1	2.8	3.5	4.2	4.9	5.6	6.3
41.2	6.8	13.7	20.6	27.4	34.3	**.2**	0.1	0.8	1.5	2.2	2.9	3.6	4.3	5.0	5.7	6.4
41.3	6.9	13.8	20.6	27.5	34.4	**.3**	0.2	0.9	1.6	2.3	3.0	3.7	4.4	5.0	5.7	6.4
41.4	6.9	13.8	20.7	27.6	34.5	**.4**	0.3	1.0	1.7	2.4	3.0	3.7	4.4	5.1	5.8	6.5
41.5	6.9	13.8	20.8	27.7	34.6	**.5**	0.3	1.0	1.7	2.4	3.1	3.8	4.5	5.2	5.9	6.6
41.6	6.9	13.9	20.8	27.7	34.7	**.6**	0.4	1.1	1.8	2.5	3.2	3.9	4.6	5.3	5.9	6.6
41.7	7.0	13.9	20.9	27.8	34.8	**.7**	0.5	1.2	1.9	2.6	3.3	3.9	4.6	5.3	6.0	6.7
41.8	7.0	14.0	20.9	27.9	34.9	**.8**	0.6	1.2	1.9	2.6	3.3	4.0	4.7	5.4	6.1	6.8
41.9	7.0	14.0	21.0	28.0	35.0	**.9**	0.6	1.3	2.0	2.7	3.4	4.1	4.8	5.5	6.2	6.8
42.0	7.0	14.0	21.0	28.0	35.0	**.0**	0.0	0.7	1.4	2.1	2.8	3.5	4.2	5.0	5.7	6.4
42.1	7.0	14.0	21.0	28.0	35.1	**.1**	0.1	0.8	1.5	2.2	2.9	3.6	4.3	5.0	5.7	6.4
42.2	7.0	14.0	21.1	28.1	35.1	**.2**	0.1	0.8	1.6	2.3	3.0	3.7	4.4	5.1	5.8	6.5
42.3	7.0	14.1	21.1	28.2	35.2	**.3**	0.2	0.9	1.6	2.3	3.0	3.8	4.5	5.2	5.9	6.6
42.4	7.1	14.1	21.2	28.3	35.3	**.4**	0.3	1.0	1.7	2.4	3.1	3.8	4.5	5.2	5.9	6.7
42.5	7.1	14.2	21.3	28.3	35.4	**.5**	0.4	1.1	1.8	2.5	3.2	3.9	4.6	5.3	6.0	6.7
42.6	7.1	14.2	21.3	28.4	35.5	**.6**	0.4	1.1	1.8	2.5	3.3	4.0	4.7	5.4	6.1	6.8
42.7	7.1	14.3	21.4	28.5	35.6	**.7**	0.5	1.2	1.9	2.6	3.3	4.0	4.7	5.5	6.2	6.9
42.8	7.2	14.3	21.4	28.6	35.7	**.8**	0.6	1.3	2.0	2.7	3.4	4.1	4.8	5.5	6.2	6.9
42.9	7.2	14.3	21.5	28.6	35.8	**.9**	0.6	1.3	2.1	2.8	3.5	4.2	4.9	5.6	6.3	7.0
43.0	7.1	14.3	21.5	28.6	35.8	**.0**	0.0	0.7	1.4	2.2	2.9	3.6	4.3	5.1	5.8	6.5
43.1	7.2	14.3	21.5	28.7	35.9	**.1**	0.1	0.8	1.5	2.2	3.0	3.7	4.4	5.1	5.9	6.6
43.2	7.2	14.4	21.6	28.8	36.0	**.2**	0.1	0.9	1.6	2.3	3.0	3.8	4.5	5.2	5.9	6.7
43.3	7.2	14.4	21.6	28.9	36.1	**.3**	0.2	0.9	1.7	2.4	3.1	3.8	4.6	5.3	6.0	6.7
43.4	7.2	14.5	21.7	28.9	36.2	**.4**	0.3	1.0	1.7	2.5	3.2	3.9	4.6	5.4	6.1	6.8
43.5	7.3	14.5	21.8	29.0	36.3	**.5**	0.4	1.1	1.8	2.5	3.3	4.0	4.7	5.4	6.2	6.9
43.6	7.3	14.5	21.8	29.1	36.3	**.6**	0.4	1.2	1.9	2.6	3.3	4.1	4.8	5.5	6.2	7.0
43.7	7.3	14.6	21.9	29.2	36.4	**.7**	0.5	1.2	2.0	2.7	3.4	4.1	4.9	5.6	6.3	7.0
43.8	7.3	14.6	21.9	29.2	36.5	**.8**	0.6	1.3	2.0	2.8	3.5	4.2	4.9	5.7	6.4	7.1
43.9	7.4	14.7	22.0	29.3	36.6	**.9**	0.7	1.4	2.1	2.8	3.6	4.3	5.0	5.7	6.5	7.2
	10′	20′	30′	40′	50′		0′	1′	2′	3′	4′	5′	6′	7′	8′	9′

Double Second Diff. and Corr. (Dec. Inc. 36.0–43.9)

36.0–37.9 Diff.	Corr.	38.0–39.9 Diff.	Corr.	40.0–41.9 Diff.	Corr.	42.0–43.9 Diff.	Corr.
0.8		0.9		0.9		1.0	
2.5		2.6		2.8		3.0	
4.2		4.4		4.6		4.9	
5.9		6.2		6.5		6.9	
7.6		7.9		8.3		8.9	
9.3		9.7		10.2		10.8	
11.0		11.4		12.0		12.8	
12.7		13.2		13.9		14.8	
14.4		14.9		15.7		16.7	
16.1		16.7		17.6		18.7	
17.8		18.5		19.4		20.7	
19.5		20.2		21.3		22.7	
21.2		22.0		23.1		24.6	
22.8		23.7		25.0		26.6	
24.5		25.5		26.8		28.6	
26.2		27.3		28.7		30.5	
27.9		29.0		30.5		32.5	
29.6		30.8		32.3		34.5	
31.3		32.5		34.2			
33.0		34.3					
34.7							

The Double-Second-Difference correction (Corr.) is always to be added to the tabulated altitude.

INTERPOLATION TABLE

Dec. Inc.	Altitude Difference (d) — Tens 10′	20′	30′	40′	50′	Decimals	Units 0′	1′	2′	3′	4′	5′	6′	7′	8′	9′	Double Second Diff. and Corr.
44.0	7.3	14.6	22.0	29.3	36.6	.0	0.0	0.7	1.5	2.2	3.0	3.7	4.4	5.2	5.9	6.7	
44.1	7.3	14.7	22.0	29.4	36.7	.1	0.1	0.8	1.6	2.3	3.0	3.8	4.5	5.3	6.0	6.7	
44.2	7.3	14.7	22.1	29.4	36.8	.2	0.1	0.9	1.6	2.4	3.1	3.9	4.6	5.3	6.1	6.8	1.1 / 0.1
44.3	7.4	14.8	22.1	29.5	36.9	.3	0.2	1.0	1.7	2.4	3.2	3.9	4.7	5.4	6.2	6.9	3.2 / 0.2
44.4	7.4	14.8	22.2	29.6	37.0	.4	0.3	1.0	1.8	2.5	3.3	4.0	4.7	5.5	6.2	7.0	5.3 / 0.3
44.5	7.4	14.8	22.3	29.7	37.1	.5	0.4	1.1	1.9	2.6	3.3	4.1	4.8	5.6	6.3	7.0	7.5 / 0.4
44.6	7.4	14.9	22.3	29.7	37.2	.6	0.4	1.2	1.9	2.7	3.4	4.2	4.9	5.6	6.4	7.1	9.6 / 0.5
44.7	7.5	14.9	22.4	29.8	37.3	.7	0.5	1.3	2.0	2.7	3.5	4.2	5.0	5.7	6.5	7.2	11.7 / 0.6
44.8	7.5	15.0	22.4	29.9	37.4	.8	0.6	1.3	2.1	2.8	3.6	4.3	5.0	5.8	6.5	7.3	13.9 / 0.7
44.9	7.5	15.0	22.5	30.0	37.5	.9	0.7	1.4	2.2	2.9	3.6	4.4	5.1	5.9	6.6	7.3	16.0 / 0.8 / 18.1 / 0.9
45.0	7.5	15.0	22.5	30.0	37.5	.0	0.0	0.8	1.5	2.3	3.0	3.8	4.5	5.3	6.1	6.8	20.3 / 1.0
45.1	7.5	15.0	22.5	30.0	37.6	.1	0.1	0.8	1.6	2.4	3.1	3.9	4.6	5.4	6.1	6.9	22.4 / 1.1
45.2	7.5	15.0	22.6	30.1	37.6	.2	0.2	0.9	1.7	2.4	3.2	3.9	4.7	5.5	6.2	7.0	24.5 / 1.2
45.3	7.5	15.1	22.6	30.2	37.7	.3	0.2	1.0	1.7	2.5	3.3	4.0	4.8	5.5	6.3	7.1	26.7 / 1.3
45.4	7.6	15.1	22.7	30.3	37.8	.4	0.3	1.1	1.8	2.6	3.3	4.1	4.9	5.6	6.4	7.1	28.8 / 1.4 / 30.9 / 1.5
45.5	7.6	15.2	22.8	30.3	37.9	.5	0.4	1.1	1.9	2.7	3.4	4.2	4.9	5.7	6.4	7.2	33.1 / 1.6
45.6	7.6	15.2	22.8	30.4	38.0	.6	0.5	1.2	2.0	2.7	3.5	4.2	5.0	5.8	6.5	7.3	35.2
45.7	7.6	15.3	22.9	30.5	38.1	.7	0.5	1.3	2.0	2.8	3.6	4.3	5.1	5.8	6.6	7.4	
45.8	7.7	15.3	22.9	30.6	38.2	.8	0.6	1.4	2.1	2.9	3.6	4.4	5.2	5.9	6.7	7.4	
45.9	7.7	15.3	23.0	30.6	38.3	.9	0.7	1.4	2.2	3.0	3.7	4.5	5.2	6.0	6.7	7.5	
46.0	7.6	15.3	23.0	30.6	38.3	.0	0.0	0.8	1.5	2.3	3.1	3.9	4.6	5.4	6.2	7.0	1.2 / 0.1
46.1	7.7	15.3	23.0	30.7	38.4	.1	0.1	0.9	1.6	2.4	3.2	4.0	4.7	5.5	6.3	7.1	3.5 / 0.2
46.2	7.7	15.4	23.1	30.8	38.5	.2	0.2	0.9	1.7	2.5	3.3	4.0	4.8	5.6	6.4	7.1	5.8 / 0.3
46.3	7.7	15.4	23.1	30.9	38.6	.3	0.2	1.0	1.8	2.6	3.3	4.1	4.9	5.7	6.4	7.2	8.1 / 0.4
46.4	7.7	15.5	23.2	30.9	38.7	.4	0.3	1.1	1.9	2.6	3.4	4.2	5.0	5.7	6.5	7.3	10.5 / 0.5
46.5	7.8	15.5	23.3	31.0	38.8	.5	0.4	1.2	1.9	2.7	3.5	4.3	5.0	5.8	6.6	7.4	12.8 / 0.6
46.6	7.8	15.5	23.3	31.1	38.8	.6	0.5	1.2	2.0	2.8	3.6	4.3	5.1	5.9	6.7	7.4	15.1 / 0.7
46.7	7.8	15.6	23.4	31.2	38.9	.7	0.5	1.3	2.1	2.9	3.6	4.4	5.2	6.0	6.7	7.5	17.4 / 0.8
46.8	7.8	15.6	23.4	31.2	39.0	.8	0.6	1.4	2.2	2.9	3.7	4.5	5.3	6.0	6.8	7.6	19.8 / 0.9
46.9	7.9	15.7	23.5	31.3	39.1	.9	0.7	1.5	2.2	3.0	3.8	4.6	5.3	6.1	6.9	7.7	22.1 / 1.0 / 24.4 / 1.1
47.0	7.8	15.6	23.5	31.3	39.1	.0	0.0	0.8	1.6	2.4	3.2	4.0	4.7	5.5	6.3	7.1	26.7 / 1.2
47.1	7.8	15.7	23.5	31.4	39.2	.1	0.1	0.9	1.7	2.5	3.2	4.0	4.8	5.6	6.4	7.2	29.1 / 1.3
47.2	7.8	15.7	23.6	31.4	39.3	.2	0.2	0.9	1.7	2.5	3.3	4.1	4.9	5.7	6.5	7.3	31.4 / 1.4
47.3	7.9	15.8	23.6	31.5	39.4	.3	0.2	1.0	1.8	2.6	3.4	4.2	5.0	5.8	6.6	7.4	33.7 / 1.5
47.4	7.9	15.8	23.7	31.6	39.5	.4	0.3	1.1	1.9	2.7	3.5	4.3	5.1	5.9	6.6	7.4	36.0
47.5	7.9	15.8	23.8	31.7	39.6	.5	0.4	1.2	2.0	2.8	3.6	4.4	5.1	5.9	6.7	7.5	
47.6	7.9	15.9	23.8	31.7	39.7	.6	0.5	1.3	2.1	2.8	3.6	4.4	5.2	6.0	6.8	7.6	1.3 / 0.1
47.7	8.0	15.9	23.9	31.8	39.8	.7	0.6	1.3	2.1	2.9	3.7	4.5	5.3	6.1	6.9	7.7	3.8 / 0.2
47.8	8.0	16.0	23.9	31.9	39.9	.8	0.6	1.4	2.2	3.0	3.8	4.6	5.4	6.2	7.0	7.8	6.3 / 0.3
47.9	8.0	16.0	24.0	32.0	40.0	.9	0.7	1.5	2.3	3.1	3.9	4.7	5.5	6.3	7.0	7.8	8.9 / 0.4 / 11.4 / 0.5
48.0	8.0	16.0	24.0	32.0	40.0	.0	0.0	0.8	1.6	2.4	3.2	4.0	4.8	5.7	6.5	7.3	14.0 / 0.6
48.1	8.0	16.0	24.0	32.0	40.1	.1	0.1	0.9	1.7	2.5	3.3	4.1	4.9	5.7	6.5	7.4	16.5 / 0.7
48.2	8.0	16.0	24.1	32.1	40.1	.2	0.2	1.0	1.8	2.6	3.4	4.2	5.0	5.8	6.6	7.4	19.0 / 0.8
48.3	8.0	16.1	24.1	32.2	40.2	.3	0.2	1.1	1.9	2.7	3.5	4.3	5.1	5.9	6.7	7.5	21.6 / 0.9
48.4	8.1	16.1	24.2	32.3	40.3	.4	0.3	1.1	1.9	2.7	3.6	4.4	5.2	6.0	6.8	7.6	24.1 / 1.0
48.5	8.1	16.2	24.3	32.3	40.4	.5	0.4	1.2	2.0	2.8	3.6	4.4	5.3	6.1	6.9	7.7	26.7 / 1.1
48.6	8.1	16.2	24.3	32.4	40.5	.6	0.5	1.3	2.1	2.9	3.7	4.5	5.3	6.1	7.0	7.8	29.2 / 1.2
48.7	8.1	16.3	24.4	32.5	40.6	.7	0.6	1.4	2.2	3.0	3.8	4.6	5.4	6.2	7.0	7.8	31.7 / 1.3
48.8	8.2	16.3	24.4	32.6	40.7	.8	0.6	1.5	2.3	3.1	3.9	4.7	5.5	6.3	7.1	7.9	34.3
48.9	8.2	16.3	24.5	32.6	40.8	.9	0.7	1.5	2.3	3.2	4.0	4.8	5.6	6.4	7.2	8.0	
49.0	8.1	16.3	24.5	32.6	40.8	.0	0.0	0.8	1.6	2.5	3.3	4.1	4.9	5.8	6.6	7.4	
49.1	8.2	16.3	24.5	32.7	40.9	.1	0.1	0.9	1.7	2.6	3.4	4.2	5.0	5.9	6.7	7.5	
49.2	8.2	16.4	24.6	32.8	41.0	.2	0.2	1.0	1.8	2.6	3.5	4.3	5.1	5.9	6.8	7.6	1.4 / 0.1
49.3	8.2	16.4	24.6	32.9	41.1	.3	0.2	1.1	1.9	2.7	3.5	4.4	5.2	6.0	6.8	7.7	4.2 / 0.2
49.4	8.2	16.5	24.7	32.9	41.2	.4	0.3	1.2	2.0	2.8	3.6	4.5	5.3	6.1	6.9	7.8	7.1 / 0.3 / 9.9 / 0.4
49.5	8.3	16.5	24.8	33.0	41.3	.5	0.4	1.2	2.1	2.9	3.7	4.5	5.4	6.2	7.0	7.8	12.7 / 0.5
49.6	8.3	16.5	24.8	33.1	41.3	.6	0.5	1.3	2.1	3.0	3.8	4.6	5.4	6.3	7.1	7.9	15.5 / 0.6
49.7	8.3	16.6	24.9	33.2	41.4	.7	0.6	1.4	2.2	3.1	3.9	4.7	5.5	6.4	7.2	8.0	18.4 / 0.7
49.8	8.3	16.6	24.9	33.2	41.5	.8	0.7	1.5	2.3	3.1	4.0	4.8	5.6	6.4	7.3	8.1	21.2 / 0.8
49.9	8.4	16.7	25.0	33.3	41.6	.9	0.7	1.6	2.4	3.2	4.0	4.9	5.7	6.5	7.3	8.2	24.0 / 0.9 / 26.8 / 1.0
50.0	8.3	16.6	25.0	33.3	41.6	.0	0.0	0.8	1.7	2.5	3.4	4.2	5.0	5.9	6.7	7.6	29.7 / 1.1
50.1	8.3	16.7	25.0	33.4	41.7	.1	0.1	0.9	1.8	2.6	3.5	4.3	5.1	6.0	6.8	7.7	32.5 / 1.2
50.2	8.3	16.7	25.1	33.4	41.8	.2	0.2	1.0	1.9	2.7	3.5	4.4	5.2	6.1	6.9	7.7	35.3
50.3	8.4	16.8	25.1	33.5	41.9	.3	0.3	1.1	1.9	2.8	3.6	4.5	5.3	6.1	7.0	7.8	
50.4	8.4	16.8	25.2	33.6	42.0	.4	0.3	1.2	2.0	2.9	3.7	4.5	5.4	6.2	7.1	7.9	
50.5	8.4	16.8	25.3	33.7	42.1	.5	0.4	1.3	2.1	2.9	3.8	4.6	5.5	6.3	7.2	8.0	
50.6	8.4	16.9	25.3	33.7	42.2	.6	0.5	1.3	2.2	3.0	3.9	4.7	5.6	6.4	7.2	8.1	
50.7	8.5	16.9	25.4	33.8	42.3	.7	0.6	1.4	2.3	3.1	4.0	4.8	5.6	6.5	7.3	8.2	
50.8	8.5	17.0	25.4	33.9	42.4	.8	0.7	1.5	2.4	3.2	4.0	4.9	5.7	6.6	7.4	8.2	1.6 / 0.1
50.9	8.5	17.0	25.5	34.0	42.5	.9	0.8	1.6	2.4	3.3	4.1	5.0	5.8	6.6	7.5	8.3	4.8 / 0.2 / 8.0 / 0.3
51.0	8.5	17.0	25.5	34.0	42.5	.0	0.0	0.9	1.7	2.6	3.4	4.3	5.1	6.0	6.9	7.7	11.2 / 0.4
51.1	8.5	17.0	25.5	34.0	42.6	.1	0.1	0.9	1.8	2.7	3.5	4.4	5.2	6.1	7.0	7.8	14.5 / 0.5
51.2	8.5	17.0	25.6	34.1	42.6	.2	0.2	1.0	1.9	2.7	3.6	4.5	5.3	6.2	7.0	7.9	17.7 / 0.6
51.3	8.5	17.1	25.6	34.2	42.7	.3	0.3	1.1	2.0	2.8	3.7	4.5	5.4	6.3	7.1	8.0	20.9 / 0.7
51.4	8.6	17.1	25.7	34.3	42.8	.4	0.3	1.2	2.1	2.9	3.8	4.6	5.5	6.4	7.2	8.1	24.1 / 0.8 / 27.3 / 0.9
51.5	8.6	17.2	25.8	34.3	42.9	.5	0.4	1.3	2.1	3.0	3.9	4.7	5.6	6.4	7.3	8.2	30.5 / 1.0
51.6	8.6	17.2	25.8	34.4	43.0	.6	0.5	1.4	2.2	3.1	3.9	4.8	5.7	6.5	7.4	8.2	33.7 / 1.1
51.7	8.6	17.3	25.9	34.5	43.1	.7	0.6	1.5	2.3	3.2	4.0	4.9	5.8	6.6	7.5	8.3	36.9
51.8	8.7	17.3	25.9	34.6	43.2	.8	0.7	1.5	2.4	3.3	4.1	5.0	5.8	6.7	7.6	8.4	
51.9	8.7	17.3	26.0	34.6	43.3	.9	0.8	1.6	2.5	3.3	4.2	5.1	5.9	6.8	7.6	8.5	
	10′	20′	30′	40′	50′		0′	1′	2′	3′	4′	5′	6′	7′	8′	9′	

Dec. Inc.	Altitude Difference (d) — Tens 10′	20′	30′	40′	50′	Decimals	Units 0′	1′	2′	3′	4′	5′	6′	7′	8′	9′	Double Second Diff. and Corr.
52.0	8.6	17.3	26.0	34.6	43.3	.0	0.0	0.9	1.7	2.6	3.5	4.4	5.2	6.1	7.0	7.9	1.8 / 0.1
52.1	8.7	17.3	26.0	34.7	43.4	.1	0.1	1.0	1.8	2.7	3.6	4.5	5.3	6.2	7.1	8.0	5.5 / 0.2
52.2	8.7	17.4	26.1	34.8	43.5	.2	0.2	1.0	1.9	2.8	3.7	4.5	5.4	6.3	7.2	8.0	9.1 / 0.3
52.3	8.7	17.4	26.1	34.9	43.6	.3	0.3	1.1	2.0	2.9	3.8	4.6	5.5	6.4	7.3	8.1	12.8 / 0.4
52.4	8.7	17.5	26.2	34.9	43.7	.4	0.3	1.2	2.1	3.0	3.8	4.7	5.6	6.5	7.3	8.2	16.5 / 0.5
52.5	8.8	17.5	26.3	35.0	43.8	.5	0.4	1.3	2.2	3.1	3.9	4.8	5.7	6.6	7.4	8.3	20.1 / 0.6
52.6	8.8	17.5	26.3	35.1	43.8	.6	0.5	1.4	2.3	3.1	4.0	4.9	5.8	6.6	7.5	8.4	23.8 / 0.7
52.7	8.8	17.6	26.4	35.2	43.9	.7	0.6	1.5	2.4	3.2	4.1	5.0	5.9	6.7	7.6	8.5	27.4 / 0.8
52.8	8.8	17.6	26.4	35.2	44.0	.8	0.7	1.6	2.4	3.3	4.2	5.1	5.9	6.8	7.7	8.6	31.1 / 0.9
52.9	8.9	17.7	26.5	35.3	44.1	.9	0.8	1.7	2.5	3.4	4.3	5.2	6.0	6.9	7.8	8.7	34.7
53.0	8.8	17.6	26.5	35.3	44.1	.0	0.0	0.9	1.8	2.7	3.6	4.5	5.3	6.2	7.1	8.0	
53.1	8.8	17.7	26.5	35.4	44.2	.1	0.1	1.0	1.9	2.8	3.7	4.5	5.4	6.3	7.2	8.1	2.1 / 0.1
53.2	8.8	17.7	26.6	35.4	44.3	.2	0.2	1.1	2.0	2.9	3.7	4.6	5.5	6.4	7.3	8.2	6.2 / 0.2
53.3	8.9	17.8	26.6	35.5	44.4	.3	0.3	1.2	2.1	2.9	3.8	4.7	5.6	6.5	7.4	8.3	10.4 / 0.3
53.4	8.9	17.8	26.7	35.6	44.5	.4	0.4	1.2	2.1	3.0	3.9	4.8	5.7	6.6	7.5	8.4	14.5 / 0.4 / 18.6 / 0.5
53.5	8.9	17.8	26.8	35.7	44.6	.5	0.4	1.3	2.2	3.1	4.0	4.9	5.8	6.7	7.6	8.5	22.8 / 0.6
53.6	8.9	17.9	26.8	35.7	44.7	.6	0.5	1.4	2.3	3.2	4.1	5.0	5.9	6.8	7.7	8.6	26.9 / 0.7
53.7	9.0	17.9	26.9	35.8	44.8	.7	0.6	1.5	2.4	3.3	4.2	5.1	6.0	6.9	7.8	8.6	31.1 / 0.8
53.8	9.0	18.0	26.9	35.9	44.9	.8	0.7	1.6	2.5	3.4	4.3	5.2	6.1	7.0	7.8	8.7	35.2
53.9	9.0	18.0	27.0	36.0	45.0	.9	0.8	1.7	2.6	3.5	4.4	5.3	6.2	7.0	7.9	8.8	
54.0	9.0	18.0	27.0	36.0	45.0	.0	0.0	0.9	1.8	2.7	3.6	4.5	5.4	6.4	7.3	8.2	
54.1	9.0	18.0	27.0	36.0	45.1	.1	0.1	1.0	1.9	2.8	3.7	4.6	5.5	6.4	7.4	8.3	2.4 / 0.1
54.2	9.0	18.0	27.1	36.1	45.1	.2	0.2	1.1	2.0	2.9	3.8	4.7	5.6	6.5	7.4	8.4	7.2 / 0.2
54.3	9.0	18.1	27.1	36.2	45.2	.3	0.3	1.2	2.1	3.0	3.9	4.8	5.7	6.6	7.5	8.4	12.0 / 0.3
54.4	9.1	18.1	27.2	36.3	45.3	.4	0.4	1.3	2.2	3.1	4.0	4.9	5.8	6.7	7.6	8.5	16.8 / 0.4 / 21.6 / 0.5
54.5	9.1	18.2	27.3	36.3	45.4	.5	0.5	1.4	2.3	3.2	4.1	5.0	5.9	6.8	7.7	8.6	26.4 / 0.6
54.6	9.1	18.2	27.3	36.4	45.5	.6	0.5	1.5	2.4	3.3	4.2	5.1	6.0	6.9	7.8	8.7	31.2 / 0.7
54.7	9.1	18.3	27.4	36.5	45.6	.7	0.6	1.5	2.5	3.4	4.3	5.2	6.1	7.0	7.9	8.8	36.0
54.8	9.2	18.3	27.4	36.6	45.7	.8	0.7	1.6	2.5	3.5	4.4	5.3	6.2	7.1	8.0	8.9	
54.9	9.2	18.3	27.5	36.6	45.8	.9	0.8	1.7	2.6	3.5	4.5	5.4	6.3	7.2	8.1	9.0	
55.0	9.1	18.3	27.5	36.6	45.8	.0	0.0	0.9	1.8	2.8	3.7	4.6	5.5	6.5	7.4	8.3	
55.1	9.2	18.3	27.5	36.7	45.9	.1	0.1	1.0	1.9	2.9	3.8	4.7	5.6	6.6	7.5	8.4	
55.2	9.2	18.4	27.6	36.8	46.0	.2	0.2	1.1	2.0	3.0	3.9	4.8	5.7	6.7	7.6	8.5	2.9 / 0.1
55.3	9.2	18.4	27.6	36.9	46.1	.3	0.3	1.2	2.1	3.1	4.0	4.9	5.8	6.8	7.7	8.6	8.6 / 0.2
55.4	9.2	18.5	27.7	36.9	46.2	.4	0.4	1.3	2.2	3.1	4.1	5.0	5.9	6.8	7.8	8.7	14.4 / 0.3 / 20.2 / 0.4
55.5	9.3	18.5	27.8	37.0	46.3	.5	0.5	1.4	2.3	3.2	4.2	5.1	6.0	6.9	7.9	8.8	25.9 / 0.5
55.6	9.3	18.5	27.8	37.1	46.3	.6	0.6	1.5	2.4	3.3	4.3	5.2	6.1	7.0	8.0	8.9	31.7 / 0.6
55.7	9.3	18.6	27.9	37.2	46.4	.7	0.6	1.6	2.5	3.4	4.3	5.3	6.2	7.1	8.0	9.0	37.5
55.8	9.3	18.6	27.9	37.2	46.5	.8	0.7	1.7	2.6	3.5	4.4	5.4	6.3	7.2	8.1	9.1	
55.9	9.4	18.7	28.0	37.3	46.6	.9	0.8	1.8	2.7	3.6	4.5	5.5	6.4	7.3	8.2	9.2	
56.0	9.3	18.6	28.0	37.3	46.6	.0	0.0	0.9	1.9	2.8	3.8	4.7	5.6	6.6	7.5	8.5	
56.1	9.3	18.7	28.0	37.4	46.7	.1	0.1	1.0	2.0	2.9	3.9	4.8	5.7	6.7	7.6	8.6	
56.2	9.3	18.7	28.1	37.4	46.8	.2	0.2	1.1	2.1	3.0	4.0	4.9	5.8	6.8	7.7	8.7	3.6 / 0.1
56.3	9.4	18.8	28.1	37.5	46.9	.3	0.3	1.2	2.2	3.1	4.0	5.0	5.9	6.9	7.8	8.8	10.9 / 0.2
56.4	9.4	18.8	28.2	37.6	47.0	.4	0.4	1.3	2.3	3.2	4.1	5.1	6.0	7.0	7.9	8.9	18.2 / 0.3 / 25.5 / 0.4
56.5	9.4	18.8	28.3	37.7	47.1	.5	0.5	1.4	2.4	3.3	4.2	5.2	6.1	7.1	8.0	8.9	32.8 / 0.5
56.6	9.4	18.9	28.3	37.7	47.2	.6	0.6	1.5	2.4	3.4	4.3	5.3	6.2	7.2	8.1	9.0	40.1
56.7	9.5	18.9	28.4	37.8	47.3	.7	0.7	1.6	2.5	3.5	4.4	5.4	6.3	7.3	8.2	9.1	
56.8	9.5	19.0	28.4	37.9	47.4	.8	0.8	1.7	2.6	3.6	4.5	5.5	6.4	7.3	8.3	9.2	
56.9	9.5	19.0	28.5	38.0	47.5	.9	0.8	1.8	2.7	3.7	4.6	5.6	6.5	7.4	8.4	9.3	
57.0	9.5	19.0	28.5	38.0	47.5	.0	0.0	1.0	1.9	2.9	3.8	4.8	5.7	6.7	7.7	8.6	
57.1	9.5	19.0	28.5	38.0	47.6	.1	0.1	1.1	2.0	3.0	3.9	4.9	5.8	6.8	7.8	8.7	
57.2	9.5	19.0	28.6	38.1	47.6	.2	0.2	1.1	2.1	3.1	4.0	5.0	5.9	6.9	7.9	8.8	
57.3	9.5	19.1	28.6	38.2	47.7	.3	0.3	1.2	2.2	3.2	4.1	5.1	6.0	7.0	8.0	8.9	5.0 / 0.1
57.4	9.6	19.1	28.7	38.3	47.8	.4	0.4	1.3	2.3	3.3	4.2	5.2	6.1	7.1	8.0	9.0	15.0 / 0.2
57.5	9.6	19.2	28.8	38.3	47.9	.5	0.5	1.4	2.4	3.4	4.3	5.3	6.2	7.2	8.1	9.1	25.0 / 0.3
57.6	9.6	19.2	28.8	38.4	48.0	.6	0.6	1.5	2.5	3.4	4.4	5.4	6.3	7.3	8.2	9.2	35.1
57.7	9.6	19.3	28.9	38.5	48.1	.7	0.7	1.6	2.6	3.5	4.5	5.5	6.4	7.4	8.3	9.3	
57.8	9.7	19.3	28.9	38.6	48.2	.8	0.8	1.7	2.7	3.6	4.6	5.6	6.5	7.5	8.4	9.4	
57.9	9.7	19.3	29.0	38.6	48.3	.9	0.9	1.8	2.8	3.7	4.7	5.7	6.6	7.6	8.5	9.5	
58.0	9.6	19.3	29.0	38.6	48.3	.0	0.0	1.0	1.9	2.9	3.9	4.9	5.8	6.8	7.8	8.8	
58.1	9.7	19.3	29.0	38.7	48.4	.1	0.1	1.1	2.0	3.0	4.0	5.0	5.9	6.9	7.9	8.9	
58.2	9.7	19.4	29.1	38.8	48.5	.2	0.2	1.2	2.1	3.1	4.1	5.1	6.0	7.0	8.0	9.0	
58.3	9.7	19.4	29.1	38.9	48.6	.3	0.3	1.3	2.2	3.2	4.2	5.2	6.1	7.1	8.1	9.1	
58.4	9.7	19.5	29.2	38.9	48.7	.4	0.4	1.4	2.3	3.3	4.3	5.3	6.2	7.2	8.2	9.2	8.2 / 0.1 / 24.6 / 0.2
58.5	9.8	19.5	29.3	39.0	48.8	.5	0.5	1.5	2.4	3.4	4.4	5.4	6.3	7.3	8.3	9.3	41.0
58.6	9.8	19.5	29.3	39.1	48.8	.6	0.6	1.6	2.5	3.5	4.5	5.5	6.4	7.4	8.4	9.4	
58.7	9.8	19.6	29.4	39.2	48.9	.7	0.7	1.7	2.6	3.6	4.6	5.6	6.5	7.5	8.5	9.5	
58.8	9.8	19.6	29.4	39.2	49.0	.8	0.8	1.8	2.7	3.7	4.7	5.7	6.6	7.6	8.6	9.6	
58.9	9.9	19.7	29.5	39.3	49.1	.9	0.9	1.9	2.8	3.8	4.8	5.8	6.7	7.7	8.7	9.7	
59.0	9.8	19.6	29.5	39.3	49.1	.0	0.0	1.0	2.0	3.0	4.0	5.0	5.9	6.9	7.9	8.9	
59.1	9.8	19.7	29.5	39.4	49.2	.1	0.1	1.1	2.1	3.1	4.1	5.1	6.0	7.0	8.0	9.0	
59.2	9.8	19.7	29.6	39.4	49.3	.2	0.2	1.2	2.2	3.2	4.2	5.2	6.1	7.1	8.1	9.1	16.2 / 0.1
59.3	9.9	19.8	29.6	39.5	49.4	.3	0.3	1.3	2.3	3.3	4.3	5.3	6.2	7.2	8.2	9.2	48.6
59.4	9.9	19.8	29.7	39.6	49.5	.4	0.4	1.4	2.4	3.4	4.4	5.4	6.3	7.3	8.3	9.3	
59.5	9.9	19.8	29.8	39.7	49.6	.5	0.5	1.5	2.5	3.5	4.5	5.5	6.4	7.4	8.4	9.4	
59.6	9.9	19.9	29.8	39.7	49.7	.6	0.6	1.6	2.6	3.6	4.6	5.6	6.5	7.5	8.5	9.5	
59.7	10.0	19.9	29.9	39.8	49.8	.7	0.7	1.7	2.7	3.7	4.7	5.7	6.6	7.6	8.6	9.6	0.0 / 0.0
59.8	10.0	20.0	29.9	39.9	49.9	.8	0.8	1.8	2.8	3.8	4.8	5.8	6.7	7.7	8.7	9.7	48.2
59.9	10.0	20.0	30.0	40.0	50.0	.9	0.9	1.9	2.9	3.9	4.9	5.9	6.8	7.8	8.8	9.8	
	10′	20′	30′	40′	50′		0′	1′	2′	3′	4′	5′	6′	7′	8′	9′	

The Double-Second-Difference correction (Corr.) is always to be added to the tabulated altitude.

Example of a Three-Star Fix

On the morning of November 4 the navigator obtained sextant altitudes of three stars during morning civil twilight. Use of the star finder had indicated that several stars would be available and a good spread in azimuth could be obtained by using Arcturus, Capella, and Sirius. The DR position was 37° 12′ north latitude and 72° 15′ west longitude. A split-second timer was used; it was started on the time tick so that no watch error would be involved. By starting the timer on the exact hour before the start of the observations, the minutes and seconds were correct for either zone time or GMT. Starting with the time and sextant altitude of the three stars and the DR position given above, the student can work the problem out on the blank form in Figure 9-1 and check the answers with the solution given in Figure 9-2. The fix is plotted in Figure 9-3.

Example of a Sun Line

On November 4, at 14 44 23 zone time +5, in DR latitude 37° 40′N, longitude 71° 20′W, an observation of the sun was made. The IC of the sextant was +0′.2, and the height of eye of the observer was 11 feet. Sextant altitude was 19° 43′.5. Referring as necessary to the tables cited at the beginning of this chapter, the student should follow through each entry in Figure 9-4 to determine how it was obtained. The plotting of the LOP representing the sun line is shown in Figure 9-5. Note that the symbol $\odot$ is used for the name of the body in the form; this indicates that a lower-limb sun observation was made. On the rare occasion when an upper-limb observation is made the symbol would be $\odot$.

Example of a Planet LOP

On November 4, at 17 19 20 zone time +5, an observation was made of the planet Jupiter. (If additional stars had been observed, and if these sights had been combined with the planet observation made during this twilight period, a multiple-star fix would have resulted.) The IC of the sextant was +0′.2, and the height of eye was 11 feet. Sextant altitude was 33° 20′.6. The complete solution is shown on the sight reduction form, Figure 9-4, and the resulting LOP is shown in Figure 9-7. Referring as necessary to the tables cited at the beginning of the chapter, follow through Figure 9-4 to determine how all the entries were obtained. But, first work the problem separately on the blank form provided in Figure 9-6; then, compare the answers with those in Figure 9-4.

SIGHT REDUCTION

Date	4 NOV.
Body	ARCTURUS
Lat. DR	N 37° 12′
λ	W 72° 15′

W. time +5	05 56 04
Corr.	+5
GMT	10 56 04

hs	20 33.7
I 0	
IC + .2	
Dip 11 FT.	
ha	
R	
Corr.	
Corr.	
Ho	

GHA ♈	
Corr.	
SHA-v	
GHA	
a λ	
LHA	
t (E)(W)	

Dec.	
d + −	
Dec.	
a L	

ht	
d corr.	
corr.	
Hc	
Ho	
a A or T	

Az	
Zn	

Date	4 NOV.
Body	CAPELLA
Lat.	N 37° 12′
λ	W 72° 15′

W. time +5	05 56 58
Corr.	+5
GMT	10 56 58

hs	47 47.7
I 0	
IC + .2	
Dip 11 FT.	
ha	
R	
Corr.	
Corr.	
Ho	

GHA	
Corr.	
SHA-v	
GHA	
a λ	
LHA	
t (E)(W)	

Dec.	
d + −	
Dec.	
a L	

ht	
d corr.	
corr.	
Hc	
Ho	
a A or T	

Az	
Zn	

Date	4 NOV.
Body	SIRIUS
Lat.	N 37° 12′
λ	W 72° 15′

W. time +5	05 57 50
Corr.	+5
GMT	10 57 50

hs	27 07.7
I 0	
IC + .2	
Dip 11 FT.	
ha	
R	
Corr.	
Corr.	
Ho	

GHA	
Corr.	
SHA-v	
GHA	
a λ	
LHA	
t (E)(W)	

Dec.	
d + −	
Dec.	
a.L	

ht	
d corr.	
corr.	
Hc	
Ho	
a A or T	

Az	
Zn	

FIGURE 9-1   Student's sight reduction form for three-star fix.

SIGHT REDUCTION

Date	4 NOV.
Body	ARCTURUS
Lat. DR	N 37° 12'
λ	W 72° 15'

W. time +5	05 56 04
Corr.	+5
GMT	10 56 04

hs	20 33.7
I 0	
IC +.2	+0.2
Dip 11 FT.	– 3.2
ha	20 30.7
R	– 2.6
Corr.	
Corr.	
Ho	20 28.1

GHA ♈	193 16.1
Corr.	14 03.3
SHA-v	146 22.5
GHA	353 41.9
a λ W	72 41.9
LHA	281
t (E)(W)	

Dec.	N 19 18.8
d + –	
Dec.	N 19 18.8
a L	N 37

ht	19 52.7
d corr. +33	+ 9.4
corr.	+ 0.9
Hc	20 03.0
Ho	20 28.1
a A or Ⓣ	25.1

Az	80.5
Zn	80°5

Date	4 NOV.
Body	CAPELLA
Lat.	N 37° 12'
λ	W 72° 15'

W. time +5	05 56 58
Corr.	+5
GMT	10 56 58

hs	47 47.7
I 0	
IC +.2	0.2
Dip 11 FT.	– 3.2
ha	47 44.7
R	– 0.9
Corr.	
Corr.	
Ho	47 43.8

GHA ♈	193 16.1
Corr.	14 16.8
SHA-v	281 16.9
GHA –360°	128 49.8
a λ	71 49.8
LHA	57
t (E)(W)	

Dec.	N 45 58.4
d + –	
Dec.	N 45 58.4
a L	N 37

ht	47 08.9
d corr. +9.9	+ 9.7
corr.	
Hc	47 18.6
Ho	47 43.8
a A or Ⓣ	25.2

	360
Az	59.5
Zn	300°5

Date	4 NOV.
Body	SIRIUS
Lat.	N 37° 12'
λ	W 72° 15'

W. time +5	05 57 50
Corr.	+5
GMT	10 57 50

hs	27 07.7
I 0	
IC +.2	0.2
Dip 11 FT.	– 3.2
ha	27 04.7
R	– 1.9
Corr.	
Corr.	
Ho	27 02.8

GHA ♈	193 16.1
Corr.	14 29.9
SHA-v	258 59.1
GHA –360°	106 45.1
a λ	71 45.1
LHA	35
t (E)(W)	

Dec.	S 16 40.8
d + –	
Dec.	S 16 40.8
a.L	N 37

ht	27 34.8
d corr. –51.5	– 34.0
corr.	– 1.0
Hc	26 59.8
Ho	27 02.8
a A or Ⓣ	3.0

	360
Az	142
Zn	218°

FIGURE 9-2   Solution to three-star fix.

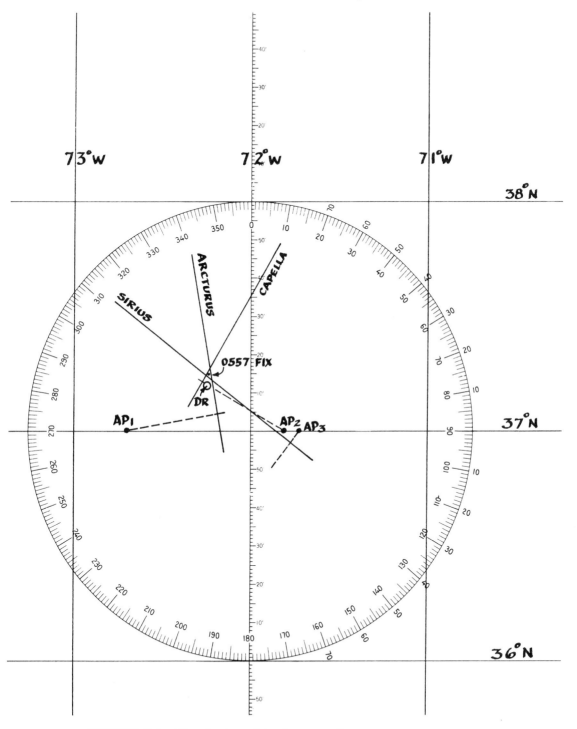

FIGURE 9-3 The plotting of the three-star fix.

Date	4 NOV.
Body	☉
Lat. DR	N 37° 40'
λ	W 71° 20'

Date	4 NOV.
Body	JUPITER
Lat.	N 37° 50'
λ	W 71° 10'

W. time	14 44 23
Corr.	+5
GMT	19 44 23

W. time	17 19 20
Corr.	+5
GMT	22 19 20

hs	19 43.5	
I		
IC +.2	+	.2
Dip 11 FT.	−	3.2
ha	19	40.5
R	+	13.6
Corr.		
Corr.		
Ho	19	54.1

hs	33 20.6	
I		
IC +.2	+	.2
Dip 11 FT	−	3.2
ha	33	17.6
R	−	1.5
Corr.		
Corr.		
Ho	33	16.1

GHA	109	06.0
Corr.	11	05.8
SHA-v		
GHA	120	11.8
a λ	71	11.8
LHA	49	
t (E)(W)		

GHA	33	35.9
Corr.	4	50.0
SHA ⓥ 2.5		0.8
GHA	38	26.7
a λ	71	26.7
LHA	327	
t (E)(W)	33	

Dec.	S 15 25.9	
d ⊕ 0.8	+	0.6
Dec.	S 15	26.5
a L	N 38	

Dec.	S 9 49.6	
d + −		
Dec.	S 9	49.6
a L	N 38	

ht	19 52.7
d corr. −46.6	− 17.7
corr.	− 2.9 / 20.6
Hc	19 32.1
Ho	19 54.1
a A or Ⓣ	22.0

ht	33 48.6
d corr. −51.5	− 41.3
corr.	− 1.2 / 42.5
Hc	33 06.1
Ho	33 16.1
a A or Ⓣ	10

360

Az	129.5
Zn	230.5

Az	140
Zn	140

FIGURE 9-4   Solution to sun line and planet LOP.

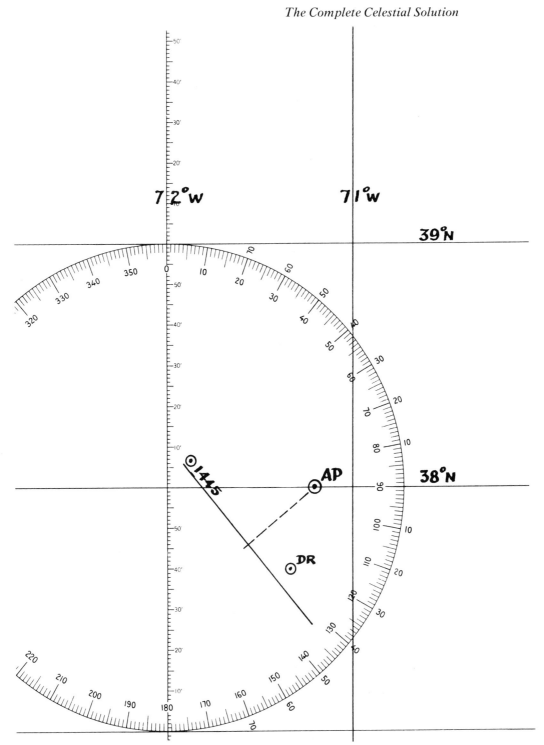

FIGURE 9-5 *The plotting of the sun line.*

SIGHT REDUCTION

Date			Date			Date	
Body			Body			Body	
Lat.			Lat.			Lat.	
λ			λ			λ	

W. time			W. time			W. time	
Corr.			Corr.			Corr.	
GMT			GMT			GMT	

hs			hs			hs	
I			I			I	
IC			IC			IC	
Dip			Dip			Dip	
ha			ha			ha	
R			R			R	
Corr.			Corr.			Corr.	
Corr.			Corr.			Corr.	
Ho			Ho			Ho	

GHA			GHA			GHA	
Corr.			Corr.			Corr.	
SHA-v			SHA-v			SHA-v	
GHA			GHA			GHA	
a λ			a λ			a λ	
LHA			LHA			LHA	
t (E)(W)			t (E)(W)			t (E)(W)	

Dec.			Dec.			Dec.	
d + −			d + −			d + −	
Dec.			Dec.			Dec.	
a L			a L			a.L	

ht			ht			ht	
d corr.			d corr.			d corr.	
corr.			corr.			corr.	
Hc			Hc			Hc	
Ho			Ho			Ho	
a A or T			a A or T			a A or T	

Az			Az			Az	
Zn			Zn			Zn	

FIGURE 9-6   *Student's sight reduction form for planet LOP.*

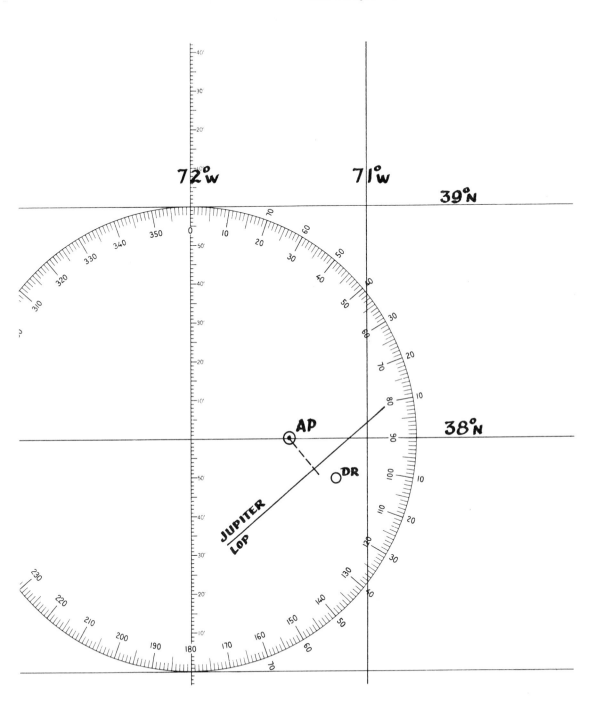

FIGURE 9-7 *The plotting of the planet LOP.*

Appendix I

Illustrations on the Plane of the Observer's Celestial Meridian

Throughout this text the coordinates used in celestial navigation have been shown on the time diagram and by schematic drawings illustrating the various coordinates on a sphere. Another method of illustrating problems is to use the plane of the observer's celestial meridian. This method is generally used to illustrate the horizon system of coordinates, but it can also be used with the celestial equator system of coordinates. The method uses an orthographic projection in which the point of projection is at infinity. The outer circumference of the circle always represents the observer's meridian.

When used to illustrate the horizon system, the components of this method are as follows:

1. A horizontal straight line through the center is the horizon.
2. A vertical straight line through the center is the prime vertical. This line passes through the zenith, the nadir, and the east and west points of the horizon.
3. The north point on the horizon is by custom at the left, and the south point is at the right.
4. The zenith of the observer is at the top, and the nadir is at the bottom.
5. Straight lines parallel to the horizon are altitude circles.

6. Vertical circles other than the prime vertical are sections of ellipses, but are often illustrated as arcs of circles for simplicity in sketching.

Figure A-1 illustrates the above coordinates.

When the celestial equator system of coordinates is projected on the plane of the observer's celestial meridian, the components of the method are as follows:

1. The horizontal straight line through the center represents the celestial equator.

2. A vertical straight line through the center represents the celestial meridian or hour circle with an LHA of 90° or 270°.

3. Straight lines parallel to the equator represent parallels of declination.

4. Celestial meridians and hour circles are shown as sections of ellipses passing through the north and south celestial poles, but are often drawn as arcs of circles for simplicity.

5. The North Pole is shown at the top of the illustration and the South Pole at the bottom.

These coordinates are shown in Figure A-2. If the two systems of coordinates are placed together and rotated to the correct point, the spherical triangle can be illustrated on the plane of the observer's meridian (see Figure A-3).

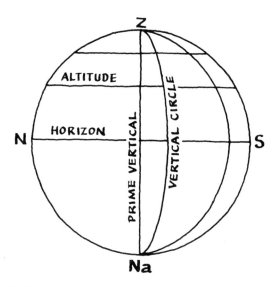

FIGURE A-1   The horizon system of coordinates.

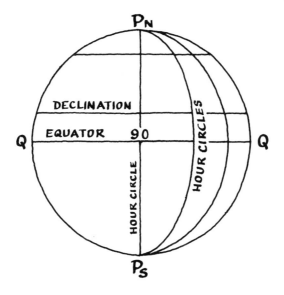

FIGURE A-2 The celestial equator system of coordinates.

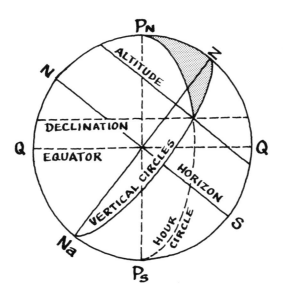

FIGURE A-3 The combined coordinate systems, illustrating a celestial triangle.

Appendix II

Conversion of Arc to Time

0°–59°		60°–119°		120°–179°		180°–239°		240°–299°		300°–359°			0′.00	0′.25	0′.50	0′.75
°	h m	°	h m	°	h m	°	h m	°	h m	°	h m	′	m s	m s	m s	m s
0	0 00	60	4 00	120	8 00	180	12 00	240	16 00	300	20 00	0	0 00	0 01	0 02	0 03
1	0 04	61	4 04	121	8 04	181	12 04	241	16 04	301	20 04	1	0 04	0 05	0 06	0 07
2	0 08	62	4 08	122	8 08	182	12 08	242	16 08	302	20 08	2	0 08	0 09	0 10	0 11
3	0 12	63	4 12	123	8 12	183	12 12	243	16 12	303	20 12	3	0 12	0 13	0 14	0 15
4	0 16	64	4 16	124	8 16	184	12 16	244	16 16	304	20 16	4	0 16	0 17	0 18	0 19
5	0 20	65	4 20	125	8 20	185	12 20	245	16 20	305	20 20	5	0 20	0 21	0 22	0 23
6	0 24	66	4 24	126	8 24	186	12 24	246	16 24	306	20 24	6	0 24	0 25	0 26	0 27
7	0 28	67	4 28	127	8 28	187	12 28	247	16 28	307	20 28	7	0 28	0 29	0 30	0 31
8	0 32	68	4 32	128	8 32	188	12 32	248	16 32	308	20 32	8	0 32	0 33	0 34	0 35
9	0 36	69	4 36	129	8 36	189	12 36	249	16 36	309	20 36	9	0 36	0 37	0 38	0 39
10	0 40	70	4 40	130	8 40	190	12 40	250	16 40	310	20 40	10	0 40	0 41	0 42	0 43
11	0 44	71	4 44	131	8 44	191	12 44	251	16 44	311	20 44	11	0 44	0 45	0 46	0 47
12	0 48	72	4 48	132	8 48	192	12 48	252	16 48	312	20 48	12	0 48	0 49	0 50	0 51
13	0 52	73	4 52	133	8 52	193	12 52	253	16 52	313	20 52	13	0 52	0 53	0 54	0 55
14	0 56	74	4 56	134	8 56	194	12 56	254	16 56	314	20 56	14	0 56	0 57	0 58	0 59
15	1 00	75	5 00	135	9 00	195	13 00	255	17 00	315	21 00	15	1 00	1 01	1 02	1 03
16	1 04	76	5 04	136	9 04	196	13 04	256	17 04	316	21 04	16	1 04	1 05	1 06	1 07
17	1 08	77	5 08	137	9 08	197	13 08	257	17 08	317	21 08	17	1 08	1 09	1 10	1 11
18	1 12	78	5 12	138	9 12	198	13 12	258	17 12	318	21 12	18	1 12	1 13	1 14	1 15
19	1 16	79	5 16	139	9 16	199	13 16	259	17 16	319	21 16	19	1 16	1 17	1 18	1 19
20	1 20	80	5 20	140	9 20	200	13 20	260	17 20	320	21 20	20	1 20	1 21	1 22	1 23
21	1 24	81	5 24	141	9 24	201	13 24	261	17 24	321	21 24	21	1 24	1 25	1 26	1 27
22	1 28	82	5 28	142	9 28	202	13 28	262	17 28	322	21 28	22	1 28	1 29	1 30	1 31
23	1 32	83	5 32	143	9 32	203	13 32	263	17 32	323	21 32	23	1 32	1 33	1 34	1 35
24	1 36	84	5 36	144	9 36	204	13 36	264	17 36	324	21 36	24	1 36	1 37	1 38	1 39
25	1 40	85	5 40	145	9 40	205	13 40	265	17 40	325	21 40	25	1 40	1 41	1 42	1 43
26	1 44	86	5 44	146	9 44	206	13 44	266	17 44	326	21 44	26	1 44	1 45	1 46	1 47
27	1 48	87	5 48	147	9 48	207	13 48	267	17 48	327	21 48	27	1 48	1 49	1 50	1 51
28	1 52	88	5 52	148	9 52	208	13 52	268	17 52	328	21 52	28	1 52	1 53	1 54	1 55
29	1 56	89	5 56	149	9 56	209	13 56	269	17 56	329	21 56	29	1 56	1 57	1 58	1 59
30	2 00	90	6 00	150	10 00	210	14 00	270	18 00	330	22 00	30	2 00	2 01	2 02	2 03
31	2 04	91	6 04	151	10 04	211	14 04	271	18 04	331	22 04	31	2 04	2 05	2 06	2 07
32	2 08	92	6 08	152	10 08	212	14 08	272	18 08	332	22 08	32	2 08	2 09	2 10	2 11
33	2 12	93	6 12	153	10 12	213	14 12	273	18 12	333	22 12	33	2 12	2 13	2 14	2 15
34	2 16	94	6 16	154	10 16	214	14 16	274	18 16	334	22 16	34	2 16	2 17	2 18	2 19
35	2 20	95	6 20	155	10 20	215	14 20	275	18 20	335	22 20	35	2 20	2 21	2 22	2 23
36	2 24	96	6 24	156	10 24	216	14 24	276	18 24	336	22 24	36	2 24	2 25	2 26	2 27
37	2 28	97	6 28	157	10 28	217	14 28	277	18 28	337	22 28	37	2 28	2 29	2 30	2 31
38	2 32	98	6 32	158	10 32	218	14 32	278	18 32	338	22 32	38	2 32	2 33	2 34	2 35
39	2 36	99	6 36	159	10 36	219	14 36	279	18 36	339	22 36	39	2 36	2 37	2 38	2 39
40	2 40	100	6 40	160	10 40	220	14 40	280	18 40	340	22 40	40	2 40	2 41	2 42	2 43
41	2 44	101	6 44	161	10 44	221	14 44	281	18 44	341	22 44	41	2 44	2 45	2 46	2 47
42	2 48	102	6 48	162	10 48	222	14 48	282	18 48	342	22 48	42	2 48	2 49	2 50	2 51
43	2 52	103	6 52	163	10 52	223	14 52	283	18 52	343	22 52	43	2 52	2 53	2 54	2 55
44	2 56	104	6 56	164	10 56	224	14 56	284	18 56	344	22 56	44	2 56	2 57	2 58	2 59
45	3 00	105	7 00	165	11 00	225	15 00	285	19 00	345	23 00	45	3 00	3 01	3 02	3 03
46	3 04	106	7 04	166	11 04	226	15 04	286	19 04	346	23 04	46	3 04	3 05	3 06	3 07
47	3 08	107	7 08	167	11 08	227	15 08	287	19 08	347	23 08	47	3 08	3 09	3 10	3 11
48	3 12	108	7 12	168	11 12	228	15 12	288	19 12	348	23 12	48	3 12	3 13	3 14	3 15
49	3 16	109	7 16	169	11 16	229	15 16	289	19 16	349	23 16	49	3 16	3 17	3 18	3 19
50	3 20	110	7 20	170	11 20	230	15 20	290	19 20	350	23 20	50	3 20	3 21	3 22	3 23
51	3 24	111	7 24	171	11 24	231	15 24	291	19 24	351	23 24	51	3 24	3 25	3 26	3 27
52	3 28	112	7 28	172	11 28	232	15 28	292	19 28	352	23 28	52	3 28	3 29	3 30	3 31
53	3 32	113	7 32	173	11 32	233	15 32	293	19 32	353	23 32	53	3 32	3 33	3 34	3 35
54	3 36	114	7 36	174	11 36	234	15 36	294	19 36	354	23 36	54	3 36	3 37	3 38	3 39
55	3 40	115	7 40	175	11 40	235	15 40	295	19 40	355	23 40	55	3 40	3 41	3 42	3 43
56	3 44	116	7 44	176	11 44	236	15 44	296	19 44	356	23 44	56	3 44	3 45	3 46	3 47
57	3 48	117	7 48	177	11 48	237	15 48	297	19 48	357	23 48	57	3 48	3 49	3 50	3 51
58	3 52	118	7 52	178	11 52	238	15 52	298	19 52	358	23 52	58	3 52	3 53	3 54	3 55
59	3 56	119	7 56	179	11 56	239	15 56	299	19 56	359	23 56	59	3 56	3 57	3 58	3 59

The above table is for converting expressions in arc to their equivalent in time ; its main use in this Almanac is for the conversion of longitude for application to L.M.T. (*added* if *west*, *subtracted* if *east*) to give G.M.T. or vice versa, particularly in the case of sunrise, sunset, etc.

Appendix III

Speed, Time, and Distance Table

Min-utes	Speed in knots																Min-utes
	0.5	1.0	1.5	2.0	2.5	3.0	3.5	4.0	4.5	5.0	5.5	6.0	6.5	7.0	7.5	8.0	
	Miles	Miles	Miles	Miles	Miles	Miles	Miles	Miles	Miles	Miles	Miles	Miles	Miles	Miles	Miles	Miles	
1	0.0	0.0	0.0	0.0	0.0	0.0	0.1	0.1	0.1	0.1	0.1	0.1	0.1	0.1	0.1	0.1	1
2	0.0	0.0	0.0	0.1	0.1	0.1	0.1	0.1	0.2	0.2	0.2	0.2	0.2	0.2	0.2	0.3	2
3	0.0	0.0	0.1	0.1	0.1	0.2	0.2	0.2	0.2	0.2	0.3	0.3	0.3	0.4	0.4	0.4	3
4	0.0	0.1	0.1	0.1	0.2	0.2	0.2	0.3	0.3	0.3	0.4	0.4	0.4	0.5	0.5	0.5	4
5	0.0	0.1	0.1	0.2	0.2	0.2	0.3	0.3	0.4	0.4	0.5	0.5	0.5	0.6	0.6	0.7	5
6	0.0	0.1	0.2	0.2	0.2	0.3	0.4	0.4	0.4	0.5	0.6	0.6	0.6	0.7	0.8	0.8	6
7	0.1	0.1	0.2	0.2	0.3	0.4	0.4	0.5	0.5	0.6	0.6	0.7	0.8	0.8	0.9	0.9	7
8	0.1	0.1	0.2	0.3	0.3	0.4	0.5	0.5	0.6	0.7	0.7	0.8	0.9	0.9	1.0	1.1	8
9	0.1	0.2	0.2	0.3	0.4	0.4	0.5	0.6	0.7	0.8	0.8	0.9	1.0	1.0	1.1	1.2	9
10	0.1	0.2	0.2	0.3	0.4	0.5	0.6	0.7	0.8	0.8	0.9	1.0	1.1	1.2	1.2	1.3	10
11	0.1	0.2	0.3	0.4	0.5	0.6	0.6	0.7	0.8	0.9	1.0	1.1	1.2	1.3	1.4	1.5	11
12	0.1	0.2	0.3	0.4	0.5	0.6	0.7	0.8	0.9	1.0	1.1	1.2	1.3	1.4	1.5	1.6	12
13	0.1	0.2	0.3	0.4	0.5	0.6	0.8	0.9	1.0	1.1	1.2	1.3	1.4	1.5	1.6	1.7	13
14	0.1	0.2	0.4	0.5	0.6	0.7	0.8	0.9	1.0	1.2	1.3	1.4	1.5	1.6	1.8	1.9	14
15	0.1	0.2	0.4	0.5	0.6	0.8	0.9	1.0	1.1	1.2	1.4	1.5	1.6	1.8	1.9	2.0	15
16	0.1	0.3	0.4	0.5	0.7	0.8	0.9	1.1	1.2	1.3	1.5	1.6	1.7	1.9	2.0	2.1	16
17	0.1	0.3	0.4	0.6	0.7	0.8	1.0	1.1	1.3	1.4	1.6	1.7	1.8	2.0	2.1	2.3	17
18	0.2	0.3	0.4	0.6	0.8	0.9	1.0	1.2	1.4	1.5	1.6	1.8	2.0	2.1	2.2	2.4	18
19	0.2	0.3	0.5	0.6	0.8	1.0	1.1	1.3	1.4	1.6	1.7	1.9	2.1	2.2	2.4	2.5	19
20	0.2	0.3	0.5	0.7	0.8	1.0	1.2	1.3	1.5	1.7	1.8	2.0	2.2	2.3	2.5	2.7	20
21	0.2	0.4	0.5	0.7	0.9	1.0	1.2	1.4	1.6	1.8	1.9	2.1	2.3	2.4	2.6	2.8	21
22	0.2	0.4	0.6	0.7	0.9	1.1	1.3	1.5	1.6	1.8	2.0	2.2	2.4	2.6	2.8	2.9	22
23	0.2	0.4	0.6	0.8	1.0	1.2	1.3	1.5	1.7	1.9	2.1	2.3	2.5	2.7	2.9	3.1	23
24	0.2	0.4	0.6	0.8	1.0	1.2	1.4	1.6	1.8	2.0	2.2	2.4	2.6	2.8	3.0	3.2	24
25	0.2	0.4	0.6	0.8	1.0	1.2	1.5	1.7	1.9	2.1	2.3	2.5	2.7	2.9	3.1	3.3	25
26	0.2	0.4	0.6	0.9	1.1	1.3	1.5	1.7	2.0	2.2	2.4	2.6	2.8	3.0	3.2	3.5	26
27	0.2	0.4	0.7	0.9	1.1	1.4	1.6	1.8	2.0	2.2	2.5	2.7	2.9	3.2	3.4	3.6	27
28	0.2	0.5	0.7	0.9	1.2	1.4	1.6	1.9	2.1	2.3	2.6	2.8	3.0	3.3	3.5	3.7	28
29	0.2	0.5	0.7	1.0	1.2	1.4	1.7	1.9	2.2	2.4	2.7	2.9	3.1	3.4	3.6	3.9	29
30	0.2	0.5	0.8	1.0	1.2	1.5	1.8	2.0	2.2	2.5	2.8	3.0	3.2	3.5	3.8	4.0	30
31	0.3	0.5	0.8	1.0	1.3	1.6	1.8	2.1	2.3	2.6	2.8	3.1	3.4	3.6	3.9	4.1	31
32	0.3	0.5	0.8	1.1	1.3	1.6	1.9	2.1	2.4	2.7	2.9	3.2	3.5	3.7	4.0	4.3	32
33	0.3	0.6	0.8	1.1	1.4	1.6	1.9	2.2	2.5	2.8	3.0	3.3	3.6	3.8	4.1	4.4	33
34	0.3	0.6	0.8	1.1	1.4	1.7	2.0	2.3	2.6	2.8	3.1	3.4	3.7	4.0	4.2	4.5	34
35	0.3	0.6	0.9	1.2	1.5	1.8	2.0	2.3	2.6	2.9	3.2	3.5	3.8	4.1	4.4	4.7	35
36	0.3	0.6	0.9	1.2	1.5	1.8	2.1	2.4	2.7	3.0	3.3	3.6	3.9	4.2	4.5	4.8	36
37	0.3	0.6	0.9	1.2	1.5	1.8	2.2	2.5	2.8	3.1	3.4	3.7	4.0	4.3	4.6	4.9	37
38	0.3	0.6	1.0	1.3	1.6	1.9	2.2	2.5	2.8	3.2	3.5	3.8	4.1	4.4	4.8	5.1	38
39	0.3	0.6	1.0	1.3	1.6	2.0	2.3	2.6	2.9	3.2	3.6	3.9	4.2	4.6	4.9	5.2	39
40	0.3	0.7	1.0	1.3	1.7	2.0	2.3	2.7	3.0	3.3	3.7	4.0	4.3	4.7	5.0	5.3	40
41	0.3	0.7	1.0	1.4	1.7	2.0	2.4	2.7	3.1	3.4	3.8	4.1	4.4	4.8	5.1	5.5	41
42	0.4	0.7	1.0	1.4	1.8	2.1	2.4	2.8	3.2	3.5	3.8	4.2	4.6	4.9	5.2	5.6	42
43	0.4	0.7	1.1	1.4	i.8	2.2	2.5	2.9	3.2	3.6	3.9	4.3	4.7	5.0	5.4	5.7	43
44	0.4	0.7	1.1	1.5	1.8	2.2	2.6	2.9	3.3	3.7	4.0	4.4	4.8	5.1	5.5	5.9	44
45	0.4	0.8	1.1	1.5	1.9	2.2	2.6	3.0	3.4	3.8	4.1	4.5	4.9	5.2	5.6	6.0	45
46	0.4	0.8	1.2	1.5	1.9	2.3	2.7	3.1	3.4	3.8	4.2	4.6	5.0	5.4	5.8	6.1	46
47	0.4	0.8	1.2	1.6	2.0	2.4	2.7	3.1	3.5	3.9	4.3	4.7	5.1	5.5	5.9	6.3	47
48	0.4	0.8	1.2	1.6	2.0	2.4	2.8	3.2	3.6	4.0	4.4	4.8	5.2	5.6	6.0	6.4	48
49	0.4	0.8	1.2	1.6	2.0	2.4	2.9	3.3	3.7	4.1	4.5	4.9	5.3	5.7	6.1	6.5	49
50	0.4	0.8	1.2	1.7	2.1	2.5	2.9	3.3	3.8	4.2	4.6	5.0	5.4	5.8	6.2	6.7	50
51	0.4	0.8	1.3	1.7	2.1	2.6	3.0	3.4	3.8	4.2	4.7	5.1	5.5	6.0	6.4	6.8	51
52	0.4	0.9	1.3	1.7	2.2	2.6	3.0	3.5	3.9	4.3	4.8	5.2	5.6	6.1	6.5	6.9	52
53	0.4	0.9	1.3	1.8	2.2	2.6	3.1	3.5	4.0	4.4	4.9	5.3	5.7	6.2	6.6	7.1	53
54	0.4	0.9	1.4	1.8	2.2	2.7	3.2	3.6	4.0	4.5	5.0	5.4	5.8	6.3	6.8	7.2	54
55	0.5	0.9	1.4	1.8	2.3	2.8	3.2	3.7	4.1	4.6	5.0	5.5	6.0	6.4	6.9	7.3	55
56	0.5	0.9	1.4	1.9	2.3	2.8	3.3	3.7	4.2	4.7	5.1	5.6	6.1	6.5	7.0	7.5	56
57	0.5	1.0	1.4	1.9	2.4	2.8	3.3	3.8	4.3	4.8	5.2	5.7	6.2	6.6	7.1	7.6	57
58	0.5	1.0	1.4	1.9	2.4	2.9	3.4	3.9	4.4	4.8	5.3	5.8	6.3	6.8	7.2	7.7	58
59	0.5	1.0	1.5	2.0	2.5	3.0	3.4	3.9	4.4	4.9	5.4	5.9	6.4	6.9	7.4	7.9	59
60	0.5	1.0	1.5	2.0	2.5	3.0	3.5	4.0	4.5	5.0	5.5	6.0	6.5	7.0	7.5	8.0	60

Min-utes	Speed in knots																Min-utes
	8.5	9.0	9.5	10.0	10.5	11.0	11.5	12.0	12.5	13.0	13.5	14.0	14.5	15.0	15.5	16.0	
	Miles	*Miles*	*Miles*	*Miles*	*Miles*	*Miles*	*Miles*	*Miles*	*Miles*	*Miles*	*Miles*	*Miles*	*Miles*	*Miles*	*Miles*	*Miles*	
1	0.1	0.2	0.2	0.2	0.2	0.2	0.2	0.2	0.2	0.2	0.2	0.2	0.2	0.2	0.3	0.3	1
2	0.3	0.3	0.3	0.3	0.4	0.4	0.4	0.4	0.4	0.4	0.4	0.5	0.5	0.5	0.5	0.5	2
3	0.4	0.4	0.5	0.5	0.5	0.6	0.6	0.6	0.6	0.6	0.7	0.7	0.7	0.8	0.8	0.8	3
4	0.6	0.6	0.6	0.7	0.7	0.7	0.8	0.8	0.8	0.9	0.9	0.9	1.0	1.0	1.0	1.1	4
5	0.7	0.8	0.8	0.8	0.9	0.9	1.0	1.0	1.0	1.1	1.1	1.2	1.2	1.2	1.3	1.3	5
6	0.8	0.9	1.0	1.0	1.0	1.1	1.2	1.2	1.2	1.3	1.4	1.4	1.4	1.5	1.6	1.6	6
7	1.0	1.0	1.1	1.2	1.2	1.3	1.3	1.4	1.5	1.5	1.6	1.6	1.7	1.8	1.8	1.9	7
8	1.1	1.2	1.3	1.3	1.4	1.5	1.5	1.6	1.7	1.7	1.8	1.9	1.9	2.0	2.1	2.1	8
9	1.3	1.4	1.4	1.5	1.6	1.6	1.7	1.8	1.9	2.0	2.0	2.1	2.2	2.2	2.3	2.4	9
10	1.4	1.5	1.6	1.7	1.8	1.8	1.9	2.0	2.1	2.2	2.2	2.3	2.4	2.5	2.6	2.7	10
11	1.6	1.6	1.7	1.8	1.9	2.0	2.1	2.2	2.3	2.4	2.5	2.6	2.7	2.8	2.8	2.9	11
12	1.7	1.8	1.9	2.0	2.1	2.2	2.3	2.4	2.5	2.6	2.7	2.8	2.9	3.0	3.1	3.2	12
13	1.8	2.0	2.1	2.2	2.3	2.4	2.5	2.6	2.7	2.8	2.9	3.0	3.1	3.2	3.4	3.5	13
14	2.0	2.1	2.2	2.3	2.4	2.6	2.7	2.8	2.9	3.0	3.2	3.3	3.4	3.5	3.6	3.7	14
15	2.1	2.2	2.4	2.5	2.6	2.8	2.9	3.0	3.1	3.2	3.4	3.5	3.6	3.8	3.9	4.0	15
16	2.3	2.4	2.5	2.7	2.8	2.9	3.1	3.2	3.3	3.5	3.6	3.7	3.9	4.0	4.1	4.3	16
17	2.4	2.6	2.7	2.8	3.0	3.1	3.3	3.4	3.5	3.7	3.8	4.0	4.1	4.2	4.4	4.5	17
18	2.6	2.7	2.8	3.0	3.2	3.3	3.4	3.6	3.8	3.9	4.0	4.2	4.4	4.5	4.6	4.8	18
19	2.7	2.8	3.0	3.2	3.3	3.5	3.6	3.8	4.0	4.1	4.3	4.4	4.6	4.8	4.9	5.1	19
20	2.8	3.0	3.2	3.3	3.5	3.7	3.8	4.0	4.2	4.3	4.5	4.7	4.8	5.0	5.2	5.3	20
21	3.0	3.2	3.3	3.5	3.7	3.8	4.0	4.2	4.4	4.6	4.7	4.9	5.1	5.2	5.4	5.6	21
22	3.1	3.3	3.5	3.7	3.8	4.0	4.2	4.4	4.6	4.8	5.0	5.1	5.3	5.5	5.7	5.9	22
23	3.3	3.4	3.6	3.8	4.0	4.2	4.4	4.6	4.8	5.0	5.2	5.4	5.6	5.8	5.9	6.1	23
24	3.4	3.6	3.8	4.0	4.2	4.4	4.6	4.8	5.0	5.2	5.4	5.6	5.8	6.0	6.2	6.4	24
25	3.5	3.8	4.0	4.2	4.4	4.6	4.8	5.0	5.2	5.4	5.6	5.8	6.0	6.2	6.5	6.7	25
26	3.7	3.9	4.1	4.3	4.6	4.8	5.0	5.2	5.4	5.6	5.8	6.1	6.3	6.5	6.7	6.9	26
27	3.8	4.0	4.3	4.5	4.7	5.0	5.2	5.4	5.6	5.8	6.1	6.3	6.5	6.8	7.0	7.2	27
28	4.0	4.2	4.4	4.7	4.9	5.1	5.4	5.6	5.8	6.1	6.3	6.5	6.8	7.0	7.2	7.5	28
29	4.1	4.4	4.6	4.8	5.1	5.3	5.6	5.8	6.0	6.3	6.5	6.8	7.0	7.2	7.5	7.7	29
30	4.2	4.5	4.8	5.0	5.2	5.5	5.8	6.0	6.2	6.5	6.8	7.0	7.2	7.5	7.8	8.0	30
31	4.4	4.6	4.9	5.2	5.4	5.7	5.9	6.2	6.5	6.7	7.0	7.2	7.5	7.8	8.0	8.3	31
32	4.5	4.8	5.1	5.3	5.6	5.9	6.1	6.4	6.7	6.9	7.2	7.5	7.7	8.0	8.3	8.5	32
33	4.7	5.0	5.2	5.5	5.8	6.0	6.3	6.6	6.9	7.2	7.4	7.7	8.0	8.2	8.5	8.8	33
34	4.8	5.1	5.4	5.7	6.0	6.2	6.5	6.8	7.1	7.4	7.6	7.9	8.2	8.5	8.8	9.1	34
35	5.0	5.2	5.5	5.8	6.1	6.4	6.7	7.0	7.3	7.6	7.9	8.2	8.5	8.8	9.0	9.3	35
36	5.1	5.4	5.7	6.0	6.3	6.6	6.9	7.2	7.5	7.8	8.1	8.4	8.7	9.0	9.3	9.6	36
37	5.2	5.6	5.9	6.2	6.5	6.8	7.1	7.4	7.7	8.0	8.3	8.6	8.9	9.2	9.6	9.9	37
38	5.4	5.7	6.0	6.3	6.6	7.0	7.3	7.6	7.9	8.2	8.6	8.9	9.2	9.5	9.8	10.1	38
39	5.5	5.8	6.2	6.5	6.8	7.2	7.5	7.8	8.1	8.4	8.8	9.1	9.4	9.8	10.1	10.4	39
40	5.7	6.0	6.3	6.7	7.0	7.3	7.7	8.0	8.3	8.7	9.0	9.3	9.7	10.0	10.3	10.7	40
41	5.8	6.2	6.5	6.8	7.2	7.5	7.9	8.2	8.5	8.9	9.2	9.6	9.9	10.2	10.6	10.9	41
42	6.0	6.3	6.6	7.0	7.4	7.7	8.0	8.4	8.8	9.1	9.4	9.8	10.2	10.5	10.8	11.2	42
43	6.1	6.4	6.8	7.2	7.5	7.9	8.2	8.6	9.0	9.3	9.7	10.0	10.4	10.8	11.1	11.5	43
44	6.2	6.6	7.0	7.3	7.7	8.1	8.4	8.8	9.2	9.5	9.9	10.3	10.7	11.0	11.4	11.7	44
45	6.4	6.8	7.1	7.5	7.9	8.2	8.6	9.0	9.4	9.8	10.1	10.5	10.9	11.2	11.6	12.0	45
46	6.5	6.9	7.3	7.7	8.0	8.4	8.8	9.2	9.6	10.0	10.4	10.7	11.1	11.5	11.9	12.3	46
47	6.7	7.0	7.4	7.8	8.2	8.6	9.0	9.4	9.8	10.2	10.6	11.0	11.4	11.8	12.1	12.5	47
48	6.8	7.2	7.6	8.0	8.4	8.8	9.2	9.6	10.0	10.4	10.8	11.2	11.6	12.0	12.4	12.8	48
49	6.9	7.4	7.8	8.2	8.6	9.0	9.4	9.8	10.2	10.6	11.0	11.4	11.8	12.2	12.7	13.1	49
50	7.1	7.5	7.9	8.3	8.8	9.2	9.6	10.0	10.4	10.8	11.2	11.7	12.1	12.5	12.9	13.3	50
51	7.2	7.6	8.1	8.5	8.9	9.4	9.8	10.2	10.6	11.0	11.5	11.9	12.3	12.8	13.2	13.6	51
52	7.4	7.8	8.2	8.7	9.1	9.5	10.0	10.4	10.8	11.3	11.7	12.1	12.6	13.0	13.4	13.9	52
53	7.5	8.0	8.4	8.8	9.3	9.7	10.2	10.6	11.0	11.5	11.9	12.4	12.8	13.2	13.7	14.1	53
54	7.6	8.1	8.6	9.0	9.4	9.9	10.4	10.8	11.2	11.7	12.2	12.6	13.0	13.5	14.0	14.4	54
55	7.8	8.2	8.7	9.2	9.6	10.1	10.5	11.0	11.5	11.9	12.4	12.8	13.3	13.8	14.2	14.7	55
56	7.9	8.4	8.9	9.3	9.8	10.3	10.7	11.2	11.7	12.1	12.6	13.1	13.5	14.0	14.5	14.9	56
57	8.1	8.6	9.0	9.5	10.0	10.4	10.9	11.4	11.9	12.4	12.8	13.3	13.8	14.2	14.7	15.2	57
58	8.2	8.7	9.2	9.7	10.2	10.6	11.1	11.6	12.1	12.6	13.0	13.5	14.0	14.5	15.0	15.5	58
59	8.4	8.8	9.3	9.8	10.3	10.8	11.3	11.8	12.3	12.8	13.3	13.8	14.3	14.8	15.2	15.7	59
60	8.5	9.0	9.5	10.0	10.5	11.0	11.5	12.0	12.5	13.0	13.5	14.0	14.5	15.0	15.5	16.0	60

Appendix IV

Preparing the Sextant for Shipment

The sextant is a delicate instrument that can be damaged quite easily in shipment if not properly packaged. The instrument case in which all high-quality sextants are supplied is intended primarily for hand carrying and for storage of the sextant. One cannot fasten the sextant in the case and then expect it to survive the rough handling of shipping. If the following precautions are observed, the sextant can be shipped safely by common carrier:

1. Release the tangent screw from the gears on the frame, and tie the release mechanism in this position. If this is not done, the precision gear teeth can be damaged.

2. Tie the index arm to the sextant frame so that it will not swing along the arc.

3. Fasten the sextant in the holder in the instrument case.

4. Pack all extra space in the instrument case with crumpled wrapping paper or newspaper. The retaining unit in the box will not always hold if the shipping case is dropped or thrown, and this inner packing will prevent the mirrors from hitting the lid of the box.

5. Place the instrument case in a large, new cardboard shipping carton so that there are at least three or four inches of packing on all sides. The cardboard shipping carton will cushion more shocks than an outer wooden box.

Appendix V

Care of the Sextant

The marine sextant is a precision instrument and should be treated as such. If the instrument is dropped on the deck, it can easily be damaged beyond repair, as a bent frame cannot be corrected. However, with reasonable care the sextant should last the navigator's lifetime and never have to be replaced.

The sextant should always be set down on its legs; never place it face down on a surface. When removing the sextant from the box, pick it up by the frame itself, never by the index arm or mirror frames. When the sextant is not being used, store it in the instrument case and keep the case in a secure spot so that it will not drift free in rough weather.

Clean the mirrors with lens paper or, lacking this, a well-worn clean linen handkerchief. Never use man-made fabrics, such as rayon, as they tend to scratch the mirror surface. If salt spray blows onto the mirrors, rinse it off with a small amount of clean water.

The sextant arc and micrometer drum assembly should be kept lubricated. Any fine instrument oil or a light household oil will suffice for this. When the index arm tends to bind or stick rather than run smoothly along the arc, this is almost always due to a lack of proper lubrication. Apply a few drops of oil to the arc, and rub off the excess with a clean cloth. All exposed screw heads should also be wiped off occasionally with a cloth containing oil. These are the points where corrosion tends to start after long exposure to salt air and salt spray. By using these precautions and keeping the sextant clean and oiled, one should never have to replace any of the sextant parts, except for the mirror. The reverse side of sextant mirrors is covered with a protective lacquer, but the elements occasionally eat through this and cause black spots on the mirror. This generally occurs when the sextant has been used in small boats and a large amount of wind-driven spray has accumulated on it; some of this spray finds its way behind the mirror, where it cannot be wiped off. When purchasing new mirrors, be sure to obtain the original type—made of optical glass—as the reflecting surfaces must be ground plane-parallel; inexpensive pocket mirrors do not have this optical characteristic.

Appendix VI

Blank Sight Reduction Forms

Date	
Body	
Lat.	
λ	

Date	
Body	
Lat.	
λ	

Date	
Body	
Lat.	
λ	

W. time	
Corr.	
GMT	

W. time	
Corr.	
GMT	

W. time	
Corr.	
GMT	

hs	
I	
IC	
Dip	
ha	
R	
Corr.	
Corr.	
Ho	

hs	
I	
IC	
Dip	
ha	
R	
Corr.	
Corr.	
Ho	

hs	
I	
IC	
Dip	
ha	
R	
Corr.	
Corr.	
Ho	

GHA	
Corr.	
SHA-v	
GHA	
a λ	
LHA	
t (E)(W)	

GHA	
Corr.	
SHA-v	
GHA	
a λ	
LHA	
t (E)(W)	

GHA	
Corr.	
SHA-v	
GHA	
a λ	
LHA	
t (E)(W)	

Dec.	
d + −	
Dec.	
a L	

Dec.	
d + −	
Dec.	
a L	

Dec.	
d + −	
Dec.	
a.L	

ht	
d corr.	
corr.	
Hc	
Ho	
a A or T	

ht	
d corr.	
corr.	
Hc	
Ho	
a A or T	

ht	
d corr.	
corr.	
Hc	
Ho	
a A or T	

Az	
Zn	

Az	
Zn	

Az	
Zn	

138

Appendix VII

(The H.O. 249) Sight Reduction Tables for Air Navigation

H.O. 249 is published in three volumes. Volumes II and III are somewhat similar to H.O. 229 in that the entering arguments are assumed latitude, declination, and LHA. The principal difference is that page opening is by latitude and column headings are in terms of declination. Separate pages are used for "Declination Same Name as Latitude" and "Declination Contrary Name to Latitude." The values extracted by inspecting the main tables are Hc, to the nearest minute of arc, d the difference in Hc between successive integral degrees of declination columns, and Z, the azimuth angle. Volumes II and III include a table for obtaining the "Correction to Tabulated Altitude for Minutes of Declination" by combining d with its sign, as taken from the main table, with minutes of declination. Volume II is used for latitudes 0°–39°, and Volume III is used for latitudes 40°–89°. These volumes are intended primarily for use with the bodies in the solar system (the sun, the moon, and the planets), and the range of declination represented in them is only from 0° to 29°. They cannot be used with stars having a declination greater than 29°.

Volume I of H.O. 249 contains sight reduction tables for selected stars; it cannot be used for other bodies. A sample page is reproduced in Table A-1 of the present text. Page entry is by latitude: north latitude

LAT 33°N

LAT 33°N

LHA ♈	Hc	Zn	Hc	Zn	Hc	Zn	Hc	Zn	Hc	Zn	Hc	Zn	Hc	Zn
	*VEGA		Alphecca		ARCTURUS		*SPICA		REGULUS		*POLLUX		Dubhe	
180	13 49	052	43 49	083	57 06	106	41 41	152	56 45	238	35 24	283	59 37	346
181	14 29	053	44 39	083	57 55	107	42 05	153	56 02	239	34 35	284	59 25	346
182	15 09	053	45 29	084	58 43	108	42 27	154	55 19	240	33 46	284	59 13	345
183	15 50	054	46 19	084	59 30	109	42 48	156	54 35	241	32 58	284	58 59	344
184	16 31	054	47 10	085	60 18	110	43 08	157	53 50	242	32 09	285	58 45	343
185	17 11	055	48 00	085	61 05	111	43 27	158	53 06	243	31 20	285	58 30	342
186	17 52	055	48 50	086	61 52	112	43 45	160	52 20	244	30 32	286	58 15	342
187	18 34	055	49 40	086	62 38	113	44 02	161	51 35	245	29 43	286	57 58	341
188	19 15	056	50 30	087	63 24	115	44 18	162	50 49	246	28 55	286	57 42	340
189	19 57	056	51 20	087	64 10	116	44 33	163	50 03	247	28 07	287	57 24	340
190	20 39	056	52 11	088	64 55	117	44 47	165	49 16	248	27 19	287	57 07	339
191	21 21	057	53 01	088	65 39	119	45 00	166	48 29	249	26 31	288	56 48	338
192	22 03	057	53 51	089	66 23	120	45 11	168	47 42	250	25 43	288	56 29	338
193	22 45	058	54 42	089	67 06	122	45 21	169	46 55	251	24 55	289	56 10	337
194	23 28	058	55 32	090	67 49	123	45 30	170	46 07	252	24 07	289	55 50	336
	*Kochab		VEGA		Rasalhague		*ANTARES		SPICA		*REGULUS		Dubhe	
195	46 31	011	24 10	058	24 51	091	12 49	134	45 38	172	45 19	252	55 30	336
196	46 40	010	24 53	059	25 41	091	13 25	134	45 45	173	44 31	253	55 09	335
197	46 48	010	25 36	059	26 31	092	14 01	135	45 50	174	43 43	254	54 48	335
198	46 57	010	26 20	059	27 22	092	14 36	136	45 54	176	42 54	255	54 26	334
199	47 05	009	27 03	060	28 12	093	15 11	136	45 57	177	42 06	256	54 04	334
200	47 13	009	27 46	060	29 02	094	15 46	137	45 59	179	41 17	256	53 41	333
201	47 21	009	28 30	060	29 52	094	16 20	138	46 00	180	40 28	257	53 18	333
202	47 28	008	29 14	061	30 42	095	16 53	139	45 59	182	39 39	258	52 55	332
203	47 35	008	29 58	061	31 33	095	17 26	139	45 57	183	38 49	258	52 32	332
204	47 41	007	30 42	061	32 23	096	17 59	140	45 54	184	38 00	259	52 08	331
205	47 48	007	31 26	061	33 13	097	18 31	141	45 49	186	37 11	260	51 44	331
206	47 54	007	32 10	062	34 03	097	19 02	142	45 44	187	36 21	260	51 19	331
207	47 59	006	32 54	062	34 52	098	19 33	142	45 37	189	35 31	261	50 54	330
208	48 05	006	33 39	062	35 42	098	20 04	143	45 29	190	34 42	262	50 29	330
209	48 10	006	34 23	063	36 32	099	20 33	144	45 19	191	33 52	262	50 04	330
	*Kochab		VEGA		Rasalhague		*ANTARES		SPICA		*REGULUS		Dubhe	
210	48 15	005	35 08	063	37 22	100	21 03	145	45 09	193	33 02	263	49 38	329
211	48 19	005	35 53	063	38 11	100	21 31	146	44 57	194	32 12	263	49 13	329
212	48 23	004	36 38	063	39 01	101	21 59	146	44 44	195	31 22	264	48 47	329
213	48 26	004	37 23	064	39 50	102	22 27	147	44 30	197	30 32	265	48 20	329
214	48 30	004	38 08	064	40 39	102	22 54	148	44 15	198	29 42	265	47 54	328
215	48 33	003	38 53	064	41 28	103	23 20	149	43 59	199	28 52	266	47 28	328
216	48 35	003	39 39	064	42 17	104	23 46	150	43 42	201	28 01	266	47 01	328
217	48 37	002	40 24	065	43 06	105	24 11	151	43 24	202	27 11	267	46 34	328
218	48 39	002	41 10	065	43 55	105	24 35	152	43 04	203	26 21	268	46 07	327
219	48 41	002	41 55	065	44 43	106	24 59	152	42 44	205	25 31	268	45 40	327
220	48 42	001	42 41	065	45 31	107	25 22	153	42 22	206	24 40	269	45 12	327
221	48 43	001	43 27	066	46 19	108	25 44	154	42 00	207	23 50	269	44 45	327
222	48 43	000	44 13	066	47 07	109	26 05	155	41 37	208	23 00	270	44 17	327
223	48 43	000	44 59	066	47 55	109	26 26	156	41 13	209	22 09	270	43 50	327
224	48 43	359	45 45	066	48 42	110	26 46	157	40 47	211	21 19	271	43 22	326
	DENEB		VEGA		*ALTAIR		ANTARES		*SPICA		Denebola		*Dubhe	
225	25 54	051	46 31	066	19 34	092	27 05	158	40 21	212	42 51	259	42 54	326
226	26 33	052	47 17	067	20 24	093	27 24	159	39 54	213	42 01	260	42 26	326
227	27 13	052	48 03	067	21 14	093	27 41	160	39 27	214	41 12	260	41 58	326
228	27 52	052	48 49	067	22 04	094	27 58	161	38 58	215	40 22	261	41 30	326
229	28 32	052	49 36	067	22 55	094	28 15	162	38 29	216	39 32	262	41 02	326
230	29 12	053	50 22	067	23 45	095	28 30	163	37 59	217	38 43	262	40 34	326
231	29 52	053	51 09	067	24 35	096	28 44	164	37 28	218	37 53	263	40 06	326
232	30 33	053	51 55	068	25 25	096	28 58	165	36 56	219	37 03	264	39 38	326
233	31 13	053	52 42	068	26 15	097	29 11	166	36 24	220	36 13	264	39 09	326
234	31 53	054	53 28	068	27 05	097	29 23	167	35 51	221	35 22	265	38 41	326
235	32 34	054	54 15	068	27 55	098	29 34	168	35 18	222	34 32	265	38 13	326
236	33 15	054	55 02	068	28 44	099	29 44	169	34 43	223	33 42	266	37 45	326
237	33 56	054	55 48	068	29 34	099	29 54	170	34 08	224	32 52	267	37 16	326
238	34 37	055	56 35	068	30 24	100	30 02	171	33 33	225	32 02	267	36 48	326
239	35 18	055	57 22	068	31 13	100	30 10	172	32 57	226	31 11	268	36 20	326
	*DENEB		ALTAIR		Nunki		*ANTARES		SPICA		ARCTURUS		*Alkaid	
240	35 59	055	32 03	101	17 45	140	30 16	173	32 20	227	62 45	247	60 20	314
241	36 40	055	32 52	102	18 18	141	30 22	174	31 43	228	61 59	248	59 44	313
242	37 21	055	33 41	102	18 49	141	30 27	175	31 06	229	61 12	249	59 07	313
243	38 03	056	34 30	103	19 20	142	30 31	176	30 27	230	60 25	250	58 30	312
244	38 44	056	35 19	104	19 51	143	30 34	177	29 49	231	59 37	251	57 52	312
245	39 26	056	36 08	104	20 21	144	30 36	178	29 10	231	58 50	252	57 15	312
246	40 08	056	36 57	105	20 51	144	30 38	179	28 30	232	58 02	253	56 37	311
247	40 50	056	37 45	106	21 20	145	30 38	180	27 50	233	57 14	254	56 00	311
248	41 31	056	38 34	107	21 48	146	30 37	181	27 10	234	56 25	255	55 22	311
249	42 13	056	39 22	107	22 16	147	30 36	182	26 29	235	55 36	256	54 43	311
250	42 55	057	40 10	108	22 43	148	30 34	183	25 47	235	54 48	256	54 05	310
251	43 37	057	40 58	109	23 10	149	30 30	184	25 06	236	53 59	257	53 27	310
252	44 19	057	41 45	110	23 36	149	30 26	185	24 24	237	53 10	258	52 48	310
253	45 01	057	42 32	110	24 01	150	30 21	186	23 41	238	52 20	259	52 10	310
254	45 44	057	43 19	111	24 26	151	30 15	187	22 59	238	51 31	259	51 31	310
	*DENEB		ALTAIR		Nunki		*ANTARES		ARCTURUS		*Alkaid		Kochab	
255	46 26	057	44 06	112	24 50	152	30 08	188	50 41	260	50 52	310	45 45	348
256	47 08	057	44 53	113	25 13	153	30 00	189	49 52	261	50 14	310	45 35	348
257	47 50	057	45 39	114	25 35	154	29 52	190	49 02	262	49 35	309	45 24	347
258	48 33	057	46 25	115	25 57	155	29 42	191	48 12	262	48 56	309	45 13	347
259	49 15	057	47 10	116	26 18	156	29 32	192	47 22	263	48 17	309	45 01	347
260	49 57	057	47 55	117	26 39	157	29 20	193	46 32	264	47 38	309	44 50	347
261	50 39	057	48 40	118	26 58	158	29 08	194	45 42	264	46 59	309	44 38	346
262	51 22	057	49 25	119	27 17	158	28 55	195	44 52	265	46 20	309	44 26	346
263	52 04	057	50 09	120	27 35	159	28 41	196	44 02	265	45 41	309	44 14	346
264	52 46	057	50 52	121	27 53	160	28 27	197	43 12	266	45 02	309	44 02	346
265	53 29	057	51 35	122	28 09	161	28 11	198	42 22	267	44 23	309	43 49	345
266	54 11	057	52 18	123	28 25	162	27 55	199	41 31	267	43 44	309	43 36	345
267	54 53	057	53 00	124	28 40	163	27 38	200	40 41	268	43 05	309	43 23	345
268	55 35	057	53 41	125	28 54	164	27 20	201	39 51	268	42 26	309	43 10	345
269	56 17	057	54 22	126	29 07	165	27 01	202	39 00	269	41 47	309	42 56	344

LHA ♈	Hc	Zn	Hc	Zn	Hc	Zn	Hc	Zn	Hc	Zn	Hc	Zn	Hc	Zn
	*DENEB		ALTAIR		*Nunki		ANTARES		ARCTURUS		*Alkaid		Kochab	
270	56 59	056	55 02	128	29 19	166	26 42	203	38 10	270	41 08	309	42 43	344
271	57 41	056	55 42	129	29 31	167	26 22	204	37 20	270	40 30	310	42 29	344
272	58 23	056	56 20	130	29 41	168	26 01	205	36 29	271	39 51	310	42 15	344
273	59 04	056	56 58	132	29 51	169	25 39	206	35 39	271	39 12	310	42 01	344
274	59 46	056	57 36	133	30 00	170	25 17	207	34 49	272	38 33	310	41 47	344
275	60 27	055	58 12	135	30 08	171	24 54	208	33 59	272	37 55	310	41 33	343
276	61 09	055	58 47	136	30 15	172	24 30	209	33 08	273	37 16	310	41 18	343
277	61 50	055	59 22	138	30 21	173	24 05	209	32 18	273	36 38	310	41 04	343
278	62 31	054	59 55	139	30 27	174	23 40	210	31 28	274	36 00	310	40 49	343
279	63 12	054	60 27	141	30 31	175	23 14	211	30 38	274	35 21	311	40 34	343
280	63 52	053	60 59	143	30 35	177	22 48	212	29 47	275	34 43	311	40 19	343
281	64 32	053	61 28	144	30 37	178	22 21	213	28 57	275	34 05	311	40 04	342
282	65 12	052	61 57	146	30 39	179	21 53	214	28 07	276	33 27	311	39 49	342
283	65 52	052	62 24	148	30 40	180	21 25	215	27 17	276	32 49	311	39 33	342
284	66 31	051	62 50	150	30 40	181	20 56	215	26 27	277	32 11	311	39 18	342
	*Alpheratz		Enif		ALTAIR		*ANTARES		ARCTURUS		*Alkaid		Kochab	
285	25 36	071	45 58	112	63 15	152	20 27	216	25 37	277	31 34	312	39 02	342
286	26 24	071	46 45	113	63 37	154	19 57	217	24 47	278	30 56	312	38 47	342
287	27 12	072	47 31	114	63 58	156	19 26	218	23 58	278	30 19	312	38 31	342
288	28 00	072	48 16	115	64 18	158	18 55	219	23 08	279	29 41	312	38 15	342
289	28 47	072	49 02	116	64 36	161	18 24	219	22 18	279	29 04	313	38 00	342
290	29 35	073	49 47	117	64 52	163	17 52	220	21 28	280	28 27	313	37 44	342
291	30 24	073	50 31	118	65 05	165	17 19	221	20 39	280	27 50	313	37 28	342
292	31 12	074	51 15	119	65 18	167	16 46	222	19 49	281	27 14	313	37 12	341
293	32 00	074	51 59	120	65 28	170	16 12	222	19 00	281	26 37	313	36 56	341
294	32 49	074	52 42	121	65 36	172	15 38	223	18 11	282	26 01	314	36 40	341
295	33 37	075	53 25	122	65 42	174	15 04	224	17 21	282	25 24	314	36 24	341
296	34 26	075	54 07	124	65 45	177	14 29	224	16 32	283	24 48	314	36 07	341
297	35 15	076	54 49	125	65 47	179	13 53	225	15 43	283	24 12	315	35 51	341
298	36 03	076	55 30	126	65 47	182	13 17	226	14 54	284	23 37	315	35 35	341
299	36 52	076	56 10	127	65 44	184	12 41	226	14 05	284	23 01	315	35 19	341
	*Mirfak		Alpheratz		*FOMALHAUT		ALTAIR		Rasalhague		*Alphecca		Kochab	
300	13 02	038	37 41	077	14 40	141	65 40	186	50 52	247	32 51	283	35 03	341
301	13 34	039	38 30	077	15 11	142	65 33	189	50 05	248	32 02	283	34 46	341
302	14 05	039	39 19	078	15 41	143	65 24	191	49 18	249	31 13	284	34 30	341
303	14 37	040	40 09	078	16 11	144	65 14	193	48 31	250	30 24	284	34 14	341
304	15 09	040	40 58	078	16 41	144	65 01	196	47 44	251	29 35	284	33 58	341
305	15 42	040	41 47	079	17 10	145	64 46	198	46 56	252	28 47	285	33 41	341
306	16 14	041	42 37	079	17 39	146	64 30	200	46 08	252	27 58	285	33 25	341
307	16 47	041	43 26	080	18 07	147	64 11	202	45 20	253	27 09	286	33 09	341
308	17 20	041	44 16	080	18 34	147	63 51	205	44 32	254	26 21	286	32 53	341
309	17 54	042	45 05	080	19 01	148	63 30	207	43 43	255	25 33	287	32 37	341
310	18 27	042	45 55	081	19 27	149	63 06	209	42 55	256	24 45	287	32 20	341
311	19 01	042	46 45	081	19 52	150	62 42	211	42 06	256	23 57	287	32 04	341
312	19 35	043	47 34	082	20 17	151	62 15	213	41 17	257	23 09	288	31 48	341
313	20 09	043	48 24	082	20 42	151	61 47	214	40 28	258	22 21	288	31 32	341
314	20 44	043	49 14	083	21 06	152	61 18	216	39 39	258	21 33	289	31 16	342
	*Mirfak		Hamal		Diphda		*FOMALHAUT		ALTAIR		*VEGA		Kochab	
315	21 19	044	23 24	077	16 21	125	21 29	153	60 48	218	60 27	292	31 00	342
316	21 53	044	24 13	077	17 02	126	21 51	154	60 17	220	59 40	292	30 44	342
317	22 28	044	25 02	077	17 42	127	22 13	155	59 44	221	58 53	292	30 29	342
318	23 04	045	25 51	078	18 23	127	22 34	156	59 10	223	58 07	292	30 13	342
319	23 39	045	26 40	078	19 02	128	22 54	157	58 35	224	57 20	292	29 57	342
320	24 15	045	27 30	079	19 42	129	23 14	157	58 00	226	56 33	292	29 42	342
321	24 50	045	28 19	079	20 21	130	23 33	158	57 23	227	55 46	292	29 26	342
322	25 26	046	29 09	080	20 59	130	23 51	159	56 46	229	55 00	292	29 11	342
323	26 02	046	29 58	080	21 37	131	24 09	160	56 07	230	54 13	292	28 55	342
324	26 38	046	30 48	081	22 15	132	24 25	161	55 28	231	53 26	292	28 40	342
325	27 15	046	31 37	081	22 52	133	24 41	162	54 49	233	52 40	292	28 25	342
326	27 51	047	32 27	082	23 29	133	24 57	163	54 08	234	51 53	292	28 10	343
327	28 28	047	33 17	082	24 06	134	25 11	164	53 27	235	51 07	293	27 55	343
328	29 05	047	34 07	083	24 41	135	25 25	165	52 46	236	50 20	293	27 40	343
329	29 42	047	34 57	083	25 17	136	25 38	166	52 03	238	49 34	293	27 25	343
	*Mirfak		Hamal		Diphda		*FOMALHAUT		ALTAIR		*VEGA		Kochab	
330	30 19	048	35 47	083	25 51	137	25 50	167	51 21	239	48 48	293	27 10	343
331	30 56	048	36 37	084	26 26	138	26 01	167	50 37	240	48 01	293	26 56	343
332	31 33	048	37 27	084	26 59	138	26 12	168	49 54	241	47 15	293	26 41	343
333	32 11	048	38 17	085	27 33	139	26 22	169	49 10	242	46 29	294	26 27	344
334	32 48	048	39 07	085	28 05	140	26 30	170	48 25	243	45 43	294	26 13	344
335	33 26	049	39 57	086	28 37	141	26 39	171	47 40	244	44 57	294	25 59	344
336	34 04	049	40 47	086	29 08	142	26 46	172	46 55	245	44 11	294	25 45	344
337	34 42	049	41 38	087	29 39	143	26 52	173	46 09	246	43 25	294	25 31	344
338	35 20	049	42 28	087	30 09	144	26 58	174	45 23	246	42 39	295	25 17	344
339	35 58	049	43 18	088	30 39	145	27 02	175	44 37	247	41 54	295	25 04	344
340	36 36	049	44 08	088	31 07	146	27 06	176	43 50	248	41 08	295	24 50	345
341	37 14	049	44 59	089	31 35	147	27 09	177	43 03	249	40 22	295	24 37	345
342	37 52	050	45 49	089	32 03	148	27 11	178	42 16	250	39 37	296	24 24	345
343	38 31	050	46 39	090	32 29	149	27 13	179	41 29	251	38 52	296	24 11	345
344	39 09	050	47 30	091	32 55	150	27 13	180	40 41	251	38 06	296	23 58	345
	*CAPELLA		ALDEBARAN		Diphda		*FOMALHAUT		ALTAIR		*VEGA		Kochab	
345	20 47	048	14 09	079	33 20	151	27 13	181	39 53	252	37 21	296	23 45	346
346	21 24	048	14 59	080	33 44	152	27 11	182	39 05	253	36 36	297	23 33	346
347	22 02	049	15 49	080	34 08	153	27 09	183	38 17	254	35 51	297	23 20	346
348	22 40	049	16 38	081	34 30	154	27 06	184	37 29	254	35 06	297	23 08	346
349	23 18	049	17 28	081	34 52	155	27 02	185	36 40	255	34 22	297	22 56	346
350	23 56	049	18 18	082	35 13	156	26 58	186	35 52	256	33 37	298	22 44	346
351	24 34	050	19 08	082	35 33	157	26 52	187	35 03	257	32 53	298	22 33	347
352	25 13	050	19 57	083	35 52	158	26 46	188	34 14	257	32 08	298	22 21	347
353	25 51	050	20 47	083	36 11	159	26 39	189	33 25	258	31 24	299	22 10	347
354	26 30	051	21 37	084	36 28	160	26 30	190	32 35	259	30 40	299	21 59	347
355	27 09	051	22 28	084	36 44	161	26 22	191	31 46	259	29 56	299	21 48	348
356	27 48	051	23 18	085	37 00	163	26 12	192	30 56	260	29 12	299	21 37	348
357	28 28	051	24 08	085	37 15	164	26 01	193	30 07	260	28 28	300	21 26	348
358	29 07	052	24 58	086	37 28	165	25 50	193	29 17	261	27 45	300	21 16	348
359	29 47	052	25 48	086	37 41	166	25 38	194	28 28	262	27 01	300	21 06	348

TABLE A-1 A sample page from the H.O. 249 sight reduction tables.

pages are in the front of the publication, and south latitude pages are in the back. These pages are not interchangeable; the north page must be used when operating in north latitudes. Column entries are by star name, and line entry is by LHAΥ. Because these tables use the star name instead of declination as an entering argument, the familiar correction table for minutes of declination that is used in other tables is not applicable here. The tabulated value of Hc taken from the main tables is the final Hc; it requires no further correction.

At any one time and place, determined by the latitude of the observer and LHAΥ, 7 stars are listed. These are brighter stars and are well spaced in azimuth; in fact, distribution in azimuth was the primary concern in choosing the stars. Volume I is undoubtedly the simplest method of sight reduction for stars, but it is limited to the 7 tabulated stars. These stars can be obscured by clouds while other, nontabulated stars are visible, a problem that does not exist to as great an extent in air navigation, for which these tables were designed. The values extracted are Hc, to the nearest minute of arc, and Zn, the true azimuth to the nearest degree. Not only is this volume very useful for sight reduction, it serves as an excellent star finder, determining which stars will be above the horizon and well spaced for multiple-star fixes.

Appendix VIII

The Air Almanac

If the *Nautical Almanac* is not available, the *Air Almanac* can easily be substituted in marine navigation. The data extracted from the two publications are basically the same: GHA and declination of the various bodies and the GHA of Aries. However, a different format is used in the *Air Almanac:* GHA and declination are tabulated for each ten minutes rather than for each hour; thus, the larger "Increments and Corrections" section of the *Nautical Almanac* is unnecessary. The corrections to GHA for any ten-minute period is included in a half-page table inside the front cover and is also duplicated on a fold-out sheet. The principal drawbacks to the use of the *Air Almanac* are that each edition covers only four months and that the volume is generally difficult to obtain very far in advance. The total cost per year is also considerably more than that of the *Nautical Almanac.*

The sextant corrections in the *Air Almanac* are designed for ease of use with the aircraft bubble sextant at flight altitude. For the mariner, they are not as convenient or precise as the correction tables in the *Nautical Almanac.* Complete details of these correction tables will not be given here; they are explained in the *Air Almanac* itself, which permits the transition to be made quite simply once the need for corrections, as explained in this text, is understood.

GHA of the Sun and of Aries is tabulated to one-tenth minute of arc, and the GHA of the planets and of the moon is tabulated to the nearest minute of arc. SHA of the principal navigation stars is tabulated once for the entire four-month period, to the nearest minute of arc, rather than on the daily pages, as in the *Nautical Almanac.* A sample daily page from the *Air Almanac* is reproduced in Table A-2 of the present text.

For maximum accuracy, ease of use, and lower cost, the *Nautical Almanac* is recommended for marine navigation.

GMT	☉ SUN GHA	☉ SUN Dec.	ARIES GHA ♈	VENUS−3.5 GHA	VENUS−3.5 Dec.	MARS−1.4 GHA	MARS−1.4 Dec.	JUPITER−2.2 GHA	JUPITER−2.2 Dec.	○ MOON GHA	○ MOON Dec.	Lat.	Moon-rise	Diff.
h m	° ′	° ′	° ′	° ′	° ′	° ′	° ′	° ′	° ′	° ′	° ′	N	h m	m
00 00	180 47.9	N 4 41.9	349 52.3	144 47	S10 54	312 26	N11 06	44 36	S20 18	20 34	S 8 08			
10	183 18.0	41.8	352 22.7	147 17		314 56		47 07		22 59	06	72	18 05	−12
20	185 48.0	41.6	354 53.2	149 47		317 27		49 37		25 25	04	70	18 00	−08
30	188 18.1 ·	41.5	357 23.6	152 17 ·	·	319 57 ·	·	52 08 ·	·	27 50 ·	02	68	17 55	−05
40	190 48.1	41.3	359 54.0	154 47		322 27		54 38		30 16	8 00	66	17 50	−02
50	193 18.1	41.2	2 24.4	157 17		324 58		57 09		32 41	7 58	64	17 47	00
01 00	195 48.2	N 4 41.0	4 54.8	159 47	S10 55	327 28	N11 07	59 39	S20 18	35 07	S 7 56	62	17 44	+02
10	198 18.2	40.8	7 25.2	162 16		329 58		62 09		37 32	54			
20	200 48.2	40.7	9 55.6	164 46		332 29		64 40		39 58	52	60	17 41	04
30	203 18.3 ·	40.5	12 26.0	167 16 ·	·	334 59 ·	·	67 10 ·	·	42 23 ·	50	58	17 39	05
40	205 48.3	40.4	14 56.4	169 46		337 29		69 41		44 49	48	56	17 37	06
50	208 18.3	40.2	17 26.8	172 16		340 00		72 11		47 14	46	54	17 35	07
02 00	210 48.4	N 4 40.0	19 57.3	174 46	S10 56	342 30	N11 07	74 42	S20 18	49 40	S 7 44	52	17 33	08
10	213 18.4	39.9	22 27.7	177 16		345 01		77 12		52 05	41	50	17 31	09
20	215 48.5	39.7	24 58.1	179 46		347 31		79 42		54 31	39	45	17 28	11
30	218 18.5 ·	39.6	27 28.5	182 16 ·	·	350 01 ·	·	82 13 ·	·	56 56 ·	37	40	17 25	13
40	220 48.5	39.4	29 58.9	184 46		352 32		84 43		59 22	35	35	17 22	15
50	223 18.6	39.3	32 29.3	187 16		355 02		87 14		61 47	33	30	17 20	16
03 00	225 48.6	N 4 39.1	34 59.7	189 46	S10 58	357 32	N11 07	89 44	S20 18	64 13	S 7 31	20	17 16	18
10	228 18.6	38.9	37 30.1	192 16		0 03		92 15		66 38	29	10	17 12	20
20	230 48.7	38.8	40 00.5	194 46		2 33		94 45		69 04	27	0	17 09	22
30	233 18.7 ·	38.6	42 31.0	197 16 ·	·	5 03 ·	·	97 16 ·	·	71 29 ·	25	10	17 06	25
40	235 48.7	38.5	45 01.4	199 46		7 34		99 46		73 55	23	20	17 02	26
50	238 18.8	38.3	47 31.8	202 16		10 04		102 16		76 20	21			
04 00	240 48.8	N 4 38.1	50 02.2	204 46	S10 59	12 35	N11 07	104 47	S20 18	78 46	S 7 18	30	16 58	29
10	243 18.9	38.0	52 32.6	207 16		15 05		107 17		81 11	16	35	16 56	30
20	245 48.9	37.8	55 03.0	209 46		17 35		109 48		83 37	14	40	16 53	32
30	248 18.9 ·	37.7	57 33.4	212 16 ·	·	20 06 ·	·	112 18 ·	·	86 02 ·	12	45	16 50	34
40	250 49.0	37.5	60 03.8	214 46		22 36		114 49		88 28	10	50	16 47	36
50	253 19.0	37.4	62 34.2	217 16		25 06		117 19		90 53	08			
05 00	255 49.0	N 4 37.2	65 04.7	219 46	S11 00	27 37	N11 07	119 49	S20 18	93 19	S 7 06	52	16 45	37
10	258 19.1	37.0	67 35.1	222 15		30 07		122 20		95 44	04	54	16 43	38
20	260 49.1	36.9	70 05.5	224 45		32 37		124 50		98 10	02	56	16 41	39
30	263 19.2 ·	36.7	72 35.9	227 15 ·	·	35 08 ·	·	127 21 ·	·	100 35 ·	7 00	58	16 39	41
40	265 49.2	36.6	75 06.3	229 45		37 38		129 51		103 01	6 57	60	16 36	43
50	268 19.2	36.4	77 36.7	232 15		40 08		132 22		105 26	55			
06 00	270 49.3	N 4 36.2	80 07.1	234 45	S11 01	42 39	N11 07	134 52	S20 18	107 52	S 6 53	S		
10	273 19.3	36.1	82 37.5	237 15		45 09		137 22		110 17	51			
20	275 49.3	35.9	85 07.9	239 45		47 40		139 53		112 43	49			
30	278 19.4 ·	35.8	87 38.3	242 15 ·	·	50 10 ·	·	142 23 ·	·	115 08 ·	47			
40	280 49.4	35.6	90 08.8	244 45		52 40		144 54		117 34	45			
50	283 19.4	35.5	92 39.2	247 15		55 11		147 24		119 59	43			
07 00	285 49.5	N 4 35.3	95 09.6	249 45	S11 02	57 41	N11 07	149 55	S20 18	122 25	S 6 41			
10	288 19.5	35.1	97 40.0	252 15		60 11		152 25		124 50	39			
20	290 49.6	35.0	100 10.4	254 45		62 42		154 55		127 16	36			
30	293 19.6 ·	34.8	102 40.8	257 15 ·	·	65 12 ·	·	157 26 ·	·	129 42 ·	34			
40	295 49.6	34.7	105 11.2	259 45		67 42		159 56		132 07	32			
50	298 19.7	34.5	107 41.6	262 15		70 13		162 27		134 33	30			
08 00	300 49.7	N 4 34.3	110 12.0	264 45	S11 04	72 43	N11 07	164 57	S20 18	136 58	S 6 28			
10	303 19.7	34.2	112 42.5	267 15		75 14		167 28		139 24	26			
20	305 49.8	34.0	115 12.9	269 45		77 44		169 58		141 49	24			
30	308 19.8 ·	33.9	117 43.3	272 15 ·	·	80 14 ·	·	172 29 ·	·	144 15 ·	21			
40	310 49.8	33.7	120 13.7	274 44		82 45		174 59		146 40	19			
50	313 19.9	33.6	122 44.1	277 14		85 15		177 29		149 06	17			
09 00	315 49.9	N 4 33.4	125 14.5	279 44	S11 05	87 45	N11 07	180 00	S20 18	151 31	S 6 15			
10	318 20.0	33.2	127 44.9	282 14		90 16		182 30		153 57	13			
20	320 50.0	33.1	130 15.3	284 44		92 46		185 01		156 22	11			
30	323 20.0 ·	32.9	132 45.7	287 14 ·	·	95 16 ·	·	187 31 ·	·	158 48 ·	09			
40	325 50.1	32.8	135 16.2	289 44		97 47		190 02		161 13	07			
50	328 20.1	32.6	137 46.6	292 14		100 17		192 32		163 39	04			
10 00	330 50.1	N 4 32.4	140 17.0	294 44	S11 06	102 48	N11 08	195 03	S20 18	166 04	S 6 02			
10	333 20.2	32.3	142 47.4	297 14		105 18		197 33		168 30	6 00			
20	335 50.2	32.1	145 17.8	299 44		107 48		200 03		170 55	5 58			
30	338 20.3 ·	32.0	147 48.2	302 14 ·	·	110 19 ·	·	202 34 ·	·	173 21 ·	56			
40	340 50.3	31.8	150 18.6	304 44		112 49		205 04		175 46	54			
50	343 20.3	31.7	152 49.0	307 14		115 19		207 35		178 12	52			
11 00	345 50.4	N 4 31.5	155 19.4	309 44	S11 07	117 50	N11 08	210 05	S20 19	180 37	S 5 50			
10	348 20.4	31.3	157 49.8	312 14		120 20		212 36		183 03	47			
20	350 50.4	31.2	160 20.3	314 44		122 50		215 06		185 28	45			
30	353 20.5 ·	31.0	162 50.7	317 14 ·	·	125 21 ·	·	217 36 ·	·	187 54 ·	43			
40	355 50.5	30.9	165 21.1	319 44		127 51		220 07		190 19	41			
50	358 20.5	30.7	167 51.5	322 14		130 22		222 37		192 45	39			
Rate	15 00.2	S0 01.0		14 59.7	S0 01.2	15 02.2	N0 00.1	15 02.6	0 00.0	14 33.1	N0 12.6			

Moon's P. in A.

Alt. °	Corr. + ′	Alt. °	Corr. + ′
0	56	55	31
7	55	56	30
12	54	58	29
16		59	28
20	53	60	27
22	52	61	26
25	51	62	25
27	50	64	24
29	49	65	23
31	48	66	22
33	47	67	21
35	46	68	20
37	45	69	19
38	44	70	18
40	43	71	17
42	42	72	16
43	41	73	15
45	40	74	14
46	39	76	13
47	38	77	12
49	37	78	11
50	36	79	10
51	35	80	
53	34		
54	33		
55	32		
56	31		

Sun SD 15.′9
Moon SD 15′
Age 14d

TABLE A-2   *A sample daily page from the* Air Almanac.

Appendix IX

Azimuth of the Sun by Amplitudes

Amplitude is "the angular distance north or south of the prime vertical; the arc of the horizon between the prime vertical and a vertical circle containing the body, measured north of south from the prime vertical." Amplitude measurements are therefore measured from east or west rather than from the traditional north point. They are given the prefix E if the body is rising or W if the body is setting. They are given the suffix N if the body rises or sets north of the prime vertical (that is, if the declination of the body is north) or S if it rises or sets south of the prime vertical (if the declination of the body is south). If, for example, the amplitude is E15°N, the azimuth is 90° minus 15°, or 75°.

In practical navigation, amplitudes are generally taken of the sun, although other bodies can be used. When the center of the body is observed on the celestial horizon, the amplitude is taken directly from Bowditch table 27; declination and latitude are used as the entering arguments. Since it is difficult to determine by observation when the body is on the celestial horizon, Bowditch table 28 contains a correction to be applied when the body is observed on the visible horizon. For the sun, the center of the body is on the celestial horizon when the lower limb is a little more than half its diameter above the visible horizon. When using table 28 for the sun, the correction is applied in the direction away from the elevated pole; the azimuth angle is thereby increased. Since it is relatively easy to observe an azimuth of the sun when it is rising or setting and when the tables are available, the use of amplitudes represents the simplest method of checking the compass each morning and evening. This is particularly true if one is using a gyrocompass, in which the error is generally the same on all headings, as opposed to a magnetic compass in which the deviation is generally different on various headings. If tables are not available, amplitudes can be worked quite easily by slide rule or pocket calculator. Use the formula sin A = sec L sin d, where A is the amplitude, L is the latitude of the observer, and d is the declination of the celestial body.

Glossary

The definitions given in this glossary are adapted primarily from H.O. Publication No. 220, *Navigation Dictionary*.

Altitude intercept (a).   The difference between observed altitude and computed altitude. It is labeled T (toward) or A (away) from the direction of the true azimuth. If the computed altitude is greater than the observed altitude, the intercept is away.

Apparent altitude (ha).   Sextant altitude corrected for dip and for inaccuracies in the reading (index, instrument, and personal errors) but not for other errors, such as refraction, parallax, semidiameter, and so forth. Apparent altitude is also known as *rectified altitude.*

Apparent time.   Time based upon the rotation of the earth relative to the apparent or true sun. This is the time shown by a sundial. Apparent time may be designated as either local or Greenwich, depending on whether the local or Greenwich meridian is used as the reference.

Assumed latitude.   The latitude at which the observer is assumed to be located for purposes of computing or reducing celestial observations. Generally it is the integral degree of latitude closest to the dead reckoning latitude.

Assumed longitude.   The longitude at which an observer is assumed to be located for purposes of computing or reducing celestial observations. When using modern tables, the minutes of longitude are so chosen that, when combined with the minutes of

GHA, the resulting LHA will be in integral degrees with no minutes of arc.

Assumed position (AP). That point on the surface of the earth for which the computed altitude is determined; the point from which the altitude intercept is plotted when using modern sight reduction tables.

Azimuth angle (Az or Z). Azimuth measured either east or west from a reference direction of either north or south. Measured from 0° at the north or south reference direction clockwise or counterclockwise through 90° or 180°.

Celestial equator. The primary great circle of the celestial sphere, everywhere 90° from the celestial poles; the intersection of the extended plane of the equator and the celestial sphere; also called the equinoctial.

Circle of equal altitude. A circle on the surface of the earth, on every point of which the altitude of a given celestial body is the same at a given instant of time. The center of this circle is the geographical position of the body, and the great-circle distance from this center to the circumference of the circle is the zenith distance of the body.

Computed altitude (Hc). Altitude of the center of a celestial body above the celestial horizon at a given time and place, as determined by computation, table, mechanical device, graphics, or calculator.

Dead reckoning position (DR). A position determined by advancing a previous position for courses steered and distances run.

Declination (dec.). Angular distance north or south of the celestial equator; the arc of an hour circle between the celestial equator and a point on the celestial sphere, measured north or south from the celestial equator through 90°, and labeled *N* or *S* to indicate the direction of measurement.

Dip (D). The dip of the horizon; the vertical angle, at the eye of an observer, between the horizontal and the line of sight to the visible horizon. The dip varies with the height of the eye of the observer above the surface of the earth. The correction for dip is always minus and is tabulated in the almanacs.

First point of Aries (*T*). The Vernal equinox; that point of intersection of the ecliptic and the celestial equator that is occupied by the sun as it changes from south to north declination on or about March 21. Sidereal hour angle (SHA) is measured west from the hour circle of the first point of Aries.

Geographic position (GP). In celestial navigation, that point on the earth at which a given celestial body is in the zenith at a specified time.

Greenwich hour angle (GHA). Angular distance west of the Greenwich celestial meridian; the arc of the celestial equator, or the angle at the celestial pole, between the upper branch of the Greenwich celestial meridian and the hour circle of a point on the celestial sphere, measured west from the Greenwich celestial meridian through 360°.

Greenwich Mean Time (GMT). Local mean time at the Greenwich meridian; the arc of the celestial equator, or the angle at the celestial pole, between the lower branch of the Greenwich celestial meridian and the hour circle of the mean sun, measured west from the lower branch of the Greenwich celestial meridian through 24 hours. Greenwich Mean Time is also called *universal time.*

Horizontal parallax. The geocentric parallax when a body is in the horizon. The term is used only in connection with the moon, and its values are tabulated in the almanacs.

Hour circle. A great circle on the celestial sphere passing through the celestial poles and a celestial body or point on the sphere. With respect to the earth the hour circle moves with the body, whereas a celestial meridian remains fixed with respect to the earth.

Index correction (IC). The correction that must be made to the sextant altitude due to index error. The correction carries the reverse sign of the error.

Index error (IE). The error in a reading of a marine sextant due primarily to a lack of parallelism of the index mirror and the horizon glass when the index is set at zero.

Line of position (LOP). A celestial line of position is a staight line representing a small section of a circle of equal altitude. A line on some point of which a vessel may be presumed to be located, as a result of a celestial observation.

Local apparent noon (LAN). The instant at which the apparent sun is over the upper branch of the local meridian.

Local hour angle (LHA). Angular distance between the upper branch of the local celestial meridian and the hour circle of a point on the celestial sphere, measured west from the local celestial meridian through 360°. The local hour angle at longitude 0° is called the Greenwich hour angle.

Mean time. Time based upon the rotation of the earth relative to the mean sun. Mean time may be designated as local or Greenwich depending on whether the local or Greenwich meridian is used as the reference. Greenwich mean time is used in the almanac as the time reference for tabulations of the position of celestial bodies.

Meridian angle (*t*). The angular distance between the upper branch of the local celestial meridian and the hour circle of a celestial body, measured east or west from the local celestial meridian through 180°, and labeled E or W to indicate the direction of the measurement.

Observed altitude (Ho). Corrected sextant altitude; angular distance of the center of a celestial body above the celestial horizon of an observer, measured along a vertical circle through 90°.

Parallax correction (P). A correction due to parallax, particularly the sextant altitude correction due to the difference between the apparent position of a celestial body viewed from the surface of the earth and the position of the body with respect to the center of the earth.

Refraction correction (R). The correction to apparent altitude caused by atmospheric refraction as the light rays from a celestial body pass through the atmosphere. The correction is always minus and varies with the altitude of the body above the horizon.

Semidiameter correction (SD). A correction due to semidiameter; in particular, the sextant altitude correction resulting from observation of the upper or lower limb of a celestial body rather than the center of the body.

Sextant altitude (hs). The altitude reading taken from the sextant before any corrections are applied.

Sidereal hour angle (SHA). Angular distance west of the vernal equinox; the arc of the celestial equator, or the angle at the celestial pole, between the hour circle of the first point of Aries and the hour circle of a point on the celestial sphere, measured west from the hour circle of the first point of Aries through 360°.

Sight reduction tables. Tables for performing sight reduction, particularly those used to determine azimuth and computed altitude. These two values are compared with the observed altitude of a celestial body to determine the altitude difference that is used in establishing a line of position.

Spherical triangle. A closed figure having arcs of three great circles as its sides. In celestial navigation, the *navigational triangle* is formed on the celestial sphere by the great circles connecting the elevated pole, the zenith of the assumed position of the observer, and a celestial body.

Time diagram. A diagram drawn on the plane of the celestial equator, or equinoctial. The celestial equator appears as a circle, the celestial meridians and hour circles as radial lines. The time diagram is used to facilitate solution of time problems and other problems involving arcs of the celestial equator or angles at the pole; it does so by indicating the relations between the various quantities involved.

True azimuth (Zn). Azimuth relative to true north; the arc of the horizon, or the angle at the zenith, between the north part of the celestial meridian and a vertical circle containing the position of the celestial body; measured from 000° at the reference clockwise through 360°.

149

Vertical circle. A great circle of the celestial sphere that extends through the zenith and the nadir. Vertical circles arc perpendicular to the horizon. Sextant altitude is measured along the arc of a vertical circle. The prime vertical circle, which is called the *prime vertical*, passes through the east and west points of the horizon.

Zenith. That point on the celestial sphere that is directly over the observer. The point 180° from the zenith is called the *nadir*.

Zenith distance (ZD). Angular distance from the zenith; the arc of a vertical circle between the zenith and a point on the celestial sphere, measured from the zenith through 90° for bodies above the horizon. Zenith distance is the same as coaltitude, or 90° minus the altitude of a body above the celestial horizon.

Zone time (ZT). The local mean time of a reference meridian whose time is kept throughout a designated zone. The zone meridian is usually the nearest meridian whose longitude is exactly divisible by 15°.

Index